Ideas of poverty in the Age of Enlightenment

Manchester University Press

STUDIES IN EARLY MODERN EUROPEAN HISTORY

This series aims to promote challenging and innovative research in all areas of early modern European history. For over twenty years it has published monographs and edited volumes that make an original contribution to our understanding of the period and is particularly interested in works that engage with current historiographical debates and methodologies, including race, emotions, materiality, gender, communication, medicine and disability, as well as interdisciplinary studies. Europe is taken in a broad sense and the series welcomes projects on continental (Western, Central and Eastern Europe), Anglo-European and trans-cultural, global histories that explore the world's relationship with Europe during the sixteenth to eighteenth centuries.

SERIES EDITORS
Sara Barker, Laura Kounine and William G. Naphy

Full details of the series and all previously published titles are available at https://manchesteruniversitypress.co.uk/series/studies-in-early-modern-european-history/

Ideas of poverty in the Age of Enlightenment

Edited by

Niall O'Flaherty and R. J. W. Mills

MANCHESTER UNIVERSITY PRESS

Copyright © Manchester University Press 2024

While copyright in the volume as a whole is vested in Manchester University Press, copyright in individual chapters belongs to their respective authors, and no chapter may be reproduced wholly or in part without the express permission in writing of both author and publisher.

Published by Manchester University Press
Oxford Road, Manchester, M13 9PL

www.manchesteruniversitypress.co.uk

British Library Cataloguing-in-Publication Data
A catalogue record for this book is available from the British Library

ISBN 978 1 5261 6677 7 hardback

First published 2024

The publisher has no responsibility for the persistence or accuracy of URLs for any external or third-party internet websites referred to in this book, and does not guarantee that any content on such websites is, or will remain, accurate or appropriate.

Typeset
by Cheshire Typesetting Ltd, Cuddington, Cheshire

Contents

List of figures	vi
List of contributors	vii
Acknowledgements	ix
Ideas of poverty in an age of Enlightenment: an introduction – R. J. W. Mills and Niall O'Flaherty	1
1 'Welfare for whom?' The place of poor relief in the theory and practice of the Enlightened absolutist state – T. J. Hochstrasser	17
2 Economic *bienfaisance* and the Physiocratic rhetoric of charity – Arnault Skornicki	36
3 Poverty, rights and the social contract in Enlightenment Austrian-Habsburg Lombardy – Alexandra Ortolja-Baird	60
4 An economic regalism: poverty and charity in eighteenth-century Spain – Jesús Astigarraga and Javier Usoz	84
5 The embarrassment of poverty: Dutch decline, liberalism, patriotism and the duties of the state around 1800 – Koen Stapelbroek	106
6 Montesquieu, Smith and Burke on the 'labouring poor': an eighteenth-century debate – Anna Plassart	128
7 Beyond a charitable design? Robert Wallace as a theorist of poverty and population growth – Conor Bollins	148
8 Conceptions of Polish and Russian poverty in the British Enlightenment – Ben Dew	168
9 Desolation and abundance: poverty and the Irish landscape, c. 1720–1820 – James Stafford	188
10 A new moral economy: the early reception of Malthus – Niall O'Flaherty	212
11 Poverty, autonomy and control: Patrick Colquhoun's *Treatise on Indigence* (1806) – Joanna Innes	232
Index	254

List of figures

3.1 Giacomo Ceruti (known as 'Il Pittocchetto'), *Group of Beggars*, c. 1737, © Museo Nacional Thyssen-Bornemisza, Madrid.   70
3.2 Giacomo Ceruti, *Errand Boy Seated on a Basket*, c. 1735, © Pinacoteca di Brera, Milano.   72
3.3 Giacomo Ceruti, *Scuola di ragazze*, c. 1720–1725, Pinacoteca Tosio Martinengo © Archivio fotografico Civici Musei di Brescia/ Fotostudio Rapuzzi.   73
11.1 Map of paupers per hundred population. From Colquhoun's *Treatise on Indigence*.   245

List of contributors

Jesús Astigarraga is a Full Professor at the University of Zaragoza, Spain.

Conor Bollins is a Visiting Lecturer at the University of East Anglia.

Ben Dew is Associate Head of School at the Faculty of Arts and Humanities, University of Coventry.

T. J. Hochstrasser is Associate Professor in the Department of International History, The London School of Economics and Political Science.

Joanna Innes is Professor Emeritus of Modern History at the University of Oxford and a Senior Research Fellow at Somerville College.

R. J. W. Mills is an Honorary Fellow at the Institute of Intellectual History, University of St Andrews.

Niall O'Flaherty is Senior Lecturer in the History of European Political Thought, King's College London.

Alexander Ortolja-Baird is Lecturer in Digital History and Culture, University of Portsmouth and a Visiting Researcher at the British Museum.

Anna Plassart is Senior Lecturer in History at the Open University.

Arnault Skornicki is an Associate Professor in Political Science at the University of Paris Nanterre.

James Stafford is Assistant Professor in the Department of History, Columbia University.

Koen Stapelbroek is Professor of Humanities and Dean of the College of Arts, Society & Education, James Cook University, Australia.

Javier Usoz is an Associate Professor at the University of Zaragoza, Spain.

Acknowledgements

The editors would first like to thank Manchester University Press, especially Meredith Carroll and Laura Swift, for their generous support and professionalism throughout the process. They are also grateful to Gareth Stedman Jones, Adela Halo, Samantha Williams, David Hitchcock, Alysa Levene, Tawny Paul, James Harris, Julia Nicholls, Emma Barker, Rich Lizardo and David Womersley for their participation in the conference at King's College London in September 2018 from which this collection emerged. Special thanks go to Talitha Ilacqua for helping to run the event. The conference was generously supported by the King's College London Faculty of Humanities Research Grant Programme, Department of History Research Fund and Centre for Enlightenment Studies; University College London's History Department Events Fund; and the Royal Historical Society.

Ideas of poverty in an age of Enlightenment: an introduction

R. J. W. Mills and Niall O'Flaherty

Surveying the history of economic theory in 1890, the English economist Alfred Marshall claimed that the 'chief motive' of the French Physiocratic school of political economy was to 'diminish the suffering and degradation which was caused by extreme poverty'.[1] The Physiocrats gave the burgeoning field of economics its 'aim of seeking after such knowledge as may help to raise the quality of human life'.[2] Marshall's confident assertion that the modern economics that emerged in the 1760s was motivated by a desire to eradicate poverty prompts reflection. Does our current picture of the European Enlightenment sufficiently incorporate the issue of destitution? The emergence of political economy, certainly, is viewed as one of the Enlightenment's greatest achievements.[3] But Karl Polanyi's sense that the Enlightenment's 'discovery of society' had poverty as its central theme has not been reiterated by the vast majority of subsequent studies.[4] Most major recent overviews of the Enlightenment do not present the material conditions of the poor as a central concern of the age.[5] Similarly, the major treatments of changing Western conceptions of poverty tend to stress radical disjuncture at the end of eighteenth century from the preceding Enlightenment.[6]

We can question whether Marshall is an adequate source for assessing changes to eighteenth-century thinking on poverty, but it would a mistake to ignore the evidence of mounting interest across Europe in alleviating or eradicating poverty, especially from the 1740s onwards. Indeed, Jonathan Israel has argued that the debate over poverty and inequality was one of the 'central intellectual dramas of modernity and most enduringly relevant aspects of the Western Enlightenment'.[7] According to economist Martin Ravallion, Europe went through the first of two 'Poverty Enlightenments' between 1740 and 1800, the second starting in the 1960s.[8] The most significant achievement of the 'First Poverty Enlightenment' was to establish the 'moral case for the idea of public effort toward eliminating poverty'.[9] Ravallion detailed how interest in Britain about poverty as a social issue grew from the 1740s, with a similar pattern occurring in France about wealth inequality and subsequently also poverty, interest which reached a crescendo in both countries in the late 1780s and 1790s. Similar developments took place across Europe, though we lack comparable statistical research. But Ravallion's identification of widespread discussion of poverty indicates that the eighteenth century's 'sea change in attitudes towards the poor' goes beyond the confines of well-known debates between Turgot, Adam Smith, Condorcet, William Godwin, Thomas Paine and T. R. Malthus.[10] The transformation of how poverty was conceptualised should be viewed as one of the key humanitarian goals of an Enlightenment concerned with temporal well-being.

To this end, the chapters that follow examine changing conceptualisations of the causes, character and consequences of poverty, as well as proposals for its amelioration. The collection seeks to provide the perspective of the intellectual historian on an issue that has long been the preserve of social historians (though surprisingly, not economic historians), and to suggest that poverty was more central to Enlightenment-era thought than the current literature suggests.[11] Our contributors have sought to situate conceptualisations of poverty within their original social, political and philosophical contexts, and to view those conceptualisations as contributions to pan-European debates over the paths to prosperity and improvement. Through reconstructing the major themes of Enlightenment-era thought about poverty, the following chapters avoid viewing these debates in terms of early twenty-first-century concepts and categories. Equally importantly, our contributors have been encouraged to explore how changing notions of poverty inform political and social action and thereby demonstrate the crucial interplay between Enlightened ideas and political practices.

A core objective of *Ideas of Poverty* is to demonstrate what intellectual history can add to our understanding of the topic. The chapters address questions that are of crucial significance to the social and political history of the period such as: how far did paternalist assumptions subsume all thinking about 'the poor' before the 1790s? Did the political thought of the Enlightenment reinforce or undermine those assumptions? How did attitudes to poverty vary in the different states of Europe and how did they change in the period? How did poverty figure in the emergence of political economy? By attempting to recover the meaning of a crucial category in social, political and religious thought, we hope the collection has important implications for the history of eighteenth-century Europe. The urgency of the issues that the collection examines goes without saying, but our aim is to recover Enlightened discussions through placing them in their historical contexts. This avoids the anachronistic reading of these debates in terms of our own ideological concerns. Our dual focus on intellectually sophisticated discussions about poverty and social policy and the direct application of Enlightened thinking means the volume discusses a wide variety of historical actors. Focus ranges from the writings of leading philosophers to the plans of private reformers to the activities of economic societies and academies to the policy decisions of state actors across Europe.

As such, the following chapters challenge both the narrow periodisation and geographical focus on England and France in the 1790s and the limited place that poverty is given in general overviews of the European Enlightenment. The nature of poverty and its amelioration was of pan-European interest, and one that concerned the newly secular, Enlightened bureaucracies of modernising absolutist monarchies as much as it did radical *philosophes* on the outside of the centres of power. The very act of compiling a chapter collection on a topic from a variety of angles, however, prevents drawing many generalisations. This is partly the point. Attempts to think about poverty anew were not limited to Adam Smith in the 1770s or Condorcet in the early 1790s; there were a variety of new things going on in different parts of Enlightenment Europe. Admittedly, before the end of the eighteenth century, the study of poverty did not evolve into a discrete subtopic of the 'science of society', whereby hardship was viewed as the consequence of interrelated social and economic factors which could be studied empirically with statistical data. There are instances here and there across Europe of such studies being undertaken. But, more substantially, poverty was increasingly conceived as the consequence of human decision-making, rather than as a fixed feature of life on Earth, and thus as something that could be ameliorated, if not eradicated, if dealt with in different ways. Poverty was approached with a new social purpose and intellectual energy across Europe from the 1740s onwards. This pan-European moment lasted until the end of the Napoleonic Wars when it was eclipsed by the ideological battle between socialism and laissez-faire liberalism. The fact that poverty was of greater concern in High Enlightenment socio-economic thinking than is commonly understood takes us away from a sense that things changed dramatically at the end of the century. It instead encourages us to recognise an Enlightenment moment on poverty – indeed, a 'First Poverty Enlightenment' – lasting into the early nineteenth century, which requires us to reconsider the post-1790s in light of what came before.

The geographical coverage, as much as chronological coverage, of Enlightenment-era thought on poverty needs to be expanded if we are to capture the moment accurately. It is understandable that our focus often turns to the emergence of British and French political economy, debate over the English poor laws and French revolutionary experiments in reducing poverty. Yet this distorts our picture by giving the misleading sense that the only loci of innovation and reform were Britain and France and by encouraging the tendency to view the 1790s as the key turning point in a 'before and after' picture of European notions of poverty. To realise that ameliorating impoverishment was a major concern for Enlightened thinkers in other parts of Europe and often long before the purportedly transformative developments in England or France, suggests that some of the grand stories about modern notions of poverty and the rise of capitalism, or poverty and the industrial revolution, need to be taken with a grain of salt. While there was intellectual transmission between European states, the discussion over poverty and reform developed according to local circumstances and in response to specific problems. Political reformers and economists in the Dutch Republic or Habsburg Milan did not walk in step with their British or French counterparts. Conversely, we can identify a broad divide here based on the established religion of European states. In Catholic Europe, the Enlightened reconceptualisation of poverty was usually framed in conflict with established ecclesiastical structures and a desire, by some at least, for the state to wrest control of the issue from the Church. In Protestant Europe, the issue related more to developing new schemes for welfare within existing state institutions. In Catholic Europe, poverty was an issue often subsumed into a debate about secularisation, whereas in Protestant Europe, it tended more to be a debate within political economy.

While we wish to ward off anachronism, the Enlightenment's debate over poverty is more than a topic for antiquarian research. It can help illuminate current concerns of the relationship between, to borrow the title of one contribution to the field, 'progress, poverty and population'.[12] What is at stake is whether 'the Enlightenment', especially in the form of the newly emergent practice of political economy, had malign or benign effects on the poor. At the grand scale, the question feeds into big issue debates about the trajectory of 'Western' societies and the nature of 'capitalism'. Several commentators claim the Enlightenment investigation into poverty was characteristic of a brief social democratic moment that was soon overrun, more by the global turmoil wrought by the Revolutionary Wars and related military demands on resources, than the emergence of liberal political economy, and which was soon replaced by the rival extremes of socialism and free-market capitalism. To Gareth Stedman Jones, contemporary social democratic thinking should 'revisit its original birthplace and resume the ambition of the late and democratic Enlightenment to combine the benefits of individual freedom and commercial society with a republican ideal of greater equality, inclusive citizenship and the public good'.[13] Similarly, Jonathan Israel holds that radical Enlightenment discourse viewed the causes and continuation of poverty as resulting from political and religious institutions that privileged the landed elite over the populace at large, whereas the socialist ideas that followed viewed working-class interests as antagonistic to those of the commercial middle class. To many Enlightenment radicals, Israel argued, inequality could be lessened and the unnatural frictions between social classes smoothed. This necessitated government action focused on increasing general happiness by undoing entrenched privilege in ways that enabled commerce to function freely.[14]

Inspired by the work of Michel Foucault and E. P. Thompson, another prominent interpretation has claimed that Enlightened thought served to increase the exploitation and impoverishment of the lower orders. The luminaries of the Enlightenment provided the ideological scaffolding necessary to move away from the well-ordered police state, including paternalistic intervention in the lives of the needy, and towards 'liberal forms of governmentality' in which the poor were subjected to the social control of free markets forced onto them by states.[15] Eighteenth-century policies towards the poor thus should be viewed in terms of increasing social discipline of the lower orders required by the need to provide goods for consumer markets and pliable workers and soldiers for expanding militaries and growing empires, and in response to ideological threats to the established society of ranks. According to this perspective, much so-called 'Enlightened' thought is not to be viewed as liberating but as facilitating extended control of populations for reasons of economic exploitation.[16] Purportedly Enlightened states adopting cameralist thought, for example, have been redescribed as 'ravenous fiscal-judicial chamber[s] that devoured everything in [their] path', headed by privileged elites who talked of the commonweal but acted only to secure their own riches and power.[17] The position has been criticised for overlooking the radical quality of much Enlightenment philanthropic discussion, especially that promulgated in absolutist monarchies, the inapplicability of the argument across many of the varied states of Enlightenment Europe and its all-explanatory – indeed, conspiratorial – framing. Similarly, critics had observed that there is little evidence of pre-existing paternalism or a 'moral economy' governing social behaviour, and that predominant instead were concerns to marshal the lower orders and to get them to work.

There are, then, strongly divergent interpretations about the Enlightenment's discourse on poverty. This is exemplified by the conflicting positions on the influence of Adam Smith's economic thought. To Thompson, Smith brought about the replacement of 'moral economy' with a de-moralised 'political economy', concerned with profit and without regard for people, and, with it, the removal of the safety next of the Old Poor Laws.[18] To Ravallion, by contrast, Smith's *Wealth of Nations* (1776) encouraged states to view 'progress against poverty' as desirable for economic development, rather than being a threat to it. The social philosophy underpinning the Old Poor Laws viewed the poor as a static aspect of society and served to protect the existing social order, not improve the material conditions of the less fortunate beyond existing levels. Enlightenment political economy, epitomised by Smith, sought to discover ways to increase prosperity to the benefit of all – the 'nation' in the *Wealth of Nations* meant the population at large, not the propertied elite. Moreover, Enlightenment-era political economy granted status to the individual, regardless of social position, as an autonomous moral agent able to make decisions about how to spend their time and money, and in ways that, in the aggregate, needed to matter to statesmen. One need not be an apologist for capitalism to make this judgement about Smith. The Marxist historian Richard Ashcraft could write that 'Smith transformed poverty from being a precondition for economic development into a symptom of economic decline' resulting from a 'structural defect of the economic system', though one to be treated through changing the workings of the system rather than ameliorating its current consequences through welfare.[19]

The afterlives of Smith's *Wealth of Nations* reveal another way of thinking about changing Enlightenment conceptions of poverty. Smith influenced many of the leading commentators on the issue of poverty, running the gamut from Paine and Condorcet to Burke and Malthus. Smith influenced revolutionaries and conservatives, informed policies of income redistribution and of leaving the poor to fend for themselves in free labour markets. Historians of the reception of Smith's thought, however, often point to how the radical elements of the *Wealth of Nations* were downplayed or ignored by early nineteenth-century readers. Smith's radicalism about state education provision, intense suspicion of merchants and the dangers of political corruption resulting from inequalities of wealth was lost, even if much of the remaining analysis adopted.[20] The dominant attitude amongst post-Smith political economists was that the laws of the market dictated the level and character of poverty. The narrow reading of Smith by the early 1800s illustrates one way we can think about the Enlightenment debate on poverty: that it was of short duration, covering the final decades of the eighteenth century and the very beginning of the nineteenth, but came quickly to an end as the rival schema of free-market liberalism and socialism took over. Moreover, it shows that these two subsequent perspectives, not least as they stand as critical attitudes adopted today, act as misleading vantage points from which to look back on the Enlightenment debate about poverty. Smith has been viewed as a radical egalitarian concerned with the prosperity of the poor or an ideological apologist for exploitative capitalism. He was neither and these characterisations are emblematic of how we must understand the Enlightenment's debate on poverty on its own terms.

Clearly, examining changing attitudes towards poverty in Europe during the second half of the long eighteenth century also raises questions about actual material changes in the number and conditions of the poor. Were the intellectual developments identified in the chapters that follow prompted by observable social change? It does not seem like there was a dramatic increase in poverty across Europe in the mid-eighteenth century. The picture is not clear, however. Partly this is due to the nature of the question – the extent of poverty in early modern Europe – raising so many problems of definition, the nature and availability of evidence and best methods to study that evidence. As one leading economic historian explains, once we seek to measure 'the prevalence of poverty across time and in different societies, the subject matter immediately becomes very complicated and somewhat disconcerting'.[21] Still, as with debates over the ideology of political economy, the extent of poverty in early modern Europe is subject to competing interpretations upon which larger issues about the costs and benefits of 'capitalism' or 'Western civilisation' rest.

One prominent interpretation stresses that nearly all Europeans existed at subsistence levels, as had all of humankind going back millennia, and that the situation only changed with the Industrial Revolution.[22] Relatedly, another views Europe as experiencing sustained economic improvement during the early modern period leading, eventually, to a 'Great Divergence' from the rest of the world, with it being assumed that such progress, the proverbial rising tide, led to reductions in poverty.[23] In direct contrast to this position is the argument for the growing volume of poverty in early modern Europe, as improvement-led gains in prosperity were syphoned off by the already wealthy or the well-positioned, leading to increasing levels of economic inequality across the early modern period.[24] This has been explained in terms of the emergence of a capitalist economic system that concentrated wealth in the hands of an increasingly prosperous merchant elite. Similarly recently an argument has gained support that claims that 'the rise of the fiscal-military state served to increase economic inequality' due to the regressive nature of new forms of taxation and the use of tax revenue primarily on military expenditure, rather than welfare.[25]

One possible answer to the question of the relationship between the Enlightenment debate on poverty and actually existing poverty, however, is to take seriously the idea of a pan-European Enlightenment committed to improving human well-being as much as marshalling resources for the state. This encourages us to view the increased interest in the amelioration of poverty across the continent not as the result of the shared experience of economic problems, but as a shared intellectual moment. Indeed, it is in an argument in favour of the existence of a pan-European Enlightenment that we see similar Enlightened debates across countries experiencing different economic fortunes. The prevalence of poor households in England remained somewhat constant between 1400 and 1800 (around 20–25 per cent), whereas the figure seems to have been on the rise across the continent during the same period, yet the problem of poverty became a preoccupation for social commentators and statesmen throughout Europe around the same time.[26] It is to this preoccupation that the following chapters are dedicated.

Our contributors address the Enlightenment's debate over poverty from a variety of thematic, temporal and geographical angles. Tim Hochstrasser's Chapter 1 acts as a scene-setting discussion. He assesses whether the absolutist states of eighteenth-century Europe were genuinely concerned with alleviating poverty and in the process introduces several of the themes of the collection. Critical of the Marxian perspective which viewed Enlightened absolutism as unable to modernise without endangering itself, Hochstrasser argues there were tentative signs of reform, underpinned by a new secular and scientific sense of poverty. Epitomising our need to view the topic of poverty in terms of reformers as much as thinkers, this development was led less by the intellectual luminaries of the age, than by powerful civil servants. Turgot led the way in 1770s France, Johann Heinrich Gottlob von Justi (1717–1771) in 1760s Prussia and Wenzel Anton, Prince Kaunitz (1711–1794) and Joseph von Sonnenfels (1732–1817) in the Habsburg Monarchy. Across absolutist Europe in the mid-eighteenth century, perceptions of the poor were shifting towards the promotion of welfare, with Frederick II, Catherine II and Joseph II all seeking to alter policy towards the poor. Local circumstances, however, determined the rate of change: Frederick achieved little, while Catherine and Joseph achieved much, though on a smaller scale than their grandiose projects had intended. But the fact that it was Joseph II who undertook some of the most radical policies of the age indicates that our narrow focus on either England or France might be wide of the mark.

Hochstrasser's analysis indicates that much new Enlightened thought about poverty was framed in newly secular terms. Obviously, this came at the expense of the established Christian conceptualisation which viewed poverty as fixed, natural and often benign; with the rich as duty-bound to help the deserving poor, though more to redeem their own souls than for the benefit of the receiver; and the church as the institution to dole out relief.[27] This older tradition of the fixity of poverty shifted from the mid-century, as reformers increasingly thought of hardship as a social problem resulting from the 'faulty organization of human affairs' rather than providential design, and thus something that could be reduced through appropriate action.[28] We must be careful, however, to avoid the grand narrative of secular liberal enlighteners battling a complacent, corrupt Church given that clergy and believers played significant roles in new conceptualisations and approaches to poverty in the second half of the eighteenth century, even if they did so with increasingly secular language and as participants in extra-ecclesiastical institutions.[29] But criticism of ecclesiastical charitable provision and the theological underpinnings of dominant conceptualisations of poverty itself was a transnational element of Enlightenment social thought. Especially important here is the critique emerging out of political economy that criticised religious foundations for locking up capital and labour without much benefit and, as opined by at least some reformers, rewarded idleness out of misplaced notions of benevolence.[30]

The *philosophes* developed the concept of '*bienfaisance*' from the 1760s in direct opposition to established theological notions of charity, a switch from Christian duty to secular humanitarian concern. As Arnault Skornicki's Chapter 2 shows, the new Physiocratic system of political economy needed to develop concepts and arguments that explained how it served the poor better than traditional modes of relief. While there was disagreement amongst the Physiocrats on precise welfare policy recommendations, they shared the view that the most important expedient was to increase employment by creating a free market economy, and, in particular, a perfectly free grain trade. This required modifying the language of '*bienfaisance*' to communicate the altruistic intentions behind such 'capitalistic' solutions, partly to fend off allegations of hardheartedness when they criticised traditional almsgiving as encouraging beggary. A new political language was developed to support the Physiocrats' arguments for removing controls and allowing the economy to return to its natural order and, with it, to aid the long-run well-being of the poor. This was a crucial moment in the history of Enlightenment ideas of poverty, as it represented one of the most significant systematic attempts to address the problem directly, rather than as a part of wider project to improve administration or increase national wealth.

Similar themes about the secularisation of concepts of poverty and the interplaying between reformers and governments are found in Alexandra Ortolja-Baird's survey of the Enlightened discourse on poverty in Austrian-Habsburg Lombardy from the 1760s to the 1780s in Chapter 3. To an extent, the political economists of Milan were fellow travellers with the Physiocrats in establishing political economy as the foremost Enlightened 'science of man'. But Ortolja-Baird's chapter indicates the benefits of drawing upon a wider geographical range of studies of changing Enlightened conceptions of poverty. Exemplified by Cesare Beccaria's discussion in *On Crimes and Punishments* (1764), the Milanese Enlightenment viewed poverty as one factor in a larger political critique of existing social privilege and the moral corruptions of the nobility and the inadequacies of Church benevolence. This discussion had some influence on the decision-making of the Habsburg-Lombard court. In Beccaria's work especially, the *Illuministi* developed solutions not only of undoing the society of ranks and ensuring equal access to economic opportunity, but also schemes for free health care. The solutions proposed did not involve social insurance schemes or the redistribution of wealth, but ensuring equal access to opportunity, based on a rights doctrine emerging from a social contractarian outlook. The radical reformist outlook of the *Illuministi* discussed in this chapter bears resemblance to the 'social economy' of the radical *philosophes* in Paris but was developed within its own Milanese, as much as wider European, context.

The same attempts at reform, including challenging ecclesiastical authority, identified in the Bourbon, Habsburg, Prussian and Russian monarchies, also took place in Enlightened absolutist Madrid. Jesus Astigarraga and Javier Usoz Otal in Chapter 4 assess the emergence of 'economic regalism' in mid-eighteenth-century Spain. This was a new Enlightened approach to poverty developed by reforming civil servants. It rejected the Catholic Church's control of poor relief and framed the issue in the new language of political economy. Poverty was to be reconceived not in Christian terms, but as a problem resulting from a workforce characterised by idleness and limited skills, and a backward society of only limited economic development. Want could be ameliorated through industry, education and market-orientated policies. This secular language of economic reform in the interests of the poor and at the expense of the Church was initially developed by government ministers and state officials in support of absolutism. Ultimately, however, the new language of egalitarianism and ameliorating the condition of the poor served to undermine the legitimacy of *ancien regime* Spain and would go on to inform the construction of the fated liberal Constitution of 1812.

The discourse on poverty in each national context shared much with the general conversation taking place across Europe, but national socio-economic circumstances could frame, in fundamental ways, the timing of when and reasons why poverty became a significant concern. A good example of these processes is that of the Dutch Republic, as discussed in Koen Stapelbroeck's Chapter 5. Borne out of its comparative wealth, a common myth in early eighteenth-century Europe was that poverty did not exist in the Republic. The emergence of poverty as an issue of economic and political debate occurred in tandem with attempts, especially in the 1770s and 1780s, to understand and stall Dutch economic decline. Two opposing discourses crystallised at this time: one which understood poverty as a mismatch of factors of production that needed to be dealt with to ensure the state's prosperity; and another which positioned poverty as an issue of moral economy, viewing it as a duty of the state to provide labour and subsistence to its citizenry. These positions provide through-lines to the rival positions of liberalism and socialism in the nineteenth-century Republic.

If several of our chapters encourage readers to move away from treating England and France as the main loci of changing conceptions of poverty, several others encourage caution against viewing the 1790s as the radical turning point in the history of Western social thought on the issue. Anna Plassart in Chapter 6 places Edmund Burke's famous mockery of the notion of the 'labouring poor' as 'political canting language' in the context not of the French Revolution, but of an ongoing eighteenth-century debate among Enlightened social theorists about the character of poverty in modern commercial states. Burke's indictment did not symbolise the end of paternalism and the beginning of free market liberalism. Certainly, it was a rhetorical move in response to radicalism in 1795. But he was participating in an ongoing conversation about the concept of the 'labouring poor'. To Burke, there were only the 'idle' poor: the purported 'labouring poor' were the expected productions of economic laws and their situation was unalterable. The framing of the labouring poor as an oxymoron was deployed by Burke, Frederick Eden, Patrick Colquhoun and Jeremy Bentham, but they were all, directly or indirectly, relying on the formulation found half a century earlier in Montesquieu's *Spirit of the Laws* (1748). In identifying the Montesquieuian origins of this critique, Plassart encourages us to think beyond the stark or binary analyses of the radical 1790s and to assess the changing status of long-established arguments.

Examining the decades before the 1790s uncovers key Enlightened debate for thinking anew about poverty that did not endure into the nineteenth century. As Conor Bollins shows in Chapter 7, one important example here is the debate over ancient and modern demography. He investigates the mid-century activities of the Scottish minister and philosopher Robert Wallace (1697–1771), who developed a Widow's Fund as a test policy for larger schemes of social insurance. Like many Enlightened thinkers, Wallace believed that modern Europe was experiencing depopulation and was facing the prospect of civilisational collapse. He attributed this to rising poverty. In response, Wallace developed both new theories and concrete solutions to create a more equitable distribution of land and resources, in the hope of encouraging families to grow. Demography emerges as a separate field of discourse to political economy in which issues of poverty were debated and the means for its amelioration or alleviation proposed. Moreover, Wallace was an innovative thinker working out schemes of social insurance, with some success, long before the radicalism of the 1790s. On the topic of demography, at least, we do find that a 'before and after' approach works: the common eighteenth-century belief that the trend of population decline could be and should be arrested by ameliorating levels of poverty was fatally undermined by the arguments of Malthus, though he was not the first to insist on the necessity of ensuring that population was proportioned to the food supply.[31]

Another locus for new eighteenth-century ways of thinking about poverty was to be found in the 'philosophical histories' of the High Enlightenment, though unlike ideas of demographic decline, notions of historical progress endured into the following century. Ben Dew in Chapter 8 shows that much Enlightened historical writing focused on charting socio-economic progress in ways that implied trajectories of the 'natural' progress of society from poverty and savagery, via feudalism based on slavery, to commercial prosperity and civility. While the reduction of poverty was something achieved over the *longué durée* due to incremental economic improvement, it could be aided by reforming or abandoning the socio-economic structures and institutions of earlier forms of society. Dew examines how British travel writers on eighteenth-century Poland and Russia understood the level of poverty in those countries as analogous to that experienced in feudal Western Europe. Thinking about how Europe emerged out of serfdom and slavery informed discussion of how Eastern Europe could do the same. Moreover, accounts of serf-holding societies in Eastern Europe were utilised, in turn, by British critics of slavery and other exploitative aspects of Britain's growing commercial empire. What is profoundly significant here is that changes in European understanding of the trajectory of history – the very notions of improvement over time – were necessary as a precondition to any conceptualisation of poverty as something subject to human control and potentially eradicable.

How to think about the relationship between poverty and empire informs James Stafford's Chapter 9. In an ongoing conversation spanning the eighteenth into the nineteenth centuries, competing visions of economic progress in Ireland gave rise to rival imaginaries of a well-ordered countryside. Following the dispossession of the Catholic aristocracy, the 'new English' ruling class rested their hopes of civilising the native population on encouraging a shift from grazing to tillage. The barbarous modes of life endemic to pasturage, it was thought, would give way to the industry, prosperity and passivity exemplified by the English peasantry. When the turn to tillage took off in the 1770s, however, it took a different path from that taken in England. The emergence of the so-called 'cottier system' – whereby tenants rented cabins and a small plot of land to grow potatoes – was heralded by some commentators as a bright new dawn. For the potato provided a sure and nourishing subsistence, while rendering the labourer's condition impervious to the price hikes that so often disturbed civil peace in the English countryside. Yet this 'celebratory narrative', too, came under attack at the beginning of the nineteenth century, as some critics pointed to its tendency to stifle enterprise by encouraging the labourer to be content with a bare subsistence and to encourage 'surplus population'.

While the bulk of the chapters explore the largely unchartered territory of ideas of poverty before the 1790s, the volume also revisits the question of why and how many governments and men of letters began to address poverty as a social problem in the 1790s. A core aim of the final two chapters is to challenge the binary characterisation of debates in the period as a struggle between humanitarian radicals and cold-hearted reactionaries. Efforts of recent scholarship to discredit the widespread view of T. R. Malthus as helping to instigate a shift from a generous paternalistic view of poverty relief to an amoral cost–benefit credo have been undermined by the contention that the cure for poverty set out in the second edition of his *Essay on the Principle of Population* (1803) was invariably either misconstrued or ignored altogether, and that it failed, therefore, to dislodge the gloomier outlook of the first edition of 1798 in the public imagination. Niall O'Flaherty shows in Chapter 10, however, that the optimistic message of the second edition was both well understood and celebrated in the decade after its publication, not only by its numerous reviewers but also by those at the forefront of the campaign to reform the English relief system in parliament. There was a foundation, in other words, for a new approach to poverty that was at once anti-paternalist and humanitarian.

In Chapter 11, Joanna Innes undertakes an investigation of polymath and reformer Patrick Colquhoun's *Treatise on Indigence* (1806). She reminds us of the need to be aware of how the reconceptualisation of poverty in the late eighteenth and early nineteenth centuries was not always in the realm primarily of abstract political economy. Treating Colquhoun as one of a generation of British metropolitan reformers and thinkers reconceptualising poverty and crime, Innes outlines what was distinctive about his thought while acknowledging that he was not necessarily the most sophisticated or innovative of commentators. What is interesting about Colquhoun is how we can chart his professional engagement with poverty and his use of new empirical data to inform his arguments about how indigence might be ameliorated. Colquhoun was no armchair political economist but someone with sustained first-hand experience of both the labouring and indigent poor. But he was one of a clique of connected philanthropists who informed the attitudes of a subsequent even larger generation of reformers and commentators who broke with the vision of the Old Poor Laws.

Although the Age of Enlightenment is known for the development of radically new approaches to the study of society and politics, the current scholarly understanding is that the existence of poverty was rarely problematised by eighteenth-century thinkers, writers and officials – not withstanding that 'the poor' made up the vast majority of Europe's population. This picture is supposed to have only substantially changed in the transformative decade of the 1790s. The chapters that follow bring together historians with a wide range of geographical and theoretical expertise to reassess this claim, and to examine anew the ways in which poverty was conceptualised in the social, economic and political discourses of eighteenth-century Europe. Though poverty did not emerge as a distinct field of study, the theme of poverty played an important role in many of the era's critical debates and many of the traditional assumptions about 'the poor' were coming under sustained attack. Our hope is that the insights garnered in the chapters collected here will not only encourage intellectual historians of the era to reconsider the position of poverty within Enlightenment thought, but also spark a conversation with social and cultural historians, and social scientists interested in the history of poverty in the Western world.

Notes

1 Alfred Marshall, *Principles of Economics* (London: Macmillan, 1890), p. 55.
2 *Ibid.*
3 John Robertson, *The Case for the Enlightenment: Scotland and Naples, 1680–1760* (Cambridge: Cambridge University Press, 2005), pp. 377–405; Jonathan Israel, *A Revolution of the Mind: Radical Enlightenment and the Intellectual Origins of Modern Democracy* (Princeton, NJ: Princeton University Press, 2011).
4 Karl Polanyi, *The Great Transformation: The Political and Economic Origins of Our Time* (Boston, MA: Beacon Press, 1957).
5 Ritchie Robertson, *The Enlightenment: The Pursuit of Happiness, 1680–1790* (London: Penguin, 2021); Anthony Pagden, *The Enlightenment and Why it Still Matters* (London: Random House, 2013); Margaret Jacob, *The Secular Enlightenment* (Princeton, NJ: Princeton University Press, 2019).
6 John Riddoch Poynter, *Society and Pauperism: English Ideas on Poor Relief, 1795–1834* (London: Routledge & Kegan Paul, 1969); Gertrude Himmelfarb, *The Idea of Poverty: England in the Early Industrial Age* (London: Faber, 1984); Gareth Stedman Jones, *An End to Poverty? A Historical Debate* (London: Profile, 2004).
7 Jonathan Israel, *The Enlightenment That Failed* (Oxford: Oxford University Press, 2019), p. 355.
8 Martin Ravallion, *The Economics of Poverty: History, Measurement and Policy* (Oxford: Oxford University Press, 2016), Part I.
9 Ravallion, *Economics of Poverty*, p. 47.
10 Samuel Fleischacker, *A Short History of Distributive Justice* (Harvard, MA: Harvard University Press, 2004), p. 53.
11 See, for example, Samantha A. Shave, *Pauper Policies: Poor Law Practice in England, 1780–1850* (Manchester: Manchester University Press, 2017).
12 John Avery, *Progress, Poverty and Population: Re-reading Condorcet, Godwin and Malthus* (London: Frank Cass, 1997); David Charles Stove, *What's Wrong with Benevolence: Happiness, Private Property and the Limits of Enlightenment* (London: Encounter, 2011); Sharon K. Vaughan, *Poverty, Justice, and Western Political Thought* (Plymouth: Lexington Books, 2008), esp. pp. 63–103.

13 Stedman Jones, *End to Poverty?*, p. 235.
14 Israel, *The Enlightenment That Failed*, Ch. 12 esp. pp. 372–389.
15 Michel Foucault, 'Governmentality', in Graham Burchell, Colin Gordon and Peter Miller (eds), *The Foucault Effect. Studies in Governmentality* (Chicago, IL: University of Chicago Press, 1991), pp. 87–104; E. P. Thompson, *Customs in Common* (London: Merlin Press, 1991), esp. pp. 185–258. See also Mitchell Dean, *The Constitution of Poverty: Towards a Genealogy of Liberal Governance* (London: Routledge, 1991); Larry Frohman, *Poor Relief and Welfare in Germany from the Reformation to World War I* (Cambridge: Cambridge University Press, 2008), esp. pp. 43–52; and Wolf Rainer Wendt *Geschichte der Sozialen Arbeit 1: Die Gesellschaft vor der sozialen Frage 1750 bis 1900* (Weisbaden: Springer, 2017), pp. 21–55.
16 Mary Lindeman, *Patriots and Paupers: Hamburg, 1712–1830* (Oxford: Oxford University Press, 1990), pp. 74–77.
17 Andre Wakefield. *The Disordered Police State: German Cameralism as Science and Practice* (Chicago, IL: University of Chicago Press, 2009), p. 25.
18 Thompson, *Customs in Common*, esp. pp. 201–202.
19 Richard Ashcraft, 'Lockean Ideas, Poverty, and the Development of Liberal Political Theory', in John Brewer and Susan Staves (eds), *Early Modern Conceptions of Property* (Oxford: Routledge, 1995), pp. 43–61 at p. 54.
20 See, for example, Paul Sagar, *Adam Smith Reconsidered: History, Liberty and the Foundations of Modern Politics* (Princeton, NJ: Princeton University Press, 2022).
21 Guido Alfani, 'The Economic History of Poverty, 1450–1800', in David Hitchcock and Julia McClure (eds), *The Routledge History of Poverty in Europe, c.1450–1800* (London: Routledge, 2021), pp. 21–38 at p. 21.
22 Gregory Clark, *A Farewell to Alms: A Brief Economic History of the World* (Princeton, NJ: Princeton University Press, 2007).
23 Keith Pomeranz, *The Great Divergence: China, Europe, and the Making of the Modern World Economy* (Princeton, NJ: Princeton University Press, 2000).
24 Alfani, 'Economic History of Poverty'; Guido Alfani, 'Economic Inequality in Preindustrial times: Europe and Beyond', *Journal of Economic Literature*, 59:1 (2021), 3–44.
25 Guido Alfani and Matteo Di Tullio, *The Lion's Share: Inequality and the Rise of the Fiscal State in Preindustrial Europe* (Cambridge: Cambridge University Press, 2019).
26 Stephen Broadberry, Bruce Campbell, Alexander Klein, Mark Overton and Bas van Leeuwen, *British Economic Growth 1270–1870* (Cambridge: Cambridge University Press, 2015), p. 329. Similarly, each European state had its own trajectory with regard to GDP per capita (compare Britain's rapid growth with Spain's stagnation and Portugal's decline), yet thinkers in nearly all states participated in the debate over poverty.
27 Himmelfarb, *Idea of Poverty*, p. 41; Daniel Roche, 'A Pauper Capital: Some Reflections on the Parisian Poor in the 17th and 18th Centuries', *French History* I (1987), 182–209.

28 David Garrioch, 'Making a Better World: Enlightenment and Philanthropy', in Martin Fitzpatrick, Peter Jones, Christa Knellwolf and Ian McCalman (eds), *The Enlightenment World* (London: Routledge, 2004), pp. 486–502 at p. 497.
29 Joanna Innes, 'State, Church and Voluntarism in European Welfare 1690–1850', in Hugh Cunningham and Joanna Innes (eds), *Charity, Philanthropy and Reform from the 1690s to the 1860s* (Basingstoke: Macmillan, 1998), pp. 15–65; Brian Pullan, 'Charity and Poor Relief in Early Modern Italy', in Martin Dauton (ed.), *Charity, Self-Interest and Welfare in the English Past* (London: UCL Press, 1996), pp. 48–66.
30 Characteristic examples of these criticisms can be found in Lodovico Ricci, *Riforma degl'istituti pii della città di Modena* (Modena, 1787). See also Sandra Cavallo, 'Conceptions of Poverty and Poor Relief in Turin in the Second Half of the Eighteenth Century', in S. J. Woolf (ed.) *Domestic Strategies: Work and Family in France and Italy, 1600–1800* (Cambridge: Cambridge University Press, 1991), pp. 148–199.
31 See James Steuart's discussion of 'Population and Agriculture', in *An Inquiry into the Principles of Political Economy* (1767), esp. pp. 17–49.

1

'Welfare for whom?' The place of poor relief in the theory and practice of the Enlightened absolutist state

T. J. Hochstrasser

Mandeville's disruptive 1723 *Essay on Charity and the Charity Schools* is the most challenging and startling contemporary perspective on poor relief, one which then went on to set up a debate for or against the view that the utility of the labouring poor and a low-wage economy were essential to economic flourishing and national greatness:

> The more man's knowledge increases in [civil society], the greater will be the variety of labour required to make him easy. It is impossible that a society can long subsist, and suffer many of its members to live in idleness, and enjoy all the ease and pleasure they can invent, without having at the same time great multitudes of people that will condescend to be quite the reverse, and by use and patience inure their bodies to work for others and themselves besides. Obsequiousness and mean services are required ... they are never so cheerfully nor so heartily perform'd as from inferiors ... a wise legislature would cultivate the breed of them with all imaginable care.[1]

But while this dynamic clearly had a shaping influence within the Enlightened discourse of political economy, it is less clear that it weighed heavily on the minds of policy makers in the absolutist states of Continental Europe for whom the scope and outreach of government itself, and the broader meaning of collective 'welfare', presented more pressing problems. Did those governments offer any serious theoretical or practical initiatives that focused on alleviation of poverty in concerted fashion? Or were such measures mere wishful thinking, examples of the flowers that garlanded those invisible chains that Rousseau suggested bound all social orders? Was a 'society of orders' necessarily, even if unconsciously, founded on an inevitable measure of social degradation by virtue of its fixed stratification that allowed for little or no social mobility? Could alleviation of poverty ever rise to a conscious policy priority given its scale – as Tocqueville asked rhetorically in his *Memoir on Poverty* (1835): 'In a country where the majority is ill-clothed, ill-housed, ill-fed, who thinks of giving clean clothes, healthy foods and comfortable quarters to the poor?'[2]

That is certainly the view argued by historians of a broadly Marxist perspective, such as Perry Anderson and Michael Mann, who have viewed Enlightened absolutism as a necessary failure because of its social contradictions.[3] How could wealth be redistributed and aristocratic power over the peasantry be challenged by those at the apex of the social pyramid without disrupting and demolishing the broad foundation of that pyramid on which that elite rested and subsisted? If the poor were tied into complex structures of agricultural service, fiscal extraction and compulsory military service, all run by local administrative elites on which central government relied, how could the government then unravel a system on which it depended? Did not the fate of Joseph II's reforms prove the point?

I would like to suggest that there is a bit more to it than that, if one disaggregates these issues. It is really important to separate out *two* different sets of priorities in respect of poverty and to assert that they apply in Continental Europe just as much as they do in Georgian England.[4] The first set concerns who should receive relief, and on what terms, and whether that should include or exclude beggars. Linked to that of course is the question of who should then provide such relief – the state, the Church or other sources of secular philanthropy – or some mix of the three. And then alongside that is the second set of parallel concerns surrounding the promotion of national improvement, the boat within which the poor as well as the rich may ideally float upwards to prosperity, albeit on different decks. On this basis the promotion of 'welfare' of different kinds becomes no longer a measure of individual charity but a project of collective utility focused on making the state and its working population as efficient, healthy and productive as possible.

In both these areas, the practice of poor relief and its justification in the absolutist states begin to show movement in new directions in the middle decades of the eighteenth century, including some vestigial but tangible sense that the poor were or could become full citizens at least in an economic and productive sense; and that the obstacles in the way of that outcome both could and should be removed. This is not yet the full moral revaluation and validation of the poor as 'the people', but at least in the aspirations of Joseph II and some of his associates we see traces of this emerging possibility; and it is certainly the case that there is some spill over between these projects and the work of Condorcet and the *idéologues* during the revolutionary decades.

Poverty was hardly a new phenomenon in the long eighteenth century. But there is clear evidence that it worsened in measurable ways across the century, and that this was noticed by contemporaries. The key issues in play were sustained population growth and the huge rise in food prices that this caused. As a result, the ranks of the chronically poor were inflated by number and degree. As various historians have argued, we see a shift from *structural* poverty, involving the aged, disabled, mentally ill or orphaned members of any given society to *conjunctural* poverty that included the under- or unemployed able-bodied across both town and country.[5]

These were victims of economic instability caused by population growth that productivity could not rise to provide for. While widespread famine was largely avoided except at moments of drastic harvest failure, the phenomenon was widely misunderstood not least because so many officials and writers believed populations levels to be falling rather than rising across Europe. The problems of chronic undernourishment were worst in the countryside where it was harder to measure and assess the scale of the problems. At least in the towns there was more of a focused infrastructure of administration to launch remedial initiatives; but, as Tocqueville records, rural villages were uniquely exposed to both bureaucratic exploitation and indifference:

> In the eighteenth century, a village is a community whose members are all poor, ignorant and coarse; its magistrates are as unpolished and as despised as the inhabitants: its syndic does not know how to read, by himself its tax-collector cannot balance the accounts on which his own fortune and that of his neighbours depend. Not only does his old lord no longer have the right to govern him, but he now considers it a kind of degradation to take part in the government of the village. To assess the taxes, raise the militia, regulate the corvées, these are servile duties, the syndic's work. There is no longer anyone but the central government which is interested in the village, and since it is very far away, and has nothing to fear from its inhabitants, it is only interested in making a profit out of it. Come see now what becomes of an abandoned class, which no one has any desire to tyrannise, but which no one is interested in educating and serving.[6]

As is familiarly known, in the towns, workhouses became the reflexive response for confining and corralling the 'idle' poor; but that hardly spoke to the countryside where such institutions were rare. In Britain there was some understanding of the concept of the 'labouring poor' – in work, but unable to support a family – which became institutionalised through such experiments as the Speenhamland system. But in the absolute monarchies of Europe the issues were still largely seen as moral, with punishment as the first and often only response. Only very gradually and grudgingly was this superseded by a more holistic concern for the health and welfare of the community and, even then, governments struggled to find the right blend of local initiatives and central incentives to make a real difference. Given the inevitable dominance in the countryside of the landlord and the parish priest, more often than not reform in this area was bound up with the success or failure of measures to bring the nobility and clergy more under the fiscal and administrative outreach of the state.

One area where the administrative state, rather than philosophers, broke new ground was in *counting* the poor, or at least attempting accurate statistics on poverty. Gregory King in Great Britain initiated a census of the poor, taken further by the Board of Trade; and in France there were regular surveys making use of the unique vantage point of the intendants in French provincial society. This was a step towards regarding the poor as a collective social category within the remit of the state, rather than a set of atomised individuals in need of specific and piecemeal religious charity.

While the Enlightenment never entirely broke free from the moralising view of poverty or attained a clear understanding of its causes, it did contribute significantly in other respects to recategorise it as a secular issue. Many writers redefine the language itself. Increasingly discussion is framed in terms, not of charity expressing the religious piety of the donor motivated by a desire for God's blessing, but *bienfaisance*, a wholly secular category of wishing to do good to other human beings.[7]

This more secular and scientific perspective follows through into the way in which these institutions for the poor are to be run and funded. In his article on hospitals in the *Encyclopédie*, Diderot makes it clear that these institutions should only be occupied by the genuinely sick, with the structural poor and indigent cared for at home instead. Moreover, he stated in the same article that the funding of these institutions should come from the redistribution of Church lands rather than state or private funds, thus making an early link between Church expropriation and social policy that was to be delivered at the end of the century.[8]

That said, for the most famous *philosophes*, poverty was not in the main a priority for discussion. It mattered more to those like Turgot or German cameralists, such as Justi and Sonnenfels, whose work was closely connected with administration, fiscal issues and wealth creation. Voltaire's *Le Siècle de Louis XIV* contains, in contrast, several dismissive remarks about the poor, whether about accepting the inevitability of poverty or the need to maintain it if workers are to be held to their work.[9] Nor does he take the issue further in *Candide*: while there are attacks on slavery and many social injustices are attributed to the practices of the Church, little is said about poverty in the abstract or particular.[10] Similarly, in *Émile*, Rousseau does not take the opportunity to make the poor the likely beneficiaries of his scheme of 'natural education'. While there are peasants who appear in the book, they have little agency and are marginal to the arguments. He appears to take the view that education is an irrelevance to the poor, rather than a potential ladder out of their poverty.

An important response to Mandeville's challenge about the relation between the poor and the state comes indirectly in Turgot's famous essay '*Fondation*' from the *Encyclopédie*. Writing in 1757, and also focusing on charitable giving, he acknowledges that the key defect of state policy on welfare was that it was reactive and fragmented, and based on traditional notions of moral economy that were worse than useless in a modern commercial society. By simply reacting on an *ad hoc* basis to grain shortages, by providing relief for mendicity as it occurred, the state tackled symptoms rather than causes and, in some respects, did more general social harm than it gained credit for incidental good. Relief of dearth may have responded to traditional Christian notions of charity and good works, but in seeking to replace the traditional and sporadic role of the monks and the churches in this area, the state was reading the broader problem incorrectly. Removing the obstacles to industry constituted the core of true welfarism, which would ultimately ameliorate poverty through removing the obstacles to wealth creation and implicate the poor as consumers as much as creators of prosperity.[11]

He goes on to offer a long analysis of the way in which wide access to charity in Spain and parts of Italy had led to further immiseration, a rise in the numbers of beggars, a decline in the numbers of the active labour force and ultimately to de-population, and concludes as follows: 'What the state owes to each of its members is the destruction of obstacles which might hinder them in their industriousness, or which might trouble them in their enjoyment of the fruits which are the reward.'[12] There is therefore a way for the poor to escape poverty, which is partly to dismantle the many restrictive and arbitrary practices of *ancien régime* administration so as to enable economic growth and the broadening of the social pyramid; but it is also a matter of working to improve the setting of their lives in the form of public works and institutions of broad social benefit.

This is a perspective that combines economic theory with a great confidence in the capacity of good administration to overcome the notorious problems of legal implementation within the *ancien régime*. We see both its possibilities and limitations working themselves out in the French debates over the so-called *dépôts de mendicité*, which Turgot sought to reform in his brief administration at the start of Louis XVI's reign. It was felt that government compromises, hostility to the *intendants* and local fears of the disruptive potential of beggars had served to neuter the more humanitarian goals of *bienfaisance* and proto-utilitarian concepts of citizenship that lay behind the original imposition of the system. What Turgot sought to do was to set up cooperation between local parishes and the agents of the state. Cases of genuine hardship would be tackled locally through alms bureaus promoted by the *intendants* or the Church, and appropriate residential arrangements should be made for genuine invalids and children. The able-bodied beggars should be put to work in creating useful manufactures, especially clothing, so that they could gain skills and contribute to the overall welfare of society. Thus, he sought to distinguish the genuinely needy from idle vagabonds and resolve the paradox that lay at the heart of mendicity – the requirement that it be stigmatised as voluntary immorality, while still making provision for those who quite clearly did not choose to be beggars.[13]

Unfortunately, these reforms largely came to grief in the failure of his *Six Edicts*. As so often in Enlightened reform projects, progress in one area was dependent on parallel progress in others before implementation could be sustained overall. Workhouse reforms required a new municipal structure, and once that failed as a result of opposition from a constellation of the usual suspects of vested interests in the church, *parlements* and other local layers, then the prospect of a new pattern of poor relief driven by Turgot's vision of administrative Enlightenment died with it. However, it should be said that many of the experiences gained by those involved in the management of the depots did filter through to the Committee on Mendicity created by the Constituent Assembly in the revolutionary years. A statement of obligations to provide both work and relief for the poor even made it into the 1793 constitution.[14]

Despite the focus on solving specific local problems, there is a common determination among practical reformers from the 1760s onwards in promoting welfare that ultimately also promoted wealth. The end of a generation of European warfare and the abolition of the Jesuits created a set of practical circumstances conducive to a focus on welfare, education and the sources of domestic prosperity. We can see this emerging at the theoretical level in the debate over the morality of luxury and consumerism and the (alleged) leisure preferences of the poor. This was in a way a debate that played one aspect of Mandeville's thought (the beneficial role of luxury) against another (the need to keep the poor in immiseration). Certainly, in England the balance of the debate in both philosophical and official circles ended up endorsing the view that even on narrow commercial grounds the poor too could become consumers who would stimulate demand through their own spending.[15]

With the effective end of feudal structures of mutual obligation, it was no longer clear who had the legal responsibility to take care of the poor anymore, and especially the rural poor. While the government may have grandly taken upon itself that obligation in theory, in some countries it was hard to see how this could mean much in practice without deliberate fostering of local structures that could channel what funds were sent from the centre for relief of the poor. This problem was particularly apparent to former *intendants*, such as Turgot, caught in the crossfire, and a manifest concern to those who called themselves cameralists and had a commitment to *Polizei*.

This last is one of those elusive concepts that has to be understood in particular context if it is to have meaning. While at one end of the spectrum it could mean direct methods of social discipline, it could as often be deployed in a philanthropic sense. Both state and local administrations across Europe had to respect or at least pay lip-service to the web of traditional expectations of support that E. P. Thompson usefully defined as the 'moral economy of the crowd', and there is often little distinction to be drawn between what we would call humanitarian motives and the management of human resources.[16] As Johann von Loen wrote, 'If a prince wishes to keep his forests in good condition, he must watch over them attentively and have good care taken of the saplings. It is just the same with the plantation of human beings: it requires protection, attention and care, if it is to thrive and prosper.'[17]

This in turn implies that a lack of clarity is inherent in the concept of *Polizei*, its particular categories varying according to what is identified as specifically missing in local examples of *Glückseligkeit*.[18] As Justi states in the preface to his large textbook, cameralism is 'the science whose object is the constant maintenance of an exact correspondence and relations between the welfare of individual families and the common good'.[19] That balance requires constant adjustment, which helps to explain how hard it is to pin down motivation and intention in social reform inspired by cameralist sources, which can seem both hard-heartedly driven by statistics and empathetic to local grievances in rapid alternation. But either way it implied top-down regulation rather than trusting to local administration to come up with answers on its own.

If one compares the many texts of political economy that emerged from the middle decades of the eighteenth century, what becomes clear is that whether they are labelled cameralist, or physiocratic or neither, there are several common themes arranged around the promotion of welfare. But it is more the welfare of the community than the rights or benefits of the individual that is the focus. Measures to boost population, improve public health, translate agricultural manuals and implement their proposals, together with plans to reduce or abolish tariffs and tolls and improve communication links, are presented as reforms that will benefit the utility of the whole community. Legal codification is part of the story too, as is the extension of new court structures into the localities staffed by civil servants rather than the local elite. Those goals apply equally to educational reforms. Abbot Felbiger, who advised both Frederick and Catherine II, was certainly determined that school curricula should become more practical, useful and uniform; but what ultimately mattered was that the skills taught reflected the economic needs of the state rather than any sense of social mobility or fresh aspirations for the pupils beyond the level to which they were born.[20]

State emulation and consolidation plays its part too, as rulers competed to attract skilled immigrants, subsidise the production of particular local luxury goods and trades and discover new resources to be mined and land to be taken into cultivation. All measures that claimed a patina of welfare also had behind them aspirations that were natural to the Enlightened absolutist state: the extension of uniformity and state authority in place of a merely theoretical claim of sovereignty, and the displacement of magnate control by the state's own agents. In the larger states, the poor could be forgiven for preferring the older system in some respects, when the state's newly enhanced presence and greater efficiency led only to a higher level of exactions.

Perhaps it was better to be poor in a small German principality run by a high-minded prince-bishop with few secular ambitions, or in a port city such as Hamburg where the city authorities were able to coordinate a community-wide cameralist response? In the latter, a Patriotic Society was founded in 1765 to debate measures on poor rates, workhouse foundation, pension schemes and new vocational training. Considerable funding was needed to bring this about, but even in the disrupted revolutionary decade at the end of the century the public health system and poor relief measures that were implemented lasted well. Teams of officials covered different areas of the city systematically, and the city fathers took on the direct administrative tasks involved in the schooling of the children of the poor, relief for beggars and new labour initiatives. This collective, coordinated and well-funded initiative showed that it was possible to move beyond piecemeal and unpredictable religiously inspired philanthropy, but only where there was a secular will to involve and potentially benefit the whole community.[21]

Of course, that was a single, tightly defined urban example, hard to replicate within the largest Enlightened absolutist states. If we turn now to offer a brief survey of the position of the poor in Prussia, Russia and the Habsburg Monarchy, and the measures taken on their behalf, we see not only much more difficulty in coordinating the centre and the localities, but also some revealingly sharp distinctions within the broad cameralist framework of economic analysis.

Frederick II was certainly the least responsive on these issues, largely because the particular military–fiscal complex of the Prussian state made it essential for the monarch to support the local nobility in their multiple roles in the army, administration and management of local agriculture. There were measures of poor relief and agricultural improvement on the Crown estates where the monarch had freedom to experiment; and traditional notions of *Polizei* – 'moral economy' – insured that grain stores were maintained in all main garrison towns against the possibility of harvest failure and dearth. There were also measures to promote a healthy and larger population. But poverty, its causes and handling, was not a popular or favoured topic in the debates and lecture series of the Academy of Sciences in Berlin.

As so often is the case with Frederick II, there is a gap between the theory and rhetoric on the one hand and the measures implemented on the other. He offered several denunciations of serfdom which raised hopes that when he was free from the distraction and alternative focus of the wars of the 1740s and 1750s he would take action to shift the balance of power in the countryside. The test of these aspirations came after the end of the Seven Years' War, when suddenly there were no obstacles any more in the way of a focus on domestic reforms. But when Frederick moved to abolish serfdom in Pomerania, as part of his plan for post-war reconstruction in a particularly damaged province, his cabinet order was simply ignored without repercussions by the Junker aristocracy.[22]

The structure of rural poverty was too closely enmeshed in the pattern of military procurement that required both aristocrat and serf to double in army roles. Dismantle one, and the other became equally infeasible. It is true that the loss of free labour service on already marginal noble estates was also an issue, as Frederick himself admitted: '... in wishing to abolish at a stroke this abominable system, we would entirely overturn the agricultural economy, and it would be necessary to compensate the nobility, in part, for the loss of revenues it would suffer'.[23] But this was a matter of resources, whereas the structural links between serfdom and army service were the essential framework of the Prussian state, which no monarch could afford to disturb.

There were a few other measures that might have improved matters at the margins, if Frederick had been willing to allow the peasants to purchase noble lands, and if he had encouraged more social mobility to and within the towns. But his social conservatism ensured the towns remained essentially providers of services to the armed forces with little or no free agency. The best that could be achieved was to improve the legal standing of the peasants on the Crown estates by granting secure tenancies and trusting to the self-interest of the aristocracy in supporting healthy peasants who were also required to be effective soldiers.[24]

For Catherine II, the policy outcomes were broadly similar but arrived at by a different route. There was no chance at this stage of the Russian peasantry, whether Church, state or noble, becoming a major player in economic growth as producers or consumers; so instead the government tried to foster the emergence of a new urban culture which ultimately might act as a counterweight to its reliance on the aristocracy. In one of her memoranda written for discussion with Diderot, Catherine dismisses the poor in the following terms:

> As for the common people, all they think of is the bread that nourishes them and the religion that consoles them. Their ideas will always be as primitive as their nature. The prosperity of the state, progress, the next generation, are words which cannot affect them; they are connected with society only by their hardships, and of all that vast period of time which is called the future, they never conceive of anything except the next day. They are deprived by their poverty of a loftier interest.[25]

Diderot, needless to say, did not share this perspective. In both his conversations with Catherine during his stay in St Petersburg in 1773–1774, and in his subsequent *Observations on the Nakaz*, he argued that future state prosperity depended on widening the ownership of land and giving the peasants fresh incentives to labour. In section 82 of the *Observations*, he takes specific issue with the Mandevillian perspective that only repressive means including perpetuated poverty could compel the serf to accept the reality of his serfdom:

> I personally heard this appalling stupidity spoken by a provincial Intendant ... that the condition of a peasant was so painful that only extreme poverty or the fear of death could keep him in it. Public minister though he was, he still did not know that no danger or work frightens a man when he is compensated by the result ... It had never entered that minister's mind that in all professions the income which makes it possible to obtain help takes away the fatigue; and that callously to exclude the peasant from the class of landowners is to halt the progress of the first of the arts ... He governed a province and knew nothing of man.[26]

That said, much of Diderot's energy in the *Observations* is directed towards refutation of the Physiocrats, so the general drift of his remarks on poverty tends towards a critique of their view that the opulence derived from removing restrictions on free trade, especially the free trade of grain, would itself resolve the problem of poverty. Without a thorough revolution in property holding, that, Diderot thought, would indeed be cold comfort for the peasantry.[27] If it is the case that 'property alone opens the door to cultivation of one's intelligence, talents and tastes, which in turn provide the qualifications necessary for citizenship', then that means education is vital as a means of transforming social attitudes in this direction.[28] Though the *Observations* marked Diderot's increasing disillusionment with the possibilities of reform from above through Enlightened absolutism, he did continue to contribute to the cause of educational reform in Russia promoted by General Betskoy.[29]

In the wake of the Pugachev Revolt the era of 'blue skies' thinking represented by the *Nakaz* came to an end. There was to be no significant reform of serfdom thereafter. Instead, Catherine refocused her attention on creating a new corporate structure so that by accelerated *fiat* she could bring into being a 'society of orders' that had taken centuries to evolve in the West, thereby creating the intermediate structures which could ease the task of implementing central government policy in the provinces. This would serve to capture the kernel of Montesquieu's thought which had been a key aspect of her preparations for the *Nakaz*. Within the structures of the *Statute of Local Administration* (1775) and the *Charters for the Nobility and the Towns* that followed ten years later were contained many initiatives that were of lasting relevance to alleviating the impact of poverty, though the final charter devoted to the peasants, which would have had most salience to the relief of poverty, was ultimately never promulgated.[30]

As noted at the start of this chapter, we need to distinguish between grand policy towards poverty and changes and adjustments to welfare on the ground. Russia is a case study where separating out the two strands offers rather different perspectives. Hartley, Dixon and Madariaga have shown in several recent studies that an apparent focus on other priorities at the top did not prevent significant changes at the bottom.[31] While these measures mattered most to Catherine for purposes of uniform government and regular, standardised administration, it was the structures dealing with primary education, welfare distribution and regular justice that made more difference to the practical lives of peasants and townsfolk.

There were substantial initiatives in creating foundling homes in the main cities, drawn from German models, though mortality rates remained as high as in other European cities.[32] There was a serious attempt to replace Church welfare provision after the secularisation of Church lands in 1764; and in the wake of the 1775 Statute new boards of public welfare were created on the same template in every Russian province, coordinating administration of hospitals, alms houses, asylums and orphanages and schools. Careful thought went into the modelling of these institutions – there was an initial grant of 15,000 roubles to every board, but each was encouraged to act in an entrepreneurial fashion in coordination with local elites, inviting top-up charitable donations and also offering loans to promising local initiatives. Further funding for schools came in the 1780s.[33]

As with so many early modern initiatives in the area of welfare the question immediately arises of how much difference these measures made. Were they dissipated and neutralised in the sands of local indifference and corruption, or did they bring about lasting changes? The results seem to have been mixed, with more promising outcomes, as you might expect, in St Petersburg, Moscow and Kiev, and fewer in rural provinces. One aspect that receives surprisingly little attention in the literature is the reluctance of many of the intended beneficiaries of welfare to come forward to receive it, whether in terms of placing orphans in schools or foundling hospitals, or in accepting hospital care in place of home remedies. It was not simply a matter of state underfunding – take-up and suspicion of state-sponsored initiatives remained endemic.[34] In some ways this should not surprise us, especially in the Russian context, where the peasant commune was constructed to be a self-sufficient structure suspicious of outside initiatives which were familiarly focused on conscription or fiscal exactions.[35] Even attempts through a land survey to rationalise agricultural practices on Catherine's own estate at Tsarskoe Selo in 1772 ran into problems that anticipated the kind of opposition to change that Joseph II experienced in the Habsburg lands during his own later abolition of serfdom.[36]

As so often in early modern welfare policies, the fundamental problem lay in a lack of coordination not just between central and local institutions but also between the various key objectives of state policy. For example, the acquisition by the state of Church lands at the start of Catherine's reign (ratifying a policy initiated by her predecessor) provided a uniquely resourced opportunity to open up a free market in land that could potentially have transformed the productivity of Russian agriculture, while also yielding the state a substantial windfall income as lands were sold off. However, the exigencies of the Turkish War of 1768–1774 ensured that the government simply subsumed the Church lands into its own portfolio, spending the income on financing war, with only a small fraction returned to the Church to fund philanthropy.[37]

Nevertheless, a corner had been turned. Catherine had fulfilled the undertaking made in the *Nakaz*, that the state and no longer the Church had the primary responsibility for the care of the elderly, the chronically unwell and orphans. Given the obstacles facing any attempt at the reform of serfdom, welfare was an area where progress could reasonably be made, and to an extent was. In some respects, Catherine restated traditional nostrums, including an equivocal view of mendicity – suggesting that the genuinely destitute should be cared for while the physically capable should be made to work. But in the language in which welfare was discussed there was now a clear humanitarian purpose and aspiration, even if it is at times tempered by a moralising determination to use labour, whether voluntary or compelled, to improve and correct the behaviour of wayward individuals. As Hartley states, 'It could be said that the provisions on welfare institutions in the Statute on Provincial Administration reflect both the influence of the Enlightenment – in establishing state, secular, responsibility for the aged, sick and insane, and in the humanitarian and moral ideals put forward – and the features of the *Polizeistaat* in its regulatory nature.'[38]

It is in the Habsburg Monarchy that we see the most sustained effort by the central government to alter the practice of poor relief and to reconceptualise the place of the poor in society. There were two reasons why this was more fertile ground for change. First, the state simply had more discretion to act – the landowning class was not so embedded in the state apparatus in the way it was in Prussia and Russia and the civil service was in large measure independent of it. Despite the lack of uniform control over its disparate territories, there were greater opportunities for a sustained 'welfarist' programme to stick. Second, the existing system of poor relief and education rested much more heavily on the Church and the monasteries and religious brotherhoods than was the case elsewhere. Once the Jesuit order was suppressed in 1772 and the programme of monastic closures began to gather pace, something inevitably had to be done to reconstruct the foundations of poor relief as well.

As early as 1771, in a letter to Maria Theresia, the Emperor sketched out the possibilities that such redistribution of assets might open up – 'what funds would be available for foundlings' homes, orphanages, correctional institutions, workhouses, penitentiaries and hospitals in which young people would be brought up as true Catholics and members of the state ... orphans would be provided for, the idle removed from society, the wicked punished and rehabilitated, and finally the weary and aged provided for'.[39]

This was coupled, as I have indicated, to a more elevated sense of how the poor might be integrated into the body corporate of society. In the introduction to his charter abolishing serfdom in 1785, there is already a clear statement that national improvement and development of civic rights go hand-in-hand:

> We understand and recognise that improving agriculture and encouraging enterprise are the two best methods of achieving [the happiness] of the peoples subject to us, but that it is impossible to bring this about unless personal freedom, which belongs to every man by nature and according to the state, is granted to the subjects in general, and the right to own property which they occupy ... is assured and consolidated.[40]

Though ultimately reversed, this document was a harbinger of things to come, not least in its assertion that freedom was granted both by nature *and* the state.

While responsibility for the most important initiatives rests with Joseph II, crucial steps were also taken during the preceding co-regency with his mother, Maria Theresia. From the mid-1760s onwards, when one ministerial generation gave way to Kaunitz, Sonnenfels and others receptive to new ideas, state social policy coalesced around an agenda that prioritised population growth, agricultural improvement and manufacturing enterprises based on import-substitution. The fact that neither of the co-regents espoused interest in the theory of cameralism did not mean that they were not fully on board with a pragmatic cameralist agenda in line with their overarching desire to apply uniform governance to the disparate domains of the monarchy. This can be seen most clearly in the agrarian reforms in Bohemia in the 1770s.

Discontent in a number of provinces focused attention on the most onerous aspect of serfdom, namely the *Robot* or *Urbarium*, which required peasants to work a specified number of days without reward on the landlord's estate. Rather than tackle the overall institution of serfdom, attention focused instead on setting up procedures whereby the peasants could negotiate new labour contracts with the nobility with a variety of ceilings set by the government. Additionally, the state official F. A. Raab pioneered a system on royal estates whereby the peasants could commute their labour obligations for a cash payment instead, leading ultimately to secure leases on the land. These measures did not challenge the balance of power in the countryside, but still introduced a new flexibility into labour relations. The government's role remained one of light-touch enforcement and dispute reconciliation. Given the dangers of pushing the nobility too far and risking revolt or refusal to pay taxes, this was perhaps the best incremental progress that could be achieved in the countryside, and similar *Robot* patents were extended to most provinces.[41] Unfortunately, this was not enough for Joseph II, when he was free to act alone.

One result of this commutation of labour days was that peasants were able to supplement their income from local manufacturing projects. Such cottage industry began to flourish after the *Robotpatent* because it could operate free of urban guild regulation and draw on a labour force galvanised by a desire to earn money to enable early marriage. With these incentives the population of Bohemia rose by up to 50 per cent in the later decades of the eighteenth century whereas in the other Habsburg lands the increase was only 10 per cent. And all this had come about without pushing the nobility too far – indeed they had benefited from the greater productivity of a freer and freshly incentivised peasantry.[42]

Joseph's measures to abolish serfdom gathered pace during his ten years of personal rule. It is important to note that the actual abolition of serfdom was one of only several measures that were aimed at reconfiguring the social order; nor was it necessarily the most important. Abolition changed legal status and facilitated labour mobility; but it has to be seen as part of a broader whole, where the chief goals were to alter the fiscal foundation of the state and extend the outreach of central government into the countryside. The attacks on the *Robot* system extended commutation of labour days outside the Crown lands and required the nobility to accept cash or crop alternatives, and to have peasant tenants on demesne land who would be paid a wage. The final straw – for the nobility – was the Tax and Agrarian Regulation of 1789, which undertook to reduce taxes on peasants to a maximum of 30 per cent, all to be assessed on a new universal cadastre.

While not identified as a physiocratic measure, in essence this was the single land-tax espoused by Quesnay and Turgot for France in the 1760s. It aimed both to liberate peasant productivity and the public treasury simultaneously through simplifying tax collection for the state. This was cold comfort for the nobility across all regions of the monarchy for whom potential increases in agricultural productivity counted little against the actual and keenly felt loss of property rights in the here and now. Ultimately the economic wisdom of this approach could not be assessed as Joseph postponed its implementation until late in 1790, by which time he had died. His brother was quick to reverse the policy and return to the incremental supervisory role that had worked well enough during the co-regency.[43]

These major institutional measures to ameliorate rural poverty and raise agrarian prosperity were only part of the story and have to be seen alongside the more successful attempts to redistribute wealth from the abolition and sequestration of the monasteries.[44] These funds remained in the first instance in the religious sphere – for the payment of pensions, the funding of parish reorganisation and the creation of general seminaries to train priests, seen as crucial to the continuing provision of primary education, something of clear and central relevance to the poor. Though there were ironic exceptions, such as the maintenance of the mendicant Franciscans on account of the quality of their pastoral work, despite Joseph's desire to outlaw elsewhere the very mendicity on which the order was founded.[45]

As we move towards the later years of the 1780s, it was the aftershock of abolition for other religious institutions that brought the practical results of Joseph's religious policies to bear on the towns and villages of Lower Austria and the parishes of Vienna itself. The suppression of religious brotherhoods brought in a huge sum – there were reckoned to be over 4,500 in the central lands of the Monarchy, and those in Vienna were worth around 700,000 florins alone. Half of the assets were assigned to a new *Institute for the Poor* whose role was to organise and supervise both poor relief and education using existing parish structures. This relied on the parish priest and other local officials to decide on the sums appropriate to each individual and to administer the handouts usually at a specific church service each week. Direction of the project was entrusted to a Bohemian nobleman, Count Buquoy, who had pioneered a similar scheme a decade earlier on his own estates. He had been heavily influenced by the writings of Muratori, and particularly his view that religious faith and practice should be built around practical altruism. Each week a collection was to be taken in the parish for the poor, with the levels of support decided by the parish priest and a couple of other local notables and administered in church. The poor were to be graded according to four levels of indigence, and the biggest daily pay-outs amounted to a third of a labourer's weekly wage.[46]

A number of features stand out in these measures. Joseph's rebranding of the parish clergy as agents of the state demonstrates again how expanding the state's role into religious and educational affairs was all of a piece with this attempt to rationalise poor relief. More evidence of this resides in the fact that the scheme was extended in 1786 beyond Christian parishes into the Jewish community of Prague as well. Also, it is clear that this kind of enterprise relied and built upon existing structures rather than new bureaucracies. So, it had economies of scale, though with significant imperial oversight. There was also a new element of moral control apparent as well, in that the behaviour of the poor was now likely to be influenced by the attitudes of those responsible for deciding pay-outs.

Registration of all recipients implied a degree of social control too, and the role of the parish priest, now officially a state servant, in coordinating both welfare and education linked these reforms to Joseph's other great redeployment of Church resources, namely primary education, so that the poor could gain the skills for advancement in society as well.[47] One other lesson that seems clear is that such reforms had a much better chance of grafting successfully in an urban setting where there were clearly articulated parish administrative structures already in place. These are top-down paternalist measures *par excellence*, but they do indicate at least a utilitarian valuation of the potential contribution of the poor within society; and though much of Joseph's work perished with him, these elements continued into the Napoleonic era, as did the enhanced parish primary education system.

The Institute for the Poor and the experimental prototype that preceded it have received little study to date, but they are representative of the best that the Enlightened absolutist state, amid all its contradictions, could provide as an approach to poor relief. Moreover, it is a rare example of a reform scheme that emerged from below rather than from above, and which was then co-opted by the administration in Vienna and repurposed more generally. As Paul Bernard has shown, the aristocratic estates of Bohemia were essentially self-governing and thus well placed to innovate on their own terms, drawing on the older paternalistic views of charity but revitalising them with new cameralist rigour.[48]

While we should not idealise their practices or motivations, it is a reminder that the aristocracy were by no means obscurantist opponents of reform: self-interest and genuine humanitarian concerns could join forces in promoting a more healthy and productive work force with an adequately calibrated system of poor relief. Beales concludes: 'In working out his plans he [Buquoy] saw the parish as the unit, and the parish clergy as the instruments of both education and poor relief. This was just the mix of religion and economics, utilitarianism and benevolence, high mindedness and practicality which appealed to many of the most responsible landlords across Europe.'[49]

It is in this instance, perhaps, that continental thinking and practice in respect of the poor most closely approached the blend of public and private, state and local initiatives that characterised the differently configured approach to the poor in England. Neither approach ever successfully reconciled the tensions between provision for the genuinely indigent and the danger of encouraging the very leisure preference that the system was intended to prevent; nor did either system overcome the difficulties involved in linking local and central government to produce an efficiently delivered level of support. But at least by very different routes there was a common recognition of the challenges involved.[50]

Despite its sometimes patronising tenor, the combined demands of international state building, national self-improvement and a desire to rationalise and recalibrate mendicity led to several developments in absolutist states that anticipate and indeed fed into revolutionary and nineteenth-century innovations and discourse. It may not have been possible to reform the structures of wealth creation in the countryside, but it was now clearer who was considered deserving of charity and who not, and how ideally the poor should be integrated into society as productive members rather than simply stigmatised by exclusion.

Notes

1 Bernard Mandeville, 'An Essay on Charity, and Charity Schools', in Bernard Mandeville, *The Fable of the Bees*, ed. Philip Harth (London: Penguin, 1989), pp. 261–326, at p. 294.
2 Alexis de Tocqueville, *Memoir on Pauperism*, trans. Seymour Drescher and intro. Gertrude Himmelfarb (London: Institute of Economic Affairs, 1997), p. 24.
3 Perry Anderson, *Lineages of the Absolutist State* (London: New Left Books, 1974); Michael Mann, *The Sources of Social Power. Volume 2: The Rise of Classes and Nation States 1760–1914* (Cambridge: Cambridge University Press, 1993).
4 I owe this observation to Jo Innes.
5 Thomas Munck, *The Enlightenment: A Comparative Social History 1721–1794* (London: Arnold, 2000), pp. 181–186.
6 Alexis de Tocqueville, *The Old Regime and the Revolution. Volume 1: The Complete Text*, eds François Furet and Françoise Mélonio (Chicago, IL: University of Chicago Press, 1998), pp. 182–183.
7 Colin Jones, *Charity and Bienfaisance: The Treatment of the Poor in the Montpellier Region 1740–1815* (Cambridge: Cambridge University Press, 1982). See also Chapter 2 by Arnault Skornicki in this book.

8 Denis Diderot, 'Hôpital (1765)', in Jean d'Alembert and Denis Diderot (eds), *Encyclopédie ou Dictionnaire raisonné des sciences, des arts et des métiers, par une Société de Gens de lettres*, 17 vols (1751–1765), vol. viii, pp. 293–294.
9 Voltaire, *Oeuvres Historiques*, ed. R. Pomeau (Pléiade: Paris, 1961), pp. 995–996.
10 Irvin Ehrenpreis, 'Poverty and Poetry: Representations of the Poor in Augustan Literature', in Louis T Milic (ed.) *Studies in Eighteenth-Century Culture: The Modernity of the Eighteenth Century* (Case Western Reserve University: Cleveland & London, 1971), pp. 18–19.
11 Anne-Robert-Jacques Turgot, 'Fondation (1757)', *Encyclopédie*, vol. vii, pp. 72–75.
12 Ibid., p. 74.
13 Thomas McStay Adams, *Bureaucrats and Beggars: French Social Policy in the Age of the Enlightenment* (Oxford: Oxford University Press, 1990), pp. 30–134; Olwen H. Hufton, *The Poor of Eighteenth-Century France 1750–1789* (Oxford: Clarendon Press, 1974), pp. 221–244.
14 Alan Forrest, 'Bienfaisance ou repression : l'état révolutionnaire et la question de la pauvreté', in *Studies on Voltaire and the Eighteenth Century*, 311 (1993), 327–338.
15 John Hatcher, 'Labour, Leisure and Economic Thought Before the Nineteenth Century', *Past & Present*, 160 (1998), 64–115.
16 Ritchie Robertson, *The Enlightenment: The Pursuit of Happiness, 1680–1790* (London: Penguin Books, 2020), pp. 400–412.
17 Ibid., p. 406.
18 Keith Tribe, *Strategies of Economic Order: German Economic Discourse 1750–1950* (Cambridge: Cambridge University Press, 1995), pp. 8–31.
19 Robertson, *Enlightenment*, p. 405.
20 H. M. Scott, 'Reform in the Habsburg Monarchy 1740–90', in Hamish M. Scott (ed.), *Enlightened Absolutism: Reform and Reformers in Later Eighteenth-Century Europe* (Basingstoke: Palgrave, 1990), pp. 175–176; Michael Printy, *Enlightenment and the Creation of German Catholicism* (Cambridge: Cambridge University Press, 2009), p. 147.
21 Mary Lindemann, *Patriots and Paupers: Hamburg 1712–1830* (Oxford: Oxford University Press, 1990).
22 Klaus Epstein, *The Genesis of German Conservatism* (Princeton, NJ: Princeton University Press, 1966), 211–213.
23 Frederick the Great, 'Essay on the Forms of Government and the Duties of Sovereigns', in ibid., *Philosophical Writings*, ed. Avi Lifschitz (Princeton, NJ: Princeton University Press, 2021), pp. 195–207 at p. 203.
24 T. C. W. Blanning, 'Frederick the Great and Enlightened Absolutism', in Scott, *Enlightened Absolutism,* pp. 265–288 at p. 272.
25 Catherine II, 'Memorandum to Diderot (1774)', first published in Maurice Tourneux, *Diderot et Catherine II* (Paris, 1899), p. 538, translated in ed. Anthony Lentin, *Enlightened Absolutism (1760–1790): A Documentary Sourcebook* (Newcastle-upon-Tyne: Avero Publications, 1985), p. 76.

26 Denis Diderot, 'Observations sur le Nakaz', in ibid., *Political Writings*, eds John Hope Mason and Robert Wokler (Cambridge: Cambridge University Press, 1992), pp. 77–164 at pp. 128–129.
27 Anthony Strugnell, *Diderot's Politics: A Study of the Evolution of Diderot's Political Thought after the Encyclopédie* (The Hague: Martinus Nijhoff, 1973), pp. 186–190.
28 Ibid., pp. 187–188.
29 Robert Zaretsky, *Catherine & Diderot: The Empress, The Philosopher, and the Fate of the Enlightenment* (Cambridge, MA: Harvard University Press, 2019), pp. 180–182; Isabel de Madariaga, *Catherine the Great: A Short History* (London: Yale University Press, 1990), pp. 104–117.
30 Madariaga, *Catherine the Great*, pp. 126–130.
31 Janet M. Hartley, *A Social History of the Russian Empire, 1650–1825* (London: Longman, 1999); Madariaga, *Catherine the Great*; Simon Dixon, *Catherine the Great* (Harlow: Longman, 2001).
32 Hartley, *Social History of Russia*, p. 146.
33 Ibid.; Dixon, *Catherine the Great*, pp. 124–135.
34 Hartley, *Social History of Russia*, pp. 147–148.
35 Dixon, *Catherine the Great*, pp. 89–91.
36 Roger Bartlett, 'J. J. Sievers and the Russian Peasantry under Catherine II', *Jahrbücher für Geschichte Osteuropas*, 32:1 (1984), 16–33.
37 Simon Dixon, *The Modernisation of Russia 1676–1825* (Cambridge: Cambridge University Press, 1999), pp. 67–71.
38 Janet M. Hartley, 'Philanthropy in the Reign of Catherine the Great: Aims and Realities', in Roger Bartlett and Janet M. Hartley (eds), *Russia in the Age of the Enlightenment: Essays for Isabel de Madariaga* (London: Macmillan, 1990), pp. 167–202, at p. 179.
39 'Letter from Joseph II to Maria Theresa (1771)', in Lentin, *Enlightened Absolutism*, p. 146.
40 'Joseph II: Serfdom Patent (1785)', in Lentin, *Enlightened Absolutism*, p. 86.
41 Derek Beales, *Joseph II*, 2 vols (Cambridge: Cambridge University Press, 1987–2009), vol. i, pp. 346–358; Charles W. Ingrao, *The Habsburg Monarchy 1618–1815* (Cambridge: Cambridge University, 2000), pp. 185–188.
42 Ingrao, *Habsburg Monarchy*, p. 205, p. 214.
43 Ibid., pp. 205–210; Beales, *Joseph II*, vol. ii, pp. 239–270.
44 Beales, *Joseph II*, vol. ii pp. 271–306.
45 Ibid., vol. ii, p. 295.
46 Ibid., vol. ii, pp. 316–319.
47 Ibid., vol. ii, Ch. 7; T. C. W. Blanning, *Joseph II* (London: Longman, 1994), pp. 67–70.
48 Paul P. Bernard, 'Poverty and Poor Relief in the Eighteenth Century', in Charles W. Ingrao (ed.), *State and Society in Early Modern Austria* (West Lafayette, IN: Purdue University Press, 1994), pp. 238–251.
49 Beales, *Joseph II*, vol. ii, pp. 318–319.
50 Joel Mokyr, *The Enlightened Economy: An Economic History of Britain 1700–1850* (London: Yale University Press, 2009), pp. 440–445.

2

Economic *bienfaisance* and the Physiocratic rhetoric of charity

Arnault Skornicki

During the second half of the eighteenth century in France, the Physiocratic school participated in a notable way in debates about poverty. Studies that have appeared on the topic of assistance have generally considered the contribution of the Physiocrats to represent the new liberal approaches advanced by Enlightened elites.[1] However, few specialised works on Physiocracy have been accorded sustained attention to the issues of poverty and assistance in the group's thought. Historian Sébastien Duchesne has analysed finely the pluralism of the 'Economists' on these matters and he concluded that all of them had betrayed the principles of their master, François Quesnay.[2] Economist and historian of ideas, Alain Clément, studied the contribution of *abbé* Nicolas Baudeau in detail, a man whose originality was to have elaborated a complete social programme for the indigent.[3] However, all of these studies have neglected sources that are as significant as the writings of Quesnay and of his closest collaborator, the Marquis de Mirabeau, as well as the main Physiocratic journal, the *Éphémérides du Citoyen*. Not only is this important corpus overflowing with discourse about poverty and charity but, from the middle of the 1760s, it reveals an overwhelming aspect of rhetoric which has hardly given rise to any commentary: that of *bienfaisance*.

It is well known that the second half of eighteenth-century France saw an outpouring and spread of discourses referring to *bienfaisance* ('beneficence'), a newly crafted term that denoted charity and virtue in contemporary France.[4] The invention of the word is commonly attributed to the *abbé* de Saint-Pierre, a major proponent of reformism who had written several texts on poverty and charity.[5] The idea derives from the noun *'le bienfait'*, that is, the good deed. In particular, *bienfaisance* referred to social virtue and love of humanity, whereas *charity* emphasised love of God. In every sense, this new commonplace could be defined as the joys of doing good to others.[6] It stressed a new sensibility grounded in a principle of humanity and fraternity. This moral watchword appeared eminently compatible with political reform in favour of prosperity, social utility and public happiness.

Its utilitarian complexion carried a critique of the traditional approach of Christian charity: 'There is magnanimity in generosity; but there is a more continuous usefulness in *bienfaisance*.'[7] Alms, in this conception, without necessarily being condemned, were devalued, for the rich man should worry less about his soul than about contributing to social utility. Poverty was no longer considered as a fatality, an object of shame or as a virtue, but as a social ill that the collectivity could combat. Traditional public assistance was criticised as inhumane and ineffective: henceforth, it would be right to render the poor useful without humiliating them. These views did not deny the action of the Church, but it was called to be overseen and coordinated by the public authorities. Both concrete acts and institutional achievements accompanied the discourse of *bienfaisance* over the final two decades of the Ancien Régime. Public authorities launched numerous enquiries and reforms concerning aid of beggars and hospital organisation. The propaganda of the monarchy developed the theme of 'royal *bienfaisance*', in which Louis XVI was called *le bienfaisant*.[8] The cultural phenomenon also encouraged new forms of private charity to appear, alongside those framed by the Church (alms, bequests, *hôtels-Dieu* or general hospitals), and this involved the creation of entirely secular philanthropic societies by representatives of the Enlightened elites.[9] Finally, the Revolution created a great Book of *Bienfaisance* in 1794 that organised aid for the poor in the French countryside, followed by *les bureaux de bienfaisance* in 1796, as part of a national policy of public assistance.[10]

However, the discourse of *bienfaisance* was by no means a coherent ideology. Rather, it can be seen as part of a common vocabulary of the French Enlightenment that framed a debate – contradictory in nature – about how to reduce poverty. For example, the debate set Turgot in opposition to the Physiocrats, on the one hand, and to Jacques Necker, on the other. Among the former, many of the *Économistes* – Dr Quesnay and his disciples – precociously endorsed the discourse of *bienfaisance*. The present chapter considers the Physiocrats as the clique of acquaintances that surrounded Quesnay and Mirabeau for a considerable time and that formed a group whose public aim was to develop and promote 'rural philosophy'; in particular – as regards the present subject – this group included Quesnay and Mirabeau themselves, Pierre-Samuel Du Pont, Nicolas Baudeau and Guillaume-François Le Trosne.[11] The Physiocratic position is both central and original in the debate about diminishing poverty. On the one hand, like Montesquieu and other Enlightened thinkers, the Physiocrats shared a liberal optimism about the beneficial effects of commercial society on poverty reduction.[12] In this view, the indigent did not need alms, but decently paid jobs. As Melon claimed, 'a charitable man gives alms; a statesman gives opportunities for working'.[13] Likewise, the Physiocrats supported free labour and proposed breaking with the punitive and mercantilist approach to poverty that had guided most European policy since the sixteenth century. The latter could be seen in the examples of British workhouses, the general hospital in Paris, founded in 1656, intended for the detention of vagrants[14] or the *dépôts de mendicité* (1767) for the confinement of beggars in France.[15] It was for this reason that they supported the new social policy of their close friend, the Minister of Finance Turgot (1774–1776), who had replaced the *dépôts de mendicité* with 'charity workshops' particularly devoted to roadworks. Conversely, a number of the *Économistes* went even further by radically disapproving the stigmatisation of poverty. Contrary to many contemporaries, and Malthus later, they firmly condemned the distinction between the wicked poor and virtuous poor: in their view, poverty had global economic causes and could not generally be attributed to the immorality of individuals. In this conception, it was the responsibility of the government to give the poor access to work. Yet, for this purpose, the Physiocrats insisted much more than Montesquieu or Melon upon the necessity of the absolute freedom of trade and the pursuit of self-interest.

Their rhetoric of *bienfaisance*, and the original way in which they expressed it, was precisely suited to this liberal view. If one could consider certain ideas as attempts to legitimise questionable actions,[16] one might discern the collective intention that guided the Physiocratic reappropriation of the lexicon of *bienfaisance*. The Jansenists, such as Pierre Nicole or Pierre de Boisguilbert, opposed economic interest and charity, valuing (in a proto-Smithian vein) the superiority of the former over the latter in reducing poverty.[17] In the opposite direction, the *Économistes* tried to describe Enlightened self-interest as true charity itself. This was an audacious rhetorical move as their economic *bienfaisance* was different not only from the traditional idea of charity, but also from the mainstream idea of *bienfaisance*, which implied at least Enlightened goodwill from devoted philanthropes. On the contrary, Physiocratic *bienfaisance* was supposed to produce beneficial but impersonal and unintentional effects through the free market. Yet, the Physiocrats were aware that this characterisation would be highly controversial, for what would *bienfaisance* mean without the intention to do good? Their response was threefold. Far from being mere superficial trickery to moralise selfish conduct, their lexicon of *bienfaisance* led them: first, to reappraise the morality of rational economic behaviour as opposed to narrow, impulsive egoism; second, to propose a social programme designed to solve a set of problems that the simple free market could not answer – the question of the unemployed poor during a transition phase towards liberalisation, and the incapacitated and ill poor; and third, to build a genuine theory of compassion compatible with their anthropological premises. This chapter shows that their rhetorical strategy was a weapon wielded in political battles to provide a greater dimension of humanity to conceptions founded on 'self-interest' and the defence of private property, ideas that their opponents accused of being insensitive to the sufferings of the people. At the same time, the chapter also demonstrates the doctrinal significance of this strategy. Rhetoric, or the art of persuading, may also be seen as the art of arguing: invoking grand principles and noble values is all the more convincing when it is not done solely to condemn, but when accompanied by arguments and propositions that have the capacity to bolster agreement.[18]

Physiocratic debate on poverty and the making of a social programme

Quesnay employed the term 'poverty' in a broad sense ('straitened means', material discomfort, vulnerability to conjunctural moments) and in a narrow sense (extreme indigence that required assistance). This latter definition was shared by many Enlightenment thinkers, like the *encyclopédiste* Louis de Jaucourt who described the condition as follows: 'POOR, Poverty (…) These words are taken ordinarily in Scripture to mean a state of indigence which necessitates the assistance of others, in the absence of a person's ability to be able to earn his livelihood through work.'[19] Surprisingly, in Georg Simmel's definition, the poor man was not so much one of the needy, as *he who receives, or should receive, assistance for his daily subsistence*. It was therefore collective behaviour and the type of assistance provided or promised which defined poverty.[20] Nevertheless, it was easy to tumble from discomfort to indigence due to the frequency of subsistence crises.[21] Although great famines and epidemics had ceased, the poor as a whole comprised a considerable proportion of the French population in 1789 (at least a third). The social question was particularly burning during the final two decades of the Ancien Régime, which saw an expansion in the number of people living in misery, of abandoned children and of rural criminality.[22]

From 1747 onwards, before his first, properly speaking, economic writings, Quesnay condemned tax-financed public assistance as an attack on property. Even if he admitted private charity, 'assistance from *bienfaisant* men (…)',[23] it also presented drawbacks. Not only did alms appear less as donation than extorsion by threatening beggars,[24] but they also diverted a proportion of capital away from investment and from '(…) the distribution of salaries, which enable men to subsist (…)'.[25] In Quesnay's view, almsgiving was legitimate '(…) in order to provide for the urgent needs of the indigent person, who is unable to provide for them by himself',[26] but because it remained a damaging cost for the community, it was necessary to reduce it as much as possible. Mirabeau, harsher still, judged that it was alms that created begging by giving rise to vocations. Therefore, it should only be 'of a moment' and reserved for life-threatening emergencies, not 'fixed' and institutionalised over time.[27]

One should not be misled by this apparent severity. Quesnay refused to blame the poor and denounced 'the maxims of those fierce men, who claim that it is necessary to reduce the common people to misery so as to force them to work'.[28] Following a cost–benefit analysis, it was perfectly rational to choose idleness and begging rather than activity if working did not provide enough means to live. As Mirabeau put it in an undated manuscript, 'he who lacks the incentive of desire confounds his pleasures and condenses them into a single one – idleness. In that way, all of his attraction is limited to what is strictly necessary with the least effort possible.'[29] Only wealth could maintain the desire to work.[30] In this conception, the causes of poverty were not moral, but economic and, above all, political. Quesnay fully agreed with a commonplace of eighteenth-century social policy debate; that is, that the government 'should not make men poor'.[31] Henceforth, the duty of government was to provide access to work, not to give alms.

Thus, the only right solution to the issue of poverty was economic growth, good wages and full employment, which would provide jobs for the needy and raise the wages of the mass of workers. One may observe that this liberal optimism was shared with other Enlightened thinkers, like Montesquieu.[32] Yet, for this purpose, Quesnay claimed that the best method was deregulation of the grain trade; that is, the key sector of the French economy. He deliberately placed the spotlight on the interests of landowners and farmers to the detriment of consumers, such as when he stated that '[o]ne should not annoy the rich in the enjoyment of their wealth or of their income for it is the enjoyment of the rich that gives birth to and that perpetuates wealth'.[33] He believed that the poverty of common consumers could not be an excuse for price regulation, and that such a protection would even be counterproductive, because it would dissuade investment in the only productive sector: agriculture. This was a clear critique of traditional police paternalism and the subsistence pact, which held that the king had a duty to ensure access to food for his people.[34]

Quesnay's social policy essentially amounted to the liberalisation of both the grain market and the charity of individuals. Certain neglected passages of *Despotism in China* (1767) offer nuance to this statement.[35] It was true that the Chinese case posed a particular difficulty: if – as Quesnay conceived it – China represented a model for economic government, how could there be so many indigent there?[36] In a first answer, Quesnay asserted that the gigantic population of China was proof of the country's general and overall affluence,[37] because population attunes itself to the level of resources, and not the contrary. If misery persisted, it was due to the restricted size of the country's territory, which entailed an excess in population with regard to available resources.[38] However, this explanation only increased the problem: if China was a victim of its success, did poverty not appear to be inevitable, therefore? 'Everywhere there are men in indigence', the doctor answered, reprising a thesis of Richard Cantillon according to which population size always tended to surpass the level of subsistence.[39] Even the best economic government in the world would not be able to escape this demographic law. It was for this reason that China offered the cruel spectacle of miserable people reduced to abandoning their children and to selling themselves as slaves. The solutions envisaged by Quesnay for eliminating this persistent indigence were of two orders: birth control through delaying the legal age of marriage, similar to the case of the Incas in Peru, or emigration of this excess population to the 'colonies' of the neighbouring islands, which were only waiting to be exploited.

These propositions with regard to *residual* poverty in a country that was generally and on the whole prosperous were scarcely pursued by the disciples of Quesnay. Rather they explored blind spots in his analysis about two other forms of poverty: one transitory and accidental, the other structural. On the one hand, Quesnay's analysis offered no plan for a current group of able-bodied poor who might be awaiting prosperity during a transition phase towards economic equilibrium, during which price increases might be more rapid than wage increases. Their friend Turgot noted thus that 'trade needed time to rise'.[40] As *intendant* of Limousin, he had been able to observe the gap between theory and practice, as well as seeing obstacles to the liberalisation of the grain trade that had been approved in 1763–1764. The brutal increase in prices could also have accidental causes, like climatic vagaries that might provoke fluctuations in production. If establishing 'natural order' would put '(…) our wealth on par with our population'[41] in such a way as to eliminate the greatest portion of begging and vagrancy, the government should definitely do something about these matters in the meantime. During this transition period, work would not allow everyone to earn a sufficient living due to lack of posts, the insufficient level of wages or the high cost of bread. Itinerant workers, with low and irregular incomes, were thus particularly exposed to precarity (stonemasons, chimney sweeps, water carriers, peddlers and so on).[42]

On the other hand, even if the free market did increase prosperity, how could one make provision for those who were really unable to work, whether temporarily or permanently? The incapacitated poor (the disabled, the aged, the ill or foundlings) would still need assistance. The problem of the 'economic government' of indigence could not be entirely resolved by deregulation and the free market. Quesnay's followers did not avoid those difficulties. *What kind of assistance could be expected from a rational economic government?* For them, only work gave men the right to obtain their own portion of wealth. Consequently, the state had no duty to assist the needy, and had no right to tax property and the rich in this context. Yet, economic government could not remain passive when great poverty both hurt common feelings of humanity and threatened social order, that is 'liberty, property and safety' (according to the Physiocratic motto).[43] As Mirabeau claimed, 'Far from excluding *bienfaisance*, the natural order prescribes it, and makes it complementary with the social order.'[44]

The problem of begging and of vagabondage presented itself cruelly after the Seven Years War. The French defeat led to economic difficulties and the demobilisation of thousands of soldiers, who threatened public order in the countryside. Minister Bertin called on the expertise of the agricultural societies in 1763.[45] Le Trosne, a Physiocrat, responded to the appeal by anonymously publishing a polemical tract against vagabondage, of which he had been a personal victim.[46] Alongside Le Mercier de La Rivière, he was one of two legally trained experts in the group, but he had a specific competence in criminal affairs.[47] If he espoused the current of reform in the lineage of Beccaria, he did not any less adopt a ruthless punitive approach towards popular delinquency. The vagabond was the *mauvais pauvre par excellence*: not only was he a sterile consumer, but he disturbed the production and circulation of wealth by holding farmers to ransom. Le Trosne conflated the vagabond's itinerancy with a deliberate refusal to work, and he asserted that this social crime ought to be punished by life in the galleys. In self-congratulation, he stated that his proposal had '(...) awakened the attention of the ministry', but the ministry only partially followed up on it, limiting punishment to three years in the galleys.[48] According to Foucault, Le Trosne's penal–economic utopia brought about a 'great confinement onto the workplace',[49] by radicalising general movement from the sixteenth century onwards, such as may be observed in the creation of the general hospital in Paris (1656) for the sequestration of vagabonds,[50] or the creation of *dépôts de mendicité* in 1767.[51]

This virulent stance sparked an internal debate within the Economists. Before his conversion to Physiocracy in 1766, *abbé* Baudeau, for his part, also responded to the ministry by drawing up a 'complete, general and perpetual system of patriotic charity'[52] that would be both decentralised and coordinated by a General Commission of the *Conseil du roi*. If he evolved thereafter towards a more conditional *bienfaisance*, he did not renounce his initial plans and publicly disagreed with Le Trosne (who, however, had been the main person behind his joining the Physiocrats).[53] Baudeau, too, legitimated the use of repression and of forced apprenticeship for *mauvais pauvres*, but wished these to be more proportionate and milder than Le Trosne had envisaged, and admitted the necessity of assistance *without return* for foundlings, incapacitated aged people and the ill.[54] On the other hand, the able-bodied adult indigent ('sturdy' indigent), and the partially able-bodied adult indigent would be required to work in subsidised charity workshops. Over the course of the discussion, Le Trosne altered his position, and without varying on vagabonds, he came to admit that begging should be tolerated and not punished.[55]

Despite their disagreements, Le Trosne and Baudeau confirmed the commonplace that there existed two categories of indigent: the good (virtuous, but unfortunate) and the bad (lazy and imbued with vice, whom one had the right to constrain). It was Du Pont who was probably the most faithful to Quesnay in breaking radically with this *topos*, considering that 'in order to have fewer poor to relieve, the correct recipe is not to create any, and for this, to make trade free and to proscribe indirect and arbitrary taxation'.[56] On this latter point, Du Pont showed himself to be insistent as he asserted that the great Physiocratic fiscal reform, namely a single tax on the net product of agriculture, should provide relief to consumers at the same time as facilitating investment by rich farmers. From then on, in his estimation, the role of the state would consist in building the conditions for a free and secure market. It would do so on the one hand by ensuring provision of public works so as to construct and maintain the network of roads and canals, and on the other hand, by dealing with the problem of indigence in order to assure public order. The dilemma was as follows: how could one protect the market and property from the perverse effects of great poverty without violating personal rights and at the least cost for the collectivity?

Du Pont was without doubt the best equipped to answer this question: as a close collaborator of Turgot, he possessed a wealth of experience in the royal economic administration. He was interested in the transition problem,[57] and clearly opposed punitive and disciplinary solutions, like forced labour. In the same way as he condemned *corvée* and slavery, he decried the *dépôt de mendicité* as a kind of prison for the poor, which seemed to him to be as unfair (citizens who have not committed a crime cannot be punished) as it was inefficient. He admitted that assistance for the able-bodied poor was a poverty trap and thus that 'the perfection of charity' consisted of labour and economic growth. In correspondence with the Margrave of Baden, Du Pont argued for the moral rehabilitation of beggars and for an anti-repressive policy. He believed that the vast majority did not adopt this way of life by choice or by vice, but because they were constrained to do so; worse, stigmatising them only reinforced their marginality.[58] With regard to able-bodied or partially able-bodied beggars, he saw it as the task of government to bring them conditional aid, like those numerous demobilised soldiers without employment and with no other option than to roam; for example, by helping them to find their families in order to settle down, because 'it is necessary that families are instructed about the great rule: God helps those who help themselves!' ('*Aide-toi, le Ciel t'aidera!*');[59] or by offering them paid jobs in the public works (maintenance of thoroughfares, construction of roads). This analysis was inspired perhaps by Turgot's policy as *intendant* of Limousin, which the *Éphémérides* had praised highly.[60] Although the principle of the *ateliers de charité* had been known since the sixteenth century, they became institutionalised truly in the 1770s. Once he became *Contrôleur général des Finances* in 1774, Turgot named Du Pont as *Inspecteur des manufactures* and appointed him as his close advisor.[61] In triumph Du Pont announced to the Margrave, 'Next year, all the throughfares in the kingdom will form an immense *atelier de charité* (...)', capable of absorbing the full number of able-bodied indigent.[62] Subsequent events would pour water on this typically Physiocratic enthusiasm.

Finally, Du Pont planned a professed optimal health care system for the ill poor, through a project for a new general hospital in Paris at the end of the Old Regime.[63] Like Baudeau,[64] he advocated a decentralised and flexible organisation of *assistance* that prioritised family assistance at home and through existing local institutions. In accordance with the principle of subsidiarity, public aid should only be given when family solidarity was lacking. The ill poor would thus be cared for in small local hospices, by relying on the network of parishes and private clinics within the framework of a public/private partnership. Public authority was to limit subsidies to local needs.[65]

The great chain of *bienfaisance* in *The Citizen's Almanac*

The majority of Physiocrats came together around a portmanteau-word, which simultaneously allowed their divergences to be smoothed out and them to meet their opponents head on. For these thinkers '*Bienfaisance* is a thoroughly essential article, it is a universal duty.'[66] In his brief essay on the ill poor, Du Pont employed the terms '*bienfaisance, bienfaisant/e*' five times. This lexicon became pervasive in a longer and more general work by Baudeau, in which one notes 135 instances in his *Première Introduction à la philosophie économique*,[67] as if *bienfaisance* was a manner of describing the entire doctrine of the 'Economists'. This rhetorical inflation did not appear at just any moment, but from 1767 in their principal journal *Éphémérides du citoyen*. This was also the year in which Physiocracy constituted itself officially into a school and became a political target due to its support for, and indeed its contribution to, the policy of liberalisation of the grain trade, which had been decided by the government in 1763–1764, and subsequently due to its support for Turgot's policy in 1774. In both cases, the dispute gave rise to a series of 'food riots' (including the well-known 'Flour War' in 1775) and to profuse anti-Physiocratic discourse.[68]

There is no doubt that the Physiocrats were aware of their reputation for being dogmatic, fanatical and insensitive to suffering humanity. The theme of *bienfaisance* was one of their responses to those criticisms, and it displayed affinities with the social and cultural dispositions of several of them. It was not a coincidence that the journal took the turn of '*bienfaisance*' under the direction of Baudeau. As well as *abbé* Roubaud, he was one of two clerics in the school: as a former member of the community of the Regular Canons of Saint-Augustin, and having a solid theological training, he never renounced his pre-Physiocratic projects of public assistance and he manipulated the language of *bienfaisance* long before his conversion.[69] This language was also promoted by the secular members of the clique. Mirabeau, who owed his celebrity (and his pseudonym) to his work *L'Ami des Hommes*, now gained a reputation as a philanthropist too. Not only did he launch the idea of a journal section specially devoted to the theme, but over time he built an entire (obscure) theory of *bienfaisance*. Finally, the notion chimed with the sentimentalism of Du Pont, an Enlightened Huguenot with pantheistic tendencies.[70] He systematised and enlarged the dedicated *bienfaisance* section in the *Éphémérides* when he succeeded Baudeau at the head of the journal (from January 1769, officially).

A few years later, Necker advanced a definition of *bienfaisance* in opposition to these commentators that conformed more with the monarchical tradition. He held that in case of a subsistence crisis, the sovereign ought to ensure the people's access to bread through regulating the grain trade so as to obtain a fair price.[71] He thus implied that Minister Turgot and his entourage (the Economists) were too blinded by the so-called 'evidence' of their science to hear the suffering of the people. In his response, Baudeau contested the monopoly on humanism with Necker: 'Humanity, Sir, we know it, as well as *bienfaisance* (…) One *exhorts* to *bienfaisance*; one advises the *traits of humanity*. But *laws* cannot, nor should not order them.'[72] Thus, charity was endorsed on a voluntary basis and, still more, on the condition that it would be useful and clearly distinguished from alms.

The great rhetorical achievement of the Physiocrats was to separate charity from donation, and *bienfaisance* from almsgiving. 'Private charity does not at all involve giving, therefore (…)', explained Mirabeau.[73] One finds here a striking example of the formidable technique of the *paradiastole*, according to the classic definition of Quintilian.[74] This literary device readjusted the value of morally damnable actions by describing them in favourable terms, or inversely devalued virtuous actions by imputing bad intentions to them. Thus, *giving* (direct, manual alms) was, at best, generosity without reflection engendering perverse effects,[75] at worst self-important vanity, which relieved the conscience of the giver but not the poor. 'Let them [the *bienfaiteurs*] take the trouble of being administrators at the expense of the pleasure of being compassionate', declared Mirabeau.[76] Such action was defined as the opposite of an unwise generosity that cleared one's conscience too easily. True generosity did not consist of giving, which did not improve in a lasting way the material condition of the poor, but rather in investment in public utility.[77] Among many other matters, Physiocracy clearly questioned the old moral economy of giving, seeing it as a system of humiliation.[78] *Investing*, on the other hand, was a profitable activity not only for the investor, but for the entire collectivity through the employment that it created, for the poor could both find in it a minimum of material comfort and their dignity. '*Bienfaisance* does not give anything; it advances, it sows, it will harvest', Mirabeau announced,[79] and it may thus be observed that separating charity and alms gave way to a connection between (Enlightened) interest and virtue. The duty and honour of rich landowners involved giving up 'luxury in the way of ornamentation' for the benefit of 'luxury in the way of subsistence' by allowing for their incomes to be circulated in the agricultural sector. Such was '(…) *bienfaisance*, which encompasses many more services of a reciprocal kind than free aid', Du Pont averred.[80] In this conception, the redistributive function of *bienfaisance* was transferred clearly towards the mechanisms of the market.

The *Éphémérides du Citoyen* was the 'organ of science *par excellence*',[81] according to the expression of the Marquis de Mirabeau. The Physiocratic editorial tactics of the publication led it to create an entire section that would form an 'archive of patriotic *bienfaisance*', that is, acts of 'well-understood generosity'.[82] From 1767 and its volume 4, the journal launched a call for articles and inaugurated a series of contributions that sought to portray a thorough picture of philanthropic actions: the section would be called 'the traits of *bienfaisance*'. From 1770 on, a more regular dedicated section entitled 'Public Events and Traits of *Bienfaisance*' was created, and from 1771, a sub-section called 'Praiseworthy Actions and Traits of *Bienfaisance*' was added. The journal thus placed itself at the avant-garde of a cultural phenomenon that impacted the French press.[83]

The eighteenth century commonly believed in the persuasive force of good example, or '(…) striking examples of Enlightened *bienfaisance*'.[84] The journal's *bienfaisance* section offered a wide range of cautionary tales that reported acts of patriotic devotion. Those acts formed a great vertical chain of *bienfaisance*, whose performers ranged from European sovereigns (such as the kings of Denmark or of Sweden, and the Grand Duke of Tuscany) to ordinary citizens, including lords,[85] landowners, farmers, the Pope,[86] the high clergy, simple priests, but also public and private institutions such as local authorities[87] or economic and agricultural societies, in other words 'royal *bienfaisance*', 'pastoral *bienfaisance*' and 'municipal *bienfaisance*'. This chain of *bienfaisance* appeared to conform to the hierarchy of orders and ranks.[88] All those benefactors were landowners and each, at their own level, contributed to prosperity and the fight against poverty. The Church, whose profession involved charity, was placed particularly to the fore, as in the case of the Enlightened priest who opened a school of apprentice-weavers so as to provide training for the minor beggars of his parish.[89] It was *bienfaisance royale* that captured most attention because it had the greatest number of effects – sovereigns were the institutors and protectors of the market, which needed both material infrastructure and guarantees to protect liberty and property.

The types of *bienfaisance* acts prized by the *Éphémérides* corresponded broadly to the three major components of the Physiocratic reform programme. In terms of the *economic* component: if liberalisation of the grain trade was described as *bienfaisant*,[90] it was especially fiscal reforms that held the journal's attention, in particular in the Grand Duchy of Tuscany[91] or those by Catherine the Second in Russia.[92] They were assigned an increasing place in the journal with the aim of underlining both the importance of the fiscal issue and the international success of Physiocratic ideas. The *educational* component was a less discussed theme: it was mentioned when presenting the programme implemented by the Polish authorities in 1775 that emphasised training and apprenticeship.[93]

Finally, the *social* component: those 'praiseworthy operations' that contributed to prosperity, certain directly targeted the indigent; namely, investment in public works. This achieved two things at once: maintaining and developing the 'public patrimony', in other words the public road network, indispensable for a commercial society; and also usefully assisting poor workers. Management of this policy was to be confined to elected municipal and provincial administrations connected to the parishes[94] and a partnership with ecclesiastical institutions that were charitable in nature.[95] But initiatives could come also directly from sovereigns. Leopold had thus engaged public spending in order to render a large marshy area of land[96] capable of being cultivated, or he had advanced funds for the creation of 300 craft jobs for poor female workers, in such a manner as to 'humiliate them much less in lending to them thus than in giving to them (...) Therefore, in his *bienfaisance*, the Grand Duke is uniting the most truly noble manner of proceeding with the most useful form.'[97] Du Pont considered those public works as the most socially useful way of relieving the unemployed poor: 'This use of public funds (...) is the model of *bienfaisance* that suits Sovereigns.'[98]

The economy of compassion and the theodicy of bienfaisance

As can be seen, this rhetoric of bienfaisance tended to legitimise commercial society and, more specifically, agricultural capitalism. The Physiocrats considered 'self-interest', within a competitive market, not as a private vice that would lead to public good, but as 'reasoned virtue' itself[99] – 'economic *bienfaisance*'. When Voltaire wrote that '*Among men, virtue consists in a trade of beneficences*',[100] the Physiocrats would prefer to state that freedom of trade itself was a beneficence. However, this Enlightened interest seemed to be virtuous in its *consequences* rather than in its *intention*, which continued to be no less egotistical. Three arguments can qualify this conclusion, however. First of all, the concept of economic rationality invited landowners to renounce immediate enjoyment for future prosperity – it opposed the short-sighted egoism of established *privilèges*. A sovereign who prioritised investment in the 'public patrimony' courageously acted in opposition to the interests of his own court.[101] A noble landowner who exempted peasants from *corvée* and gave up his own fiscal *privilège* in order to finance the construction of roads was taking the risk, even reasonably, of leaving the comfort of the ways things had always been done.[102] Second, economic *bienfaisance* could not be reduced simply to an unintentional consequence of prosperity, because it also *intentionally* targeted great misery when it set out '(...) to direct towards public utility the aid that they [*bienfaisant* men] give to the private needs of the poor'.[103] By employing the able-bodied indigent, one was converting alms into investment without any loss to society.

Finally, this theory of *bienfaisance* was no more than window-dressing to glorify the idea of 'self-interest' – by professing humanitarian principles in the face of criticism of their programme, the Physiocrats were forced not only to develop their social programme, but to explain compassion. Considered on the narrow basis of an anthropology of interest, the latter certainly appeared mysterious, for what leads us to aid others unconditionally? Mirabeau saw no paradox in it, asserting that '*bienfaisance* is of the same nature as all our other motives: it is interest'.[104] If a father gives generously to his children, it is because he feels that this love will be returned to him.[105] But there was still a need to explain the psychological mechanism pushing us to risk generosity without guarantee of return. Compassion, Du Pont explained, was a 'natural inclination' that lay in every human heart, because there was a specific joy in helping others insofar as we can identify with them.[106] Our commiseration is proportionate to closeness, he considered, as we always prefer to help our family and friends because we want to give back to them what they have given us: *charity begins at home*.[107] It was for this reason that a policy of assistance to the non-able-bodied poor, who were incapable of giving anything in return, should rest mainly on the compassionate micro-networks of the family – for Du Pont, 'this is not only the rigorous calculation of just and prudent economy, more than that, it is the combination of Enlightened and sentimental *bienfaisance* (...)'.[108]

However, compassion does not merge entirely with *bienfaisance*. One signifies a spontaneous generosity, limited, however, to the family; the other is a reasoned virtue to which the Physiocrats conferred an amazing vitalist, universal and even theological scope. To conform to the '(...) *natural order of general bienfaisance*'[109] was to carry out divine justice, because it was the '(...) *bienfaisant* Divinity, which wished the earth to be covered by happy men', concluded Le Mercier de La Rivière in his pivotal work.[110] Mirabeau, in his whimsical style ingrained with mysticism, particularly developed this authentic theodicy.[111] The breath of God's creative will would make up this genuine 'patrimony of *bienfaisance*',[112] and it would reach fruition through free economic cooperation, weaving links of reciprocity on the scale of the entire society, where each person would continually give and receive good deeds by his works. It would give birth to a feeling of interdependence and of belonging to a common humanity, in space (between peoples) and in time (between generations). This feeling was both sensitive and calculated in that it inclined towards *doing good without immediate return*, in particular towards the aged and foundlings. This intergenerational solidarity rested as much on our feeling of debt towards the society that raised and educated us, as on the calculation that it would return our good deeds to us. There would be no donation without donation in return, that is, 'TO DO GOOD IS TO RECEIVE IT'.[113] This moral relationship to the totality of society can appear abstract compared to the warmth of familial love. It is for this reason that Mirabeau mobilised naturalist and fraternal metaphors to give flesh to this long chain of *bienfaisance*, this '(...) inexhaustible river of love and of charity which must establish between men the communication of goods, the relief of ills, the gentleness of confraternity (...)'.[114] 'The electricity of *bienfaisance*[115] irrigates and links all parts of the social body, as far as joining together the great family of humanity': 'we are therefore brothers with all of the human race from here to Tonkin or to Panama'.[116]

These hydraulic and, moreover, electric analogies gave a seductive representation to commercial society – fast as lightning, full of life and harmonious.[117] They tended also to naturalise and soften the reality of inequalities, which seemed to be 'smoothed out' by the harmony of mutually beneficial exchanges. In doing this, they reinforced justification of social inequalities: the Economists constantly defended the idea that these latter were the consequence of natural inequalities and that the most blatant of all – great landed property – was the indispensable condition of prosperity and of improving the fate of the poor. The 'patrimony of *bienfaisance*' still supposed a hierarchy between landowners and non-landowners. Without inequality, there would be no *bienfaisance*; without land, no *bienfaiteur* or recipient of good deeds: inequality '(…) is the most powerful motivation for all useful and essential works, and it furnishes to *bienfaisance*, as much general as individual, effective power'.[118] If *bienfaisance* was a theodicy, it strongly resembled a 'theodicy of privilege'[119] so much did it justify the pre-eminence of the class of landed property owners. This pre-eminence, however, implied a double duty: to spend one's income to guarantee the optimal reproduction of wealth, and to acquit the totality from taxes. And if they failed in their duty, it would be the sovereign, final guarantor of economic *bienfaisance*, who would force them to fulfil it.[120]

Conclusion

The Physiocrats not only espoused a fashion of the moment, they also contributed to shaping and stimulating a genuine cultural phenomenon around philanthropy, which saw an evolution until the start of the French Revolution. Though this rhetoric aimed to render their doctrine of 'self-interest' acceptable, it was not cosmetic but had a theoretical scope. Three levels of *bienfaisance* derived from such rhetoric, each one stacked inside the other: compassion, which entailed *giving* without return (at the family level); Enlightened interest, which involved *investing* and stood in opposition to spontaneous egoism (at the stratum of society); the general and impersonal *bienfaisance* of the natural order, which spreads happiness over the entire planet and bequeaths the feeling of a universal brotherhood (on the scale of humanity). This natural order was not spontaneous and it implied the vigorous and continual action of sovereigns, the primary benefactors of peoples, through their making provision for public aid for the indigent when familial solidarity was lacking, by liberalising trade and maintaining the road networks through public works, and by reigning peacefully and encouraging international free-exchange.

This rhetoric was part of the originality of Physiocracy within European eighteenth-century liberalisms. On the one hand, it invented a form of liberal paternalism in the lineage of certain tendencies of the European agronomic avant-garde.[121] While criticising representation of the monarch as provider of food for the people or as 'father to the poor',[122] the Economists attempted to redefine political paternalism by reviving the figure of 'the Pastor Prince'.[123]

This 'protective and *bienfaisant* authority', more motivating than coercive, showed the poor the way to provide for their own needs, by education and freedom of trade, while making provision for a system of aid at a low cost. The flock would always need to be guided by an elite of Enlightened landowners of which the sovereign was the living incarnation.[124] On the other hand, this rhetoric implied a genuine programme against poverty and a theory about compassion. The topic of *bienfaisance* was not just a mere spark of humanity in their pro-market views. It was for this reason that in 1817 the very last representative of the Physiocratic school could show his indignation when faced with the harshness (according to him) of Thomas Robert Malthus. One could not, Du Pont exclaimed, deprive from assistance an abandoned child so as to punish the faults of its intemperate parents – he possessed '(…) a right to live by our help, since we would all be dead, if at his age, we had not received the help which we needed like him, and which saved our life! Let us pay our debts!'[125] Such was the swansong of Physiocracy at the dawn of the industrial age: *bienfaisance* supposed inequality, but symmetrically implied social responsibility from landowners and the sovereign. It was the moral crowning of a civilisation that had achieved a high degree of interdependence.

Translated by Ann-Marie Kilgallon.

Notes

1 Camille Bloch, *L'assistance et l'État en France à la veille de la Révolution: généralités de Paris, Rouen, Alençon, Orléans, Châlons, Soissons, Amiens, 1764–1790*, 1 vol. (Geneva [Paris]: Slatkine, 1974). Clarisse Fairchilds, *Poverty and Charity in Aix-en-Provence 1640–1789* (Baltimore, MA: The Johns Hopkins University Press, 1976), Ch. 6; Thomas McStay Adams, *Bureaucrats and Beggars: French Social Policy in the Age of the Enlightenment* (Oxford: Oxford University Press, 1990).

2 Sébastien Duchesne, 'Les physiocrates et les gueux ou la position des premiers économistes sur la question de la pauvreté en France (1756–1789)', Masters Thesis in History, University of Ottawa, Ottawa (2003), http://search.proquest.com/docview/305246719/?pq-origsite=primo. Accessed 4 September 2021.

3 Alain Clément, 'Nicolas Baudeau et la question des pauvres ou la naissance de l'État-providence', in Alain Clément (ed.), *Nicolas Baudeau: un 'philosophe économiste' au temps des Lumières* (Paris: M. Houdiard, 2008), pp. 72–96; Alain Clément, 'Le droit des pauvres dans l'œuvre de Nicolas Baudeau', *Cahiers d'économie politique*, 59:2 (2010), 69–88 at 69. See also Caroline Chopelin-Blanc and Alain Clément, 'L'idée de pauvreté chez deux ecclésiastiques des Lumières: Nicolas Baudeau et Adrien Lamourette', *Histoire, économie & société*, 3 (2008), 45–63.

4 'Qu'est-ce que la vertu? Bienfaisance envers le prochain', Voltaire, *Dictionnaire philosophique, portatif* (London, 1764), p. 342. See Marisa Linton, *The Politics of Virtue in Enlightenment France*, Studies in Modern History (Houndmills, Basingstoke, Hampshire; New York: Palgrave, 2001), pp. 69–79.
5 Charles-Irénée Castel de Saint-Pierre, 'Économie bienfaizante', *De la douceur* (Amsterdam and Paris, 1740), p. 4, pp. 6–7.
6 Linton, *Politics of Virtue*, p. 8.
7 Anonymous text of 1780, cited in Patrizia Oppici, *L'idea di 'bienfaisance' nel Settecento francese: o il laccio di Aglaia* (Pisa, Italy: Libreria Goliardica, 1989), p. 26. See also Isabelle Brancourt, 'La Bienfaisance en France au siècle des Lumières. Histoire d'une idée', in G. Deregnaucourt (ed.) *Société et religion en France et aux Pays-Bas. XVe–XIXe siècle* (Arras: Artois Presses Université, 2000), pp. 525–537 and Emma Barker, 'From Charity to Bienfaisance: Picturing Good Deeds in Late Eighteenth-Century France', *Journal for Eighteenth-Century Studies*, 33:3 (2010), 285–311.
8 Linton, *The Politics of Virtue in Enlightenment France*, pp. 132–137.
9 Catherine Duprat, *Le temps des philanthropes: la philanthropie parisienne des Lumières à la monarchie de Juillet*, 2 vol., Mémoires et documents 47 (Paris: Editions du C.T.H.S, 1993). Déborah Cohen, *La nature du peuple: les formes de l'imaginaire social, XVIIIe–XXIe siècles, la chose publique* (Seyssel: Champ Vallon, 2010), pp. 115–137; Colin Jones, *Charity and Bienfaisance: The Treatment of the Poor in the Montpellier Region, 1740–1815* (Cambridge: Cambridge University Press, 1982); Jean-Pierre Gutton, *La société et les pauvres en Europe : XVIe–XVIIIe siècles* (Paris: PUF, 1974), Ch. 3.
10 Alan Forrest, *La Révolution française et les pauvres* (Paris: Perrin, 1986).
11 On the functioning of the Physiocratic group and division of labour therein, see Arnault Skornicki, *L'économiste, la cour et la patrie: l'économie politique dans la France des Lumières* (Paris: CNRS Editions, 2011), Ch. 6. More recently, see Loïc Charles and Christine Théré, 'The Physiocratic Movement: A Revision', in Sophus Reinert and Steven Kaplan (eds), *The Economic Turn: Recasting Political Economy in Enlightenment Europe* (London, New York: Anthem Press, 2019), pp. 35–70.
12 Catherine Larrère, 'Montesquieu et les pauvres', *Cahiers d'économie Politique / Papers in Political Economy*, 59 (2010), 24–43.
13 Jean-François Melon, *Essai politique sur le commerce* (S. l., 1736), p. 99.
14 Christian Paultre, *De la répression de la mendicité et du vagabondage en France sous l'Ancien régime* (Geneva [Paris], Slatkine Megariotis [Champion], 1975).
15 Robert M. Schwartz, *Policing the Poor in Eighteenth-Century France* (Chapel Hill, NC: University of North Carolina Press, 1988), pp. 15–18.
16 Quentin Skinner, *Visions of Politics. I: Regarding Method* (Cambridge: Cambridge University Press, 2002), Ch. 7.
17 Gilbert Faccarello, *Aux origines de l'économie politique libérale: Pierre de Boisguilbert* (Paris: Editions Anthropos, 1986).

18 Déborah Cohen, Niall O'Flaherty and Robin Mills have kindly (and with *bienfaisance*) provided me with advice and critiques – I hope to have lived up to them. Ann-Marie Kilgallon has drawn on her competence as a historian of France and of poverty to translate this chapter: I thank her warmly.
19 Louis de Jaucourt, « PAUVRE, Pauvreté, (Critique sacrée.) *Encyclopédie, ou Dictionnaire raisonné des sciences, des arts et des métiers*, 17 vols (Le Breton/David/Briasson/Durand, 1751–1765), vol. xii, p. 209. See also Denis Diderot, 'Indigent', *idem*, 1765, vol. viii, p. 676. Contemporaries generally defined the poor as those families whose head could not provide for the household's subsistence and whose members could not ensure their own survival, cf. Olwen H. Hufton, *The Poor of Eighteenth-Century France 1750–1789* (Oxford: Clarendon Press, 1974), p. 12.
20 Georg Simmel, *Der Arme*, ed. E. Barlösius (Sesto San Giovanni: Mimesis, 2019).
21 Daniel Roche, 'Paris capitale des pauvres: quelques réflexions sur le paupérisme parisien entre XVIIe et XVIIIe siècle', *Mélanges de l'ecole française de Rome. Moyen-age, temps modernes*, 99:2 (1987), 835–837.
22 Hufton, *The Poor of Eighteenth-Century France*, pp. 11–24.
23 François Quesnay, *Essai physique sur l'œconomie animale* (1747), in ibid., *Œuvres économiques complètes et autres textes*, eds Christine Théré, Loïc Charles and Jean-Claude Perrot (Paris: Institut national d'études démographiques, 2005), vol. i, p. 5.
24 Quesnay, 'Second problème économique' (1767), in ibid., *Œuvres économiques completes*, vol. i, p. 635.
25 Quesnay, *Despotisme de la Chine* (1767), in ibid., *Œuvres économiques completes,* vol. ii, 1049.
26 Ibid.
27 '… en général l'aumone est un mal (…) en proportion de ce qu'il y aura d'aumones fixes dans un pays, il y aura des mendiants de profession et inconnus' [translation: '… in general, almsgiving is an ill (…) in proportion to the existence of fixed almsgiving in a country, there will be unknown persons who make a profession out of begging'], Victor de Riqueti, Marquis de Mirabeau, 'Notes pour l'abbé Nicoli', Archives Nationales (France), M784, no. 50. Compare with Anne R. J. Turgot, 'Fondation', *Encyclopédie*, vol. vii (1757), 72b–75b.
28 Quesnay, 'Hommes' (1757), in ibid., *Œuvres économiques complètes*, vol. i, p. 287.
29 Victor de Riqueti, Marquis de Mirabeau, 'Notes pour l'abbé Nicoli', Archives Nationales (France), M784, no. 50.
30 F. Quesnay, 'Note on "Maxime 20 du Gouvernement économique"' in *Physiocratie*, 1767–1768, vol. i, p. 164.
31 Adams, *Bureaucrats and Beggars*, p. viii. For instance, see Dupont, 'Letter to the Margave of Baden (1773)' in Victor de Riqueti, Marquis de Mirabeau and Pierre-Samuel Dupont (eds), *Carl Friedrichs von Baden brieflicher Verkehr mit Mirabeau und Dupont. Herausgegeben von der badischen historischen Commission*, vol. ii (Heidelberg: C. Winter, 1892), p. 106.

32 Catherine Larrère, 'Montesquieu et les pauvres', *Cahiers d'économie politique / Papers in Political Economy*, 59 (2010), 24–43.
33 Quesnay, 'Hommes' (1757), in ibid., *Œuvres économiques complètes*, vol. i, p. 314.
34 Steven L. Kaplan, *Bread, Politics and Political Economy in the Reign of Louis XV*, second edition (London: Anthem Press, 2015). For the Physiocratic critique of this pact, see Victor de Riqueti, Marquis de Mirabeau, 'Projet d'édit sur le commerce des grains' (1768) in Georges Weulersse (ed.), *Les manuscrits économiques de François Quesnay et du Mis de Mirabeau aux Archives nationales (M. 778 à M. 785)* (Paris: P. Geuthner, 1910), pp. 106–109; 'Letter from Dupont to the Margrave of Baden (1773)', in Mirabeau and Dupont, *Carl Friedrichs von Baden*, vol. ii, p. 132.
35 Quesnay, *Despotisme de la Chine* (1767), in ibid., *Œuvres économiques completes*, vol. ii. See, however, Adolphe Landry, 'Les idées de Quesnay sur la population', *Revue d'histoire des doctrines économiques et sociales*, 2 (1909), 71–74 and Joseph Spengler, *French Predecessors of Malthus, a Study in Eighteenth-Century Wage and Population Theory* (Durham, NC: Duke University Press, 1942), pp. 170–211.
36 Quesnay, *Œuvres économiques complètes et autres textes*, vol. ii, p. 1048. For a recent study on this work, see Gabriel Sabbagh, 'Quesnay's Thought and Influence through Two Related Texts, *Droit Naturel* and *Despotisme de La Chine*, and their Editions', *History of European Ideas*, 46:2 (2020), 131–156.
37 Quesnday, *Despotisme de la Chine* (1767), in ibid., *Œuvres économiques completes*, vol. ii, pp. 1103–1104.
38 Ibid., vol. ii, p. 1049.
39 Richard Cantillon, *Essai sur la nature du commerce en général* (Paris: Institut National d'Études Démographiques, 1997 [1755]), pp. 37–38. This case of borrowing was noted by the editors in Quesnay, *Œuvres économiques complètes*, vol. ii, p. 1112, note 241. However, the Marquis de Mirabeau had already mobilised this thesis in 1756 – see Victor de Riqueti, Marquis de Mirabeau, *L'ami des hommes*, part I (Avignon, 1756–1758), Ch. 2, pp. 16–18.
40 Anne-Robert-Jacques Turgot, 'Lettres au Contrôleur général sur le commerce des grains' (1770), in ibid., *Formation et distribution des richesses*, eds J.-T. Ravix and P.-M. Romani (Paris: Flammarion, 2013), p. 364. See Philippe Steiner, *Sociologie de la connaissance économique: essai sur les rationalisations de la connaissance économique (1750–1850)* (Paris: Presses universitaires de France, 1998), pp. 107–109.
41 *Éphémérides du citoyen* (Paris: N. A. Delalain/Lacombe, 1765–1772), 1766, vol. iii, p. 270.
42 Clément, 'Le droit des pauvres', pp. 75–76.
43 Arnault Skornicki, 'Liberté, propriété, sûreté. Retour sur une devise physiocratique', *Corpus: revue de philosophie*, 66 (2014), 16–36.
44 Victor de Riqueti, Marquis de Mirabeau, *Lettres sur la législation, ou l'ordre légal, dépravé, rétabli et perpétué*, 3 vols (Berne, Chez la Société Typographique, 1775), vol. ii, p. 509.

45 Adams, *Bureaucrats and Beggars*, p. 39; Georges Weulersse, *Le mouvement physiocratique en France de 1756 à 1770*, 2 vols (Paris: F. Alcan, 1910), vol. ii, pp. 422–423.
46 Guillaume-François Le Trosne, *Mémoire sur les vagabonds et sur les mendiants* (Soissons and Paris: Chez P. G. Simon, 1764). His house had been set on fire by vagabonds: see Weulersse, *Le mouvement physiocratique*, vol i, pp. 422–423.
47 Guillaume-François Le Trosne, *Vues sur la justice criminelle* (Paris: Debure frères, 1777). For a recent biography of Le Trosne, containing an analysis of his penal thought, see Thérence Carvalho, 'Présentation', in Guillaume François Le Trosne, *Les lois naturelles de l'ordre social*, ed. Thèrence Carvalho (Geneve: Slatkine, 2019), pp. 11–34. See also Adams, *Bureaucrats and Beggars*, pp. 39–43.
48 Letter from Le Trosne to Tscharner (Secretary of the Economic Society, Bern), Orleans, France, 7 January 1767, in August Oncken, *Der ältere Mirabeau und die oekonomische Gesellschaft in Bern* (Bern: K. J. Wyss, 1886), pp. 73–74.
49 Michel Foucault, *La société punitive: cours au Collège de France (1972–1973)* (Paris: EHESS, 2013), p. 52.
50 Christian Paultre, *De la répression de la mendicité et du vagabondage en France sous l'Ancien régime* (Geneva [Paris], Slatkine Megariotis [Champion], 1975).
51 Schwartz, *Policing the Poor*, pp. 15–18.
52 Nicolas Baudeau, *Idées d'un citoyen sur les besoins, les droits et les devoirs des vrais pauvres* (Amsterdam & Paris: Chez Barthelemy Hochereau, 1765), p. 14.
53 Dupont, 'Notice abrégée des différens Ecris modernes qui ont concouru en France à former la Science de l'économie politique', *Éphémérides du citoyen*, 1769, vol. v, pp. xxx–xxxii.
54 Clément, 'Le droit des pauvres dans l'œuvre de Nicolas Baudeau'. See also ibid., 'Nicolas Baudeau et la question des pauvres ou la naissance de l'État-providence', in Clément, *Nicolas Baudeau*, pp. 72–96.
55 Letter from Le Trosne in *Éphémérides du citoyen*, 1766, vol. iii, p. 270. Later, he recommended confiding assistance of the indigent to the municipal authorities – see Guillaume-François Le Trosne, *De l'administration provinciale et de la réforme de l'impôt* (Basle, Paris, 1779), pp. 530–534.
56 Dupont, 'De l'incendie de l'Hôtel-Dieu de Paris et de divers projets auxquels il donne occasion pour le bien ou pour le mal des pauvres' (1773), in Mirabeau and Dupont, *Carl Friedrichs von Baden*, vol. ii, p. 531.
57 Pierre-Henri Goutte, 'Economie et transitions: l'œuvre de Dupont au début de la Révolution française 1789–1792', in Jean-Michel Servet (ed.), *Idées économiques sous la Révolution (1789–1794)* (Lyon: Presses universitaires de Lyon, 1989), pp. 145–234.
58 Letter to the Margrave of Baden (1773), in *Carl Friedrichs von Baden*, vol. ii, pp. 99–107.
59 Pierre-Samuel Dupont, *Idées sur les secours à donner aux pauvres malades dans une grande ville* (Philadelphia and Paris: Moutard, 1786), pp. 15–16.

60 Dupont praised Turgot for having established *ateliers de charité* and obtaining funds destined for '(…) providing an occupation for the poor during the winter on public works', in *Éphémérides du citoyen*, 1772, pp. 194–206. On this influence of Turgot on Dupont, see Duchesne, 'Les physiocrates et les gueux', pp. 155–157.

61 Adams, *Bureaucrats and Beggars*, pp. 123–133. Anne-Robert-Jacques Turgot, *Œuvres de Turgot et documents le concernant*, ed. Gustave Schelle, 5 vols (Paris: F. Alcan, 1913), vol. iv, pp. 499–520. See Anne Conchon, 'Les travaux publics comme ressource : les ateliers de charité dans les dernières décennies du xviiie siècle', *Mélanges de l'École française de Rome. Italie et Méditerranée*, 123:1 (2011), 173–180 and Alain Clément, 'La politique sociale de Turgot : entre libéralisme et interventionnisme', *L'actualité économique*, 81:4 (2007), 725–745.

62 Dupont to Carl Friedrich, Paris, 4 September 1775, in *Carl Friedrichs von Baden*, vol. ii, p. 182.

63 Dupont, *Idées sur les secours*.

64 Clément, 'Le droit des pauvres dans l'œuvre de Nicolas Baudeau', p. 79.

65 Jean-Baptiste Masméjan, 'Dupont et la question hospitalière: un éclairage des enjeux sanitaires à la fin du XVIIIe siècle', in A. Mergey and Arnault Skornicki (eds), *Le siècle de Du Pont. Politique, droit & histoire des lumières à la Restauration* (Liverpool: Liverpool University Press: Oxford University Studies in the Enlightenment (forthcoming)).

66 Victor de Riqueti, Marquis de Mirabeau, 'article de Bienfaisance pour le mois de 7bre' (1767?), Archives Nationales (France), M784, No. 51.

67 Nicolas Baudeau, *Première introduction à la philosophie économique, ou analyse des états policés, par un disciple de l'ami des hommes* (Paris: Didot l'aîné, 1771).

68 See, for instance, the special issue of *The European Journal of the History of Economic Thought*, 22:3 (2015), 'Antiphysiocratic Perspectives in Eighteenth-century France'.

69 See Chopelin-Blanc and Clément, 'L'idée de pauvreté chez deux ecclésiastiques', 45–63; Catherine Chopelin-Blanc, 'L'abbé Baudeau théologien: la physiocratie au service de l'utopie chrétienne', in Clément, *Nicolas Baudeau*, pp. 49–71; and Alain Clément, 'Nicolas Baudeau et la question des pauvres ou la naissance de l'État-providence', in ibid., *Nicolas Baudeau*, pp. 72–96.

70 Julien Vincent, '"Un Dogue de forte race": Dupont, ou la physiocratie réincarnée (1793–1807)', *La Révolution française*, 14 (18 June 2018), https://doi.org/10.4000/lrf.2005. Accessed 10 September 2021. On sensibility and the Physiocrats, see Liana Vardi, *The Physiocrats and the World of the Enlightenment* (Cambridge: Cambridge University Press, 2012).

71 Jacques Necker, *Sur la législation et le commerce des grains* (Roubaix: Edires, 1986), pp. 145–146.

72 Nicolas Baudeau, *Eclaircissements demandés à M. N**, sur les principes économiques et sur ses projets de législation, au nom des propriétaires fonciers et des cultivateurs françois* (S. l., 1775), p. 84. See Léonard Burnand, 'Nicolas

Baudeau polémiste. *Les Éclaircissements demandés à M.N.*', in Clément, *Nicolas Baudeau*, pp. 306–317.
73 Victor de Riqueti, Marquis de Mirabeau, 'Lettre de M. B. à l'Auteur des Éphémérides, contenant des réflexions sur la manière d'exercer la Bienfaisance envers les Pauvres', in *Éphémérides du citoyen*, 1767, vol. vii, p. 187.
74 See Quintilian's *Institutio Oratoria*, and the analysis of Skinner, *Visions of Politics. I: Regarding Method*, pp. 183–185.
75 For example, Pierre-Samuel Dupont, 'Grande et coûteuse Charité très dangereuse parce qu'elle est mal entendue en un point', *Éphémérides du citoyen*, 1770, vol. iv, pp. 185–201.
76 Mirabeau, 'Lettre de M. B. à l'Auteur des Éphémérides', *Éphémérides du citoyen*, 1767, vol. vii, p. 189.
77 *Éphémérides du citoyen*, 1767, vol. iv, p. 182.
78 *Éphémérides du citoyen*, 1768, vol. v, p. 263.
79 Victor de Riqueti, Marquis de Mirabeau, *Entretiens d'un jeune prince avec son gouverneur* (Londres: Moutard, 1785), vol. ii, p. 559.
80 Pierre-Samuel Dupont, 'Grande et coûteuse Charité très dangereuse parce qu'elle est mal entendue en un point', *Éphémérides du citoyen*, 1770, vol. iv, p. 190.
81 Victor de Riqueti, Marquis de Mirabeau, *Lettre à Frédéric de Sacconay*, Paris, 7 May 1767, Private collection. According to the transcription established by Lumières. Lausanne (Université de Lausanne), http://lumieres.unil.ch/fiches/trans/281/. Accessed 20 september 2021. On this journal, see Ferdinand Pélissier, 'Les Éphémérides du citoyen', *Recherches et travaux*, 8 (1979), 12–19; Pierre-Henri Goutte, 'Les *Éphémérides du citoyen*, instrument périodique de l'ordre naturel (1765–1772)', *Dix-huitième siècle*, 26 (1994), 139–161; Bernard Herencia, *Les Éphémérides du citoyen et les nouvelles Éphémérides économiques (1765–1788). Documents et table complète*, Ferney-Voltaire, Centre international d'étude du XVIIIe siècle, 2014. See also Bernard Herencia's website: www.bernard-herencia.com/ephemerides/. Accessed 20 September 2021.
82 Nicolas Baudeau, 'Traits de bienfaisance économique', *Éphémérides du citoyen*, 1767, vol. iv, p. 186.
83 Two big journals created their own *bienfaisance* section over the following years: the *Mercure de France* from 1768 and the *Journal encyclopédique* from 1772. See Oppici, *L'idea di "bienfaisance" nel Settecento francese*, p. 31.
84 *Éphémérides du citoyen*, 1767, vol. iv, p. 182. On pedagogy by means of exemplary acts of *bienfaisance*, and its Rousseauist inspiration, see Oppici's analysis in Oppici, *L' idea di "bienfaisance" nel Settecento francese*, pp. 138–144.
85 'Bienfaisance de M. le Prince de Rohan', *Éphémérides du citoyen*, 1770, vol. xii, pp. 199–201.
86 'Bienfaisance du Pape', *Éphémérides du citoyen* 1771, vol. v, p. 207.
87 *Éphémérides du citoyen*, 1771, vol. ii, p. 160.
88 This chain appears clearly in the traits of *bienfaisance* series described in *Éphémérides du citoyen*, 1771, vol. v, pp. 190–269.

89 'Copie d'une lettre écrite en 1765, au sujet de M. de Bois-Gruel, Curé de Saint Victor-de-Chrétienville' *Éphémérides du citoyen*, 1767, pp. 169–191.
90 For example, the law which established the free export of grain in France was described as 'edit bienfaisant qui rend la Liberté du Commerce des Bleds', *Éphémérides du citoyen*, 1770, vol. i, p. 20.
91 In particular, the abolition of taxes on Companies of Tradesmen within the territory. See 'Édits de bienfaisance en Toscane', pp. 194–202, or ending the 'general farm' system of tax collection, *Éphémérides du citoyen*, 1770, vol. x, pp. 171–213. See also 1771, vol. i, pp. 129–158.
92 'Suppression de plusieurs Impôts en Russie', *Nouvelles éphémérides économiques, ou Bibliothèque raisonnée de l'histoire, de la morale et de la politique* (Paris: Lacombe, 1774), 1775, vol. vii, pp. 183–205.
93 'Statuts & programme du tribunal souverain de l'education nationale en Pologne', *Nouvelles éphémérides économiques, ou Bibliothèque raisonnée de l'histoire, de la morale et de la politique*, vol. viii, pp. 167–196.
94 On public works in Physiocratic thought and, more generally, their plans for local assemblies, see Anthony Mergey, *L'État des physiocrates: autorité et décentralisation* (Aix-en-Provence: Presses Universitaires d'Aix-Marseille, 2010), esp. pp. 258–266.
95 Such as an Enlightened priest who opened a school of apprentice-weavers to provide vocational training to the minor beggars of his parish, 'Copie d'une lettre écrite en 1765, au sujet de M. de Bois-Gruel, Curé de Saint Victor-de-Chrétienville', *Éphémérides du citoyen*, 1767, vol. iv, pp. 169–191.
96 *Éphémérides du citoyen*, 1771, vol. i, pp. 130–158.
97 *Éphémérides du citoyen*, 1771, vol. v, p. 212. On the spread of Physiocracy in Tuscany and relations with Grand Duke Leopold, see Thérence Carvalho, '"L'ami des hommes et le prince pasteur". Le rôle du marquis de Mirabeau dans la diffusion et l'application des théories physiocratiques en Toscane', *Annales historiques de la Révolution française*, 394:4 (2018), 3–24.
98 'Bienfaisance royale', *Éphémérides du citoyen*, 1770, vol. xii, p. 193. See also *Éphémérides du citoyen*, 1771, vol. ii, p. 160.
99 Mirabeau, *Entretiens d'un jeune prince avec son gouverneur*, vol. ii, p. 164.
100 'La vertu entre les hommes est un commerce de bienfaits', Voltaire, *Dictionnaire philosophique*, p. 343.
101 'Economie dans les dépenses de la Maison royale' (of Denmark), *Éphémérides du citoyen*, 1771, vol. v, pp. 239–242.
102 'Exemple louable d'un Propriétaire bienfaisant, juste & éclairé', *Éphémérides du citoyen*, 1769, vol. xii, pp. 217–221.
103 *Éphémérides du citoyen*, 1767, vol. iv, p. 182.
104 Mirabeau, *Entretiens d'un jeune prince avec son gouverneur*, vol. ii, p. 540.
105 Ibid., vol. ii, p. 545.
106 Dupont, *Idées sur les secours*, p. 9.
107 Ibid., p. 12.
108 Ibid., p. 18.
109 Baudeau, *Première introduction à la philosophie économique*, p. 198.

110 Paul-Pierre Lemercier de la Rivière, *L'ordre naturel et essentiel des sociétés politiques* (Londres [Paris]: J. Nourse Desaint, 1767), vol. ii, p. 496.
111 Michael Sonenscher, 'Physiocracy as a Theodicy', *History of Political Thought*, 23:2 (2002), 326–339.
112 Mirabeau, *Entretiens d'un jeune prince avec son gouverneur*, vol. ii, pp. 159–18, pp. 535–656.
113 Victor de Riqueti, Marquis de Mirabeau, *Les économiques*. 4 vols (Amsterdam/Paris: Chez Humblot, 1771), vol. iii, p. lxxi.
114 Mirabeau, 'article de Bienfaisance pour le mois de 7bre', Archives Nationales (France), M784, No. 54. See also *Éphémérides du citoyen*, 1770, vol. xii, pp. 189–200.
115 Mirabeau, *Éphémérides du citoyen*, 1770, vol. xi, p. 199. This metaphor recurs elsewhere: *Nouvelles éphémérides économiques*, vol. iii, 1776, p. 71; Pierre-Samuel Dupont, *De l'exportation et de l'importation des grains. Mémoire lu à la Société royale d'agriculture de Soissons* (Soissons et Paris: Chez P. G. Simon, 1764), pp. 50–51.
116 Mirabeau, *Les économiques*, vol. ii, p. 267.
117 On the scientific, and particularly electrical, models of the Physiocrats, see Jessica Riskin, *Science in the Age of Sensibility: The Sentimental Empiricists of the French Enlightenment* (Chicago, IL: University of Chicago Press, 2002), pp. 105–138.
118 Pierre-Samuel Du Pont, *Examen du livre de M. Malthus sur le principe de population* (Philadelphia: P. M. Lafourcade, 1817), p. 32.
119 According to the expression of Pierre Bourdieu, *Sociologie générale* (Paris: Raisons d'agir: Seuil, 2015), p. 623.
120 Quesnay had insisted at an early stage on this duty of landowners to the extent of threatening to strip them of their wealth completely (*'dépouiller'*) if they engaged in hoarding – see 'Impôt' (1757). See Quesnay, *Œuvres économiques complètes et autres textes*, pp. 218–219. See also Victor de Riqueti, Marquis de Mirabeau, *Les devoirs* (Milan: Au monastère impérial de Saint-Ambroise, 1780), pp. 100–101.
121 Martin Stuber and Regula Wyss, 'Paternalism and Agricultural Reform; the Economic Society of Bern in the Eighteenth Century', in Koen Stapelbroek and Jani Marjanen (eds), *The Rise of Economic Societies in the Eighteenth Century: Patriotic Reform in Europe and North America* (Basingstoke: Palgrave Macmillan, 2012), pp. 157–181.
122 Priscille Aladjidi, *Le roi, père des pauvres: France, XIIIe – XVe siècle* (Rennes: Presses Universitaires de Rennes, 2008).
123 Mirabeau, *Les économiques*, vol. i, p. v.
124 Ibid., vol. iv, pp. 40–48.
125 Dupont, *Malthus sur le principe de population*, 15. See also Pierre-Samuel Dupont, *Philosophie de l'univers* (Paris: Imprimerie Pont, 1793), pp. 107–108.

3

Poverty, rights and the social contract in Enlightenment Austrian-Habsburg Lombardy

Alexandra Ortolja-Baird

> All along the way he was assailed by mendicants, – mendicants of necessity, not of choice – peasants, mountaineers, tradesmen, whole families reduced to poverty, and to the necessity of begging their bread.[1]

Alessandro Manzoni's *I promessi sposi* (*The Betrothed*, 1827) recounts the triumph of love above all odds. Set in early seventeenth-century Spanish-Habsburg Lombardy, the tale follows the humble silk-weaver Renzo and the pious villager Lucia in their quest to be rightfully married against the vicissitudes of injustice and circumstance. Beneath its romance, however, it is ultimately a story of deprivation and hardship. Along their journeys, the couple witness the devastation of famine, plague, war and corruption across Lombardy. Poverty abounds. 'Swarms' of families – 'mendicants of necessity' – flock to the cities, ragged, wretched and emaciated, in the hopes of finding bread. But their condition is inescapable. The poor have little option but to hope that their faith and suffering will be rewarded in the afterlife.

The story served to critique Manzoni's contemporary Lombardy. Fervently condemning feudal privileges, the oppression of the poor, corruption, the introspection of the political class, foreign domination and authoritarian rule, Manzoni desired to bring the forgotten millions – the '*gente di nessuno*' – into the limelight. But, although a work of historical fiction, and one heavily imbued with Manzoni's Christian beliefs, *I promessi sposi* nonetheless captured many of the social realities of its protagonists. Since the sixteenth century, the Italian states had faced widespread economic decline. The inability to keep up with English, Dutch and French competition in manufacturing, the shift in trade from the Mediterranean to the Atlantic and the conquest of much of the peninsula by the Spanish Habsburgs all contributed to a dramatic increase in poverty across the peninsula.[2] In Lombardy, the Thirty Years War, the plague of 1630 and famine and scarcity caused by poor harvests and woeful economic planning – all captured by Manzoni – resulted in vast numbers of families toppling from subsistence lifestyles into pauperism. Little had changed by the following century. The newly Austrian-Habsburg Lombardy faced a combination of devastating epidemics, subsistence crises, famine (1764–1767) and the economic drain of Habsburg wars, resulting in ever-increasing levels of unemployment, poverty, malnutrition and high mortality rates, many of which lasted into the nineteenth century.

The pauperisation of Lombardy resulted in a rapid proliferation of charitable and debtors' institutions. As elsewhere in Europe, such assistance had been typically provided by religious bodies, corporations and local communities.[3] However, as the crisis worsened mid-eighteenth century, a discernible shift in attitudes occurred towards not only the causes of poverty, but also the purpose, stewardship and forms of poor relief. Many of these mirrored changing views across the continent within the 'First Poverty Enlightenment'.[4] Poverty was no longer perceived as a purely moral weakness, but rather as contingent on structural factors; poverty was growingly seen as detrimental, not intrinsic to economic growth, nor was it an inevitable part of society; and changing views on political equality and opportunity rendered existing frameworks of poor relief insufficient, resulting in a shift from protective to promotional anti-poverty policies.[5]

It is these changing attitudes in the Milanese context that will be examined in this chapter. To do so, it will focus on the views of the Milanese philosopher, economist, jurist, grandfather and arguably inspiration to Alessandro Manzoni, Cesare Beccaria (1738–1794). Beccaria is best known for his 1764 treatise *On Crimes and Punishments*, a powerful work that condemned the arbitrary nature of eighteenth-century criminal justice, the use of torture and disproportionate retributive punishment, and which contentiously called for the outright abolition of the death penalty. His statements were celebrated by figures like Jeremy Bentham, Catherine the Great of Russia and Thomas Jefferson, but the treatise also provoked vehement criticism. It is Beccaria who first prompted the pejorative use of 'socialist', for instance, initially directed as a barbed but ultimately confused insult towards his egalitarian view of human nature and the social contract by the vociferous monk Ferdinando Facchinei.[6]

Beccaria's 'socialist' standpoint is central to his views on poverty. While the language of *On Crimes and Punishments* might suggest an impassioned humanitarian rationale behind his criticism of social and legal injustices, his arguments were driven by a vision of the social contract in which individual rights remained paramount. Distinct from existing charitable and Christian outlooks towards the poor, Beccaria instead strove to protect individuals' right to improve their status through facilitating greater social, legal and economic mobility. Moreover, he questioned why the privileges of class were tolerated when the parasitism of the nobility ultimately led to social injustice and economic stagnation. He was not alone in such an outlook. The particular dynamics of the Lombard Enlightenment, in which the local intellectual and cultural elite collaborated with the Austrian-Habsburg administration in a programme of Enlightened reformism, functioned somewhat like an echo chamber. The entanglement of Milan's philosophers – the *Illuministi* – artists and administrators both within and outside Lombardy's administrative institutions, resulted in a new but largely homogenous approach to counteracting poverty which bridged both theory and practice. While much of the Italian peninsula and Southern Europe more generally faced similar social and political concerns in the period – the changing face of absolutism, famine, the tension between Church and state – Lombardy was set apart in its commitment to moving beyond the rhetoric of improved public provision for the poor and needy to substantial intervention and bureaucratic reorganisation. Across the Italian territories, only the Habsburg-Lorraine Grand Duchy of Tuscany and, to a lesser extent, Savoy Piedmont, were able to usher in reforms that altered the management of social provisions as profoundly as in Lombardy.[7] This was due, in large part, to the dual philosopher–administrator roles of Lombard figures like Beccaria.[8] Already in the 1760s, these figures had identified poverty as a social problem entwined with questions of individual rights, the injustices caused by noble privileges and economic stagnation. Initially articulated in philosophical and literary works, these views became embedded in social policy as the *Illuministi* turned from page to practice, eventually driving the sweeping secularisation, centralisation and reconceptualisation of poor relief in Lombardy in the 1780s.

Situating poverty in the social contract

Beccaria's attitudes to poverty were shaped by his complex vision of the social contract. To appreciate his views, it is worth unpacking this social contract theory briefly, largely because it sits uncomfortably within the wider tradition as associated with Locke, Hobbes and others. Put simply, Beccaria combines the two often-considered opposing doctrines of utilitarianism and social contract theory: he frames the state's obligation towards the public good in utilitarian terms while ensuring that individual rights cannot be sacrificed to the majority.

Starting from the state of nature, Beccaria argues that individuals, tired of living in a constant state of war, come together to live in security and tranquillity. Here they are finally able to enjoy their liberty which has been, until then, rendered useless by the sheer uncertainty of retaining it.[9] To form such a union, all individuals must sacrifice the *smallest possible portion* of their liberty to the good of all which, collected together, form the sovereignty of the nation.[10] The goal of this social contract, Beccaria claims, is the preservation of 'the greatest happiness divided among the greater number'.[11] This statement, although frequently mistranslated as the 'greatest happiness of the greatest number' bears no similarity to utilitarian arguments. Rather, it requires the sovereign to ensure that the total 'greatest happiness' be fairly divided amongst all citizens, even if this means that the majority might be awarded less happiness than they would be in a utilitarian schema. As such, the public good cannot be separated from individual happiness and the purpose of government is the provision of such happiness.

According to Beccaria, happiness is simply derived from the pursuit, rather than the achievement, of pleasure.[12] However, while man is predictable in being motivated by pleasure, he is unpredictable in terms of his sensitivity to what he finds pleasurable. Thus, the social contract has to accommodate both the predictable and unpredictable parts of man's nature and facilitate the equal opportunity for each individual to pursue what their personal, idiosyncratic sensations dictate will bring pleasure, assuming that it does not cause damage to the larger community. The inability to predict or regulate what this pursuit entails thus means that the social contract is upheld by ensuring equal access to the *possible* sources of pleasures in society.

Beccaria interpreted the pursuit of pleasure in largely economic terms, as the pursuit of wealth, luxury or freedom of enterprise. He consequently claimed that all inflexible social, political and economic privileges enjoyed by the Church and the nobility which institutionalised inequality and prevented citizens from the pursuit of wealth, were abuses of the terms of the social contract. The equality of opportunity that Beccaria envisioned was thus predicated on inequality being a dynamic concept. It was something to be 'continually destroyed and reborn' between individuals, not remain fixed between classes.[13] It is in this regard that poverty, when a consequence of economic disempowerment and lack of opportunity, as opposed to individuals' poor financial management, becomes entangled in the fabric of the social contract. Beccaria did not call for the abolition of poverty on ideological or sentimental grounds, nor did he believe that it could be eradicated entirely. Rather, he wanted to prevent the systematic and institutionalised impoverishment caused by the social, legal and economic privileges held by the clergy and nobility. In impeding the equal opportunity to pursue wealth, these privileges stood in opposition to the terms of the social contract. Being born into inescapable poverty was not being born free and naturally equal, as Beccaria so interpreted humankind. Thus, by opening the circulation and pursuit of wealth to all, poverty was not necessarily remedied, but the sovereign's responsibility to ensure the greatest happiness of the greater number was at least fulfilled.

The centrality of the individual within Beccaria's social contract is striking. While Kant is often attributed with proposing the notion that all human beings must be treated 'as an end withal, never as means',[14] nascent sentiments of inherent human value and the moral parity between rich and poor can already be found in Beccaria's *On Crimes and Punishments*. Arguing that 'there is no freedom when the laws permit a man in some cases to cease to be a *person* and to become a *thing*',[15] and that it is a false idea of utility to 'impose on a multitude of sentient creatures the symmetry and order of brute inanimate matter'[16] and to 'separate the public good from the good of each individual',[17] he rebalanced society in favour of individual experience and the right of individuals to live and enjoy life as they please. However, while Beccaria emphasised the worth of the individual regardless of class, he also stressed that people should be valued by their utility to society. Although this appears to be a point of tension, for Beccaria these values are two sides of the same coin. In his mind, respect for individual rights would yield productive citizens, and the freedom to pursue individual wealth and pleasures would align private with public utility.[18] To frame this more cynically: Beccaria perceived that all individuals, nobility included, should be valued purely in terms of their labour function in society. While all were equal in birth and free to pursue their diverse private interests as they so pleased, their civic, not intrinsic, value was one of strictly economic productivity.

A sociological approach to poverty: crime, property, education

Beccaria's views on poverty stemmed from a complex understanding of the relationship between human nature and society. He identified both the causes and consequences of poverty, examining the patterns of social behaviour of those trapped in a perpetual cycle of impoverishment. He outlined the misery of the poor thus:

> Who can fail to feel himself shaken to the core by the sight of thousands of wretches whom poverty, either willed or tolerated by the laws, which have always favoured the few and abused the masses, has dragged back to the primitive state of nature ...?[19]

It is this 'willed or tolerated' poverty, he argues, which is the root cause of social delinquency and which, in turn, makes punishment futile as a deterrent against crime. If the poor are unable to escape their condition due to institutionalised injustices and are subsequently criminalised for the behaviours stemming from their inescapable poverty, then there is no incentive for them to abide by the laws of society, as they are ostensibly no longer within the bounds of the social contract.[20] Adopting the voice of the 'thief', Beccaria captures this tension in a powerful speech unpicking the psychology and sociological context of criminality:

> What are these laws which I have to obey, which leave such a gulf between me and the rich man? He denies me the penny I beg of him, brushing me off with the demand that I should work, something he knows nothing about. Who made these laws? Rich and powerful men, who have never condescended to visit the filthy hovels of the poor, who have never broken mouldy bread among the innocent cries of starving children and a wife's tears. Let us break these ties, which are pernicious to most people and only useful to a few and idle tyrants; let us attack injustice at its source. I shall return to my natural state of independence; for a while I shall live free and happy on the fruits of my courage and industry; perhaps the day for suffering and repentance will come, but it will be brief, and I shall have one day of pain for many years of freedom and pleasure. King of a small band of men, I shall put to rights the iniquities of fortune, and I shall see these tyrants blanch and cower at one whom they considered, with insulting ostentation, lower than their horses and dogs.[21]

He concludes that theft is 'generally the crime of poverty and desperation, the crime of that unhappy section of men to whom the perhaps "terrible" and "unnecessary" right to property has allowed nothing but a bare existence'.[22] In so doing, Beccaria reveals what he perceives as a root cause of poverty: the perception of property as a natural right. Property, he claims, is a social right[23] – the eldest daughter and not the mother of society[24] – which cannot exist without the social contract. Arguing that 'everyone is equal in property, that is to say, that there is no property more or less subject to the laws and that the laws that restrict this property are universal in favour of everyone against all',[25] he concludes that property should not be allowed to remain tied up in primogeniture or other social privileges. The institutions of *fidecommessi* [fidecommissum] and *mani morte* [mortmain] which legally cemented privileges among the elite, were at the heart of his criticism. These, Beccaria argued, should not be enjoyed by only the few and in perpetuity, but should be obtainable by all and with 'steady circulation should accumulate and divide continuously',[26] just as all inequality should be 'continually destroyed and reborn'. It was, above all, the liberation of the land that he was calling for. Stating that there 'ought to be as many landowners as suffice to be counted as many times over relative to the population as a whole',[27] he posited that not only was the circulation of property central to the social contract, but it would reinvigorate the economy through individual industry and wealth.

Beccaria associated social and economic privileges with political idleness or social parasitism. The politically idle were not those who, in spending their inherited fortunes, dispensed 'bread and a livelihood to the industrious poor, and who wages by means of his wealth the silent war of trade in peacetime', as were criticised by the 'stern moralists'.[28] Rather, they were those who did not serve to circulate wealth through either their own labour or the remuneration of the labour of others. Beccaria reiterated this sentiment in the Inaugural lecture for his Chair of Cameral Sciences at the Palatine School in Milan in 1769, underlining the 'chain of reciprocal service' that binds all men together and which should drive us to value individuals not for their pomp and ostentation, but for their utility.[29] Inverting the traditional social hierarchy and the trope of the indolent poor, Beccaria claimed:

> we learn how much respect is due to the proud indolence of those who lie in rags among the tattered images of their ancestors and how much to the hard-working and wholesome industry of the farmer; and, while we admire the solitary and austere monk, we do not despise the humble father who divides a loaf, earned through his sweat, between the tender children of the nation.[30]

It was the nobility that Beccaria identified as hindering the circulation of wealth and whose greed and privilege bound labourers to poverty.[31] Calling the inherent value of this class into question,[32] he argued that it was only through engaging in commerce and industry that such individuals could uphold their civic duties.

It was a concern shared by many of Lombardy's *Illuministi*. Among them, the economist and philosopher Pietro Verri, a close friend and collaborator of Beccaria, criticised the nobility's paltry economic contribution to society,[33] and stressed the importance of free commerce and the circulation of wealth for national development and the prevention of poverty. Of particular concern was the removal of monopolies. Making people dependent on the whims of a few wealthy magnates for their commodities left them vulnerable to artificial shortages, price gouging and generally arbitrary treatment.[34] For Verri, the 'soul of commerce' was rooted in freedom and competition. By freedom, however, he meant that which 'arises from the laws, not from the license', alluding to the security of property founded on clear laws not subject to arbitrariness or privilege.[35] In so doing, he echoed Beccaria's claims regarding the importance of legal equality in matters of property and commerce, pre-empting those made more famously by Adam Smith in his calls for the security of the poor and landless.[36] But both also drew on a growing Italian tradition criticising the parasitism of the nobility. In Naples, Paolo Mattia Doria had already pinned poverty on noble privileges preventing the circulation of wealth in the 1740s.[37] A decade later, Antonio Genovesi likewise emphasised the parasitism of feudal classes.[38]

Security also had a social dimension. In order for individuals to profit from and fully enjoy their rights, they needed to understand them. To this end, Beccaria edged towards a correlation between poverty, crime and education. Arguing that 'the surest but hardest way to prevent crimes is to improve education', he indicated the need for educational reform. On the one hand, this positioned education as a form of rehabilitation – as the end goal of incarceration[39] – but on the other it implied a new philosophy of civically minded, reflective education directed towards public utility. The Enlightened man cherished the social contract, understood the value of his sacrifices to society and comprehended how the laws worked to his advantage.[40] To produce such a citizen, Beccaria argued, the laws needed to be written in clear and simple vernacular languages, and printed and distributed so as to render the general public the repository of the laws.[41] Education was thus essential to ensuring that individuals could profit from their rights and contribute to society.

The cultural turn: *Il Caffè*, Giuseppe Parini, Giacomo Ceruti

Beccaria and Verri's views were indicative of evolving regional attitudes towards poverty. Much of this was driven by the Milanese intellectual elite as their place at the heart of Milan's intellectual and cultural landscape allowed their views to radiate throughout the city's public sphere. In addition to participating in discussions within various scholarly academies, many local luminaries voiced their opinions through the *Il Caffè* journal (*The Coffeehouse*) produced by Beccaria and Verri's own intellectual circle, the Accademia dei Pugni (the Academy of Fisticuffs) in the 1760s. Modelled on the *Spectator*, this satirical journal – often regarded as the 'mouthpiece of the Lombard Enlightenment' – sought to encourage social, economic and political reform in Lombardy, dedicating itself to 'things not words'; to practical improvement and public utility.[42]

Poverty was addressed at multiple points within *Il Caffè*. Unsurprisingly, it displayed a concern for poverty which was strictly structural, not moral, and its articles presented similar correlations between ideas of good citizenship and commerce, property rights and impoverishment, to those outlined by Beccaria and Verri above. It likewise communicated unflinching criticisms of institutionalised privileges in articles such as 'Reflections on the opinion that commerce denigrates the nobility', which bemoaned the social parasitism of those nobles who 'received everything from society and returned nothing to it'.[43] Published pseudonymously, the journal also espoused contentious opinions questioning the very legitimacy of the nobility and the natural right to property.[44] Above all, poverty was discussed in relation to the creation of a liberal economy which circulated wealth throughout society. This structure was not only essential to the mitigation of poverty, but to the economic improvement of the region, and could be achieved, the writers argued, by encouraging the nobility to engage in commerce and opening the economy to new groups. Women of all classes, for instance, were to play an important economic role. The financial independence of women both before and during marriage, and their increased presence in the workforce and economy, was anticipated to prevent the further impoverishment of families.[45]

The immediate alleviation of poverty was not the overarching concern driving the economic proposals made within *Il Caffè*. Nonetheless, the acknowledgement that poverty was a product of structural failings, that it could be rectified through new socio-economic models and that it could be extracted entirely from discussions regarding charity and sentimentality set *Il Caffè* apart. This is especially apparent if we situate the journal in Milan's broader literary and artistic culture of the 1760s, where poets, artists and writers alike grappled with changing perceptions of poverty. The widely popular Enlightenment poet and social commentator Giuseppe Parini (1729–1799) is an important foil in this regard. Parini echoed many of the themes addressed in *Il Caffè*, above all the critique of the nobility. Like the *Caffètisti*, he considered those nobles who languished in the wealth and status of their forebears to be social parasites. However, the Christian Parini put forward a more noticeably moralistic vision of the role of the nobility in society. We find this in his observations of their treatment of the poor. The nobles of Parini's poems trample innocent pedestrians beneath their carriages, enfamish their servants and cast them out into the cold. The nobility had, in Parini's eyes, become a class without virtue, unworthy of their place in society. While the *Il Caffè* group considered the nobility unvirtuous due to their aversion to commerce, Parini argued that the nobility had abandoned their social duty towards the welfare of the poor as well as their responsibility to provide leadership and stand as a pillar of truth and justice.[46]

Despite their critical acclaim, Parini's moralising accounts did not sit well with the *Caffètisti*. Pietro Verri, for one, criticised Parini for insufficiently depicting the depravity of the nobility.[47] Alluding to Parini's most famous poem '*Il Giorno*' (1763–1765), which satirised the fatuousness of a young lord's day, from his interminable *toilet* preparations to his fanciful social protocol in the company of women, Verri remarked that Parini's emphasis on the levity of the lord's world only made such a lifestyle appear enviable. It was only by depicting the grotesque paradoxes of the nobility, he argued- their pleading with creditors, their scheming to maintain social prowess, their inability to keep up in conversation with the *homme d'esprit* – that they could be ridiculed to social effect.[48] However, it was a mutual disregard. Parini likewise mocked what he viewed as the *Caffètisti*'s superficial focus on the social benefits of commerce and luxury and the elitism of their 'Enlightened' economic arguments, instead advocating a frugal, hardworking, largely agricultural society. Yet, their philosophical differences ultimately gave way to a shared outlook on the institutions responsible for poverty and its social effects. Inspired by Beccaria's statements connecting poverty to crime, Parini felt compelled to further Beccaria's arguments, resulting in the poem '*Il bisogno*' (*Need*). Just as Beccaria had adopted the voice of the thief in *On Crimes and Punishments*, here Parini personified the delinquent: tortured, incarcerated and treated without mercy or justice. It was those in need, Parini claimed, that turned to crime, and whose actions could be deterred through better living conditions, as well as equality before the law, as he later argued in the ode '*La magistratura*'. Poverty, for both Beccaria and Parini, was ultimately a social issue rooted in injustice.

The critiques of poverty threading through literary culture in the 1760s marked a turning point in Milan. However, attitudes towards the poor had already been evolving since the turn of the century. This is evident in the changing visual culture of period as a number of painters in Northern Italy directed their attention to the realities of poverty. Pietro Bellotti, Antonio Cifrondi and the Milan-based Giacomo Francesco Cipper (Il Todeschini) extensively depicted the poor, infirm and mendicant in styles devoid of sentimentality, judgement and Christian charity. In some respects, this turn reflected wider developments in early modern depictions of the poor. French and Spanish artists like Le Nain, Callot, Murillo and Georges La Tour created increasingly varied and complex imageries of poverty which collapsed the traditional iconographic binary of good/bad, sacred/dishonest for their subjects.[49] Similarly, in Rome, the *Bamboccianti* (the ugly dolls) produced allegorical genre paintings of peasants, peddlers and pickpockets intended to undermine the pretensions of academic artists. In Lombardy, this changing outlook was captured most clearly in the work of Giacomo Ceruti (1698–1767) – part of *Il Caffè*'s wider social circle[50] – commonly known as '*il Pitocchetto*' (little beggar), the painter of the poor. Although sympathetic, his paintings of beggars, peasants, dwarves and the impoverished fringes of Lombard society lacked the moralising, allegorical or comedic tone common to much of the genre painting of the period, as well as many of the gestural and morphological codes associated with poverty, begging and alms.[51] Ceruti neither vilified nor idealised the poor, as had been the longstanding iconography,[52] and instead drew attention to his sitters' agency and humanity by using realistic styles and natural compositions (Figure 3.1). Situating figures in their everyday surroundings, he sought to capture the 'culture of poverty'.[53] The men, women and children – beggars, orphans, washerwomen – of his paintings are depicted at moments of work, rest and leisure, at relatable human activities like card-playing and eating. Often depicted in public settings, Ceruti's sitters serve as a

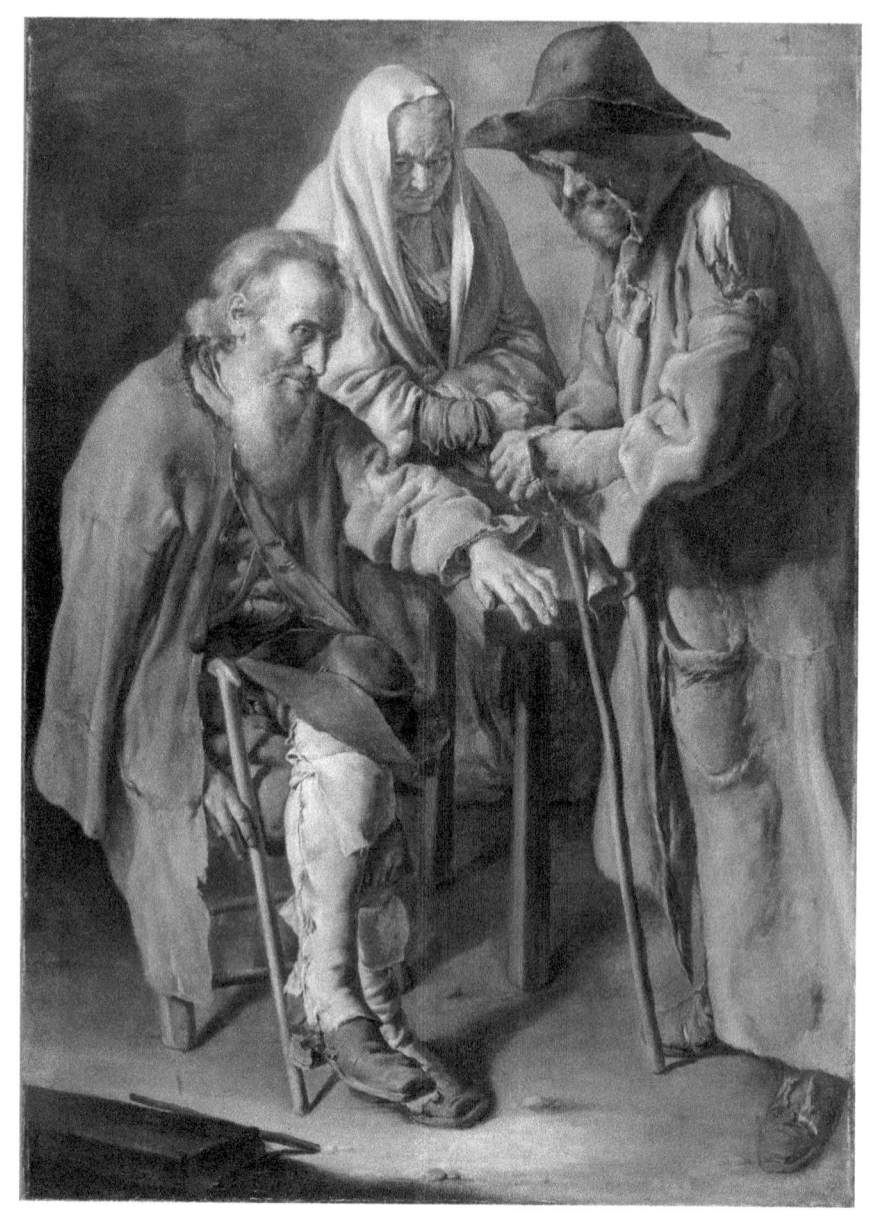

Figure 3.1 Giacomo Ceruti (known as 'Il Pittocchetto'), *Group of Beggars*, c. 1737. © Museo Nacional Thyssen-Bornemisza, Madrid.

reminder of the contradictory visibility/invisibility of urban poverty. These were individuals who were highly visible, living, working and socialising in Lombardy's public spaces – especially given the influx of rural poor into the cities – but who were invisible as individuals. By capturing these moments, Ceruti documented their presence and humanity in modes which brought individual experience to the foreground.

A number of identifiable references to Lombard society in Ceruti's paintings attest to regional concerns shaping the visual language of poverty. The prominence of urban porters in Milan due to seasonal migration from the countryside (Figure 3.2)[54] and the reliance of thousands of poor peasant women on Lombardy's silk share-cropping system and silk production within the workhouses and houses of correction,[55] are captured by sitters carrying baskets and spindles. Ceruti's focus on wounded and impoverished soldiers is similarly telling of the Lombard social climate. As part of the Habsburg Empire, Lombardy was obliged to provide two infantry regiments. These recruits were selected locally; however, the poor wages and work conditions ostensibly limited volunteers to the region's most impoverished men, as Pietro Verri, who served briefly as a Captain, recorded: 'the common soldiers are either rabble, who were sent to the regiment rather than to jail, or idlers, who in a moment of drunkenness swore their oath'.[56] The soldiers depicted by Ceruti testify to the precarity of the profession. Many of his sitters, bandaged and on crutches, their uniforms tattered, have been reduced to begging. Others sit around playing cards on up-turned military drums. While vagrant soldiers were a perennial concern in early modern Europe, their perceived threat to society is entirely absent in Ceruti's rendering. Like the silk-spinners, porters and mendicants, they too are merely individuals within the diverse social fabric of Lombardy.

Yet, although Ceruti benignly reintegrates the poor as people into the Lombard landscape, he simultaneously reveals the structures of support upon which they were reliant. His sitters are often situated against recognisable Lombard urban landmarks of poor relief, though they are never explicitly in receipt of assistance; a pilgrim sleeps outside the Church of Sant'Alessandro in Brescia, for instance, and the outfits of girls sewing and making lace clearly locate them within the orphanage of Pio Luogo della Pietà (Figure 3.3).[57] While it was not unusual for such institutions to feature in genre painting of the period, the local tone was undoubtedly important for Ceruti's audience. His sizeable paintings were purchased by the Milanese elite and prominently exhibited in their homes alongside more traditional portraits, and historic and landscape scenes.[58] This was, however, reflective of interests beyond aesthetics alone. As the following section will show, it captured the growing involvement of Lombardy's political and intellectual class in initiatives to rationalise frameworks of social assistance.

Figure 3.2 Giacomo Ceruti, *Errand Boy Seated on a Basket*, c. 1735.
© Pinacoteca di Brera, Milano.

Figure 3.3 Giacomo Ceruti, *Scuola di ragazze*, c. 1720–1725. Pinacoteca Tosio Martinengo © Archivio fotografico Civici Musei di Brescia/ Fotostudio Rapuzzi.

Calculating poverty: pestilence, policy and the productive poor

A striking dimension of the Lombard Enlightenment was the collaboration that occurred between the local elite and the Habsburg administration. After the heyday of the *Il Caffè* journal, many members of the Accademia dei Pugni took up positions within Habsburg-Lombard institutions and state bureaucracy. Cesare Beccaria, for instance, initially accepted the first chair of cameral sciences at the Palatine School in Milan, before rising to a position on the Supreme Economic Council of Lombardy in 1771, after which he became part of the Governing Council of Lombardy, responsible for areas like manufacture, commerce, the price of food, the *polices des blés*, public health, police, prisons and jurisdictional issues.

In this latter position, where he spent the majority of his career, Beccaria was confronted with the bitter social and economic costs of poverty. The growing state involvement in society, prompted by the centralising, cameralist attitudes of the ruling Habsburgs, had drawn attention to the scale of poverty's effects across the region. This was especially apparent in the field of public health. Disease naturally brought poverty in its wake, above all in agricultural communities that had limited access to health care. Faced with recurrent epidemics including cattle plague and smallpox, rural populations and local economies faced harsh existential realities. However, poverty also brought disease, especially in urban settings. Already in the 1760s, *Il Caffè* had explored this relationship at length. In an article on the location of burial sites, Luigi Lambertenghi had used mortality tables to highlight the 'tragic example' of urban beggars who, living in narrow streets where the air was thick with disease, had a much lower life expectancy than their wealthier peers.[59] Parini too, turned his attention to the unsanitary conditions in Milan caused by poverty and the neglect and greed of those in power. In the poem '*La insalubrità dell'aria*' (*The insalubrity of the air*), he depicted a disease-riddled city overwhelmed by noxious gasses arising from the nearby marshes, the stench of chamber pots emptied out of windows and streets littered with refuse and carrion. Introducing an unprecedented contrast between rural and urban health, Parini argued that while the rural poor still bore the brunt of poverty, at least they breathed fresh, salubrious countryside air.

Parini's lyrical exhortations for the introduction of sanitary reforms reflected increasingly paternalist approaches within the Habsburg-Lombard administration. The management of epidemics, failed harvests, rural squalor and stagnant waters was increasingly seen as the responsibility of the governing council. The provision and regulation of health care was also a priority, framed in terms of both economic stability and social welfare. This is visible in a 1784 proposal for the redistribution of medical services across the Milanese provinces composed by Beccaria. Using calculations from the Director of the Medical Faculty, Beccaria painted the stark reality of rural poverty: the Milanese countryside comprised 880,000 inhabitants, more than 500,000 of whom were without any medical assistance.[60] Shocked by how a 'civilised nation' could subject rural communities to such hardships, especially considering their economic contribution through agriculture and industry, Beccaria proposed increasing and dispersing medical facilities more equitably throughout the Milanese territory via the establishment of more than 100 rural clinics. However, while the proposal sought to alleviate some of the symptoms of poverty, if the poor could not afford such services, it made little difference whether it was local or not. Consequently, it was the existing, institutionalised poverty perpetuating ill-health which formed the core of Beccaria's concerns. While physicians had always been encouraged to attend to the poor without compensation, any assessment of whether patients qualified for free treatment was left to individual physicians' discretion. This, Beccaria argued, led to the discriminatory assessment of poverty, likely to be influenced by the already lowly wages paid to rural physicians. Local parishes, though ostensibly responsible for charitable alms, similarly lacked any rigorous or standardised criteria by which to assess individuals' needs. Beccaria thus proposed quantifying the entitlement to free medical treatment.[61] This financial threshold would not only make assessments easier, but also allowed the administration to forecast the percentage of free treatment required. However, this efficiency subsequently revealed a more disturbing problem. Upon calculating how many individuals would meet this financial threshold, Beccaria projected that the vast majority of the rural population would qualify as the 'deserving poor'.[62]

Beccaria's calculations formed part of a wider initiative to quantify poverty. Many *Illuministi* associated with Beccaria had similarly attempted to estimate poverty rates, though they reached strikingly different numbers. Luigi Lambertenghi calculated there to be 6.300 individuals supported by pious institutions;[63] Gian Rinaldo Carli suggested there were more than 20,000 paupers who received free bread, soup or clothing; and the Marquis Carpani claimed that around a quarter of the Porta Comasina district lived off support.[64] But without clearer definitions of poverty it was impossible to truly gauge the scale of the problem, as the Austrian Chancellor Kaunitz made clear in a letter to the Plenipotentiary of Lombardy, Count Firmian, concerning the vagaries of the term 'poor'.[65] It was a longstanding problem across Europe. Already in the seventeenth century the moralising distinction between the 'deserving' (those unable to work due to age, accident or illness) and 'idle' poor had shifted towards this latter category, which expanded to include the majority of able-bodied persons. Yet, distinguishing between poverty and indigence, between poor, subsistence labourers and those who were destitute, remained challenging. In Lombardy, part of the solution, it was proposed, was to secularise and centralise social assistance in its entirety. As elsewhere in the Habsburg Empire under Joseph II, social provisions in Lombardy were removed from the control of religious institutions, corporations and individual charity and rationalised into centralised state mechanics.[66]

The centralisation process also reframed the poverty discussion around notions of rehabilitation through work and education. In so doing, it echoed many of the arguments made by the *Illuministi*, including Beccaria, already in the 1760s. Criticising the Christian outlook of Ludovico Muratori's *Della caritá cristiana* of 1724, the *Caffètisti* argued that traditional frameworks of charity had little economic and social benefit:

> whoever provides citizens with a free and independent subsistence from fatigue renders men themselves and their country a very bad service by fomenting idleness and indolence, and by diminishing proportionately the mass of the nation's labor, in which then in substance consists of all the true wealth of a state.[67]

While indolence was more commonly presented as the disease of a nobility reluctant to engage in commerce, the *Caffètisti* were nonetheless concerned that charity hindered the economy through encouraging dependence whilst simultaneously preventing assistance from reaching those most in need. Luigi Lambertenghi's *On the idle and beggars, and on the need for a workhouse* neatly condenses this outlook.[68] Here, Lambertenghi argued that the resources of Milan's pious institutions would be better spent on subsidising artisans and labourers during times of bad harvest; that only the disabled and infirm should be supported at public expense; and that the house of correction should be transformed into a workhouse not only for prisoners but also the unemployed. Pietro Verri too, repeatedly emphasised the value of industry and industriousness for well-being, both individual and national, in his *Elements of Commerce*.[69]

The desire to secularise social provisions, separate the 'real' from the indolent poor and reintegrate the able-bodied through labour, resulted in the creation and/or reform of a number of institutions – largely compulsory – in the 1770–1790s. These included the Pio Albergo Trivulzio for the elderly, wounded, incurable, insane, mute, blind, crippled and monstrous;[70] the Pia Casa di Santa Caterina della Ruora for abandoned children; San Pietro in Gessate and the Martinitt for male orphans; the Stelline for female orphans; the Pia Casa di Abbiategrasso for the incurable (1784); the Hospice of Senavra for the insane; and the workhouse (1784).[71] These sites of Foucault's 'Great Confinement' were widely supported by the Milanese elite. The Pio Albergo Trivulzio, for instance, was founded by Prince Antonio Tolomeo Gallio Trivulzio, a close friend and follower of Beccaria and Pietro Verri. Driven by the Enlightened reformism of the Milanese Enlightenment, Trivulzio bequeathed his wealth and palace to create the first secular institution for poor relief.[72] Similarly, Attilio Lampugnani Visconti, overseer of Milan's roads and provisions (*giudice delle strade/giudice delle vettovaglie*), after originally bequeathing his wealth to the construction of a house of correction, left his legacy to the Ospedale Maggiore di Milano, of which he was deputy, and within whose walls his portrait by Ceruti remains today.[73] A similar portrait of the Marquis Guido Antonio Arcimboldi was produced by Ceruti after his nomination of the Luogo Pio della Stella as his sole heir.[74]

The socio-economic injustices causing poverty, as identified by the *Caffètisti*, do not feature in the taxonomy of poverty used to assign assistance through the above institutions, and which undoubtedly entrenched or even criminalised pathologies of destitution in the name of efficiency. However, the focus on labour and rehabilitation behind these categories echoed the *Caffètisti*'s arguments in support of industry and can be read as a move towards preventative, and away from protectionist, policies regarding poverty. For the Milanese reformers, providing work opportunities for the able-bodied gave individuals the ability to extract themselves from poverty, being no longer dependent on alms or the whims of weather, harvests or seasonal labour. While this was never explicitly framed as the right to work, as Gaetano Filangieri so demanded in Naples,[75] it was certainly entangled in understandings of the right to happiness as seen as the exercise of one's talents and the pursuit of wealth. As such, it reflected wider shifts towards rights-based understandings of social assistance, security and opportunity within Habsburg policy.[76] This was prominent in the 1784 Italian translation of Count Johann Nepomuk Buquoy's work on poverty management in the Habsburg-Bohemian states, lauded by its translator for its strict classifications of the deserving and undeserving poor.[77] Buquoy's highly regulated poor institutes had become the model for poor relief in Vienna and lower Austria under Joseph II due to their efficiency in administering aid.[78] However, they were rooted in an understanding of the relationship between rights and poverty. According to Buquoy, if individuals had contributed to society through their labour, or were rendered unable to do so by illness, age or accident, then they had a legitimate right to demand protection, public compassion and provision from the state. As poverty was an inescapable product of the state of society, Buquoy claimed that it was essential to delineate who had the right to social assistance, under which circumstances, and how these should be fulfilled by the state.[79]

The idea that poverty was ineradicable did not restrict further preventative anti-poverty policies based on ideas of rehabilitation. The activities of Milan's Patriotic Society, formed by Empress Maria Theresa in 1776, brought together scientific practitioners and reformers, including Cesare Beccaria and Pietro Verri, to improve domestic agricultural and manufacturing practices for the benefit of both the state and the rural poor.[80] The Society explored such possibilities as creating *case rustiche* (buildings to be used as storehouses and temporary accommodation for seasonal farmworkers), introducing new crops like potatoes, encouraging agricultural techniques like small-scale farming and developing new breadmaking technologies. While agricultural development had clear economic advantages for the Habsburg state, many of the proposals were intended to improve the conditions of agricultural workers and mitigate the dangers of famine and disease longer term. Prizes were offered for initiatives such as the creation of an affordable regional pharmacopeia for the poor, or insight into the causes of devastating local diseases like Pellagra, later discovered to be caused by malnutrition. Moreover, the Society's proceedings stressed the importance of disseminating useful agricultural and sanitation knowledge to rural communities through clear and vernacular instruction. Translations were commissioned for distribution,[81] including George Armstrong's *Essay on the Diseases most Fatal to Infants* and Ludwig Mitterpacher's *Elements of Agriculture* [*Elementa rei rusticæ*] in the hopes of giving the rural poor the tools needed to work their way out of precarity. Such emphasis on education was mirrored in the activities of the Lombard administration, too. From his position in the governing council, Cesare Beccaria repeatedly raised concerns regarding how the superstitions of the poor perpetuated disease and poverty by encouraging 'unscientific' health and sanitation practices. A pressing example, due to the high rate of paediatric diseases, infant mortality and orphancy in Lombardy, was the prevalence of superstitious birthing practices. Writing to the Viennese Court, Beccaria suggested that providing rural obstetricians and midwives would serve a dual purpose: not only would they ensure the safe delivery and care of infants, but their increased presence in the provinces would slowly break down 'by way of the sure value of education, the damaging prejudices often harboured by rural populations'.[82]

Education was not a panacea for either poverty or disease. However, its inclusion in a multi-pronged approach to poor relief is illustrative of the increasingly complex understanding of poverty held by the Lombard elite, which shone light on poverty's connections to wider political, social, economic and environmental factors. Likewise, it indicated the germination of rights-based ideas within policy and practice. Though these were yet to be fully articulated, the broader notion that the state had a duty to prevent poverty through providing opportunities for work and self-improvement, as well as more tangible aid, signalled shifting perceptions of the nature and scope of social rights.

Conclusion

It is a bad thing to be born poor, my dear Renzo.[83]

When Manzoni's humble silk-weaver, Renzo, asks the local priest's servant, Perpetua, for advice, she has little to offer but a reminder of the inescapable misfortune of poverty. As Renzo learns first-hand, not only was being poor a state of existential concern, but it was one coupled with legal, social and political injustices. For Beccaria and the Milanese *Illuministi*, such entrenched inequalities were anathema to a functioning society predicated on the social contract. While poverty was not necessarily something to be eradicated, and the poverty caused by the personal idleness of any class certainly did not warrant assistance or sympathy, structural poverty generated by the abuse of the social contract was an abomination of individual rights. As such, the *Illuministi* argued that a liberal economy and the removal of privileges, both legal and social, were an essential means of upholding this contract, as well as mitigating the causes and effects of poverty.

With regards to the wider history of European Enlightenment ideas of poverty, Lombardy presents a number of noteworthy considerations. First, the complex understanding of poverty as a phenomenon entangled with other social, political, economic and environmental issues, held by individuals like Beccaria, is indicative of increasingly sophisticated views on the relationship between society, economy and human nature. The correlations drawn between poverty and crime, sanitation and education reflected not just evolving attitudes towards poverty as a social issue, but to society more generally. Likewise, the fundamental questions regarding the purpose of a parasitic nobility similarly indicate shifting economic priorities. This links to another important point of reflection: the interaction between ideas and practices of poor relief in Lombardy. This was in many ways symptomatic of the specific political landscape of Habsburg-Lombardy and the collaboration between local reformers and the administration. The activities of the Lombard governing council indicate a growing acceptance of rights-based understandings of society and social assistance, which shaped policy and practice. On the one hand, the right to relief for the deserving poor – as opposed to the expectation of charity or beneficence – was increasingly acknowledged. On the other, the new programmes and institutions of industry were likewise framed in terms of the obligation of the state to provide opportunity for labour and rehabilitation. Finally, these two points lead us to a question of chronology. While the 1790s are commonly identified as a turning point in Europe towards conceptions of poverty as a social problem, Lombardy indicates that this outlook was already developing in the 1760s, if not earlier. Moreover, the Lombard rights discourse around poverty, though still nascent, was in many ways moving in the direction of the social rights that took centre stage towards the end of the eighteenth and early nineteenth century. We find the seeds of the right to work, health care and education, though, in the shadows of Habsburg paternalist attitudes and the renewed pathologising of the poor; these would take time to see light and grow.

Notes

1. Alessandro Manzoni, *The Betrothed* (London, 1834), p. 208.
2. Stuart Woolf, *The Poor in Western Europe in the Eighteenth and Nineteenth Centuries* (Oxford: Routledge, 2016), Ch. 2.
3. See Bruno Passamani, "Brescia e Ceruti: patrizi, popolo, pitocchi. Alla ricercar di 'fatti certi' e di 'persone vive' in *Giacomo Ceruti: Il Pitocchetto* (Mazzotta: Milano, 1987), p. 22; Carlo Capra, 'Il Pio Albergo Trivulzio: un'eredità del secolo dei lumi', in *La nascita del Pio Albergo Trivulzio: Orfani, vecchi e poveri a Milano tra Settecento e Ottocento* (Milan: Electa, 1993), p. 16.
4. Martin Ravallion, *The Economics of Poverty: History, Measurement and Policy* (Oxford: Oxford University Press, 2016), Part I.
5. Ibid.
6. Ferdinando Facchinei, *Note ed osservazioni sul libro intitolato Dei delitti e delle pene* (Venice, 1775), p. 188.
7. For more, see John Davies, 'Health Care and Poor Relief in Southern Europe in the 18th and 19th Centuries', in Ole Peter Grell and Andrew Cunningham (eds), *Health Care and Poor Relief in 18th and 19th Century Southern Europe* (Oxford: Routledge, 2017), pp. 10–33 at pp. 14–17.
8. See: Alexandra Ortolja-Baird, 'Cesare Beccaria: Functionary, Lecturer, Cameralist? Interpreting Cameralism in Habsburg Lombardy', in Ere Nokkala, Nicholas B. Miller and Anthony J. LaVopa (eds), *Cameralism and the Enlightenment: Happiness, Governance, and Reform in Transnational Perspective* (London: Routledge, 2020), pp. 173–200.
9. Cesare Beccaria, *On Crimes and Punishments and Other Writings*, ed. Richard Bellamy (Cambridge: Cambridge University Press, 1995), p. 11.
10. Ibid.
11. Cesare Beccaria, 'Dei delitti e delle pene', in Gianni Francioni (ed.), *Edizione Nazionale delle opere di Cesare Beccaria* (Milano: Mediobanca, 1984), vol. i, p. 23.
12. Ibid., vol. i, pp. 43–44.
13. Beccaria, *On Crimes and Punishments*, p. 51.
14. Immanuel Kant, *Groundwork of the Metaphysics of Morals*, ed. and trans. Mary Gregory (Cambridge: Cambridge University Press, [1785] 1997), p. 45.
15. Beccaria, *On Crimes and Punishments*, p. 50.
16. Ibid., p. 101.
17. Ibid., p. 112.
18. This sentiment is clearest in his inaugural lecture. See: Cesare Beccaria, 'Inaugural Lecture', in Beccaria, *On Crimes and Punishments*, p. 132.
19. Beccaria, *On Crimes and Punishments*, p. 65.
20. Ibid., p. 102.
21. Ibid., p. 69.
22. Ibid., p. 53.
23. Ibid., p. 99.

24 Cesare Beccaria, 'Elementi di economia pubblica', in Gianmarco Gaspari (ed.), *Edizione Nazionale delle opere di Cesare Beccaria* (Milano: Mediobanca, 2014), p. 237.
25 Ibid.
26 Ibid., pp. 137–138.
27 Beccaria, *On Crimes and Punishments*, p. 167.
28 Ibid., p. 56.
29 Beccaria, 'Prolusione nell'apertura della nuova cattedra', in Gaspari, *Edizione Nazionale*, p. 86.
30 Ibid., p. 87.
31 Daniel M. Klang, 'Cesare Beccaria, Pietro Verri e l'idea dell'imprenditore nell'illuminismo Milanese', in Sergio Romagnoli (ed.), *Cesare Beccaria tra Milano e l'Europa* (Milan: Cariplo – Laterza, 1990), p. 397.
32 Beccaria, 'Elementi di economia pubblica', p. 390.
33 Pietro Verri, 'Saggio d'aritmetica politica', in Gianni Francioni and Sergio Romagnoli (eds), *Il Caffè, 1764–1766* (Turin: Bollati Boringhieri, 1993), pp. 198–199.
34 Pietro Verri, *Reflections on Political Economy*, trans. Barbara McGilvray with Peter D. Groenewegen (Fairfield, NJ: Augustus M. Kelley Publishers, [1781] 1993), p. 23.
35 Pietro Verri, 'Elementi del commercio', in Francioni and Romagnoli, *Il Caffè*, p. 36.
36 Emma Rothschild discusses this at length in 'Social Security and Laissez Faire in Eighteenth-Century Political Economy', *Population and Development Review*, 21:4 (1995), 711–744.
37 Paolo Mattia Doria, *Del commercio del regno di Napoli* (1740).
38 See: Anna Maria Rao, 'The Feudal Question, Judicial Systems, and the Enlightenment', in Girolamo Imbruglia (ed.), *Naples in the Eighteenth Century* (Cambridge: Cambridge University Press, 2000), pp. 95–117.
39 For more, see Sophus Reinert, *The Academy of Fisticuffs: Political Economy and Commercial Society in Enlightenment Italy* (Cambridge, MA: Harvard University Press, 2018), pp. 330–333.
40 Beccaria, *On Crimes and Punishments*, p. 105.
41 Ibid., p. 17.
42 See: Gian Rinaldo Carli, 'Della patria degli Italiani', in Francioni and Romagnoli, *Il Caffè*, pp. 421–427.
43 Alessandro Verri, 'Alcune riflessioni sulla opinione che il commercio deroghi alla nobiltà', in Francioni and Romagnoli, *Il Caffè*, pp. 256–274.
44 Alfonso Longo, 'Osservazioni su i fedecommessi', in Francioni and Romagnoli, *Il Caffè*, pp. 115–132.
45 Sebastiano Franci, 'Difesa delle donne', in Francioni and Romagnoli, *Il Caffè*, pp. 245–256.
46 Giuseppe Parini, 'La Educazione' (1761). https://it.wikisource.org/wiki/Odi_(Parini)/La_educazione. Accessed 22 April 2022.
47 Pietro Verri, 'Sul ridicolo', in Francioni and Romagnoli, *Il Caffè*, pp. 560–566.
48 Ibid., pp. 561–563.

49 See: Robert Jütte, *Poverty and Deviance in Early Modern Europe* (Cambridge: Cambridge University Press, 2006), pp. 8–20; Tom Nichols, 'Motives of Control/Motifs of Creativity: The Visual Imagery of Poverty in Early Modern Europe', in David Hitchcock and Julia McClure (eds), *The Routledge History of Poverty 1450–1800* (Routledge: Abingdon, 2021), Ch. 8.
50 Ceruti painted Alessandro Verri's portrait, which was hung in Pietro Verri's home.
51 For more, see: Jütte, *Poverty and Deviance in Early Modern Europe*, pp. 8–20.
52 Nichols, 'Motives of Control'.
53 Bruno Passamani, "Brescia e Ceruti: patrizi, popolo, pitocchi. Alla ricercar di 'fatti certi' e di 'persone vive', in *Giacomo Ceruti: Il Pitocchetto* (Milano: Mazzotta, 1987), p. 23.
54 Luca Mocarelli estimates there to have been upwards of 1,000 porters in Milan at this time. See: Luca Mocarelli, 'The Attitude of Milanese Society to Work and Commercial Activities. The Case of the Porters and the Case of the Elites', in Josef Ehmer and Catarina Lis (eds), *The Idea of Work in Europe from Antiquity to Modern Times* (Farnham: Ashgate, 2010), fn. 31.
55 See: Margaret Hunt, *Women in Eighteenth-Century Europe* (Abingdon: Routledge, 2014), p. 187.
56 Pietro Verri, Diario Militare (Capelli: Rocca San Casciano, 1967), p. 54.
57 Passamani, 'Brescia e Ceruti', p. 25.
58 See: *Giacomo Ceruti: Il Pitocchetto*.
59 Luigi Lambertenghi, 'Sull'origine e sul luogo delle sepolture', in Francioni and Romagnoli, *Il Caffè*, pp. 481–487.
60 'Piano per le condotte mediche e chirurgiche forensi, relazione, 5 Ottobre 1784', in Rosalba Canetta (ed.), *Edizione Nazionale delle opere di Cesare Beccaria* (Milano: Mediobanca) vol. viii, no. 982, pp. 162–163.
61 Ibid., p. 184.
62 Ibid., p. 177.
63 Luigi Lambertenghi, *Sugli oziosi e mendici e Sulla necessità di una casa di travaglio*. Milano, Biblioteca Ambrosiana, Mss., Z.235 sup.
64 Capra, 'Il Pio Albergo Trivulzio', p. 17.
65 Ibid.
66 See Tim Hochstrasser's Chapter 1.
67 Pietro Secchi, 'Anecdoto chinese', in Francioni and Romagnoli, *Il Caffè*, pp. 335–336.
68 Luigi Lambertenghi, *Sugli oziosi e mendici e Sulla necessità di una casa di travaglio*. For more, see: Carlo Capra, 'LAMBERTENGHI, Luigi Stefano' in *Dizionario Biografico degli Italiani*, vol. 63 (2004). www.treccani.it/enciclopedia/luigi-stefano-lambertenghi_%28Dizionario-Biografico%29/. Accessed 22 April 2022.
69 Verri, 'Elementi del commercio'.
70 Capra, 'Il Pio Albergo Trivulzio', p. 75.
71 See: Rosalba Canetta, 'Povertà e lavoro nella Milano di metà Ottocento', in Aldo Carera, Mario Taccolini and Rosalba Canetta (eds), *Temi e questioni di*

storia economica e sociale in età moderna e contemporanea: studi in onore di Sergio Zaninelli (Milan: Vita e Pensiero, 1999), p. 266.
72　Capra, 'Il Pio Albergo Trivulzio', pp. 13–19.
73　See: https://artsandculture.google.com/asset/portrait-of-attilio-lampugnani-visconti-giacomo-ceruti-detto-il-pitocchetto/3QG9JzfKtQr4BA?hl=it. Accessed 22 April 2022.
74　See: www.lombardiabeniculturali.it/opere-arte/schede/8g060–00024/. Accessed 22 April 2022.
75　See Vincenzo Ferrone, *The Politics of Enlightenment: Constitutionalism, Republicanism, and the Rights of Man in Gaetano Filangieri* (New York: Anthem Press, 2012), pp. 207–213.
76　For more, see: Marco Bascapè, 'Gli interventi teresiani e giuseppini contro il pauperismo: dai progetti degli anni Cinquanta [del XVIII secolo] all'Istituto generale delle elemosine', in M. Bona Castellotti et al. (eds), *Cultura, religione e trasformazione sociale. Milano e la Lombardia dalle riforme all'unità* (Milan: Francoangeli, 2001), pp. 109–138.
77　*Esatto Ragguaglio dell' istituto dei poveri eretto nel 1779 nelle terre de del Signor Conte di Buquoy in Boemia. Traduzione* (Stamperia privilegiata di Giuseppe Nobile de Baumeister, 1784).
78　Martin Scheutz, 'Demand and Charitable Supply: Poverty and Poor Relief in Austria in the 18th and 19th Centuries', in Grell and Cunningham, *Health Care and Poor Relief*, pp. 63–64.
79　*Esatto Ragguaglio dell' istituto dei poveri*, pp. 206–207.
80　Lavinia Maddaluno, 'De Facto Policies and Intellectual Agendas of an Eighteenth-Century Milanese Agricultural Academy: Physiocratic Resonances in the Società Patriotica', in Sophus Reinert and Steven Kaplan (eds), *The Economic Turn: Recasting Political Economy in Enlightenment Europe* (New York: Anthem Press, 2019), p. 419.
81　Ibid.
82　'Piano per le condotte mediche e chirurgiche forensi', pp. 171–172.
83　Manzoni, *The Betrothed*, p. 22.

4

An economic regalism: poverty and charity in eighteenth-century Spain

Jesús Astigarraga and Javier Usoz

Introduction

Why did a work that addressed the ills of Spanish society in the second half of the eighteenth century say nothing about poverty, one of its greatest problems? The question arises because the book concerned, Cadalso's *Cartas marruecas* (1789), is undoubtedly a landmark work due to its sharpness and link with European modernity.[1] This chapter attempts to answer the question by showing that the eighteenth century brought with it a new secularising and economistic way of tackling poverty. This new perspective could only be embraced by those who upheld the monarch's secular authority; in other words, those who had adopted a regalist position and were thus willing to question the Catholic Church's traditional religious approaches to charity and its related institutional framework. Moreover, this stance could not have been adequately defended without the purely economistic conception that emerged in Europe during the eighteenth century, especially from 1740 onwards; a vision that was structured around the new science of political economy and required the proper use of private and public resources, particularly the labour force. From the Enlightenment political and economic viewpoint, therefore, the issue was not so much charity but combating idleness and thus promoting industry, which was understood as application to productive work.

Poverty was a fundamental issue during the Spanish Enlightenment and its importance grew with increasing awareness of the fact that it was not contingent on periods of scarcity and that the welfare system could not cope. Clearer answers to the question of how to deal with begging and unemployment appeared from the 1740s onwards, from the emerging discipline of political economy; in fact, the first systematic welfare scheme, Ward's *Obra pía*, dates from 1750. From then on the amount of literature on the subject increased, constituting a sub-genre that included translations and accounts of national and foreign experiences: if at the beginning of the century in Spain, the example of the hospice in Lyon was repeatedly evoked, during the middle decades that of Saint-Sulpice in Paris became omnipresent. Finally, at the end of the century, examples in Munich and other European cities became the testing ground for experiences by Benjamin Thompson, Count Rumford (1753–1814) (the renowned British scientist, soldier and philanthropist, originally from Massachusetts, whose welfare policy proposals, including food hygiene, were widely circulated and debated in the Europe of his day).

A major concern was how to distinguish the 'real' from the 'fake' poor; the spotlight fell on *policy* towards the poor and occupied some of the century's most brilliant minds, such as Campomanes, Jovellanos and Foronda.[2] These authors normally confined themselves to reproducing the best-known foreign texts, such as those by De la Mare (1705–1710), Duchesne (1758) and Bielfeld (1760), which were followed by Rumford and the *l'Encyclopédie Méthodique* volumes on '*Jurisprudence*' (1782–1791) towards the end of the century. Together with the reception accorded to Beccaria and other authors who were sensitive to humanist views of the treatment of criminals, this meant that the century's closing years saw a call for better conditions in poorhouses, workhouses or *hospicios*, which Foronda described as 'prisons decorated with the lovely epithet of charitable refuges'.[3]

While Spanish and European Enlightenment views on these matters differed little, the same cannot be said of the battle over poverty policy in eighteenth-century Spain, which was waged against the privileges of the Catholic Church, in whose hands lay the welfare network and the prevailing approach to the issue. This translated into a regalist movement, in which political figures such as Aranda, Campomanes and Floridablanca took part, and which used the language of political economy, provided with criteria that upheld civil governance's primacy over the Church, even though the latter's participation was essential due to the Bourbon government's institutional and financial weakness. This chapters' authors believe that a meaningful contribution to the understanding of these issues can be made by examining this battle and the important role played by economic discourse.[4]

In the *Ancien Régime* context of the Spanish Enlightenment, references to a regalist movement or *regalismo* (*regalías* were the Crown's rights vis-à-vis the Church and the nobility) are not allusions to an institutionalised social or political organisation, but to a line of ideology and political action. In Spain this orientation, which had a strong legal component, was driven by the reformism of the ministers to Philip V and his successors. Political leaders under Charles III, who had already confronted the power of Rome during his reign in Naples and the Two Sicilies prior to his accession to the Spanish throne in 1759, stood out in this respect. Nonetheless, during the eighteenth-century *regalista* ideology, which had medieval origins, transcended the monarch's specific interests and adapted to the Enlightenment objective of public happiness. *Regalismo* was thus conditioned by the desire to strengthen and centralise government power, to the detriment of the privileges enjoyed by the Church and the nobility. The issue was primarily one of creating and consolidating a government capable of carrying out far-reaching reforms while also enabling individual action, especially in economic terms, and this meant confronting the guilds and certain privileged companies.

On very few issues – usury would be another – did Enlightened Spaniards enter headlong into the ideological terrain monopolised by the Church. It is no coincidence that Spanish economic treatises repeatedly evoked the controversy over the poor laws in late sixteenth-century Scholasticism, considered a turning point in the Catholic tradition.[5] With a backdrop of natural law, the issue invoked the work of humanist Juan Vives (1520) and epigones such as Juan de Medina (1545) and Cristóbal Pérez de Herrera (1595; 1617), advocates of civil control and isolating the poor from society.[6] In the opposing ranks was the treatise by Dominican Domingo de Soto (1545), an advocate of almsgiving.[7] The choice between these double 'interventionist' and 'liberal' paths was a fundamental one since, already in the sixteenth century, mainly thanks to Vives and Medina, the path was opened to the secularisation of charity by invoking the responsibility of the state in a matter that had previously been left to individual conscience. These scholastic controversies cast their long shadow over eighteenth-century Spain, which witnessed Spanish translations of Latin texts by Pérez de Herrera (1733), Medina (1757; 1766) and Vives (1781).

However, these works were understood as something rather more than moral or theological disputes in the eighteenth century. Not unrelated was the legacy of the seventeenth-century Castilian *arbitristas*, a term that referred to the *arbitrios* (fiscal measures favouring the Royal Treasury) and was applied to early Spanish mercantilists, frequently pejoratively. These *arbitrista* authors favoured isolating the poor so that they became workers (Cellorigo, Fernández Navarrete, Moncada and Martínez de Mata) or were concerned about depopulation, which made this measure into an essential component of mercantilist power politics, as characterised by Heckscher.[8] However, like the British mercantilists, the Spanish *arbitristas* were less interested in population levels than in employment levels, even more so when the Spanish monarchy emerged as a paradigmatic case of an underdeveloped economy.[9] Thus, charity, populationism and encouragement of factory building were intertwined, so that poverty policy was considered key if the economy were to navigate its way through the sea of international 'jealousy of trade'.[10] Thus, at the end of the seventeenth century, the first civil welfare experiments were added to the activities of traditional guild brotherhoods, poor relief brotherhoods and, above all, ecclesiastical charity.[11]

The growing interest in political economy among eighteenth-century treatise writers provided them with a tool with which to oppose the exclusive charity of the Church and the wealthy, with a view to bringing Christian piety's resources under the control of civil power. This chapter takes the socio-economic treatises on poverty written during the Spanish Enlightenment as a basis for addressing three consecutive bodies of work: the writings that underpinned the regalist option; the emergence in the 1770s of the official poor relief scheme led by Campomanes and, finally, the late Enlightenment vision in the closing years of the eighteenth century.

The foundations of Enlightened regalism

This section aims to give an account of the three main contributions that underpinned the regalist and economistic perspective on the treatment of poverty during the Spanish Enlightenment. These are the works by José del Campillo, Bernardo Ward and Tomás Anzano, which appeared in that order and shared a good part of their arguments, structured around two novel approaches: incorporating an economic criterion into the struggle against idleness and critically questioning the Church's role in this sphere, in support of the regalist theory, which entailed giving power to the government bodies under the monarch's authority. This position was in line with the Bourbon reform of the state initiated after the War of Succession (1701–1715) and Philip V's implementing of the Nueva Planta Decrees (1707–1716) following his victory over the supporters of the ruling House of Austria.

The 1740s were a turning point in the political-economic culture of the Spanish Enlightenment. Several works by authors from the first half of the century (Uztáriz, Ulloa and Zavala) were reprinted during these years, and the problem of poverty began to be closely linked to the 'lack of trade'. The pioneer in this area was José del Campillo (1693–1743), a politician, economist and all-powerful minister under Philip V, in the work *Lo que hay de más y de menos en España*, which followed the line taken by two other leading politicians in the last part of Philip V's reign (1700–1746), José Carvajal and Zenón de Somodevilla, Marquis of Ensenada.[12] All advocated harsh policies to deal with vagrants and other marginal groups, which Secretary of state Floridablanca would refer to decades later as the need to keep 'the rope taut', an allusion to the gallows.[13]

'Idleness' featured as the cause of Spain's decline in Campillo's introductory 'Exordium'. Idleness was an evil that included the 'inaction' of the ruling classes and the 'great multitude of starving nobles', who, far from conforming to the stereotype of the *noblesse commerçant*, preferred to remain in a state of need rather than accepting 'jobs' that they deemed low status. In any event, the main problem was the 'abandoned or vagrants', against whom Campillo suggested using the militia, the galleys and yet to be enacted legislation – in fact, two *Pragmáticas* in 1751 and 1775 – which would entail imposing punishments, 'registration' and 'passports' to certify that individuals were not 'abandoned or vagrant', and which were required for residence purposes.

The author deals with poverty more specifically in the section on the *Casas Reales de Hospicio* – royal poorhouses, to use the regalist term – in a manner consistent with his views on the high number of unproductive 'friars' who made no contribution to the 'public purse'. The *hospicios* would look after three classes of poor: 'real', 'for their own convenience' and 'ostensible'.[14] The first group comprised individuals that were incapacitated by illness or old age, while the second and third were destined to fill prisons and galleys, unless they could prove that finding work was impossible.[15] The author proposed founding *hospicios* in the provincial capitals, starting with Madrid. They would all have 'factories' to produce goods that were protected against competition from imports, simple to produce, used local raw materials and were easy to sell. The *hospicios* would be run by a 'manager' and several expert 'officials' who would teach the inmates how to work.

Campillo shares common ground with Carvajal on all these issues, anticipating the ambitious programme of royal manufacturing companies that Carvajal would initiate from 1746 onwards as president of the Board of Trade, establishing the *hospicio*-factories as symbols of official reform during those years.[16] While Uztáriz had supported this option, Amor de Soria and Argumosa did not.[17] From exile in Vienna, Amor de Soria, an *austracista* politician, thought state manufacturing unlikely to prosper in Spain, due to the 'lack of industry', and proposed embedding the poor into the guild structure.[18] For his part, Argumosa argued that *hospicios* were 'very costly and of little value', opting to leave the fate of work for the poor in the hands of the justice system.[19]

Campillo's secularising spirit was also evident in fact that the *hospicios* were to be funded 'at the Royal Purse's expense'. Once well-established, these institutions would gradually repay the initial outlay to the state through selling their products and with contributions from the 'residents in each town'.[20] Campillo designed a self-financing national network of institutions without increasing the tax burden.

The 1740s closed with the publication of eighteenth-century Spain's most influential text on poverty, the *Obra Pía y eficaz método para remediar la miseria de la gente pobre en España* (1750), written by Bernardo Ward (?–1776), an Irishman in Ferdinand VI's service, after his arrival in Spain in the mid-1740s. Ward is believed to have been one of the Irish Jacobites who went into exile in Spain, as was Ferdinand VI's minister Ricardo Wall, who had taken Ward under his wing after they met in London.[21] The work in question was reissued in 1767, 1779 and 1787, always certainly with political aims. Ward proposed creating an institution, an '*Obra Pía*' – religious work, '*Hermandad*' – Brotherhood, or '*Cuerpo Nacional*' – National Corps made up of people of 'all estates' and supported 'without taxation' under 'Royal patronage'. Regional authorities would be involved, as well as 'bishops, town councils, cities', 'most of the nobility', 'rich merchants' and lower-status workers. Its organisation would entail setting up boards 'in all major cities', to which the 'subordinate boards' in 'large towns' would report, all accountable to the 'main board' at Court, which would direct operations and publish an annual report.[22]

This scheme would tackle 'supporting the disabled poor', 'rounding up the kingdom's vagrants' and the 'planning of industry in Spain', which would involve employing most of the two million poor that existed, in the author's estimation.[23] Ward was influenced by the example of monarchy-led policy in 'Europe's wisest nations', especially Holland and England, perceiving similarities between his *Hermandad* and the British Parliament. The English model also appears in Ward's recommendation for stable homes for beggars; however, 'we must also learn' from the French political system, because of its greater similarity to the Spanish system.[24]

The *Hermandad*'s first task would be to draw up a 'political map' of Spain, estimating the numbers of 'real poor' and *hermanos* – brothers – who could be relied on to set up and maintain fifty *hospicios* with factories.[25] Ward claimed that there were some 50,000 genuine poor people, who, once installed in the *hospicios*, would produce goods that were protected from external competition and for which there was a market of 7,500,000 inhabitants, the Spanish population.[26]

To finance his enterprise Ward devised a complex project in which both the Church and the government would participate. The sources of his funds were first, a 'voluntary annual contribution from the ecclesiastical community' to replace 'alms', estimated at 3 per cent of the Church's income, some '300,000 ducats a year'; second, contributions from the wealthy, from religious 'foundations' and towns and cities, and finally lotteries, following the example set by other countries.[27] In addition to these three sources, Ward aimed to place 'Church funds' at the service of this public cause; thus, the Church would become the guarantor of the *Obra Pía*'s investment loans, just as in England Parliament guarantees the public debt and the country's money.[28] The Church, 'in the name of Spain', would be the custodian and administrator of the funds invested by the public, who would have the added incentive of obtaining an 'annuity' in return. According to this model the Church would be answerable to private individuals and the 'cities' would in turn be answerable to the Church with 'their own and more liquid income' for the funds received on loan for the *Obra Pía*'s activities in their 'jurisdictions'. These would amount to 'five million pesos', to be repaid without interest during the first four years, after which they would yield 'five per cent of the capital, until the debt is discharged in twenty years', thanks to 'widespread movement and internal trade in all parts of the Kingdom'.[29]

Meanwhile, the *Hermandad* would have the following functions where production and trading were concerned: setting up factories in the places where 'the goods are consumed'; identifying suitable goods for inter-provincial trade and export; promoting 'means useful to the Kingdom' and 'representations' to the King on the basis of the information obtained, so that he 'facilitates the advancement of industry, trade and internal movement'; combatting idleness; creating 'awards for industry' like England, and applying 'useful inventions'.[30] In short, Ward anticipated in 1750 the functions of the future economic societies – *sociedades económicas de los amigos del país* – by proposing a *Cuerpo*, which, under the 'very orders' of the King, would harness the 'talents of all the Kingdom's men', which, in the absence of 'bodies to work in public affairs', were no use to the 'public good'.[31]

This ambitious project was put together throughout the eighteenth century and formed part of the publishing campaign in the aftermath of the Esquilache's riot and other deep social revolts in the spring of 1766; they represented a turning point in the fight against idleness and included a new house of correction in Madrid, which became the *Hospicio* of San Fernando. A translation of Medina's text emphasising the real legitimacy of isolation was published in 1766 on the initiative of the Council of Castile.[32] The following year saw the publication of a treatise by Cortines (1767); backed by Medina's authority, it was a routine proposal for the creation of royal *hospicios* in all Spain's provincial capitals. In the same year the first reprint of War's *Obra Pía* finally appeared, undertaken anonymously and with the clear aim of influencing 'public opinion'.[33] There was no more effective way to show, as the opening 'Note' did, that a French work by Nicolas Baudeau, the great populariser of Physiocracy in Europe, entitled *Idées d'un citoyen* (1765), was a 'copy' of the *Obra Pía*, although this was not in fact the truth.[34]

In 1788, Tomás Anzano, a jurist, economist and high-ranking government official (?–1795), who held senior positions in the military quartermaster's office in several Spanish territories during the second half of the eighteenth century, published *Elementos preliminares para poder formar un sistema de gobierno de hospicio general*, which followed the line taken by Campillo and Ward but contained differences that reflected the author's adherence to the welfare policy pursued by Public Prosecutor – *Fiscal* – Campomanes and the Council of Castile (see *infra*), his reputation as an author of economic texts and, finally, his first-hand knowledge of the subject, acquired while he was Director of the *Hospicio* of San Fernando in Madrid from 1771 to 1777.[35] Anzano spoke with an official voice; the work was dedicated to the Secretary of State, the Count of Floridablanca, and linked to an August 1768 *Decision* regarding the creation of the *Real Junta de Hospicios* [Royal Board of Hospices] of Madrid and San Fernando.[36] It was also the basis for reports sent by the Council of Castile to the Madrid and Murcia economic societies in 1781 to serve as a standard for the kingdom's *hospicios* and *casas de misericordia* [houses of mercy].

Following Bielfeld, Anzano linked 'public happiness' to government legislation, maintaining that anti-poverty policy was a government matter, for which reason the Church must be at the service of the public cause.[37] This entailed unifying charitable 'foundations' and making them accountable to the government; this was the only way for authority to act effectively, as 'the government has been deranged by the excessive variety of measures'.[38] 'Court leadership' must be imposed on the 'provinces' and municipalities.[39]

Anzano's plan for financing the *hospicios* diverged from the prevailing vision of Enlightened reform in Spain, adopted by Campillo and Ward and based on financial self-sufficiency. Convinced that the *hospicios* must above all fulfil a welfare and educational function, Anzano used data to show that such self-sufficiency was not possible, and believed that simply aiming to achieve this was a hindrance to obtaining resources.[40] To the lack of 'incentives' for 'workshop instructors' and 'workers' to act as they would in 'their own businesses' was added Anzano's mistrust 'of profligate, unruly people', while the 'inexperienced visitors' who inspected the factories proved ineffective.[41]

In addition to these factors, Anzano understood that subsidising the products made in the *hospicios* harmed other manufacturers, and also that a large number of 'good family fathers' would be more productive in jobs outside the *hospicios*. He therefore proposed that the *hospicios* factories should constitute a 'state education' that would train good workers, including women and girls, who essentially did spinning work.[42] The operations had to be 'simple, learned quickly and useful in a broad sense', dedicated to producing goods 'that foreigners supply us with' and at the service of local manufacturers.[43]

None of this would be feasible without sufficient and stable funding, based on reliable data and from the whole 'nation', transcending 'almsgiving'.

'All the kingdom's individuals' needed to contribute to a 'single fund', supervised by the government.[44] This is an argument of Bielfeld – his *Institutions politiques* had been translated almost entirely in 1768–1778 – but it was also put forward by Thomas Aquinas when he stated that 'part of good government is providing for the needs of the poor and widows from the common purse'.[45] The options were therefore either a general 'in proportion' contribution set by the government, or converting the alms in the Church's control into 'charity' of another kind. Anzano left the decision in the hands of the 'provinces', to their 'secular' and 'ecclesiastical' officials, but he unfailing supported the second option, which avoided increasing taxes. This meant involving the ecclesiastical sector under the King's control, and turning alms into a national fund, 'for all the provinces, in the charge of the Court'.[46]

Anzano suggested using the following means: suppressing 'canonries and dignities' and allocating their income to the fund; investing some 'local taxes' in the fund; obtaining funds from town 'assets'; creating a 'national lottery'; 'suppressing many memorial funds and pious foundations, whose legitimate legal owners have died and the objects of their foundation no longer exist, for the *hospicios*' benefit'; finding the 'most accessible, least harsh and costly means' in each region, such as the '*personados* of Cataluña' – income paid to some of the clergy in Catalonia – and the 'bull allowing meat to be eaten on Saturdays' in Aragon, Valencia, Catalonia and Majorca; using 'ten per cent of all expenditure on *cofradías*' [guilds] and applying it to 'everything that affects pious foundations of any kind or that is assigned to religions, chapters, brotherhoods in charge of suffrages, personal assistance or any other obligation'; finally, bishops, priests, confessors, preachers 'and other evangelical workers' should channel their 'last wills' towards charity.[47]

Campomanes

Anzano's book was far from immune to influence from the six volumes of *Discursos* published between 1774 and 1777 by the Count of Campomanes; a prolific jurist, economist and writer, Campomanes was a leading figure in eighteenth-century Spanish politics, especially in his role as Prosecutor of the Council of Castile. He became the main ideologist behind Carlos III's economic policy and was thus present in all its social, political and economic aspects.[48] The *Discursos* underpinned the framework for official reform on poverty,[49] a problem with which Campomanes was familiar, having been involved in the Council of Castile's legislation regarding the poor since 1762.[50] In fact, the first of the *Discursos* aimed to 'banish idleness', for which the 'universality of the people' must be employed, according to their capabilities.[51] The nation as a whole would benefit, as labour was the main source of its wealth.[52] Boosting employment meant increasing working hours and bringing women and children into the labour market, all bearing in mind agriculture's potential as a source of employment; this was understood as the first productive art and industrial activities had to be compatible with it. The widely consumed 'coarse' textiles, which could be produced with low capital endowment and by women and children, would be the 'cornerstone of Spanish industry'.[53]

Campomanes started from the government's 'indisputable right' to apply appropriate public policies using the justice system, the town councils and especially the economic societies.[54] Indeed, both the pioneering Bascongada Society (1765) and, especially, the Madrid Society (1775), set up by Campomanes as a model of how to create these societies all over Spain, took up the fight against poverty as just one more of their many tasks, which included economic promotion, advising the government and spreading useful knowledge.[55]

Campomanes proposed classifying the victims of poverty using 'clear and practicable rules', aiming to establish a network of houses of mercy that were suitable for each type, including the fact that the most troublesome individuals were destined for the militia and public works. The fundamental principle was isolation and work, by means of formulas that combined living in the *hospicios* and at home. The fact that Campomanes did not allude to Vives' strict isolation methods is highly significant; instead, he copied long fragments from the writings of Pérez de Herrera and, in particular, Medina, whose work appears many times in the notes to the *Discursos*, which included Campomanes' recommendation that it should be reissued in Spanish for the third time.

The registration, selection and final destination of the poor was in the hands of the 'poor deputations or boards', municipal bodies that revolved around quarter and neighbourhood mayors. Campomanes was well acquainted with the Madrid *hospicio* and the San Fernando correctional institution, which had years of experience in textile manufacturing, and laid down the path that Anzano would eventually follow, distancing himself from the *hospicio*-factory tradition and proposing the main aim of training men and women in crafts.[56] He also advocated founding *hospicios* in provincial capitals, if necessary combining existing institutions into one in order to reduce costs. To save money he also made no provision for salaries for their managers and proposed that management should be standardised throughout the kingdom; hence the importance of Anzano's work referred to above.

Campomanes' main innovation was the 'patriotic' or 'charity' schools, which were small textile school-workshops.[57] With this initiative, he underlined the virtuous circle between charity, labour and education. In an urban context, beyond guild control and focusing on home-based production, these 'patriotic schools' were aimed at instructing in the crafts and promoting cottage industries using linen, hemp, wool, etc. and employing beggars, women and children, whose modest wages would supplement the family budget. The underlying goal was to liberalise the labour market to integrate migrants from rural areas into the cities. These immigrants were untrained and, therefore, could not be fully absorbed by the guilds and, consequently, they became unemployed

These 'schools' would also be part of the fight against almsgiving, considered an incentive to idleness to such an extent that Gándara went so far as to state that the bishops, the 'best almsgivers in the world', bore the prime responsibility for creating the 'taste for vagrancy'.[58] Campomanes argued that alms, as they were managed at the time, were the great enemy of occupation and should be banned wherever there were *hospicios* and 'patriotic schools'. However, beyond that, their abolition was not advisable as they constituted 'the backbone of pious funds, capable of stimulating industry'.[59] Campomanes opposed the parish tax in England because of the possibilities offered by 'standardised' and 'well-managed' alms. However, the bulk should come not from voluntary but from 'necessary' alms obtained from ecclesiastical incomes and 'compulsory' alms from foundations and pious works. Campomanes waged a fierce regalist battle against alms from the Council of Castile, aiming to unify them so that they would not proliferate and would eventually die out. They should be overseen by the civil authorities and economic societies and be earmarked for *hospicios* and 'patriotic schools'. For their part, the economic societies also became the repositories of two Enlightened ideas regarding the nobility: the first was that the nobility should restore its social status by participating in charitable activities, while the second entailed dispelling contempt for manual occupations, which particularly affected the impoverished lower nobility.

Campomanes' *Discursos* were a trigger for reform activity, which was also greatly influenced by improvements at the *hospicio* of Vitoria in 1777. Its statutes were exemplary in Enlightened Spain. Foronda went so far as to write that the experiment improved on that of Saint-Sulpice in Paris.[60] With the help of the Bascongada Society, a network of cottage industries developed around the Vitoria *hospicio*, in both the city and the countryside.[61]

However, the driving force behind the reform machinery was the *Sociedad Matritense* – Madrid Society – backed by new regulations issued by the Council of Castile. In 1775, it approved a decree devised by Campomanes on the rounding up of vagrants for the militia and public works, which was followed in 1778 by a further measure setting up 'charity or neighbourhood councils' in Madrid's sixty-four neighbourhoods. The *Matritense* founded 'patriotic schools' for embroidery, spinning and linen, an example for other economic societies. These schools offered education mainly to women and girls, and, in this way, managed to train a voluminous work force of a domestic nature and outside guilds' control: six years after its foundation in 1779, Madrid spinners *Montepío* supplied raw materials to more than seven hundred workers in the poorest neighbourhoods of the city. At the same time, the *Matritense* was attempting to influence economic societies to adopt the recommendations in Campomanes' *Discursos*. This seemed to be the main aim of the Council of Castile's November 1777 request to the societies to assess the applicability of Anzano's writings in the light of Ward's work. The responses spoke of alignment with the official proposal, which was ratified in a report drafted by the prestigious Jovellanos in the name of the Society of Sevilla.[62] The *Matritense* used the Council's request to promote Campomanes' design, which eschewed the *hospicio*-factories model on the grounds that they meant dishonest competition for private producers and were in fact failed royal factories, opting instead for education as a route out of poverty.[63] Also aiming to position 'public opinion' on the side of reform, in 1781 the *Matritense* organised public prizes for charity, which met with great enthusiasm. Sempere's prize-winning memoir reiterated the harsh criticism of the practice of 'indiscreet almsgiving'.[64]

Outside the *Matritense*, this reforming activism led to the publication of texts calling for more welfare policy. In 1777, Campomanes began to draft a 'Plan to Banish Idleness' which included compiling a list of the most important European legislation on the subject. To this end he requested a translation of the chapter on Great Britain in Smith's *The Wealth of Nations* (1776), which convinced him that restrictions on the poor's geographical mobility were 'a clear violation of natural liberty and justice'.[65] Three years later, in collaboration with Campomanes, Floridablanca commissioned Sisternes' translation of a work by *Abbé* Malvaux, tailored to the official reforms.[66] However, all this foreign activity failed to overshadow the importance of Spanish treatises, especially Ward's, and Arriquíbar aligned himself with Ward's ideas in the *Recreación política*, although he did not agree that the provincial *hermandades* should culminate in a higher national version.[67]

The publication of Ward's *Proyecto económico* in the same year on Campomanes' initiative was far more important.[68] Written in 1762, the work retained the regalist line put forward by the author in the *Obra pía* (1750), which, not surprisingly, was reissued after the *Proyecto*. This line was clear from Ward's proposal that 'a quarter or a fifth' of all mortmain bequeathed 'should go to the poor', and also in the suggestion that 'every woman who pays a dowry to become a nun' should contribute 'a thousand *reales* to marry off a poor girl'.[69] However, this political line was manifested most clearly when Ward addressed the funding of his project and, more specifically, a *Junta de Mejoras* [Improvements Board], an institutional development of the proposal in the *Obra pía* and the forerunner of the emerging economic societies. The Board's functions would include experiments in agriculture and manufacturing, setting up a *Banco general* [General Bank] and American colonial policy. Ward proposed that all this activity should be covered by funds obtained from all the Spanish and American 'church livings' that became vacant, 'at no expense to the Royal Treasury', a condition that would be imposed for a year, during which their income, which he estimated at one million *pesos* a year, would go to the Board.[70]

Enlightenment reform policy followed the line of previous approaches, taking into account the examples provided by foreign regulatory and institutional experiences and promoting measures to encourage the poor and destitute to work, training in productive work and isolating the most serious and vulnerable cases. This was achieved not by setting up a major project or a national network with its epicentre at court, as Ward and Anzano had proposed, but rather through creating orphanages, hospitals and above all *hospicios*, some forty of which were established in mainland Spain by various local institutions, including economic societies. It was thus necessary to enter the terrain of the Church and its charity remit, this time in accordance with the plans of Enlightened rulers and economists.

These developments were accompanied by extensive and detailed legislation that specifically covered vagrancy and begging as well as the functioning of the *hospicios* and other institutions.[71] In the same way as Enlightened economists' writings, the range of decrees, ordinances and regulations making up the legislation distinguished between the real poor who could not work and beggars and vagrants who were able to work but unwilling to do so. The *hospicios* fulfilled different functions for the two groups, relating to charity, training, production and chastisement or punishment.

Beyond official reforms

The period between the American and French Revolutions saw the emergence of a *later* Enlightenment generation Spain that was more radical and critical of official reforms, as also occurred in other European countries. Aguirre, Cabarrús and Meléndez Valdés were among the later Enlightenment writers who addressed poverty, although their doctrinal bases differed. Aguirre's *Discurso sobre el oficio de la pobreza o mendiguez*

(1788) had Rousseau as its backdrop, while Cabarrús' *Cartas* (1795) – they were written in response to *The Agrarian Law Report* (1795) of his friend Jovellanos – referenced Physiocracy and, finally, Meléndez Valdés' *Fragmentos de un discurso sobre la mendiguez* (1802) was more in tune with an earlier legacy.[72]

Nevertheless, these three discourses were connected by several *filos rossos* [common threads]. Most importantly, they linked poverty with the social contract: if equality could be achieved in the state of nature, or in imaginary republics, as Meléndez commented, it was no more than a 'shining dream' in civil society because of its inherent wealth inequality, especially after the establishment of private property. According to Meléndez, this provided an 'inviolable order', which had to be guaranteed by the ruler.[73] Cabarrús evoked Physiocracy, arguing that rulers should confine themselves to ensuring 'personal safety, property ownership and freedom of speech', and take responsibility only for what was 'inaccessible to isolated efforts', as 'individual interest' would have to take care of the rest.[74] In a similar vein Meléndez argued that self-interest and greed were the main factors that motivated individuals to find work that matched their abilities. Legislation had to intertwine individual interests and the common good.[75]

However, the division between property owners and the landless carried within it the seeds of poverty and inequality, which were exacerbated by the 'barbarous' and 'feudal' times that had made inheritance, abuse of property and the privileges of the nobility and clergy possible. The 'rights of man' or 'humanity' to which Aguirre appealed included the poor's right to receive the means of subsistence from the state in exchange for moderate labour as part of the social contract. However, the emergence of what Aguirre calls the 'poor man's occupation', which had become 'a way of eating at others' expense', had transformed this right into an attack on the social contract and a source of poverty.[76] If the nobility, with its excessive luxury, monopoly over goods and concentration of property, was a source of inequality, the Church and its alms were even more so. On the basis of such ideas these emblematic late Spanish Enlightenment authors proposed an all-out battle against ecclesiastical power, starting from the defence of government sovereignty.[77]

The battle's main features surfaced in the managing and funding of charity. Meléndez merely reworked Ward's proposal for building a national *hermandad* based on those in the provincial, emphasising its civil, centralising and standardising sense, which would be guided by 'true economic principles'.[78] To Aguirre, the fight against poverty should fall to municipal charity boards and be funded from ecclesiastical wealth. In his proposal, the sovereign would manage the ordinary clergy's assets, and they would only receive payment to maintain 'the decency of their state' and to guarantee worship; the remainder must be given over to 'charitable funds', without affecting the contributions from *confradías* and *hermandades* as well as the nobility and 'other vassals'.

Cabarrús did not advocate levying new taxes to finance charity, instead proposing better management of existing resources at the expense of ecclesiastical privileges. He had already suggested removing the clergy's tax exemption in 1783 in one of eighteenth-century Spain's most radical works on taxation.[79] In 1795, he added the principle that 'whatever [income] is not necessary for worship and the subsistence of ministers should be allocated to the poor'.[80] Welfare policy consequently had to be financed from the sum total of three current ecclesiastical taxes, the *tercias reales*, the *excusado* and the *mitres*, to which other revenue from tithes and pious foundations was added, with a further quota from vacant posts in the diocese. The task of managing the poor and their occupation in industry and public works should fall to municipal boards made up of five local residents who were elected 'without class distinction'.[81] Cabarrús opposed alms houses, preferring cottage industries, for which the boards would act as merchants in the putting-out system.

Where the impact of these new views on poverty was concerned, the Enlightened intellectuals' slide towards radicalism during Carlos IV's reign (1788–1808) was probably more widespread than these examples show. This is borne out by the fact that in 1801, Sempere, a moderate, published an address drafted in 1788 which began with a – probably new – chapter devoted to explaining that poverty was an inevitable consequence of the division between property owners and the landless.[82] Although Sempere remained faithful to Campomanes, the years that elapsed between the paper's drafting and its actual publication may have been conducive to the new chapter's inclusion.

On the reformist side, however, there were no major signs of change, even though the existing welfare system became even more inadequate as the long growth curve that characterised the eighteenth century flattened alarmingly. The fact that in 1787 Alcalá-Galiano, an influential advisor to Minister of Finance Pedro de Lerena, circulated a translation of a text by the Physiocrat Dupont de Nemours in which he argued that hospitals should be replaced by care at home and a network of private hospitals should be set up by 'entrepreneurs' who were motivated by 'profit' need come as no surprise.[83]

In any event, the closing years of the eighteenth century heralded the end of an era. In the wake of the 1787–1789 subsistence crises, the combination of bread shortages, crop failures and inflation led to a sharp fall in real wages between 1798 and 1805 and an equally sharp increase in poverty and deprivation. By then the regalist battle had achieved a new state welfare network, which differed from the traditional religious system, but this did not prevent the collapse of the welfare system.[84] In Madrid, the arrival of a veritable 'army of misery' placed 40 per cent of the population on the edge of destitution.[85] Given this daunting context, it is not surprising that the ideas of Count Rumford, the last great foreign author to influence the welfare issue in Spain, were so well received.[86] Additional help came from the reception of Dusquenoy's compilation work (1798–1804), which was partially influenced by Rumford and aimed at reorganising the welfare system in post-Revolutionary France.[87] Rumford was particularly promoted by the Madrid Society, which published a partial translation of his writings in 1801, and by the *Semanario de Agricultura* (1797–1808), an official newspaper dedicated to disseminating useful knowledge.[88]

This all proved insufficient, however. Neither the propaganda in favour of creating new hospices in the century's last treatise on charity, for which Murcia was responsible, nor the 1803 law ordering the distribution of Rumford's *sopas económicas* [economy meals] throughout the kingdom, nor the extraordinary measures to accelerate the control of civil power over religious power, were enough to save the system from collapse; a collapse which, in the form of riots, relentless mortality and a new wave of repressive power, was simply a reflection of a much more far-reaching political crisis.[89]

Final remarks

This chapter opened with a question about the absence of the theme of poverty in Cadalso's *Cartas marruecas*. After reviewing the eighteenth century's essential contributions on this subject in Spain, two reasons emerge. The first is that the Enlightenment approach to poverty entailed harsh criticism of the Church's role, yet Cadalso avoided this, convinced that religion structured and calmed society.[90] The second reason is that, as Cadalso was not an economist, he did not appeal to the relationship between poverty, idleness, education and economic development that characterised the debate of the economic Enlightenment in Spain and Europe. He thus failed to join the avant-garde of his time, which spoke the language of political economy and in so doing questioned the ultimate legitimacy of *Ancien Régime* institutions, especially the Catholic Church.

This approach, which could be described as economic regalism in terms of its fundamental contributions, can be said to have emerged in Spain around 1740 with the economics writings of Philip V's minister José Cadalso. It was sustained, refined and finally defined in the following decade through the involvement of politician and government minister Bernardo Ward.

While still somewhat veiled, it became more radical towards the end of the 1760s thanks to the work by high-ranking official and quartermaster Tomás Anzano, which coincided with contributions from the Count of Campomanes, Prosecutor of the Council of Castile, both in terms of ideas and the implementing of specific policies on poverty during the following two decades. Nourished by the vision of political and economic liberalism, the Spanish Enlightenment was to undergo a still more advanced radicalisation through authors such as Aguirre, Cabarrús and Meléndez Valdés, which provided the impetus that would eventually crystallise in the Spain of the 1812 Liberal Constitution.

Notes

1 José Cadalso, *Cartas marruecas* (Barcelona: Edicomunicación, 1992). Deemed a 'Spanishisation' of Montesquieu's *Lettres persanes* (1721), the work was written around 1768 and published posthumously in 1789.
2 See, respectively, Pedro Rodríguez, Count of Campomanes, *Discurso sobre el fomento de la industria popular* (Madrid, 1774); ibid., *Discurso sobre la educación popular de los artesanos y su fomento* (Madrid, 1775); and ibid., *Apéndice a la educación popular*, 4 vols (Madrid, 1775–1777). Gaspar Melchor de Jovellanos, 'Copia del Informe sobre hospicios que hizo al Consejo la Real Sociedad Patriótica en la ciudad y reino de Sevilla' (1778), in ibid., *Obras completas. Vol. x. Escritos económicos*, eds Vicent Llombart and Joaquín Ocampo (Gijón: KRK ediciones, 2008) pp. 436–465; ibid., 'Discurso acerca de la situación y división interior de los hospicios con respecto a su salubridad' (1778), in ibid., *Obras publicadas e inéditas de D. Gaspar Melchor de Jovellanos*, ed. Cándido Nocedal (Madrid: M. Rivadeneyra Impresor, 1859), pp. 431–435. Valentín de Foronda, *Cartas sobre la policía* (Madrid: Imprenta de Cano, 1801).
3 Valentín de Foronda, *Cartas sobre los asuntos más exquisitos de la economía política, y sobre las leyes criminales* (1789–1794), ed. José Manuel Barrenechea (Vitoria: Gobierno Vasco, 1994), vol. ii, pp. 154–155.
4 Among the rich scholarship on pauperism in eighteenth-century Spain, see especially the works by María Rosa Pérez, *El problema de los vagos en la España del siglo XVIII* (Madrid: Confederación Española de Cajas de Ahorros, 1976); and Jacques Soubeyroux, 'Pauperismo y relaciones sociales en el Madrid del siglo XVIII', *Estudios de Historia social*, 12–13 (1980), 2–227.
5 The details can be found in Marjorie Grice-Hutchinson, *El pensamiento económico en España (1177–1740)* (Barcelona: Crítica, 1982), pp. 176–179 and pp. 184–186, who, like Joseph A. Schumpeter, *Historia del análisis económico* (Barcelona–Caracas–Méjico: Ariel, 1971), pp. 316–322, stresses the factual and sociological value of these authors' works, rather than their theoretical worth. See also José Antonio Maravall, *Estado moderno y mentalidad social. Siglos XV a XVII* 2 vols (Madrid: Revista de Occidente, 1972), vol. ii, pp. 245–249.

Poverty and charity in eighteenth-century Spain 101

Victoriano Martín, 'La controversia sobre los pobres en el siglo XVI y la doctrina sobre la propiedad', in E. Fuentes (ed.), *Economía y economistas españoles. Vol. ii. De los orígenes al mercantilismo* (Barcelona: Galaxia Gütenberg–Círculo de Lectores), pp. 295–338, at p. 298, p. 338, argues that, in contrast to Soto, Vives did not believe in the existence of a natural order and that his work was a forerunner of the 'omniscient paternalistic state'.

6 Juan Luis Vives, *Tratado del socorro de los pobres* (Valencia: Benito Monfort, [1520] 1781); ibid., *La caridad discreta practicada con los mendigos, y utilidades que logra la república en su recogimiento* (1545) (First edition: Valladolid, 1757) (Second edition: Madrid, 1766); Cristóbal Pérez Herrera, *Proverbios morales* (1595; 1617) (Madrid, 1733).

7 Domingo de Soto, *Deliberación de la causa de los pobres* (Salamanca, 1545).

8 Manuel Martín, 'Población y análisis económico en el mercantilismo español', in Fuentes, *De los orígenes al mercantilismo*, pp. 499–521; Eli Heckscher, *Mercantilism*, 2 vols (London: Allen and Unwin, 1935).

9 William Grampp, 'The Liberal Elements in English Mercantilism', *The Quarterly Journal of Economics*, 65:4 (1952), 465–501; Cosimo Perrota, 'Early Spanish Mercantilism: The First Analysis of Underdevelopment', in Lars Magnusson (ed.), *Mercantilist Economics* (London: Kluwer, 1993), pp. 17–58.

10 Istvan Hont, *The Jealousy of Trade* (Cambridge, MA: Harvard University Press, 2005).

11 José Agua and Victoria López, 'Pauperismo, protesta social y colapso del sistema asistencial en Madrid (1798–1805)', *Investigaciones históricas*, 39 (2019), 119–136.

12 José del Campillo *Lo que hay de más y de menos en España para que sea lo que debe ser y no lo que es*, ed. Antonio Elorza (Madrid: Facultad de Filosofía y Letras, [c. 1741] 1969). The poverty issue was less central to Campillo's second work, *España despierta*, ed. Antonio Elorza (Madrid: Facultad de Filosofía y Letras, [c. 1742] 1969). Neither was published during Campillo's lifetime.

13 José Miguel Delgado, *El proyecto político de Carvajal* (Madrid: CSIC, 2001), pp. 129–135; José Luis Gómez, *Víctimas del absolutismo. Paradojas del poder en la España del siglo XVIII* (Madrid: Punto de vista editores, 2020).

14 Campillo, *Lo que hay de más y de menos en España*, p. 79.

15 Ibid., p. 81.

16 Delgado, *El proyecto político de Carvajal*, p. 200.

17 Jerónimo de Uztáriz, *Teórica y práctica de comercio y de marina* (1724), pp. 188–189, pp. 472–474.

18 Juan Amor de Soria, *Enfermedad crónica y peligrosa de los reinos de España y de Indias. Aragonesismo austracista (1734–1742)*, ed. Ernest Lluch (Zaragoza: Institución Fernando el Católico, [1741] 2010, pp. 181–372.

19 Teodoro V. de Argumosa, *Erudición política* (Madrid, 1743), pp. 238–245.

20 Campillo, *Lo que hay de más y de menos en España*, p. 83.

21 Bernardo Ward, *Obra pía. Medios de remediar la miseria de la gente pobre de España* (Valencia, 1750; Second edition, Madrid, 1767; Third edition, Madrid, 1779; Fourth edition, Madrid, 1787). References to this work use the

1767 edition. Ward could have found a source of inspiration in the project to organise an *Obra pía* on a national scale in Alvaro Navia, Marquis of Santa Cruz de Marcenado, *Rapsodia económico–política monárquica* (Madrid, 1732), pp. 237–256.

22 Ibid., pp. 25, 27–28.
23 Ibid., pp. 31, 59, 90.
24 Ibid., pp. 16, 18, 19, 17.
25 Ibid., pp. 32–42. As was usual in the Spanish Enlightenment, the gypsy population was not included among the poor; they should be taken to America to 'form a colony, well away from other Spanish vassals'.
26 Ibid., pp. 62–69.
27 Ibid., pp. 76–90.
28 Ibid., pp. 109–111.
29 Ibid., pp. 121–123.
30 Ibid., pp. 130–146.
31 Ibid., pp. 158–159.
32 The author was Luis de la Valle, a member of the Council of Castile, but the scheme could have been masterminded by Campomanes.
33 On the role of political economy treatises in the creation of the public sphere and a new Enlightened politics in the eighteenth-century Spain, see Javier Usoz, 'La 'nueva política' ilustrada y la esfera pública: las introducciones a la Economía en el siglo XVIII español', *Revista de estudios políticos*, 153 (2011), 11–46; and ibid., 'Political Economy and the Creation of the Public Sphere during the Spanish Enlightenment', in Jesús Astigarraga (ed.), *The Spanish Enlightenment Revisited* (Oxford: Voltaire Foundation, 2015), pp. 105–127.
34 Nicolas Baudeau's *Idées d'un citoyen sur les besoins, les droits et les devoirs des vrais pauvres* (Amsterdam [Paris], 1766) is by no means a translation of Ward's but takes an original approach to the question of poverty, suggesting a similar institutional solution, albeit one that is tailored to circumstances in France. Moreover, as the 'printer' himself points out, the ideological starting point is different. Although the texts share a regalist position, Baudeau's is more radical with regard to the rights of the poor, which he deems to have been usurped by centuries of abuse of ecclesiastical power.
35 Tomás Anzano, *Elementos preliminares para poder formar un sistema de gobierno de hospicio general* (Madrid, 1778). On Anzano the economist, see Javier Usoz, 'La política ilustrada y el libre comercio de granos: las *Reflexiones económico–políticas* (1768) de Tomás Anzano', *Historia Agraria*, 44 (2008), 21–51, and Jesús Astigarraga and Javier Usoz, 'Política y economía en el *Análisis del comercio del trigo* (1795) de Tomás Anzano', *Hispania*, 69 (2009), 395–422.
36 Anzano, *Elementos preliminares*, p. 6.
37 Ibid., p. 27, pp. 2–7. The book cited is Jakob F. von Bielfeld's *Institutions politiques*, 2 vols (The Hague: Pierre Gosse, 1760).
38 Anzano, *Elementos preliminares*, pp. 47–48.
39 Ibid., p. 51–52.

40 He drew on the recent accounts from the Madrid and San Fernando *hospicios*, which were managed by the same 'Royal Board'. They recorded losses every year. See ibid., pp. 80–81.
41 Ibid., pp. 74–75.
42 Ibid., p. 103.
43 Ibid., pp. 93–97.
44 Ibid., pp. 138–140.
45 Ibid., p. 142.
46 Ibid., p. 149.
47 Ibid., pp. 151–156.
48 Campomanes, *Discurso sobre el fomento de la industria popular*; *Discurso sobre la educación popular de los artesanos y su fomento*; *Apéndice a la educación popular*.
49 Vicent Llombart, *Campomanes, economista y político de Carlos III* (Madrid: Alianza, 1992), pp. 261.
50 Pérez, *El problema de los vagos en la España del siglo XVIII*, pp. 323ff.
51 Campomanes, *Discurso sobre el fomento de la industria popular*, p. 2.
52 See Carmen Sarasúa, 'Una política de empleo antes de la industrialización: paro, estructura de la ocupación y salarios en la obra de Campomanes', in Francisco Comín and Pablo Martín (eds), *Campomanes y su obra económica* (Madrid: Instituto de Estudios Fiscales, 2004), pp. 171–191.
53 Campomanes, *Discurso sobre el fomento de la industria popular*, pp. 29–31, p. 107.
54 Campomanes, *Apéndice a la educación popular*, vol. ii, p. 139.
55 On these institutions, see Jesús Astigarraga, 'Economic Societies and the Politicisation of the Spanish Enlightenment', in Astigarraga, *Spanish Enlightenment Revisited*, pp. 63–81; and about the important role of all economic institutions in the development of the Enlightenment in Spain, see Jesús Astigarraga, *A Unifying Enlightenment* (Leiden: Brill, 2021).
56 José Agua, 'Manufacturas, caridad y salario en la red asistencial madrileña del Setecientos', *Mediterránea. Ricerche storiche*, 17 (2020), pp. 143–167 at pp. 153–163.
57 Campomanes, *Apéndice a la educación popular*, vol. ii, pp. 85–256.
58 Miguel A. de la Gándara, *Apuntes sobre el bien y el mal de España*, ed. J. Macías (Madrid: IEF, [c. 1762] 1988), pp. 300–301.
59 Campomanes, *Apéndice a la educación popular*, vol. ii, p. 166.
60 Valentín de Foronda, 'Paralelo de la Casa de Misericordia de Vitoria, con la Sociedad Caritativa de San Sulpicio de París', in *Miscelánea o colección de varios discursos* (Madrid, 1787).
61 Jesús Astigarraga, *Los ilustrados vascos* (Barcelona: Crítica, 2003), pp. 168–172.
62 Jovellanos, 'Copia del Informe'.
63 Anonymous, 'Memoria presentada a la Junta Particular de 12 de febrero de 1778. Por varios individuos de la Clase de Industria, para informar al Consejo sobre el recogimiento de pobres, y medios de evitar la mendicidad con el fomento de fábricas gobernadas por factorías' (1778), in *Memoria de*

la Sociedad Económica (Madrid, 1787), vol. iii, pp. 184–203; José Guevara, 'Memoria sobre el recogimiento y ocupación de los pobres' (1778), in *Memorias de la Sociedad Económica* (Madrid, 1787), pp. 1–99.

64 Juan Sempere, 'Memoria sobre el ejercicio de la caridad en el reparto de la limosna' (1784), in *Colección de las memorias premiadas [...] por [...] la Real Sociedad Económica de Amigos del País* (Madrid, 1786), pp. 1–36.

65 Vicent Llombart, *Campomanes, economista y político de Carlos III*, pp. 297–299.

66 Pierre-Claude Malvaux, *Les moyens de détruire la mendicité en France* (Chalons-sur-Marne: 1780). In 1777, this work won an award from the Academia de Chalons-sur-Marne, and a *Resumé* appeared in 1779. See Pablo Cervera, *El pensamiento económico de la Ilustración valenciana* (Valencia: Generalitat Valenciana, 2003), pp. 198–204.

67 Nicolás de Arriquíbar, *Recreación política* (1779), eds Jesús Astigarraga and José M. Barrenechea (Vitoria: Instituto Vasco de Estadística, 1987), pp. 100–102, pp. 250–252.

68 Bernardo Ward, *Proyecto económico* (Madrid: Joaquín Ibarra, 1779).

69 Ibid., p. 205.

70 Ibid., pp. 207–209.

71 See Soubeyroux, 'Pauperismo y relaciones sociale', pp. 212–227.

72 Manuel de Aguirre, 'Discurso sobre el oficio de la pobreza o mendiguez', in Antonio Elorza (ed.), *Cartas y Discursos del Militar Ingenuo al Correo de los Ciegos de Madrid* (San Sebastián: Gráficas Izarra, [1788] 1974), pp. 207–226; Francisco de Cabarrús, *Cartas sobre los obstáculos que la naturaleza, la opinión y las leyes oponen a la felicidad pública* (Vitoria, [1795] 1808); Juan Meléndez, 'Fragmentos de un discurso sobre la mendiguez', in *Discursos forenses* (Madrid, [1802] 1821), pp. 273–310.

73 Meléndez, 'Fragmentos de un discurso sobre la mendiguez', pp. 307–308.

74 Cabarrús, *Cartas sobre los obstáculos*, p. 71.

75 Meléndez, 'Fragmentos de un discurso sobre la mendiguez', pp. 290–292.

76 Aguirre, 'Discurso sobre el oficio de la pobreza', p. 212.

77 To quote Aguirre: it was 'licit to impose rules on the administration and use of the goods belonging to a body or community that lives under the protection of its power and laws, if they divert its people's good or happiness'. See Aguirre, 'Discurso sobre el oficio de la pobreza', p. 220. Cabarrus wrote: 'the state should never abandon the right and obligation to resolve all these points sovereignly'. See Cabarrús, *Cartas sobre los obstáculos*, p. 89.

78 Meléndez, 'Fragmentos de un discurso sobre la mendiguez', p. 303.

79 Francisco de Cabarrús, *Memoria al Rey Nuestro Señor Carlos III, para la extinción de la deuda nacional y arreglo de contribuciones en 1783*, in *Cartas sobre los obstáculos que la naturaleza, la opinión y las leyes oponen a la felicidad pública* (Vitoria, 1808), pp. 27, 33.

80 Cabarrús, *Cartas sobre los obstáculos*, pp. 35–36.

81 Cabarrús, *Cartas sobre los obstáculos*, pp. 40–41.

82 Juan Sempere, 'Policía de España acercas de los pobres, vagos y malentretenidos', *Biblioteca española económico–política* (Madrid, 1801), vol. i, pp. 1–150.

83 Pierre S. Dupont, *Ideas sobre la naturaleza, forma y extensión de los socorros que conviene dar a los enfermos pobres en una ciudad populosa* (Segovia, 1787), p. 45.
84 William. J. Callahan, 'Caridad, sociedad y economía en el siglo XVIII', *Moneda y Crédito*, 146 (1978), 67–79 at 73.
85 See Agua and López, 'Pauperismo, protesta social y colapso del sistema asistencial'.
86 Benjamin Thompson, Count of Rumford, *Ensayos políticos, económicos y filosóficos*, 2 vols (Madrid, 1800–1801).
87 Adrien Dusquenoy (ed.), *Recueil de mémoires sur l'établissemens d'humanité, traduits de l'allemand et de l'anglais*, 18 vols (Paris, 1798–1804).
88 Rumford, *Ensayos políticos, económicos y filosóficos*.
89 Pedro J. de Murcia, *Discurso político sobre la importancia, y necesidad de los hospicios, casas de expósitos y hospitales, que tienen todos los estados, y particularmente España* (Madrid, 1798).
90 Cadalso, *Cartas marruecas*, pp. 204–205.

5

The embarrassment of poverty: Dutch decline, liberalism, patriotism and the duties of the state around 1800

Koen Stapelbroek

Introduction: poverty and Dutch historiography

The problem of poverty in the Dutch Republic of the eighteenth century has been studied predominantly by social and economic historians, who have focused on specific cities, regions, institutions, organisations or the market for particular products in relation to poverty.[1] This literature was often influenced by theoretical questions on wider issues central to these sub-disciplines, such as modernisation, labour conflicts and social relations, mechanisation and the advent of the industrial revolution, poor relief and the institutions of charity and the activities and composition of local associations.

Poverty in the Dutch Republic was also commented on in books, pamphlets, manuscripts and magazine articles during the eighteenth century in a more general sense – often in relation to the political and economic decline of the Dutch Republic, and notably in prize essay questions that were issued in the 1770s and 1780s.[2] The writers who wrote these commentaries devised rival political and economic reform projects and held different views on how poverty could be alleviated. Moreover, these projects were developed from general perspectives on the history of trade, civilisation and the nature of the Dutch state. Ultimately, those wider perspectives had an impact on these writers' conceptions of what poverty itself *was*, what ought to be done about poverty and by whom, how to address poverty and what social, economic and political conditions characterised the end result once poverty had been successfully addressed. However, these different logics of thinking about poverty have been hard to recognise due to disciplinary impositions that have recounted history in terms of its own preoccupations and pre-determined analytical schemes of historical development. Notably, social and economic historians, influenced by Joh. de Vries's well-known study on the relative decline of Dutch trade, have replaced a more historically adequate political understanding of the role of the Dutch state in the international system with a straightforward distinction between an 'absolute' and 'relative' decline of trade volumes.[3]

While the structure of the general Dutch political and economic reform debate before 1800 has often been reduced, to some degree at least, to a dichotomous rivalry between factions – Orangists versus Patriotst – these reductionist framings have had the effect of obscuring the more fundamental and more relevant intellectual and international dimensions of a range of debates, including discussions about poverty. In particular, they have reinforced the historical disjunction between later eighteenth- and early nineteenth-century approaches to political and economic reform and collapsed intellectual continuities between the time of the end of the Republic and the emergence of the Dutch United Kingdom.

By consequence, the topic of poverty was not properly integrated into more refined narratives about national historiography and instead was assimilated into retrospective schematics that garbled any understandings of poverty previous to the later nineteenth century. Thus, it could be argued, for instance, 'that it was not until the socially-oriented liberals came to power in the late nineteenth century that the system began to significantly change for the better. Until then free-market liberals had joined their voices to confessional parties in proclaiming poor relief to be an encouragement to laziness.'[4]

This chapter loosely maps the structure of the Dutch political and economic reform debate of the later eighteenth century onto the issue of poverty to help explain how different conceptions of poverty were constituted and continued into the nineteenth century. The larger task for historians of the Dutch state is to disentangle the complex of liberalism, economic science and partisan political conceptions without reverting to entrenched national political narratives or ideological caricatures. This chapter aims to provide some starting points for this process by looking at the issue of poverty in relation to decline, the idea of the state and political ideologies around 1800.

The argument below starts with the notion that poverty did not exist in the Dutch Republic until the eighteenth century and was a phenomenon that appeared later as a political challenge than in other European states. It traces comments by Bernard de Mandeville on William Temple, the Dutch Republic after the War of the Spanish Succession and on charity, before moving on to how so-called Economic and Political Patriots in the 1770s and 1780s conceptualised poverty. Confronting their policy proposals and initiatives with the outlook on wealth, luxury and poverty that can be traced back to Isaac de Pinto and that may be recognised in the writings of Hogendorp and other self-declared liberals in the early nineteenth century, it leads to the figure of Hendrik Willem Tydeman, who by 1850 was the standard-bearer of the Dutch liberal conception of poverty and the duties of the state before it was attacked as socialist by a new generation of writers.[5]

Before poverty: the Dutch Republic's Golden Age and the institution of charity

A specific and apparently peculiar starting point is the idea that there was no poverty in the Dutch Golden Age, the heyday of Dutch global proto-colonialism, urban culture and luxury trade. This is what Simon Schama argued in his well-known character sketch of the Dutch Republic, *The Embarrassment of Riches: An Interpretation of Dutch Culture in the Golden Age*, first published in 1987.[6] Schama's conceptual rhetorical scheme had rich Calvinist merchants engaged in a moral exchange relationship with society's less fortunate members, whose acceptance of charity provided the rich with 'the quiet of their souls'.[7] Any need that arose was relatively easily dealt with by the institutions of charity that were an integral part of Dutch culture and an element that was deemed over time to be a differentiating characteristic not only of the fiscal, but also of the moral make-up of the Republic compared with its monarchical neighbouring states.

The material backbone to Schama's essayistic thesis on the moral balance between Dutch wealth and poverty was a selection of studies by Jan de Vries of the 1970s and early 1980s.[8] De Vries, in these works so eagerly cited by Schama, provides an explanation for why 'Holland was indeed a striking exception in a Europe plagued by constant shortages, the pronounced loss of purchasing power among wage earners, and endemic violence in both town and country'.[9] Compared with other European societies, in the Republic 'unskilled labor was always in as good or better a position than its counterpart throughout the century extending from 1580 to 1680' because of Dutch control over and direct access to the Baltic and international grain trade, which mitigated the risks of bad harvests and famine, protected the real wages of labourers and offset the high taxation levels and rents in the cities of Holland.[10]

Long into the eighteenth century, the absence of poverty in the Dutch Republic remained something of a European myth or commonplace and observers would comment on the consumption patterns of ordinary labourers.[11] An intriguing example is Joshua Gee, who in his *The Trade and Navigation of Great Britain Considered* (1729) included a chapter called 'Propositions for better Regulating and Employing the Poor' in which he put forward Dutch fiscal policies as an incentive model for Britain to avoid poverty and stimulate industry:

and doubtless a good Example and Perseverance in the Rules of Industry will change the very Inclinations of those idle vagrant Persons, who now run about the Kingdom, and spend their Time and what Money they can any Way come at upon their Debauches. We see all wise Governments have and do follow this Practice: The Dutch have brought their Poor under such Regulations, that there is scarcely a Beggar to be seen in the whole United Provinces; for that no other Nation may under-work them, they take all imaginable Care to keep all Materials for Manufactures as low as possible, and lay their Taxes upon such Things as the People cannot subsist without, as Eatables, Firing, &c. very well knowing that Hunger and Cold will make People work to supply their Necessities.[12]

Gee's analysis of Dutch fiscal policies and their impact on human behaviour chimed with de Vries's explanation of how high wages, high taxes and high rents could stably co-exist in an urban society with primary access to the flow of goods and capital in a seventeenth-century global economy. While other countries in Europe were perennially exposed to need, uncertainty and risk, the social fallout of inequality and misfortune in the Republic was relatively limited, and could be dealt with by charity institutions that regulated social order.[13] More recently, it has been argued, in contrast with de Vries's explanation, that the exceptional economic trajectory of Dutch development lay in anterior institutional causes dating back to urbanisation and economic integration in Burgundian and Habsburg times.[14]

Whatever principles might underpin the Dutch economic historical *Sonderweg* thesis, the balance between wages and prices of living costs held out until the aftermath of the invasion of Louis XIV and outbreak of the Third Anglo-Dutch War in the so-called Disaster Year of 1672. In the absence of exposure to poverty, the institutions of charity had, so to speak, a relatively easy task to perform. This balance was still active when William Temple wrote his *Observations on the United Provinces*, published in 1672, in which he famously remarked with regard to charity that:

> Charity seems to be very National among them [the Dutch], though it be regulated by Orders of the Countrey, and not usually moved by the common Objects of Compassion. But it is seen in the admirable Provisions that are made out of it for all sorts of persons that can want, or ought to be kept in a Government. [...]. In general, All Appetites and Passions seem to run lower and cooler here, than in other Countreys where I have convesrt. Avarice may be excepted. And yet that should not be so violent, where it feeds only upon Industry and Parsimony.[15]

Yet, by then the Dutch fall from grace was about to take place and the problem of poverty – amid the decline of the staple market, accelerated urbanisation and inflexible wage and price levels – was about to kick in. If the Dutch Republic had not known need or a particular stress on charity institutions, the advent of the modern problem of poverty was going to hit as hard in the Dutch Republic as elsewhere. From the mid eighteenth century onwards, restoring the absence of need and 'solving' poverty would be seen as a political challenge.

Among the first to address the conceptual gap between charity and the full-blown appearance of poverty as a modern political challenge was the Dutch-born Bernard de Mandeville, the author of the famous *Fable of the Bees* of 1714. Mandeville's analysis of the development of the Dutch Republic between the 1670s and the end of the War of the Spanish Succession contrasted with Gee's (later) recommendation to his British audience that the Dutch fiscal policy approach to poverty provided a model to be adopted. According to Mandeville, the picture that would be sketched by Gee in the late 1720s had already become outdated by the early eighteenth century.[16]

Mandeville's target for making this argument was Temple's sketch of Dutch charity. While Temple depicted a Dutch seventeenth-century society in which wealth, poverty and charity were well-ordered and organically worked towards the same end, Mandeville signalled in the *Fable of the Bees* and in his *Essay on Charity and Charity Schools*, of 1723, that the world had changed and that charity was both fundamentally disingenuous and a problematic solvent of modern inequality, even in the Dutch Republic.[17]

Mandeville's *Fable of the Bees* had been carefully grafted on a set of reference points, among which was William Temple's *Observations*. The *Fable* revealed the moral hypocrisy and range of false emotions that lay behind what was considered virtuous. But its argument was also designed to reveal the political gap between Christian schemes of virtue and vice and the moral registers to be accommodated by policies in a competitive eighteenth-century commercial society. Likewise, Mandeville framed his work on charity as a specific application of his general outlook on the appropriate management of poverty and wealth, focused on a contrast with individual charity initiatives and their motivations.

Both the *Fable* and the *Essay on Charity and Charity Schools* exposed misguided custom-induced inclinations and policies that ultimately affected the international competitiveness of modern economies. In the *Fable*, Mandeville operationalised his message by emphasising the distance between the Dutch Republic of around 1670, as its society was described by William Temple, and that same state following the Peace of Utrecht of 1713. Mandeville noted that 'the *Dutch* indeed were then [in the days of William Temple] very frugal; but since those Days and that their Calamities have not been so pressing ... a great Alteration has been made among the better sort of People in their Equipages, Entertainments and whole manner of Living'.[18] Frugality might have been a viable national spirit half a century earlier, and have combined well with the privileged access to international markets that the Dutch enjoyed in the Golden Age of their Republic. But in the meantime, the entire reality of international trade and competition had changed. The time of the trade republics was over, and even the Dutch Republic was transforming into a commercial society that in terms of its moral psychology was an entirely different type of state.

That type of state, Mandeville argued between the *Fable* and the *Essay on Charity and Charity Schools*, needed to be built on a political foundation that understood wealth and poverty as each other's mirror image, channelling human self-interest to wealth. It could not remain stuck in a world of beliefs and social codes of esteem that no longer had any function and that were politically dysfunctional.

In this regard, poverty was a sign of imperfection, unused resource or capacity that ought to be activated politically. In the *Essay on Charity and Charity Schools*, Mandeville argued with regard to English 'Complaint and Lamentations' that '[t]here is no People yet come to higher Perfection in the Woollen Manufacture, either as to dispatch or goodness of Work, at least in the most considerable Branches, than ourselves, and therefore what we complain of can only depend on the difference in the Management of the Poor, between other Nations and ours'.[19] Somehow, wealth, poverty and charity were not properly aligned in Britain in the early eighteenth century and their interrelations were misunderstood. Mandeville, to put it differently, suggested that the 'management of the poor', as he termed it, was an indicator of the adequacy of a state's commercial politics at large.

Acts of charity, by contrast, did not correspond to a collective rationality, nor were they directly coupled with compassion. From a moral perspective, acts of charity had their basis in a self-love developed from an embryonic minimal sense of pity and were not inspired by a benefactor's desire to relieve poverty, but a performative need to be seen to care and be a good Christian. Politically, and much more significantly, relief and education did not align with political expediency and redirected labour to suboptimal productive capacity. Not only was the establishment of charity schools not organically related to collective well-being, the wider general social economic and political problem it bred was an artificially constructed mismatch at a particular moment in the development of commercial society.

Developing his argument from moral reasoning, Mandeville in the essay on charity specifically targeted caritative educational initiatives. Rather than stimulating productivity, these distorted the natural progress within a society of instruction and emancipation. Elevating poor labourers by education and improving their conditions of life was a lofty goal, but initiatives to that end had to match the development of the land and economic side of society. As Mandeville put it, different classes necessarily had to experience different discomforts and moral characteristics to be appropriately incentivised. The education of the poor by charity 'spoiled' society's labour reserve. It created a mismatch between social demands. Preparing children of workers for a life they could not sustain meant setting them up for failure and not only promoting idleness, but even rebellion against society. Instead, simplicity, labour and frugality were the moral cornerstones for boosting the wool industry. Only once the wool industry became more technologically advanced was it prudent to accommodate an educational transition and provide instruction to labourers to improve their conditions *along* with those of commercial society at large.

Pinto's 'constitutional' idea of poverty

Mandeville's historical contextualisation of education in terms of the technological and economic progress of society provided a genuine political logic to thinking about poverty. Just as the Dutch Republic had changed character between the later seventeenth and early eighteenth century, which created a need to adjust policies, so it was essential in Britain to align labour and poverty with a wider economic transition and development process. In the case of Britain, that process was dictated first and foremost by the labour demands of the wool industry. To hammer home his political message, Mandeville concluded his *Essay on Charity and Charity Schools* by considering Russia and Britain in comparison and judged that Russia had 'too few knowing men' while Britain had 'too many'.[20]

In a similar vein, Mandeville's *Fable of the Bees* included a comparison between the Dutch and the British economies, distinguishing their respective foundations and development trajectories. Mandeville argued that the economy of the Dutch Republic traditionally was held together by higher taxation levels and a greater need for frugality than the English ever required. If the Dutch by the early eighteenth century no longer lived in the reality that Temple had sketched, the British economy, according to Mandeville, required even less frugality and could be incentivised through luxury consumption, pride and social inequality.[21]

A useful figure to bring into the discussion here, whose views – like Mandeville's – have often been misrepresented or miscategorised, is Isaac de Pinto. Pinto was an Amsterdam financier and advisor to the Dutch and British East India Companies who was fantastically well connected (among his acquaintances were David Hume, Voltaire, Diderot and Jacques Necker, but he was also involved in diplomatic negotiations at the end of the Seven Years' War). Pinto disagreed with Mandeville on a number of issues around the theme of luxury, but in his unpublished policy advice to

Stadholder William IV in the late 1740s he agreed with Mandeville that the predicament of the Dutch Republic had changed enormously between the late seventeenth and the eighteenth century. Based on that historical insight around the decline of the Dutch Republic in international trade and politics, Pinto called for a series of reforms.[22]

Pinto did not publish any texts on poverty, charity or pauperism as a subject, but developed a comprehensive take on the foundations of international trade, economic growth and modern finance. Initially, he became known as an author for his *Essai sur le luxe*, an essay on card-playing addressed to Diderot and other expositions of issues within commercial society.[23] In these essays Pinto developed a social theory of wealth in terms of shared artificial values. The more members of society were brought under the same political regime of labour, wealth creation, trade politics and credit, the more 'complete' and integrated a commercial society was. Pinto's theory of commercial society was that of an economically constituted nation that progressed over time through stages as a 'commercial state'.[24] To keep this state together and optimally wealthy and powerful, it was key not to lose members or wealth due to loss of credit, bankruptcies, trade opportunities or other sources of poverty. These not only affected individuals, but the economically constituted state as a whole.

Pinto presented this political argument in his essay on luxury as a critique of Hume, Montesquieu, Melon and Mandeville, whose analyses of luxury had not been fully sensitive to the damaging effects of poverty in modern societies. While Mandeville and these other writers were no advocates for unconditional luxury, their political theory did not, Pinto felt, take into account sufficiently how personal disaster affected the good of the state.

Poverty for Pinto could be related to the state of society where people were not yet included in the social fabric of shared wealth creation, *or* when members of a fully integrated commercial society were reduced to poverty causing the collapse of pockets of wealth in society. In the latter case, the damage fell upon the general well-being of society and was to the detriment of all.

Analogous to how Pinto felt Hume and others were naïve about the political effects of state debt defaults, he felt their accounts of luxury did not reflect the social dangers of overspending. Bankruptcy was not a matter of dividing the spoils of somebody's stable property, but of an edifice tumbling down, values evaporating and credit going up into smoke. Society as whole paid for the damage, not just the bankruptee, or debtor. In his text on card-playing, Pinto addressed political theories that appraised patriotism and political virtue and that disparaged highly socialised games and fashions. Pinto argued that the latter were in fact useful interfaces for people to help them understand the new reality of commercial society, credit and investment, whereas political virtue was a primitive sentiment that could spark rebellion against the state.[25]

Given the increasing number of bankruptees in the cities of Holland in the 1750s and 1760s, Pinto took serious issue with the problem of poverty and its social consequences and proposed a regulation that forbade banks to turn its customers into lifelong cash-cows. The direct way to take the sting out of luxury would be to implement new social codes that made wealth accumulation and reinvestment, not spending, the object of admiration. But such projects carried the inherent risk of tending to 'tyranny'. A more promising approach that was 'easier in practise than one imagined and prodigiously useful' lay in the legal creation of personal spending regimes to be managed by banks issuing loans to the profligate victims of luxury in order to save their honour and credit – and prevent social capital leakages.[26]

Patriotism at the end of the Republic: republican views of poverty, property and rights

Between the early seventeenth century – and the idea of the Dutch Republic as a place that had no poverty – and the mid-nineteenth century, the relation between poverty and the state changed enormously. If we map Mandeville's critique of charity and Pinto's 'constitutional' idea of poverty onto the Dutch debate of the 1770s and 1780s, their views become instruments for the identification of new dividing lines.

The appearance of new ideas about managing poverty in the later eighteenth century had a clear reason. During the eighteenth century, the decline of Dutch foreign trade, the loss of the staple market and the impact of international changes on the reputation of the Dutch state had given rise to an internationally more similar manifestation of poverty. If the United Provinces was always an unstable entity, the continuous state debt crisis following the War of the Spanish Succession and the effective end of the Protestant alliance made the Republic vulnerable. Throughout the eighteenth century, the Dutch Republic was no longer characterised by the social and economic balances of the 'Golden Age'. Moreover, the old institutional balance of the seventeenth century had not aligned with a new reality and the Dutch economy was suffering from the international exposure of its combination of high unemployment rates, high wage levels and low interest rates. Finally, the outdated organisation of manufacturing and guild institutions impeded international competition with Britain and France. This analysis was made not only by Dutch writers and politicians, but also internationally by figures like Adam Smith, who noted his belief that tax levels in the Dutch Republic aggravated its trajectory into decline.[27] With the old equilibrium gone, the bottom had fallen away under the Dutch economy and the increasingly competitive global market system was unforgiving.

From the middle of the eighteenth century, this situation led to attempts to reform the shape of the Dutch economy by a general fiscal and tariff reform.[28] While these attempts did not bear fruit and the problem of pauperism in Dutch cities was more and more noted, a different combined approach to economic reform and poverty took shape in the second half of the eighteenth century.

The movement of 'economic patriotism' that emerged around 1770 shared Mandeville's and Pinto's recognition of poverty as a political economic problem. Developing as a national network of city-based local organisations, it sought to mobilise and channel private initiative to shape a focused outlook onto economic renewal and the transformation of idleness and unemployment into an emphatically nationalistic economic programme. As this grassroots national network institutionalised into a powerful organisation that was independent from the state, and that had its own publications, meetings and budget, it was given the name *Oeconomische Tak* in 1777 (*Tak* meaning branch in Dutch, as the organisation was an offspring from the *Hollandse Maatschappij van Wetenschappen – the Holland Society of Sciences*). The *Oeconomische Tak* developed an ideology of economic patriotism that rejected charity and infused production and consumption with a set of nationalistic values. Good citizens bought domestic wares, invested in national companies and developed projects to put poor labourers to work and promote national industriousness – notably by developing workhouses and labour colonies and by attempting to promote the Dutch textile industry. Compared with Pinto's more internationally focused and refined understanding of credit, trade and finance, the economic patriots were grassroots activists who responded to everyday observations of problems in Dutch cities.[29]

What these economic patriots aspired to, in the words of one of its main historians, was the 'marriage between philanthropy and the economy'.[30] More broadly, the aim was to use charity to force indolent citizens to serve the national economy. In the writings published through the *Oeconomische Tak*, the old attitude to charity as poor relief was considered akin to slavery, as it did not only make poor people indolent, but more fundamentally was a debasement of their true nature by making them reliant upon support for self-preservation.[31] To break the deadlock that the Republic found itself in, charity was reframed as the primary agency that could restore people's proper nature and direct them to a more purposeful life in the service of their country.

This sense of restoration was strongly related to a nostalgia for the 'Golden Age' Dutch Republic as a leading trading power. The Dutch

Republic in these later decades of the eighteenth century did not face the problem that Mandeville described for Britain in 1714 of suppressed growth because of institutional mismatch. Its predicament was closer to the British context of the late eighteenth and early nineteenth century where the dynamics of population, poverty and charity formed a political economic puzzle that in the British case led to Malthus's reflections on poverty and a protracted poor law debate. The overwhelming aim was to overcome the decline of the Republic. And poverty was seen as a manifestation of that decline first, and part of a political economic puzzle second.

The rejection of the old 'passive' attitude to charity in the sense of poor relief was also the main agreement among this patriotic movement with regard to poverty and economic reform. Everyone wanted to get rid of the old system that Temple had lauded. Charity bred indolence, perpetuated poverty, distracted people from their true nature (a religiously inspired argument) and put political and social power in the hands of charity organisations, while the poor themselves once desocialised – excluded from participating in society, from having hopes and dreams – easily could take to rebellion. In other words, the challenge was to transform the fear of the poor into a utility of the poor.

During the 1770s and 1780s, the movement of economic patriotism and the transformation of charity split, I believe, into two strands. On the one hand, there were writers – typically educated citizens – who proposed policies geared towards structural supply-side factors like technological improvement and diffusion of knowledge, along with protectionist barriers and reforms of the labour market. Within this strand of thinking, the idea was increasingly held that subsistence was to be treated as a right and that getting rid of poverty was the proper object of politics.

Part of their proposals was morally corrective and aimed at the forced coupling of the 'will to work' to the 'duty to work' and a 'right to subsistence'. The aim was to repair indolence, by setting up new workhouses and designing poor laws, to take poverty away from the charity offered by religious groups and elites in society and incorporate it instead into state regulation. This way of thinking led in the Batavian Republican period around 1800 to new – unprecedented – proposals for welfare politics. So here we move from charity via philanthropy to welfare politics: the transformation of charity into a political right to subsistence and the duty to work as part of a republican political economic reform strategy.

On the other hand, a group of writers proposed incentives in the 1770s and 1780s of a non-permanent kind to correct mismatches and revive economic growth through the integration of groups of people in society and of economic sectors and provinces – which had not only a high degree of political autonomy, but also differed enormously in their economic profiles.

New fiscal arrangements (such as were proposed since the 1750s) and initiatives to diffuse new agricultural methods and technological knowledge went along with economic policies that treated languishing industries like infant industries and attempted to 'revive' them through temporary import substitutions. Within this approach to Dutch decline, the poor and subsistence were of concern, but inherently part of a general political economic challenge of integrating the Dutch state within an emerging global economy, not an end goal or moral or social principle, politically anchored in a nostalgia for the seventeenth-century Golden Age.

Pauperism and the duty of the modern liberal state

Getting rid of poverty was not a moral duty of the state in the view of the second strand of writers. Instead, their ideas chimed more with Pinto's 'constitutional' outlook on the political costs of poverty to the state. Herman Hendrik van den Heuvel, for instance, was the main initiator behind the establishment of the *Oeconomische Tak*, and a prominent economic patriot in the early 1770s. But he never developed republican notions of representative government, equality or rights in his political or economic outlooks. Where most economic patriots made the shift from the 'marriage between philanthropy and the economy' to republican ideology, Van den Heuvel never developed pro-French, pro-National Assembly or Batavian Patriotic sentiments in the 1790s, but remained loyal to the House of Orange by default.

Underlying this political allegiance was not so much a royalist loyalty, but a scepticism towards the new French political discourses that were influential in the 1780s among economic patriots. For this reason, van den Heuvel was at one point called an 'Anglo-Patriot'.[32] Among Van den Heuvel's contacts was the young Gijsbert Karel van Hogendorp, whose family he represented as a lawyer and whom he advised to read certain political economic works, from Forbonnais to Verri and Smith.[33] Hogendorp attended meetings of the *Oeconomische Tak* in the 1770s and early 1780s, and in 1831 (amid the crisis following the Belgian breakaway from the Dutch United Kingdom) looked back upon the creation of the *Oeconomische Tak* judging that 'this association', which itself was set up with Stadholder William V as its protector, 'renewed the design of William IV' to place the Dutch national economy on a renewed fiscal and commercial foundation.[34]

If economic patriotism started as a broad church, it became emphatically associated – in the 1780s, as well as in retrospect – with republican ideologies, while Hogendorp and others styled themselves as self-declared liberals in the early nineteenth century and quickly became disenchanted with the restoration regime that had turned the Dutch Republic into a monarchy and that they themselves initially had strongly supported. And it was from that critical distance towards the Dutch state that Hogendorp's intellectual successors confronted the issue of poverty in the Dutch state of the nineteenth century.[35] Indeed, within this category of thinkers, who neither turned to republican ideology, nor uncritically stuck with the Orange restoration monarchy, a lineage (often connecting generations of families, as in the case of the Tydeman family) might be discerned that emanated from van Hogendorp and that linked a number of his successors.

Among his early successors was Hendrik Willem Tydeman, who was actually a contemporary of Hogendorp, but who published until into the 1850s, long after Hogendorp's death in 1834. Tydeman published on the subject of poverty much earlier, notably a prize essay in 1820.[36] But he was also the main author, together with his son Jan Willem Tydeman and Jan Heemskerk, of a book entitled *Denkbeelden omtrent eene wettelijke regeling van het armwezen in Nederland* (1850), which outlined a vision of the appropriate policies for dealing with poverty in the Netherlands.[37] The *Denkbeelden* started with a foreword by Tydeman senior which suggested that the recognition of the need for a national poverty law by the 1848 Dutch constitution had already been part of King William I's constitutional design which he and Hogendorp had been involved in around 1815 and was long overdue.[38]

Indeed, the issue of poverty and constitutional reform were related in the minds of both Tydeman and Hogendorp. Tydeman's main policy focus was on poverty, but he published a commentary on the constitution of 1815.[39] That same text, written by Hogendorp, identified poverty explicitly as a matter of national interest and ongoing concern. Hogendorp had in fact been writing and publishing texts on poverty since the 1790s at least.[40] In the years immediately after 1815, he wrote a set of policy memoranda about poverty in which he outlined the nature of the problem: poverty was a political problem for the state, since it affected the national labour resource and capacity, plus it created a risk for political stability and could easily inspire discontent and revolutionary sentiments. Yet, it could not follow that poor relief was a right that citizens could demand from the state. The duty of the state to address poverty and create a 'well-ordered state' thus lay somewhere in the middle, where employment might need to be created by the state to preserve the political balance.[41]

Tydeman was not a great supporter of Thorbecke's 1848 constitutional design, which included a series of layered representative political institutions, and preferred the 1815 approach to turning the former Republic into a 'well-ordered state'.[42] Yet, deep down, their political visions were grounded in the same intellectual tradition, and Tydeman's emphasis on the recognition of poverty as a political concern in both the 1815 and 1848 Constitutions alluded to their shared roots. Tydeman's aim in 1850, in publishing his *Denkbeelden*, and in heaping praise on Thorbecke's wisdom, vision and ability to see the truthfulness of his own 'system', as he called it, was to lobby for his own policies on poverty. Tydeman presented his 'system' as a new version of the plan he had put forward around 1815.[43] To clarify its wider aim and character, the *Denkbeelden* contained an embryonic history of Dutch poverty legislation from the time of Charles V onwards. The upshot of Tydeman's history was that the continuous and widespread neglect of considering poverty and inequality as part of the modern state had led to the international revolutionary movement of 1848.[44] Socialism and communism, 'rightfully hated and feared' as they were, were the dysfunctional gut responses to this international neglect, but not the solution.[45] The task to be confronted on a national scale was to 'tidy up all the bits and pieces, radical reforms and entirely one-dimensional designs'.[46]

The worst that could happen in a modern society was if members of society fell into a degree of poverty and incapacity that removed them from the economic foundation of the state. General poverty, as characterised by Tydeman, was the decrease of the 'power to labour' of the citizens of the state and caused a 'loss' of 'national capital'.[47] This did not mean that Tydeman was sympathetic to the republican law that was propounded in 1800 by the Dutch Batavian Representative Body that considered all poor to be 'children of the state' and elevated the practice of philanthropy into a moral duty of the state.[48] Tydeman's position was decidedly not that citizens had a political right to charity, but that the state had a political duty to sustain itself, which warranted the establishment of poverty laws and labour colonies to keep the poor on board as members of society: 'in a well-ordered state no one shall die of hunger or need; if this occurs, something is failing within the government of the nation'.[49]

Tydeman's eagerness to distance himself from the Dutch economic patriots who held the day in the Batavian period was not merely historically motivated. Within the context of the 1840s and the rise of a liberal economic orthodoxy that sought to pare back the duties of the state, he himself, as a proponent of 'the well-ordered state', was accused by a number of his academic colleagues of holding socialist or communist ideas. The new liberal economists understood poverty as a failure of the state to let the natural course of events, the market, run its course and determine an optimal allocation of labour and production factors. The duty of the modern state was not to intervene or to alleviate, but to abstain and thereby prevent poverty. Tydeman thus sought to carve out a political space between the moral 'children of the state' and the dogmatic anti-statism of the mainstream of Dutch economists of the time.[50]

Within the space that Tydeman occupied, he was in good company. Socially as well as intellectually and politically, he was close first to Hogendorp and later on to Thorbecke, the two standard bearers of Dutch constitutional liberalism of the nineteenth century. In the years before Hogendorp passed, Tydeman was among the people he continued to work and associate with and 'enjoyed a longstanding friendship' with.[51] Mutual professional and intellectual trust also characterised Tydeman's relationship with Thorbecke, who was one of the last people Tydeman wrote to before his death in 1863.[52] Tydeman disliked Thorbecke's representative constitutional design, but his political ideas were cut from the same cloth.[53] Like Hogendorp, Tydeman combined a detachment from Dutch political life from the 1820s onwards, with disenchantment, silently professing his 'liberal constitutional sentiments' and 'full loyalty to the Dynasty', he lamented the 'sad state of the country'.[54] In a sense, Tydeman was the 'link' between Hogendorp and Thorbecke.

This was the case in particular for their views on poverty. Similar to Tydeman's ideas about the well-ordered state, Thorbecke argued 'that a civilised state has in fact the duty to care maximally about its members not perishing due to want'.[55] It was this perspective on the duties of the state that saw Thorbecke being severely criticised in the 1840s for being a 'pseudo-liberal', a closet-socialist whose adherence to a traditional state conception made him akin to a false liberal, who was unable to see the ordering principle of self-interest as the best guide to social equilibrium.[56]

The 1840s in the Netherlands saw a major debate on the nature of poverty that was the conductor for the rise of the new political economy. Within this debate and leading up to the Dutch poverty law of 1854, anti-revolutionary Christian conservatives and the parliamentary representatives of the views held by dogmatic economic liberals formed an uneasy alliance to defeat Thorbecke's conception of poverty as integral to the duties of the modern state.[57] The Calvinist orthodoxy that philanthropy had to be separate from the realm of the political found itself in line with the new political economy in rejecting poverty as an object of the state.[58]

Simultaneous to the 1840s poverty debate producing the poverty law of 1854, the need arose for a historical understanding of the new political economy. That historical understanding had to be patriotic. A Dutch ancestor, one whose ideas connected the Dutch republican Golden Age to the era of economic liberalism, had to be found. Two decades after his death in 1834, G. K. van Hogendorp became this figure, owing to a prize essay by Otto von Rees which argued that Hogendorp was the first Dutch classical economist whose vision extended the tradition of free trade of the Dutch Republican Golden Age into the nineteenth century.[59]

While a new generation of Dutch political economic writers celebrated Hogendorp's legacy over his dead body, Tydeman was best placed to point out the errors implied in this historical revisionism. In a review of von Rees's work, Tydeman corrected a number of errors in the work, provided a much wider context for Hogendorp and defended himself from the allegation of socialism and communist in one go.[60] Indeed, Hogendorp had strongly rejected the suggestion by his friend Jan Ackersdijck that the cause of poverty lay in the obstruction of self-interested reasoning by the state and that the emancipation of labourers could do with a bit of hunger and need as adequate incentives.[61]

Instead, what had been key to van Hogendorp was 'the participation of the entire nation in the wealth of the state'. Yet, it was this political, almost constitutional, reasoning, Hogendorp complained, that a new generation of economists neglected and confused by 'more and more turning national wealth as such into the object of the science'.[62]

Conclusion: patriotism and poverty

To conclude, considering the development of Dutch discourses of patriotism and poverty in the 1770s and 1780s one can recognise a parting of two positions, in politics theory as well as on poverty, out of the common economic Patriot movement of the 1770s. Everyone wanted to get rid of unregulated charity. This no longer fit with society as it had developed, and the condition of decline warranted a new approach to and new conception of poverty.

One position sees poverty (and charity) as an object of government and connects it to rights or duties of the state to provide labour and subsistence and goes along with revolutionary and democratic representative discourses. Another sees poverty in relation to wealth as a mismatch of production factors and analyses this mismatch in terms of moral philosophical incentives, but also from a political constitutional perspective. The duty of the state was not a moral duty towards its citizens, but a political one to itself, not emanating from rights discourses, but from a sense of politics that was inherently economic and collective. Within this reasoning there was a continuity connecting the notion of the 'intrinsic power' of the state of the mid-eighteenth century to Hogendorp's early- and Tydeman's mid-nineteenth-century understanding of poverty as a duty of the state.

By 1854, in the aftermath of the 1848 upheavals and the rise of ideological reference points of communism and socialism, the idea that poverty was a political problem that was the duty of the state to address thus had been thoroughly constitutionally anchored. Yet, exactly at this time it was questioned and rejected by the first generation of Dutch classical political economists, whose theories in political reality found an ally in the traditional Calvinist scepticism towards the state.

Notes

1 For instance, Herman Diederiks, D. J. Noordam, H. D. Tjalsma, *Armoede en sociale spanning: sociaal-historische studies over Leiden in de achttiende eeuw* (Hilversum: Verloren, 1985); L. F. van Loo, 'Den arme gegeven'. *Een beschrijving van armoede, armenzorg en sociale zekerheid in Nederland, 1784–1965* (Amsterdam: Boom, 1981); Auke van der Woud, *Koninkrijk vol sloppen. Achterbuurten en vuil in de negentiende eeuw* (Amsterdam: Bert Bakker, 2010); H. F. J. M. van den Eerenbeemt, *Armoede en arbeidsdwang: werkinrichtingen voor 'onnutte' Nederlanders in de Republiek 1760–1795: een mentaliteitsgeschiedenis* (The Hague: M. Nijhoff, 1977); H. F. J. M. van den Eerenbeemt, 'Armoede in de "gedrukte" optiek van de sociale bovenlaag in Nederland 1750–1850', *Tijdschrift voor Geschiedenis*, 88 (1975), 468–500; Maarten Prak, 'Armenzorg 1500–1800', in Jacques van Gerwen and Marco van Leeuwen (eds), *Studies over zekerheidsarrangementen. Risico's risicobestrijding en verzekeringen in Nederland vanaf de Middeleeuwen* (Amsterdam: NEHA, 1998), pp. 49–90.

2 For an overview on literature on the issue of Dutch decline, see Koen Stapelbroek, 'Dutch Decline as a European Phenomenon', *History of European Ideas*, 36 (2010), 139–152 and Joris Oddens, Mart Rutjes and Arthur Weststeijn, 'Introduction: Republican Decline in Context', *Discourses of Decline. Essays on Republicanism in Honor of Wyger R. E. Velema* (Leiden: Brill, 2022), pp. 1–18.

3 Joh. de Vries, 'De economische achteruitgang der Republiek in de achttiende eeuw' (Amsterdam: PhD thesis, University of Amsterdam, 1959).

4 Ole Peter Grell, Andrew Cunningham and Robert Jütte, 'Health Care and Poor Relief in 18th and 19th Century Northern Europe', in ibid. (eds), *Health Care and Poor Relief in 18th and 19th Century Northern Europe* (Aldershot: Ashgate 2002), pp. 3–14 at p. 12; and in the same volume, Marijke Gijswijt-Hofstra, 'Dutch Approaches to Problems of Illness and Poverty between the Golden Age and the Fin de Siècle', pp. 259–276.

5 The main work on this topic is T. J. Boschloo, *De productiemaatschappij. liberalisme, economische wetenschap en het vraagstuk der armoede in Nederland, 1800–1875* (Hilversum: Verloren, 1989), which connects political economy from 1800 to the issue of poverty through a perspective on Dutch liberalism in the early nineteenth century.

6 Simon Schama, *The Embarrassment of Riches: An Interpretation of Dutch Culture in the Golden Age* (New York: Alfred A. Knopf, 1987).

7 Ibid., p. 579; Anne McCants, 'Nederlands republikanisme en de politiek van liefdadigheid', *Tijdschrift voor Sociale Geschiedenis*, 22 (1996), 443–455. For a

sociologically inspired analysis of the reciprocal logic of charity, see Marco van Leeuwen, 'Logic of Charity: Poor Relief in Preindustrial Europe', *The Journal of Interdisciplinary History*, 24 (1994), 589–613.

8 Schama referred to an unpublished paper 'Labor in the Dutch Golden Age', which appeared in a revised form as Jan de Vries, 'An Inquiry into the Behaviour of Wages in the Dutch Republic and the Southern Netherlands, 1580–1800', in *Dutch Capitalism and World Capitalism/Capitalisme Hollandais et Capitalisme Mondial*, Maurice Aymard (ed.) (Cambridge: Cambridge University Press), pp. 37–61 and his *The Dutch Rural Economy in the Golden Age, 1500–1700* (New Haven, CT: Yale University Press, 1974).
9 Ibid., p. 167.
10 Ibid., pp. 167–170.
11 Diderot, famously, was impressed by the living standards of Dutch labourers during his journey to the United Provinces. See Denis *Diderot*, 'Voyage de Holland', *Oeuvres complètes de Diderot*, eds Jules Assézat and Maurice Tourneux, 20 vols (Paris, 1876), vol. xvii, pp. 420–421.
12 Joshua Gee, *The Trade and Navigation of Great Britain Considered* (London, 1729), p. 37 and Ch. 13, 'Propositions for better Regulating and Employing the Poor', in general.
13 On poverty in general in early modern Europe, Jean-Pierre Gutton, *La société et les pauvres en Europe (XVIe–XVIIIe siècles)* (Paris: PUF, 1974). Still useful as a basic study of subsistence goods, price levels and charity institutions in the Burgundian and Habsburg Netherlands of the fourteenth, fifteenth and sixteenth centuries is W. P. Blockmans and W. Prevenier, 'Armoede in de Nederlanden van de 14e tot het midden van de 16e eeuw: bronnen en problemen', *Tijdschrift voor Geschiedenis*, 4 (1975), 501–538.
14 Jan Luiten van Zanden, 'The "Revolt of the Early Modernists" and the "First Modern Economy": An Assessment', *The Economic History Review*, 55 (2002), 619–641; Bas van Bavel and Jan Luiten van Zanden, 'The Jump-Start of the Holland Economy during the Late-Medieval Crisis, c.1350–c.1500', *The Economic History Review*, 57 (2004), 503–532.
15 William Temple, *Observations Upon the United Provinces of the Netherlands* (Cambridge: Cambridge University Press, [1672] 2011), p. 105.
16 On Mandeville's engagement with the Dutch Republic, see Alexander Bick, 'Bernard Mandeville and the "Economy" of the Dutch', *Erasmus Journal for Philosophy and Economics*, 1 (2008), 87–106.
17 On Mandeville on charity, see Francesca Pongiglione and Mikko Tolonen, 'Mandeville on Charity Schools: Happiness, Social Order and the Psychology of Poverty', *Erasmus Journal for Philosophy and Economics*, 9 (2016), 82–100; Jonathan B. Kramnick '"Unwilling to be short, or plain in any thing concerning gain": Bernard Mandeville and the Dialectic of Charity', *The Eighteenth Century*, 33 (1992), 148–175.
18 Bernard Mandeville, *The Fable of the Bees: Or, Private Vices Publick Benefits* (London, 1714), p. 169. Mandeville referred to William Temple, *Observations upon the United Provinces of the Netherlands* (London, 1673).

19 Bernard de Mandeville, 'Essay on Charity and Charity-Schools', *The Fable of the Bees and Other Writings*, ed. E. J. Hundert (Indianapolis: Hackett, [1723] 1997), p. 128.
20 Ibid., p. 128.
21 Bick, 'Bernard Mandeville and the 'Economy' of the Dutch', pp. 95–98.
22 Koen Stapelbroek, 'From Jealousy of Trade to the Neutrality of Finance: Isaac de Pinto's 'System' of Luxury and Perpetual Peace', in Béla Kapossy, Isaac Nakhimovsky and Richard Whatmore (eds), *Commerce and Peace in the Enlightenment* (Cambridge: Cambridge University Press, 2017), pp. 78–109.
23 The best take on the luxury debate is Istvan Hont, 'The Early Enlightenment Debate on Commerce and Luxury', in Mark Goldie and Robert Wokler (eds), *The Cambridge History of Eighteenth-Century Political Thought* (Cambridge: Cambridge University Press), pp. 377–418.
24 Pinto developed this vision in his *Traité de la circulation du credit [...] & Suivi d'une letter sur la jalousie du commerce, où l'on prouve que l'interêt des puissances commerçantes ne se croise point* (Amsterdam, 1771).
25 For example, Isaac de Pinto, *Essai sur le luxe* (Amsterdam, 1762), p. 10 and p. 18. See also Koen Stapelbroek, 'Commercial Sociability and the Management of Self-Interest in Isaac de Pinto's Letter on Card-Playing', in Christine Zabel (ed.), *Historicizing Self-Interest in the Modern Atlantic World* (London: Routledge, 2021), pp. 73–94.
26 Pinto, *Essai sur le luxe*, p. 24.
27 Adam Smith, *An Inquiry into the Nature and Causes of the Wealth of Nations* (Oxford: Clarendon, 1976), p. 905.
28 Koen Stapelbroek, 'Reinventing the Dutch Republic: Franco-Dutch Commercial Treaties from Ryswick to Vienna', in Antonella Alimento and Koen Stapelbroek (eds), *The Politics of Commercial Treaties in the Eighteenth Century: Balance of Power, Balance of Trade* (Basingstoke: Palgrave MacMillan, 2017), pp. 195–215.
29 Koen Stapelbroek, 'The Haarlem 1771 Prize Essay on the Restoration of Dutch Trade and the Emergence of the Oeconomische Tak of the Hollandsche Maatschappye der Weetenschappen', in Koen Stapelbroek and Jani Marjanen (eds), *The Rise of Economic Societies in the Eighteenth Century: Patriotic Reform in Europe and North America* (Basingstoke: Palgrave MacMillan, 2012), pp. 257–284.
30 See H. F. J. M. van den Eerenbeemt's discussion, published in three instalments, 'Het huwelijk tussen filantropie en economie: een Patriotse en Bataafse illusie', *Economisch- en sociaal-historisch jaarboek*, 35 (1972), 28–64; 38 (1975), 179–255; and 39 (1976), 13–100.
31 The argument recurs frequently throughout Eerenbeemt, *Armoede en arbeidsdwang*.
32 The anonymously published *Oeconomische Uitreekening van de Nationale Schuld van Engeland* was sarcastically addressed to van den Heuvel for his 'sincere Anglo-Patriotic sentiments' (s.l. 1782).
33 P. Ch. H. Overmeer, *De economische denkbeelden van Gijsbert Karel van Hogendorp (1762–1834)* (Tilburg: Gianotten, 1982), pp. 16–18.

34 G. K. van Hogendorp, *Brieven over de nationale welvaart, geschreven in de jaren 1828, 1829, september 1830, aan eenen Zuid-Nederlander* (Amsterdam, 1831), p. 103. The design of William IV Hogendorp that was referred to was the 1751 Proposal to turn the Republic into a limited free port and align its economic sectors within the changing world of international trade.
35 On the debates of this period, other than Boschloo, *De productiemaatschappij* and Eerenbeemt, *Armoede en arbeidsdwang*, see P. B. A. Melief, *De strijd om de armenzorg in Nederland 1795–1854* (Groningen: Wolters, 1955).
36 Reinhard Jansz. Scherenberg and Hendrik Willem Tydeman, 'Verhandeling ter beantwoording der Vrage: Kan de Armoede, waaronder eenige staten van Europa thans gedrukt worden, inderdaat net grond worden toegeschreven an eene te groote bevolking, in evenredigheid der middelen van bestaan', *Verhandelingen van de Hollandsche Maatschappij der Wetenchappen te Haarlem*, 1/2 (Haarlem, 1821), pp. 1–181.
37 Hendrik Willem Tydeman, Jan Heemskerk and Johan Willem Tydeman, *Denkbeelden omtrent eene wettelijke regeling van het armwezen in Nederland* (Amsterdam, 1850). The publication was followed by a critique of the 1851 proposal for a poverty law: Hendrik Willem Tydeman, Jan Heemskerk and Johan Willem Tydeman, *Het ontwerp van wet op het armbestuur van 1851* (Amsterdam, 1852).
38 Tydeman, Heemskerk and Tydeman, *Denkbeelden*, p. vi.
39 Hendrik Willem Tydeman, *Aanmerkingen op de grondwet voor de Vereenigde Nederlanden* (Dordrecht, 1815).
40 Notably, G. K. van Hogendorp, *Missive over het Armwezen* (Amsterdam, 1805), as well as six short pamphlets published with the same publisher between 1799 and 1801 under the title *Iets voor de Armen*.
41 A good overview of Hogendorp's take on poverty is in Eerenbeemt, 'Armoede in de "gedrukte" optiek van de sociale bovenlaag', pp. 468–500. For an overview of pamphlet debates in this period, see J. De Vries Jr, 'Pamfletten over het armoedeprobleem in de negentiende eeuw. Bijdrage tot de kennis van de geest der vorige eeuw', *Mensch en Maatschappij*, 14 (1938), 10–21.
42 As he made very clear in 1855 in H. W. Tydeman, 'Gijsbert Karel van Hogendorp als Staathuishoudkundige', *De Recensent*, 9/1 (1855), 250–263: 260. See also Boschloo, *De productiemaatschappij*, p. 129.
43 Tydeman, Heemskerk and Tydeman, *Denkbeelden*, pp. vii–viii.
44 Ibid., pp. 12–33, pre-empted on pp. ix–xiv.
45 Ibid., pp. xii–xiii.
46 Ibid., p. xi.
47 Ibid., p. xiii.
48 Ibid., p. 17.
49 Ibid., p. 75.
50 Perhaps the main articulation of the new approach to poverty in response to Tydeman's and Hogendorp's traditional politial understanding was Jeronimo de Bosch Kemper, *Geschiedkundig onderzoek naar de armoede in ons vaderland, hare oorzaken en de middelen, die tot hare vermindering zouden kunnen*

worden aangewend (Haarlem, 1851). The work was critically reviewed by Tydeman in the *Algemeene Konst- en Letterbode* 53/1 (1852), 121–124 and in 'Nadere Aanmerkingen op het Geschiedkundig Onderzoek naar de Armoede in ons Vaderland, hare Oorzaken', *Tijdschrift voor het Armwezen*, 3 (1853), 268–283. Tydeman argued against De Bosch Kemper, Rees, Vissering, Ackersdijck and others that the introduction of direct taxes on subsistence goods was a main cause of poverty, see Boschloo, *De productiemaatschappij*, pp. 136–142.

51 J. A. W. Tydeman, 'Levensberigt van Mr. Hendrik Willem Tydeman', *Handelingen der jaarlijksche algemeene vergadering van de Maatschappij der Nederlandsche Letterkunde te Leiden*, 61 (1863), 403–450 at 424–425. At Hogendorp's request Tydeman translated and wrote texts about the Dutch economic reform and international politics. Tydeman, 'Gijsbert Karel van Hogendorp', p. 262, felt he was able to relay Hogendorp's political sentiments 'from own experience and a more and more familiar interaction from 1816 until his death'.

52 Tydeman, 'Levensberigt', p. 449.

53 Koen Stapelbroek, Ida H. Stamhuis and Paul M. M. Klep, 'Adriaan Kluit's Statistics and the Future of the Dutch State from a European Perspective', *History of European Ideas*, 36 (2010), 217–235.

54 Tydeman, 'Levensberigt', p. 429.

55 Quoted by Boschloo, *De productiemaatschappij*, p. 77.

56 Ibid., p. 117 (by Sloet) and p. 93 (by De Bosch Kemper).

57 Tydeman was sucked into this debate in the 1840s and expressed his position in his 1846 rectoral farewell address. See Tydeman, Heemskerk and Tydeman, *Denkbeelden*, pp. vi–vii and Tydeman, 'Levensberigt', p. 434. For the 1854 law and its context, H. J. Smit, 'De armenwet van 1854 en haar voorgeschiedenis', *Historische opstellen aangeboden aan J. Huizinga op 7 december 1942 door het historisch gezelschap te's Gravenhage* (Haarlem: Tjeenk Willink, 1948), pp. 218–246; J. J. Dankers, 'Thorbecke en de Armenwet van 1854', *Geschiedenis en cultuur: achttien opstellen*, eds E. Jonker and M. Van Rossem (The Hague: SDU, 1990), pp. 119–130.

58 Boschloo, *De productiemaatschappij*, p. 75, p. 77. Thorbecke's own proposal for a poverty law of 1851 did not make it and in 1853 he became an MP himself and voted against the 1854 law. For context and international comparison, see Peter Lindert, 'Poor Relief before the Welfare State: Britain versus the Continent, 1780–1880', *European Review of Economic History*, 2 (1998), 101–140; Frances Gouda, *Poverty and Political Culture: The Rhetoric of Social Welfare in the Netherlands and France, 1815–1854* (Lanham: Rowman & Littlefield, 1995); Marco H. D. van Leeuwen, *The Logic of Charity: Amsterdam, 1800–1850* (New York: St. Martin's Press, 2000).

59 Otto van Rees, *Verhandeling over de verdiensten van Gijsbert Karel van Hogendorp als staathuishoudkundige ten aanzien van Nederland* (Utrecht, van der Post: 1854). For context, see Boschloo, *De productiemaatschappij*, pp. 144–148.

60 Tydeman, 'Gijsbert Karel van Hogendorp'. Rees was aware that his portrayal of Hogendorp did not quite fit reality but explained these problems away through the idea that Hogendorp necessarily, because of his context, was confused about the truth of his own ideas and made some errors in articulating them. See Boschloo, *De productiemaatschappij*, p. 147, p. 151.
61 W. C. Mees, 'Eene Briefwisseling tusschen Gijbert Karel van Hogendorp en prof Jan Ackersdijck', *Economisch-Historisch Jaarboek*, 12 (1926), 100–124. See also Boschloo, *De productiemaatschappij*, pp. 148–151, p. 162 and pp. 81–135 for the position of Tydeman versus his contemporaries, including Ackersdijck.
62 Mees, 'Briefwisseling Hogendorp Ackersdijck', p. 117.

6

Montesquieu, Smith and Burke on the 'labouring poor': an eighteenth-century debate

Anna Plassart

Introduction

Edmund Burke's anti-radical agenda in the 1790s is widely seen as pushing Smithian economics in a harsh free-markets direction that opposed any sort of government intervention to alleviate poverty. Consequently, he has become associated with the 'bleak possessive individualism' and 'anti-paternalist' approach to thinking about poverty that shaped nineteenth-century British welfare policy, and still finds echoes in twenty-first-century British and American conservative thought.[1] Read in this light, Burke exemplified an emerging 'reactionary' Enlightenment-inspired critique of the Old Poor Laws, and 'a new callousness, an unprecedented harshness toward the poor'.[2]

In contrast, Smith's reputation has been overhauled in the last few decades, as historians have wrestled his heritage away from decades of hero-worshipping by proponents of free-markets liberalism. Pointing to Smith's support for high wages and advocacy of elementary schooling for factory workers, historians of ideas increasingly read him as a 'compassionate observer of the plight of the poor [and a] stark critic of the corruption of our moral judgment that goes with fashionable admiration of the rich and disdain for the poor'.[3] Following the drive to draw a clear line between Smith and Burke's views of poverty, Burke has been left to shoulder at least some of the blame for '[helping] to set the trend' for the 'noticeably harsher stance towards the poor' developed from the 1790s, as historians continue to note his 'often staggering indifference to the suffering of the poor'.[4]

This chapter, however, will suggest that the approaches of Smith and Burke in fact shared many intellectual strands beyond their support for free markets, and that the innovations they are credited with (or blamed for) were part of a much larger eighteenth-century shift in understandings of poverty. The French Revolution is traditionally highlighted as heralding 'the realisation that there need no longer be such a thing as "the poor"'.[5] Yet views of poverty as sin, as resulting directly from the natural features of human psychology, or as useful (even indispensable) to prosperous commercial societies, were already being challenged throughout the Enlightenment. Political economists, following Montesquieu's lead, were developing theories that saw labour – not the absence of material goods or wealth – become central to the notion of poverty.

The chapter's starting point is Burke's striking observation that 'those who labour ... are miscalled the Poor'. It is found in his *Thoughts and Details on Scarcity* (1795), which contains a sustained critique of the expression 'labouring poor', dismissed as '[based and wicked] political canting language'.[6] The passage remains Burke's most-often cited contribution to the debate on poverty and welfare, and goes a long way towards explaining why Burke has usually been seen as anticipating the harsh turn taken by British poverty laws in the nineteenth century. It has been described as a 'momentous portent of the future' – an early attempt to introduce a formal distinction between the poor deemed deserving of compassion and charity (the old, the sick, the infirm), and those able-bodied people who could work and should therefore not be eligible for government relief.[7] While the linguistic distinction made by Burke did not take hold, his indictment of the 'labouring poor' in *Thoughts and Details* is widely identified as sharing conceptual roots with the arguments deployed against the Old Poor Laws in the early nineteenth century.

Since the seventeenth century, the Old Poor Laws had provided a legal status for those whose income was so low that they had to apply for relief – thus reflecting the early modern assessment of poverty as a normal and inevitable feature of society. Relief was administered by parishes and could either take the form of 'outdoor relief' for the able-bodied willing to work (in the form of clothing or food), or 'indoor' relief that relocated the poor in local poorhouses, workhouses, orphanages and so on. When living standards declined in the late eighteenth century, poverty rates shot up and more people applied for relief. As outlined in several of the contributions in this volume, a central question in the period therefore became that of who should be considered as deserving of charity, and who should provide relief?[8]

In any case, by the early nineteenth century the Old Poor laws were widely criticised for being too generous, and in 1834 they were replaced by the New Poor Laws: a system that aimed to strictly limit outdoor relief, and discourage claims by able-bodied claimants.[9] It is not difficult, therefore, to spot links between Burke's rejection of the label of 'labouring poor', and the nineteenth-century distinction between the 'pauper' or 'indigent' who deserved relief, and the able-bodied 'poor' who needed to be disincentivised to apply for relief. This stands in contrast to Smith's analysis in the *Theory of Moral Sentiments* (1759) and *Wealth of Nations* (1776), which frequently used the expression 'labouring poor' and analysed poverty not as an absolute measure of economic or physical well-being, but rather as a complex social, psychological and relative phenomenon which shamed and socially isolated its victims.[10]

Smith's compassionate assessment of the labouring poor is generally considered as marking a break in eighteenth-century attitudes towards poverty, and has been described as having emerged from the system of moral philosophy developed in the Scottish Enlightenment.[11] Burke's bleak approach, on the other hand, has not tended to be read in the context of Enlightenment philosophy – it has been analysed by most commentators through the prism of his engagement in the French Revolution debate in the 1790s.[12] More specifically, it has been analysed as a by-product of Burke's distrust of the radical and egalitarian discourses that flourished in the wake of the French Revolution, which have been identified as a fundamental historical turning point and 'the beginning of all modern thought about poverty'.[13] Against the radical agenda of economic redistribution and calls to support the 'labouring poor', Burke warned that poverty relief was not a legitimate function of the state, and that market mechanisms should be allowed to play out unhindered.

This chapter, however, presents Burke's discussion of the 'labouring poor' in a different context altogether: not as a reaction against the contemporary radical discourses that aimed to eradicate poverty, but rather as part of a decades-long Enlightenment debate about the nature of poverty in commercial society. Importantly, the point is not to argue that the revolutionary context was irrelevant to Burke's argument: it clearly was, if only because it directly prompted his infamous outburst against the 'labouring poor'. Rather, it is argued that Smith's thinking about poverty, and Burke's 1790s argument about the 'labouring poor', shared old and complex roots in eighteenth-century philosophical debates. Therefore, Burke's intervention should not be read as the starting point of well-known nineteenth-century debates about poverty and welfare. Rather, it should be reframed as the outcome of an all but forgotten century-long discussion about the 'labouring poor', thus providing a fresh entry point into wider eighteenth-century debates about poverty and its place in modern commercial society.

Burke on the 'labouring poor' in *Thoughts and Details on Scarcity*

Thoughts and Details on Scarcity was written by Burke at the behest of Henry Dundas, as Britain was experiencing acute political and economic challenges.[14] The country was at war, and the harvest of 1795 had once again been disappointing. In order to pre-empt the threat of new food riots and demonstrations, the government considered recommending 'regulations' to Parliament.[15] At the same time, several initiatives aimed at shielding the poor from the impact of rising food prices were being reported in British newspapers: these included the 1795 'Speenhamland laws', a locally-administered system of means-tested wage supplement tied to the price of bread, as well as the French Revolutionary Government's attempts to regulate France's internal grain trade.

Burke's memorandum, distributed to Dundas as well as William Pitt in early November 1795, argued that labour should be considered in the same light as any other commodity whose price was set by the laws of supply and demand, and that government should not intervene with market mechanisms. Therefore, it was not the duty of government, but rather the duty of charitable Christians, to alleviate the sufferings of the poor. Strikingly, and most importantly for the purpose of this chapter, Burke claimed that 'those who labour [are] miscalled the Poor', and that the expression 'labouring poor' was a nonsensical oxymoron, and 'base and ... wicked... political canting language'.[16]

Burke's memorandum remained unpublished for several years. Nevertheless, his literary executioners thought his indictment of government intervention to have been 'not wholly unproductive of good', and credited its influence for defeating various interventionist schemes, including the minimum wage bill introduced in the House of Commons by Samuel Whitbread on 9 December 1795.[17] Still, Whitbread's attempt appears to have spurred Burke to further develop his argument against wage subsidies, especially as they concerned agricultural wages. On 17 December he advertised a letter on the topic, addressed to his long-time friend Arthur Young, then Secretary to the Board of Agriculture.[18] However, news of the peace negotiations between France and England prompted him to abandon the project, instead shifting his attention towards his *Letters on Regicide Peace*. Burke's memorandum and fragments of the unfinished 'letter on agricultural wages' were eventually collated by his literary executors, scrubbed of all references to Young, and published posthumously in 1800, under the title *Thoughts and Details on Scarcity*.[19]

The way in which *Thoughts and Details on Scarcity* was framed and presented by Burke's executors in their 1800 preface goes a long way towards explaining its reception and subsequent reputation: in the preface they drew a direct link between Burke's economic argument and Adam Smith's *Wealth of Nations*, and credited Burke's memorandum with having convinced the government to drop early enquiries into mechanisms for controlling the price of grains. They framed the text as 'a solemn warning from [Burke's] grave', and identified the lingering effect of his argument in the 'excellent frame of mind [prevailing] in Government, in Parliament, and among the people' following the disastrous harvest of 1799: there was little talk of government intervention on grain supply and grain prices, and 'Little or no popular declamation was heard on the miseries of "the labouring poor"'.[20]

In a political context that saw Whig commentators strive to draw a clear line between Smithian political economy and the French Revolution's egalitarian agenda, *Thoughts and Details* was therefore presented as a Smith-inspired argument against government intervention on prices and wages, and subsequently came to be seen as a foundational text for early nineteenth-century conceptualisations of poverty.[21] Burke's enduring reputation as a 'blind defender of the interests of the landed aristocracy at the expense of the impoverished' owes much to his striking redefinition of the word 'poor', which is highlighted as 'the most significant part of his essay'.[22] It is worth noting that Burke reiterated the same point two years later, in his *Third Letter on Regicide Peace* (1797):

> the vigorous and laborious class of life has lately got from the bon ton of the humanity of this day, the name of the 'labouring poor.' ... This pulling jargon is not as innocent as it is foolish. ... Hitherto the name of poor (in the sense in which it is used to excite compassion) has not been used for those who can, but for those who cannot, labour ... when we affect to pity, as poor, those who must labour or the world cannot exist, we are trifling with the condition of mankind.[23]

Burke's striking critique of the expression 'labouring poor' has been interpreted in a few different ways. One of the earliest scholars to highlight its significance was the conservative historian Gertrude Himmelfarb, in her study of the idea of poverty in early industrial England. Himmelfarb argued that Burke's immediate target was the Speenhamland system, which extended wage support to all labourers – but beyond this, she suggested that Burke's wider target was the Elizabethan Poor Laws, which had always considered the 'labouring poor' as falling under their purview.[24] Richard Bourke and Gregory Collins have both disputed this account, and argued that Burke's outburst should be read in the context of the French Revolution and 1790s British radicalism: Burke, they argue, analysed the use of the phrase 'labouring poor' as a rhetorical move which provided coded support to Jacobin ideology, and became part of a broader argument for the sort of wealth redistribution agenda he abhorred. This is certainly convincing: the phrase was indeed adopted by the radical press in the mid-1790s, and it seems unlikely that the French Revolution would have been far from Burke's mind at the time.[25] Burke scholars, however, have tended to accept Burke's linguistic analysis of the term 'labouring poor', and his assertion that it represented a 'new idiom' or 'new coinage', contradicting the supposedly traditional understanding of the 'poor' as 'the indigents who were incapable of labour'.[26]

In fact, as already noted by Himmelfarb in the 1980s, it was not the radical sympathisers of the French Revolution who were 'proposing a radical change in conventional usage', but rather Burke himself.[27] The Elizabethan Poor Laws, she pointed out, 'had used the word "poor" precisely in the generic sense Burke deplored, the sense of the "laboring poor" ... Even those reformers who sought to make relief to the able-bodied available only in the workhouse did not presume to exclude the able-bodied from the mandate of the poor laws.'[28] Her contention is therefore that it was Burke – not the radicals – who was introducing a new distinction, by distinguishing sharply between 'labouring' and 'non-labouring' poor, and excluding the former from the broad category of 'the poor'.

Himmelfarb was certainly correct in her analysis of eighteenth-century usage. The expression 'the poor' did normally include the working or labouring poor, and Burke himself can be found to use the word 'poor' in this broad way, as can many other authors throughout the eighteenth century.[29] Yet Burke was also correct to point out that, in practice, the term 'labouring poor' had recently been increasingly used in a strategic manner for party politics purposes, to imply that many labouring people could not afford bread, to highlight the privileges of the rich, to argue for subsidising the price of provisions and for wealth redistribution, and to plead for an end to the war against France.

Regardless of its linguistic accuracy, Burke's argument about the 'labouring poor' has important ramifications. The conceptual (if not linguistic) distinction made in *Thoughts and Details* would eventually become prevalent in the early nineteenth century, and would play a large role in the movement to reform the poor laws, leading to the New Poor Law of 1834 which distinguished between the 'impotent' poor unable to support themselves because they couldn't work, and the 'able-bodied' poor who needed to be disincentivised from relief and pushed towards work. This is why Burke's indictment of the 'political cant' language of the 'labouring poor' has usually been interpreted as announcing an important shift – as an indictment of the Elizabethan Poor Laws devised in reaction to the new egalitarian discourses inspired by the French Revolution, and as a precursor to nineteenth-century ideas about poverty and welfare. But as we will now see, Burke was in fact building upon a century-long discussion about the 'labouring poor': his indictment of the 'labouring poor' was not only the starting point of a nineteenth-century debate about welfare, but also the end point of an Enlightenment discussion about the labouring poor, commercial society and the role of the state.

The emergence of the 'labouring poor'

To any contemporary reader of Burke's 1790s writings, it would have been obvious that his claim about the recent emergence of the term 'labouring poor' was not meant to be taken at face value. The expression has been claimed to date back to Tudor England, when the medieval emphasis on Christ's exaltation of the poor and on the duty of charity was being slowly phased out in favour of a new view of the poor as naturally idle and therefore 'culpable', and as Elizabethan legislation attempted to determine who deserved government assistance by drawing distinctions between 'deserving' and 'undeserving' poor.[30] While still comparatively rare, the phrase (alongside the less frequent 'labourious poor', 'labouring poor men' and 'working poor') was certainly in regular use throughout the eighteenth century, before its adoption by radicals in the revolutionary decade.

One notable early adopter of the expression 'labouring poor' was the Irish pamphleteer Daniel Defoe, who used it in almost a dozen different essays in the late seventeenth and early eighteenth centuries. In these essays Defoe criticised several of the workhouse experiments developed in the late seventeenth century to limit parishes' spending on outdoor relief. Workhouses, he argued, were not the best way to 'for ever Banish Beggery and Poverty out of the Kingdom'.[31] Instead he put forward 'rational proposals for the more effectual cure of this grand disease [poverty]': poverty had two main causes, 'natural or accidental impotence as to labour', and idleness. It was the latter that Defoe proposed to tackle. In *Giving Alms no Charity* (1704) he bemoaned 'a general Taint of Slothfulness upon our Poor', who worked only to earn enough money to 'then go and be idle, or perhaps drunk, till 'tis all gone'. In other words, the 'labouring poor' were only poor because they chose to limit their own labour: "'Tis the men that *won't work*, not the men that *can get no work*, which makes the numbers of our poor. ... I can give an incredible number of Examples in my own Knowledge among our Labouring Poor.'[32]

Defoe was writing at a time when the idea that the able-bodied poor should be denied economic support in order to incentivise them to work was gaining traction: in 1680, Louis XIV's minister Jean-Baptiste Colbert wrote to local *intendants* that 'nothing encourages laziness like public charity', and encouraged religious orders to put charity recipients to work, because 'nothing is so damaging to the state as the beggary of able-bodied poor who are able to work'.[33] In turn, the approach was theorised by eighteenth-century political economy, most famously by Bernard Mandeville. One notable feature of his 1714 *Fable of the Bees* was its treatment of poverty: far from considering the poor as a separate category that would display uniquely corrupt or deficient morals, Mandeville argued that the tendency to laziness was a universal feature of humankind. Therefore, charity always incentivised idleness rather than work. In Mandeville's mercantilist understanding of the wealth of nations, this represented a major challenge: England was wealthy because the labour of its low-paid workers made it competitive on the international stage. Indeed, 'the surest Wealth consists in a Multitude of laborious Poor ... the Bulk of the Nation [should] every where consist of Labouring Poor that are unacquainted with anything but their work'.[34] Therefore, he argued, there was an economic need for the 'bulk of the people' not only to be working, but also to be kept in poverty. This could be achieved through low wages or high taxation, in order to counterbalance humankind's natural laziness and incentivise the poor to work: 'I have laid down as Maxims never to be departed from, that the Poor should be kept strictly to Work, and that it was Prudence to relieve their Wants, but Folly to cure them.'[35]

Later dubbed the 'utility of poverty' thesis, Mandeville's argument soon became commonplace in eighteenth-century economic discourse.[36] Among many examples, it is found later in the century in Young's 1771 assertion that 'everyone but an idiot knows that the lower classes must be kept poor or they will never be industrious', or Joseph Townsend 1786 view that 'in proportion as you advance the wages of the poor, you diminish the quantity of their work'.[37] It was particularly associated with mercantilist writers: as national wealth was understood to be dependent upon manufacturing exports, it was also dependent upon low-paid labour by the poor.

The logical consequence of Mandeville's 'utility of poverty' argument was that the duty of the state was not to feed the poor, but rather to keep them at work. This was the argument made by Jean-François Melon in his 1734 *Essai politique sur le commerce*. Melon distinguished between individual charity, and the duty of the state, which was to provide work: 'charitable men give alms, statesmen give work'.[38] Rousseau took a similar line in his 1755 *Discours sur l'économie politique*.[39]

By the mid-eighteenth century, the 'labouring poor' was therefore a well-established category of analysis – most often on the understanding that poor labourers lived on a continuum from destitution to relative comfort, depending on their ability and willingness to find work. There was, in any case, no suggestion that the category of the 'poor' did not include many low-paid working people. One feature shared by these accounts was a common understanding of poverty in terms of a lack of wealth or income: to be poor was to have barely enough (or not enough) to purchase the basic necessities of life. It is Montesquieu, as we are about to see, who broke decisively with this approach.

Montesquieu on the 'labouring poor'

While undoubtedly successful, the 'utility of poverty' doctrine also had its opponents. Against mercantile principles, the London-based political economist Jacob Vanderlint argued in 1734 that low wages depressed consumption, and that 'the working people can and will do a great deal more work than they do, if they were sufficiently encouraged [by higher wages]'.[40] Along similar lines, George Berkeley believed that 'the creating of wants' was 'the likeliest way to produce industry in people'.[41] The same argument was picked up by Montesquieu in Book XIII of *Spirit of the Laws*: 'It is ease of speaking and inability to examine that have caused it to be said that … the more one is burdened with imposts, the more one puts oneself in a position to pay them: two sophisms that have always ruined and will forever ruin monarchies.'[42]

But Montesquieu's 1748 *Spirit of the Laws* also put forward a highly innovative discussion of poverty.[43] Like Mandeville, Montesquieu considered human nature to be universally uniform, and laziness to be a natural inclination of humankind. Laziness developed either as the consequence of climate ('the bad effects of the climate, that is, natural laziness'),[44] or of bad government ('Because the laws were badly made, lazy men appeared').[45] Widespread, structural poverty was similarly described as being linked to the species of government, whether despotic regimes or virtuous republics.

Montesquieu, however, broke with Mandeville, and with traditional discourse about poverty, in his explicit rejection of the category of the 'labouring poor'. He did so by tying poverty directly to work, thus distinguishing between the 'poor' who don't work and need charity, and the common people who work for wages. In his account the 'labouring poor' therefore became an oxymoron:

> A man is not poor because he has nothing, but because he does not work. The one who has no goods and who works is as comfortable as the one who has a hundred ecus of revenue without working. Whoever has nothing and has a craft is no poorer than he who has ten arpents of land of his own and who has to work them to continue to exist. The worker who has given his art to his children for an inheritance has left them a good which multiplies in proportion to their number. It is not the same for the one who has ten arpents of land to live on and divides them among his children.[46]

This represented a striking break with previous definitions of poverty. From Ancient Greece to early modern Europe, the poor had usually been defined as those 'without income from property or profession and, therefore, dependent upon their manual labour for living': poverty was 'the harsh compulsion to toil'.[47] Montesquieu turned this definition on its head: the poor, he insisted, were not those who depended upon their manual labour for subsistence, but rather those who did not work. Those who work, Montesquieu explained, cannot be 'poor', because they possess – at the very least – their ability to work, maybe even specific skills. This is, in some ways, more valuable than money because it can be passed on to the next generation without splitting its value. Here, Montesquieu's argument about individual wealth and poverty was directly reflecting his critique of mercantilism as a zero-sum game played between nations, where wealth consisted in the accumulation of bullion: the formation of wealth, he countered, was a dynamic process of interdependent growth spurred on by industry and commerce – citing the colonial riches of Spain as a counter example, he explained it to be 'a bad kind of wealth … which does not depend on the industry of the nation, the number of inhabitants, nor the cultivation of the earth'.[48]

Montesquieu's critique of mercantilism and praise of free trade would only be amplified in the second half of the century, most notably by Adam Smith – but also by Burke.[49] His reframing of the concept of poverty also finds obvious echoes in Burke's infamous claim, half a century later, that 'those who labour [are] miscalled the Poor'.[50] Yet Montesquieu and Burke drew starkly different conclusions from this shared conceptual premise. Montesquieu, indeed, was far from suggesting that the labouring poor should be left to their own devices, or that they were the remit of individual charity: rather, he concluded, it was the state's duty to manage its affairs well enough that all able-bodied people would be able to earn a living wage. Here Montesquieu drew an important distinction between 'particular' poverty as an individual phenomenon, and 'general' poverty as the structural outcome of the poverty of a country. Only the former, he explained, was compatible with the existence of commercial monarchies: 'republics end in luxury; monarchies, in poverty'.[51]

The duty of the state, he explained, was therefore less to provide relief for 'particular' poverty, than it was to establish good government that would eradicates 'general poverty' by increasing the national riches and providing work for everyone.

> A few alms given to a naked man in the streets does not fulfil the obligations of the state, which owes all the citizens an assured sustenance, nourishment, suitable clothing, and a kind of life which is not contrary to health.[52]

Montesquieu's analysis of poverty as a problem to be solved not by welfare schemes, but rather by the good administration of the state which would eradicate structural poverty by increasing the wealth of the nation, would most famously be developed by Smith. Yet, Montesquieu acknowledged, even good administration would never fully eradicate 'particular poverty':

there would always be people physically unable to work, and there would always be at least some workers in need of temporary relief. For these particular cases, he suggested that it was indeed the state's duty to prevent sufferings and provide relief. This left him arguing that government relief was necessary, but that it was best applied when the state is already well administered ('*bien policé*').[53] Montesquieu does not say 'I shall make my empire so rich that it will not need poorhouses', but rather 'I shall begin by making my empire rich, and I shall build poorhouses'.[54]

At its core, Montesquieu's redefinition of poverty should therefore be read as a critique of the mercantilist 'utility of poverty' theories that recommended maintaining the 'labouring poor' in poverty, in order to incentivise work. Instead, he suggested that prosperity should be diffused through all the ranks, from the poor to the wealthy, with real but limited inequalities.[55] This was best encouraged by the spirit of commerce characteristic of wealthy commercial monarchies, which 'brings with it the spirit of frugality, economy, moderation, work, wisdom, tranquillity, order, and rule'.[56] Fostering this 'spirit of commerce' was the real structural answer to laziness, which cannot be eradicated by either charity or governmental management policies such as workhouses: 'The effect of the wealth of a country is to fill all hearts with ambition; the effects of poverty is to bring them to despair. Ambition is excited by work; poverty is consoled by laziness.'[57] As we will see, Montesquieu's argument was to have a long afterlife in the second half of the eighteenth century.

The 'labouring poor' in mid-eighteenth-century Britain

By mid-century, a new economic landscape was beginning to take shape. Britain was experiencing both impressive commercial growth, and significant popular economic distress, due to unemployment, high food prices and the effect of enclosures. As a result, in the concluding decades of the century 'the laboring poor represented the majority of both internal migrants and poor relief recipients'.[58] It is therefore not surprising that Montesquieu's theorisation of poverty as lack of work should not have found immediate echoes in Britain: if anything, the expression 'labouring poor' was used more frequently in the second half of the century.[59] The list of works using the expression in the mid to late eighteenth century is a lengthy one: it includes literary works such as Richardson's *Clarissa* (1748), which reminded its readers that charity should be directed to 'the honest, industrious, labouring Poor, when sickness, lameness, unforeseen losses, or other accidents, disable them from following their lawful calling'.[60] It also includes economic and political texts, such as Josiah Tucker's *Elements of Commerce* (1755) and Richard Price's *Observations on reversionary payments* (1772). Smith used the expression frequently in the 1776 *Wealth of Nations*, referring to 'the labouring poor' as shorthand for 'the great body of the people': the 'scanty maintenance of the labouring poor', he argued, was a 'natural symptom' of economic stagnation, while increasing national wealth ensured 'the liberal reward of labour'.[61] The expression was also adopted by a number of Scottish writers including Henry Home, Lord Kames, George Chalmers and the radical William Ogilvie. It is worth noting that it was not specifically associated with radical discourse: it is found, for example, in Joseph Townsend's 1786 *A Dissertation on the Poor Law*, which built upon traditional moral critiques of poverty to berate the 'labouring poor' for their poor lack ethic and lack of frugality. As the 'labouring poor' came into sharper focus in the second half of the century, so did emerging critiques of the Mandevillian approach. This has usually been associated with Adam Smith: the *Wealth of Nations* is widely viewed as a landmark challenge for utility-of-poverty approaches.[62] The most effective incentive to effort, Smith argued, was not external constraint, but rather 'The natural effort of every individual to better his own condition, [which] is so powerful a principle, that it is alone, and without any assistance, [capable] of carrying on the society to wealth and prosperity.'[63] Like Montesquieu, Smith was therefore arguing that there was no need to keep ordinary working people in poverty – quite the contrary, since individual prosperity was a driving factor of national commercial prosperity. Consequently, Smith advocated high wages, and argued that it was both the duty and the interest of the state to protect the interests of wage earners through legislation that allowed for fair wages covering essential needs.

Smith's argument has been highlighted as a decisive break in eighteenth-century views of poverty, as his 'optimistic' approach to poverty opened the way to seeing the end of poverty 'as a goal of development, rather than a threat to it'.[64] But it also illustrates a broader trend, as per Tim Hochstrasser's contribution to this volume in Chapter 1, towards a conception of 'welfare' as 'a project of collective utility focused on making the state and its working population as efficient, healthy and productive as possible', which would see the poor 'integrated into society as productive members rather than stigmatised by exclusion.'[65] Indeed, Smith's position grew out of a wide array of anti-Mandevillian arguments dating back at least to Montesquieu. Since the publication of *Spirit of the Laws*, several writers had also argued that the increasing wealth of European (or at least of the English) nation was eradicating exactly the type of 'general poverty' Montesquieu had been hoping to make redundant. As outlined in Arnault Skornicki's Chapter 2, in the 1760s the French physiocrats were arguing for a 'protective and *bienfaisant* authority' that would motivate rather than coerce the poor to provide for their own needs – their master Quesnay denouncing the 'maxims of those ferocious men who pretend that the lower ranks must be reduced to poverty, so that they must work ... All men look to comfort and wealth, and they are never lazy when these are attainable: their laziness only reflects their powerlessness, and their powerlessness is the consequence of [bad] government.'[66]

In England, debates about poverty flared up in the 1760s, in the wake of rising food prices. Benjamin Franklin, an admirer of 'the great Montesquieu' who had been settled in London since 1757 as an envoy of the Pennsylvania Assembly, witnessed the growing unrest that followed the disappointing wheat crop of 1766.[67] In an anonymous letter published in the *Morning Chronicle*, he argued for the respect of free-market principles that would allow farmers to benefit from the situation by setting higher prices: calls to forbid exports, or to regulate prices, would not serve the poor's best interest in the long run:

> I think the best way of doing good to the poor, is not making them easy *in* poverty, but leading or driving them *out* of it. In my youth I travelled much, and I observed in different countries, that the more public provisions were made for the poor, the less they provided for themselves, and of course became poorer. Repeal that law, and you will soon see a change in their manners. St. Monday, and St. Tuesday, will cease to be holidays.[68]

Franklin pushed his anti-Mandevillian argument further in a follow-up article entitled 'On the Laboring Poor', published in the *Gentleman's Magazine* in 1768. The article opened with a sentence that could have been written by Burke in 1795: 'I have met with much invective in the papers for these two years past, against the hard-heartedness of the rich, and much complaint of the great oppressions suffered in this country by the labouring poor.'[69] These complaints, Franklin argued, were misguided. For one thing, he pointed out, 'the condition of the poor here is by far the best in Europe' and was still improved by the 'many laws for the support of our labouring poor, made by the rich, and continued at their expence'.[70]

Franklin was not alone in arguing that Britain was on the way to eliminating the structural or 'general' poverty identified by Montesquieu. One of the writers who most enthusiastically embraced the expression 'labouring poor' in the mid to late eighteenth century was Burke's friend Arthur Young, a careful reader of Franklin, who used it repeatedly in several works published between 1767 and 1780. His early use of the expression was strongly tinted by the mercantilist theories that linked the labouring poor to the wealth of nations: 'It is agreed, by the most sensible politicians, that the true riches of any state consists in the employment of the labouring poor; and all countries will flourish in proportion to the quantity and value of their labour.'[71] However, he also hinted at a substantial difference in outlook when he cautioned that the term 'labouring poor' did not necessarily imply low standards of living:

> Whenever therefore, the terms of 'labouring poor' are used, we should always understand the average of families ... the prices of the *necessaries of life* are by no means so high, that the industrious cannot only live, but live well.[72]

He added that 'the labouring poor, in general, earn *now* sufficient to live decently cloathed, and in good health; some, I know, are not able, but such their parish assists'.[73]

Young's call to caution when using the term 'labouring poor' soon gave way to a much starker argument: in his 1770 *Six Months Tour through the North of England*, he presented cost of living data based on the price of staple expenses, which led him to state that 'the labouring poor in this kingdom are by no means severely burthened in any of these articles of expence'.[74] 'The *labouring poor*', he went on, 'is a term that none but the most superficial of reasoners can use; it is a term that means nothing.'[75]

Young's stern assertion immediately calls to mind Burke's similar outburst, more than two decades later. But it also calls to mind Montesquieu's striking redefinition of poverty as the state of 'the man who does not work': in Young's statistical account, Britain's economy ensures living wages for all who work. Therefore, only those who do *not* work can properly be called 'poor', and the 'labouring poor' is an oxymoron. In another 1770 work, which argued, along the same lines as Franklin, for the free export of grain, Young therefore argued that poverty was the direct product of either inability or unwillingness to work. 'It is a fact well known through all the manufacturing towns of this kingdom, that the labouring poor work no more days in a week than are sufficient to maintain themselves: the remainder is spent in idleness.'[76] The price of staple goods, Young asserted again in 1772, were in themselves low enough to maintain the 'labouring poor' in comfortable circumstances, as long as they were willing to increase their labour: 'Provisions certainly may rise to such a height all over the kingdom, that the labouring poor must work six days in the week to be able to live, and even good hours every day. That is precisely the proper height of prices.'[77]

This was an almost exact reformulation of Franklin's argument about 'Saint Monday'. Britain, Young argued, had reached the precise level of prosperity identified by Montesquieu as the mark of a country that had eliminated 'general' poverty. Wages were sufficiently high to ensure decent living standards to those who were able and willing to work, and therefore only relief for 'particular' poverty – the old, the sick, the momentarily unemployed – should be required. This was, in effect, a defence of free-market mechanisms and commercial prosperity as the solution to structural poverty – a position very similar to that of Smith, who had argued in his

Theory of Moral Sentiments that in modern commercial monarchies, 'The wages of the meanest labourer ... afford him food and clothing, the comfort of a house, and of a family.'[78] A few years later the *Wealth of Nation* made the same point again: 'In Great Britain the wages of labour seem, in the present times, to be evidently more than what is precisely necessary to enable the labourer to bring up a family', and that the 'labouring poor ... [were] much more at their ease now' than in previous centuries.[79] This was also a position argued at some length by Burke in his *Thoughts and Details*.

Montesquieu, Smith and Burke therefore agreed on several fundamental points: they all opposed the then-widespread Mandevillian 'utility of poverty' thesis and understood poverty as a societal problem that could be solved structurally by a general increase in commercial prosperity, which raised living standards for the mass of the population. Here Smith departed from Montesquieu and Burke, by taking the logic of the argument in a different direction: the labouring poor, he agreed, were no longer 'poor' in the absolute sense of 'economic destitution', but they were poor, he argued, in a social and relative sense. Perhaps this emphasis explains his apparent lack of interest about state assistance to the poor, in contrast with Montesquieu's argument that poor relief formed part of the state's duty. As for Burke, he took Montesquieu's redefinition of poverty in a direction which Montesquieu never intended, drawing entirely different policy conclusions in his explicit preference for individual Christian charity to relieve 'particular' poverty.

Conclusion: Burke's intervention in eighteenth-century context

In the 1780s, and more so in the 1790s, the phrase 'labouring poor' came to be used more frequently by reformists – including John Wilkes, William Ogilvie, Joseph Priestley, Mary Wollestonecraft and more. When Burke characterised it as new 'political cant' in 1795, he was referring to its increasing popularity in the reformist press – and he was correct, in the sense that radicals did adopt the expression in support of their political agenda. Yet, as this chapter has demonstrated, the 'labouring poor' had in fact been extensively discussed throughout the eighteenth century.

Burke's rhetorical move against the 'labouring poor' in the 1790s has received significant scholarly attention for its provocative formulation, and for arguably signalling a shift towards the debates that would inform the New Poor Laws. But Burke's argument had not emerged, fully formed, out of the revolutionary debate. Views of the poor had shifted significantly from the seventeenth century onward, from religious outlook to moral critique, to 'utility of poverty' theories that remained widespread at the end of the eighteenth century. At the same time, concerns mounted about rising poverty levels and the effect of cyclical economic downturns. It is within this broader context that arguments about the 'labouring poor' were developed: these initially closely paralleled traditional moral critiques of poverty, and later, the mercantilist 'utility of poverty' reasonings popularised by Mandeville.

The real conceptual break was effected not by Burke, but rather by Montesquieu, whose redefinition of poverty as the absence of work effectively made the existence of the labouring poor a logical impossibility. Montesquieu's primary aim was to challenge the Mandevillian argument about the necessity of a large supply of 'labouring poor', by showing that structural poverty should not exist in a well-run commercial society. His argument was to be taken in two different directions: in Adam Smith's interpretation, the central point was that commercial states had a duty to incentivise individual industry by establishing opportunities for decently paid work. The *Spirit of the Laws* provided all the ingredients not only for a repudiation of the mercantilist doctrine of the 'utility of poverty', but also for the idea, usually associated with the French Revolution era, that widespread poverty was not a natural, inevitable or necessary fact, but rather a feature of pre-modern societies that could and should be eradicated in prosperous commercial societies.

But conceptually reframing poverty as the absence of work could also provide the basis for a different type of argument. Burke took the premise in an entirely different direction to Montesquieu and Smith, to argue that only the non-working poor should be entitled to relief or charity. In this very specific sense, Montesquieu's redefinition, combined with a Mandevillian logic of incentivisation to work, did unwittingly provide some of the ingredients for the poor laws of the nineteenth century.

To return to Burke's infamous 1790s outburst against the 'labouring poor' as fashionable 'political cant': while it should undoubtedly be read in the context of the French Revolution, it can therefore equally be analysed as the tail end of a century-long Enlightened debate about poverty, in which Montesquieu played a seminal role. While Smith is rightfully identified as a central figure who inspired both the post-revolutionary radical agenda for eradicating poverty, and a harsh free-market approach to managing the poor, Montesquieu can also be recast as a central figure in Enlightenment views of poverty, whose heritage was contested by both Smith and Burke.

Notes

1 Gareth Stedman Jones, *An End to Poverty? A Historical Debate* (London: Profile Books, 2004), Ch. 2.

2 Samuel Fleischacker, *A Short History of Distributive Justice* (London: Harvard University Press, 2005), p. 84.
3 Alexander Schmidt, 'The Enlightenment Origins of the Democratic Welfare State', in *A Cultural History of Democracy in the Age of Enlightenment*, ed. M. Mosher and A. Plassart (London: Bloomsbury, 2021), pp. 87–107 at p. 90. See also Emma Rothschild, *Economic Sentiments: Adam Smith, Condorcet and the Enlightenment* (London: Harvard University Press, 2001) and Fleischacker, *A Short History of Distributive Justice*.
4 Jennifer Pitts, *A Turn to Empire: The Rise of Imperial Liberalism in Britain and France* (Princeton, NJ: Princeton University Press, 2006), p. 62.
5 Stedman Jones, *An End to Poverty*, p. 10.
6 Edmund Burke, *Thoughts and Details on Scarcity, Originally Presented to the Right Hon. William Pitt, in the Month of November, 1795* (London, 1800), pp. 2–3.
7 Gertrude Himmelfarb, *The Idea of Poverty* (London: Faber and Faber, 1984), p. 68.
8 See Tim Hochstrasser's Chapter 1 in this volume.
9 Bernard Harris, *The Origins of the British Welfare State: Social Welfare in England and Wales, 1800–1945* (Basingstoke: Palgrave Macmillan, 2004).
10 Geoffrey Gilbert, 'Adam Smith on the Nature and Causes of Poverty', *Review of Social Economy*, 55:3 (1997), 273–291.
11 Donald Winch, 'Poverty and Pauperism: From Smith to Malthus', *Kumamoto Journal of Economics*, 3:4 (1998), 1–15 at 1.
12 See, for example, Winch, 'Poverty and Pauperism'; Richard Bourke, *Empire and Revolution: The Political Life of Edmund Burke* (Princeton, NJ: Princeton University Press, 2015); Stedman Jones, *An End to Poverty*.
13 Stedman Jones, *An End to Poverty*, p. 10.
14 Burke to Pitt, 7 Nov. 1795, in *The Correspondence of Edmund Burke*, 10 vols, ed. R. B. McDowell (Cambridge: Cambridge University Press, 1969), vol. viii, pp. 337–338.
15 Parliamentary History XXXII, col. 142. Cited in Bourke, *Empire and Revolution*, p. 887.
16 Burke, *Scarcity*, pp. 2–3.
17 Ibid., p. xi.
18 Geoffrey M. Collins, *Commerce and Manners in Edmund Burke's Political Economy* (Cambridge: Cambridge University Press, 2020), p. 42.
19 Burke, *Thoughts and Details*, p. x.
20 Ibid., p. xii.
21 On Smith, see Emma Rothschild, 'Adam Smith and Conservative Economics', *The Economic History Review*, 45:1 (1992), 74–96; Stedman Jones, *An End to Poverty*.
22 Himmelfarb, *The Idea of Poverty*; Collins, *Commerce and Manners*, p. 108.
23 Edmund Burke, *A Third Letter to a Member of the present Parliament, on the Proposals for Peace with the Regicide Directory of France* (London, 1797), p. 109.

24 Himmelfarb, *The Idea of Poverty*, p. 69.
25 Bourke, *Empire and Revolution*, p. 891.
26 Ibid. Gregory Collins provides a nuanced interpretation. He argues that Burke aimed to 'challenge the public tendency in the late eighteenth century to indiscriminately expand the definition of the "labouring poor" beyond the conceptual integrity of its traditional understanding'. It is debatable, however, whether such 'conceptual integrity' ever existed in the first place, or whether Burke's aim in his critique of the phrase 'labouring poor', was truly 'clarifying its meaning'. Collins, *Commerce and Manners*, p. 94.
27 Himmelfarb, *The Idea of Poverty*, p. 71.
28 Ibid., p. 69.
29 See, for example, in *Vindication of Natural Society*: 'The poor by their excessive labour, and the rich by their enormous luxury, are set upon a level, and rendered equally ignorant of any knowledge which might conduce to their happiness.' Burke, *Writings and Speeches*, vol. i, p. 180.
30 On this subject, see M. K. McIntosh, 'Poverty, Charity, and Coercion in Elizabethan England', *The Journal of Interdisciplinary History*, 53:3 (2005), 457–479; Paul Slack, *Poverty and Policy in Tudor and Stuart England, Themes in British Social History* (London: Longman, 1988). See also E. Royston Pike, *Human Documents of Adam Smith's Time* (London: George Allen & Unwin, 1974), p. 154. In any case, the expression was certainly in use by the late seventeenth century – for example in a 1678 pamphlet proposing to 'set up Manufacture for the labouring Poor [and] provide Maintenance for the Impotent'. M. L. D. D., *Proposals to the King and Parliament* (London, 1678), p. 26.
31 Daniel Defoe, *Essays upon Several Projects: Or, Effectual Ways for Advancing the Interest of the Nation* (London, 1702), p. 171.
32 Daniel Defoe, *Giving Alms No Charity, And Employing the Poor A Grievance to the Nation* (London, 1704), p. 7.
33 Jean-Baptiste Colbert, 'Lettre de Jean-Baptiste Colbert (Contrôleur Général des Finances) à René de Marillac (Intendant de Poitiers) datée du 28 Novembre 1680, à Versailles.', in *Lettres, Instructions et Mémoires de Colbert*, ed. P. Clément, vols (Paris, 1861–73), vol. ii, pp. 714–715 at p. 714.
34 Bernard Mandeville, *The Fable of the Bees: Or, Private Vices Publick Benefits*, ed. F. B. Kaye, 2 vols (Oxford: Oxford University Press, 1924), p. 302.
35 Ibid., p. 248.
36 The same principle was cited, and cautiously endorsed, by Hume. See David Hume, 'Of Taxes', in *Essay Moral, Political, and Literary*, ed. E. F. Miller (Indianapolis, IN: Liberty Fund, 1987), pp. 342–348.
37 Cited in E. P. Thompson, *The Making of the English Working Class* (London: Victor Gollancz, 1963), p. 358; J. Townsend, *A Dissertation on the Poor Laws* (London, 1786), p. 24.
38 Jean-François Melon, *Essai Politique Sur Le Commerce [1734]* (Amsterdam, 1735), p. 114. My translation.
39 Jean-Jacques Rousseau, *Discourse on Political Economy and The Social Contract*, ed. C. Betts (Oxford: Oxford University Press, 1994), p. 25.

40 Jacob Vanderlint, *Money Answers All Things*, printed for T. Cox (London, 1734), p. 122.
41 George Berkeley, *The Querist, Containing Several Queries Proposed to the Consideration of the Public* (London, 1736), p. 3, cited in Cosma Orsi, 'The Political Economy of Inclusion: The Rise and Fall of the Workhouse System', *Journal of the History of Economic Thought*, 39:4 (2017), 453–481 at 80.
42 C. L. de Secondat Montesquieu Baron de, *The Spirit of the Laws*, eds A. Cohler, B. Miller and H. Stone (Cambridge: Cambridge University Press, 1989), p. 434.
43 Catherine Larrère, 'Montesquieu et les pauvres', *Cahiers d'économie Politique*, 59 (2010), 24–43.
44 Montesquieu, *Spirit of the Laws*, p. 237.
45 Ibid., p. 253.
46 Ibid., p. 455.
47 Cited in Orsi, 'The Political Economy of Inclusion', p. 455; Raymond Cowherd, *Political Economists and the English Poor Laws: A Historical Study of the Influence of Classical Economics on the Formation of Social Welfare Policy* (Athens, OH: Ohio University Press, 1977), pp. 1–2. M. I. Finley, *The Ancient Economy* (Berkeley and Los Angeles, CA: University of Chicago Press, 1974), p. 41.
48 Montesquieu, *The Spirit of the Laws*, p. 396.
49 See Collins, *Commerce and Manners*, pp. 211–212.
50 Burke, *Thoughts and Details on Scarcity*, pp. 2–3.
51 Ibid., p. 100.
52 Montesquieu, *The Spirit of the Laws*, p. 455.
53 My translation. '*Bien policé*' is translated as 'with a good police' in the 1989 Cambridge edition. Ibid., p. 455.
54 Ibid.
55 Ibid., p. 48.
56 Ibid.
57 Ibid., p. 214.
58 Orsi, 'The Political Economy of Inclusion', p. 460. See Paul A. Fideler, *Social Welfare in Pre-Industrial England: The Old Poor Law Tradition* (Basingstoke: Palgrave Macmillan, 2006), p. 147.
59 While neither database is comprehensive, both Google NGram and Eighteenth Century Collections Online suggest a rise in usage from the 1760s.
60 Samuel Richardson, *Clarissa. Or, the History of a Young Lady* 8 vols (London, 1751), vol. viii, pp. 110–111.
61 Adam Smith, *An Inquiry into the Nature and Causes of the Wealth of Nations*, R. H. Campbell, A. S. Skinner and W. B. Todd, 2 vols (Indianapolis IN: Liberty Fund, [1776] 1981), vol. I, p. 91. See also David Hume, 'Of Commerce', in ibid., *Essays: Moral, Political, and Literary*, pp. 253–267 at pp. 266–267.
62 Martin Ravallion, *The Idea of Antipoverty Policy*, NBER Working Paper Series, no. w19210 (Cambridge, MA: National Bureau of Economic Research, 2013); Winch, 'Poverty and Pauperism'; Stedman Jones, *End to Poverty?*; Fleischacker, *Short History of Distributive Justice*.

63 Smith, *Wealth of Nations*, vol. i, p. 540.
64 Ravallion, *The Idea of Antipoverty Policy*, p. 15.
65 See Tim Hochstrasser's Chapter 1 in this volume.
66 F. Quesnay, *Oeuvres économiques complètes et autres textes*, eds C. Théré, L. Charles and J.C. Perrot, 2 vols. (Paris: Ined, 2005), vol. i, p. 295. My translation. See Arnault Skornicki's Chapter 2 in this volume.
67 'From Benjamin Franklin to the Comtesse de Golowkin, 1 February 1781', in *The Papers of Benjamin Franklin*, ed. B. B. Oberg (New York and London: Yale University Press, 1998), xxxiv, pp. 331–332; https://founders.archives.gov/documents/Franklin/01-34-02-0247. Accessed 12 May 2022.
68 Benjamin Franklin, '"*Arator*": *On the Price of Corn, and Management of the Poor [29 November 1766]*', 1766, Founders Online, National Archives https://founders.archives.gov/documents/Franklin/01-13-02-0194. Accessed 12 May 2022.
69 Benjamin Franklin, '*On the Laboring Poor [April 1768]*', 1768, Founders Online, National Archives https://founders.archives.gov/documents/Franklin/01-15-02-0064. Accessed 12 May 2022.
70 Burke, *Writings and Speeches of Edmund Burke*, vol. ix, p. 122; Franklin, '*On the Laboring Poor [April 1768]*'.
71 Arthur Young, *The Farmer's Letters to the People of England: Containing the Sentiments of a Practical Husbandman, on Various Subjects of Great Importance* (Dublin, 1768), p. 279. Notably, Young cites Franklin in his discussion of labour and wages. Young, *Political Essays Concerning the Present State of the British Empire*, pp. 235, 271. Burke greatly admired Young's work and corresponded with both him and Franklin.
72 Young, *Farmer's Letters*, p. 208.
73 Ibid., p. 201.
74 Arthur Young, *A Six Months Tour through the North of England: Containing, an Account of the Present State of Agriculture, Manufactures and Population, in Several Counties of This Kingdom [1770]* (London: 1771), p. 289.
75 Ibid., p. 298.
76 Arthur Young, *The Expediency of a Free Exportation of Corn at This Time: With Some Observations on the Bounty, and Its Effects*, Second edition (London, 1770), p. 29.
77 Arthur Young, *Political Essays Concerning the Present State of the British Empire* (London, 1772), p. 220.
78 Adam Smith, *The Theory of Moral Sentiments*, ed. D. D. Raphael and A. L. Macfie (Indianapolis, IN: Liberty Fund, 1982), p. 50.
79 Smith, *Wealth of Nations*, vol. i, p. 91, p. 94.

7

Beyond a charitable design? Robert Wallace as a theorist of poverty and population growth

Conor Bollins

Robert Wallace returned home victorious in 1744. As a minister based in Edinburgh, he had been formally commissioned by the General Assembly of the Church of Scotland to travel to London. Here, he was to convince the Parliament of Great Britain to grant legal status to the first Scottish widows insurance scheme.[1] The scheme offered to provide cover for the widows of members of Scottish universities and churches. Not only had Wallace helped underwrite the scheme, but he also went on to successfully lobby Scottish Members of Parliament to unanimously promote it as a bill in the House of Commons. Much to the delight of the General Assembly, this was then passed into legislation and the fund was established. This was a personal achievement for Wallace, which cemented his reputation among his contemporaries.

Wallace travelled to London alongside George Wishart, who was a friend from his time as a student at the University of Edinburgh. William Grant, a Scottish politician, judge and one-time clerk to the General Assembly, was among those who wrote to Wallace and Wishart to offer congratulations upon the completion of their task.[2] Indeed, Wallace's overall reputation was greatly improved as a result of this endeavour. Many of the collaborators involved with setting up the widows' fund subsequently maintained a strong network of political, academic and religious contacts. For Wallace, however, there was a much more profound significance to their success. Within a few years of his involvement with the scheme, Wallace suggested that the fund could feasibly provide a template for creating social insurance on a national scale. In his wider work, Wallace went as far to envisage a society that sought to eradicate poverty and enjoy a far more equitable distribution of wealth. In fact, he believed that the survival of Scottish society depended on such proposals.

The work of Wallace and his collaborators marked one of the most serious attempts to confront how best to ameliorate national poverty in early eighteenth-century Scotland. Curiously, however, Wallace has rarely been the subject of focused scholarly attention. Nicholas Phillipson, it should be said, identified Wallace as having belonged to the circle of intellectuals responsible for the development of a culture of improvement that came to characterise what has become known as the Scottish Enlightenment. For Phillipson, Wallace's generation established the institutional and cultural style of discussing the improvement of Scottish society that paved the way for the intellectual breakthroughs of the period between the 1750s and the 1770s.[3] For John Robertson, in Scotland and elsewhere, the Enlightenment was chiefly defined by an interest in securing human betterment in the material world, and one of the ways that this manifested itself was through the emergence of political economy as a field of enquiry.[4] Returning to Wallace provides an interesting case study in not only how Scotland's culture of improvement linked to broader Enlightenment currents of thought, but also concrete policy proposals. Moreover, as I shall argue, Wallace's work was concerned with tackling the specific, immediate and concrete issue of poverty rather than economic improvement or human betterment in a more general or abstract sense. Therefore, revisiting Wallace may even reinvite a reappraisal of how poverty was itself conceptualised in the eighteenth century.

Although there is very little detailed scholarship on Wallace, there has always persisted a vague sense that there was a significance to his debate with David Hume about the populousness of the ancient world.[5] In a paper delivered to the Edinburgh Philosophical Society, Wallace argued that the ancient world had enjoyed a vaster human population than existed in the present. Against this, Hume contended that the world had become more densely populated since antiquity.[6] Ultimately, Wallace feared that the world was suffering from extensive population decline and that this represented widespread ruination. For Wallace, as I shall show, poverty was fuelling this level of depopulation. Due to the fact that Europe actually went on to experience an increase in population growth that has more or less continued to the present day, and because of the nineteenth-century interest in overpopulation, earlier fears about depopulation have come to be seen as antiquated, inaccurate or even bizarre to subsequent generations of historians.[7] Wallace's work has been largely neglected for this reason. Increasing population growth and reducing poverty were the two most central, interlinked themes of Wallace's work. Taking Wallace's fears about depopulation seriously provides the key to understanding his broader political and theoretical aims. This chapter will explore how Wallace's desire to see an increase in population growth correlated to his attitude towards poverty. This will require a contextualisation of Wallace's work in relation to the social and economic context of early to mid eighteenth-century Scotland. I will focus on Wallace's major projects of the 1740s to illustrate his solutions to depopulation and poverty. I hope for this to offer a fresh perspective on the importance of Wallace's contribution to Scottish Enlightenment debates about poverty.

Wallace had interests in politics, mathematics, history and theology. As a divinity student, he had been involved with setting up an informal society known as the Rankenian Club. This group was founded in around 1717 and based in Edinburgh, where Wallace later became a minister. Members of the Rankenian Club had a stake in the Calvinist theological debate over whether charity provided a stronger bond between Christians than agreement on particular points of doctrine.[8] Wallace became involved in the management of the General Assembly of the Presbyterian Kirk of Scotland, from around 1742 until 1746. This was only shortly after the Porteous Affair of 1736 to 1738, which had seen many Kirk ministers refuse to comply with a statute requiring them to condemn the riots of 1736.[9] Nevertheless, in this period, many fellow ministers such as Alexander Webster used their sermons to preach in defence of the recently consecrated Hanoverian regime.[10]

Over the course of his life, many of Wallace's published and unpublished writings addressed how to provide stability to the British polity. Wallace described himself as a Whig. Even into the 1750s, his work regularly included defences of the Glorious Revolution of 1688 as well as the 1707 Acts of Union between England and Scotland. That is not to say that Wallace was uncritical of the Hanoverian regime or its political and constitutional underpinnings. Yet, particularly in the 1740s, he remained acutely aware that the permanence of the regime could not be taken for granted and implied that its implosion would be a disaster. Similarly, Wallace's perspective on any particular state or its government has to be studied alongside his broader position on the depopulation of the modern world. Wallace consistently sought to demonstrate that the social, economic and moral foundations of the entire European state system was responsible for population decline. So, it stood to reason that he hoped to see reforms take place in Britain.

Wallace articulated his ideas about the relationship between population growth, poverty and political stability in his most well-known text. This was his *Dissertation on the Numbers of Mankind in Ancient and Modern Times*. Although published in 1753, it is important to note that this text was first drafted in around 1745. The original manuscript provided the material that Wallace shared with the Edinburgh Philosophical Society as the aforementioned paper. Accurately dating the text is important for a number of historiographical reasons. Chiefly, it establishes that Wallace's *Dissertation* should be read in the context of the turmoil of the 1740s. As I shall show, this helps to explain why Wallace felt that the situation was so dire for Scotland, Britain and even Europe at large.

From the outset, Wallace's *Dissertation* summarised his views on the populousness of the modern world. He proclaimed that: 'in most of those countries whose antient and present state is best known, there have been fewer inhabitants in later ages, are fewer at present, than were in more antient times, and that these countries were better peopled before the Roman empire was established, than they have ever been at any succeeding period'.[11] This verdict echoed sentiments that had been previously expressed by Montesquieu, especially in his *Lettres persanes* of 1721. Although Wallace conceded that 'an opinion in favour of antiquity may be carried too far',[12] he largely subscribed to the conceptual basis of Montesquieu's contention that the ancient world had been more densely populated.[13]

Unlike Montesquieu's, Wallace's history of human population growth took into consideration the 'first peopling of the world'[14] narrated in sacred history. At an early stage in the *Dissertation*, Wallace provided a series of calculations and tables of figures to depict how quickly he estimated human population sizes had grown following the creation of Adam and Eve described in the Book of Genesis, and then after the Flood. In short, these were designed to show that population growth occurred at an exponential rate under optimal conditions. According to Wallace, the ancient world only witnessed depopulation due to the 'mighty change wrought on the world by the conquests of Alexander the Great, and his successors, and afterwards by the Roman Empire'.[15] Thus, it remained for Wallace to investigate the reasons behind this 'mighty change' in the world's total human population.

Wallace contended that these reasons behind the modern world's 'paucity of inhabitants, and [mankind's] irregularity of increase, are manifold'.[16] Essentially, they all coalesced around one central premise. Wallace explained that 'the number of people in every nation depends most immediately on the number and fruitfulness of marriages'.[17] As such, states with conditions that made it easier for people to marry and raise families would have higher populations. Wallace's *Dissertation* explored at great length the theoretical circumstances under which individuals would be most likely to marry. For Wallace, the most significant influences on population growth were 'moral causes, which arise from the passions and vices of men'.[18] These 'moral causes' constituted the variables capable of stimulating population growth that were directly within the control of human societies or their governments.

Wallace looked at a wide variety of supposed moral causes of depopulation. For example, he was very interested in how different religious practices had affected marriage and propagation across regions and throughout history.[19] For the purposes of this chapter, I will focus on the moral cause of depopulation that Wallace was most preoccupied with. Above all, Wallace deemed levels of poverty and access to subsistence good to be the most deciding factor as to why the modern world was less populous than its ancient counterpart. All other things being equal, Wallace argued, then:

> In every country, there shall always be found a greater number of inhabitants [...] in proportion to the plenty of provisions it affords, as plenty will always encourage the generality of people to marry.[20]

This argument presupposed that the most powerful impediment to marriage was related to people's subsistence needs. Put simply, Wallace assumed that individuals afflicted by poverty would be unlikely to marry as they would not believe themselves capable of affording to raise a family. While Wallace had rebuked Montesquieu for being slightly too captivated with an image of an exceptionally densely populated antiquity, he also favoured the notion that the ancient world had been 'more crouded and magnificent'.[21] Primarily, Wallace reasoned, this was because ancient societies had displayed a greater aptitude for meeting the subsistence requirements of their inhabitants.

In practical terms, this meant that ancient societies had been better at both the production and the distribution of subsistence goods. Wallace's fixation on the production of subsistence goods revealed a slight bias towards favouring agriculture over commerce. This was somewhat tempered in Wallace's later work, but he largely remained of the opinion that agricultural production was too low in the modern world. In the *Dissertation*, he stated that, 'to have the greatest possible number of inhabitants in all the world, all mankind should be employed directly in providing food'.[22] Maximising food production would ensure that there was a greater amount of available resources to share amongst a society. Wallace found it self-evident that 'if the lands of any country be neglected, the world in general must suffer'.[23] Furthermore, he maintained that in a world insufficiently geared towards agriculture, 'the earth must contain a smaller number of inhabitants, in proportion to the numbers which might be supported by these uncultivated lands'.[24] Overall, Wallace concluded that the modern world had failed to produce the subsistence goods needed to prompt renewed population growth, and that this failure was international in scope.

Wallace conceded that there were also potential 'physical causes' of depopulation. Certain geographical factors, in other words, could prevent a state from producing subsistence goods at a desirable rate. Conceivably, the forces of nature could even cause 'a fruitful land' to 'become a desart'.[25] Plagues and famines had to be taken into consideration as well. Nevertheless, Wallace did not think that these physical factors could adequately explain the 'phænomenon of so great a decay of people'[26] that he perceived. Hypothetically, societies with strong social, economic and moral foundations should have been able to mitigate against the worst excesses of an injurious geography.

It was not simply a case of producing subsistence goods, however. For there to be population growth, these same goods also had to be adequately shared out among a state's inhabitants. Wallace retained a commitment to advocating equality and redistribution throughout his life. In the *Dissertation*, he set out to defend the 'institutions concerning the division of lands'[27] that had existed in antiquity. Wallace asserted that:

> when any antient nations divided its lands into small shares, and when even eminent citizens had but a few acres to maintain their families, tho' such a nation had but little commerce [...] it must have abounded greatly in people.[28]

Owning farmland enabled families to tend to their own subsistence. It seemed to Wallace that divisions of land into small shares provided security to a greater number of married couples. In turn, this encouraged potential parents to raise children, and therefore contributed to population growth.

To Wallace, the Roman Republic epitomised the 'superior populousness of many ancient nations'.[29] The *Dissertation* portrayed the Roman Republic as a model of excellence whose 'industry, which in ancient times was directed to the provision of food, caused a wonderful plenty'.[30] Wallace conjectured that Rome had been heavily populated because this 'wonderful plenty' had also been equitably distributed. On the other hand, Wallace held the rise of the Roman Empire to be responsible for the collapse of this greatness. Under its excessive, acquisitive emperors, Rome acquired a taste for elegance and riches. Consequently, Wallace argued, Rome's equality and focus on agriculture 'decayed gradually, as luxury and a false taste prevailed'.[31] This led to 'great tracts of land being left uncultivated', such that 'food [...] became scarce and dear'.[32] As a result, the state began to depopulate as 'many would not choose to subject themselves to the incumbrance of a family'.[33] Ultimately, Wallace judged this chain of events to have set the preconditions for the low population growth of the modern world.

It could be said that Wallace's analysis of population growth intersected with the wider eighteenth-century debate on the effects of luxury and commerce on modern society. In fact, Wallace even concluded his *Dissertation* with an attack on Mandeville. In his *The Fable of The Bees: or, Private Vices, Publick Benefits*, published first in 1714 and then again in 1723, Mandeville argued that a flourishing economy built upon the production and consumption of luxuries provided the basis of national power in the modern world.[34] In contrast, Wallace had sought to show that 'the introduction of a corrupted and luxurious taste [...] contributed in a great measure to diminish the numbers of mankind in modern days'.[35] Wallace regarded his work as having demonstrated that a predilection towards agriculture, frugal manners and a great degree of equality could guarantee a high level of population growth. It was this formula, he concluded, which makes the public flourish: and [...] private vices are far from being, what a notable writer has employed the whole force of his genius to demonstrate them to be, public benefits'.[36]

Conversely, Wallace did not necessarily mean that there was no place for commerce and the manufacture of luxuries in a thriving society. He conceded that 'whenever the earth shall happen to be as richly cultivated as is possible, then there will be room for those arts that tend only to ornament'.[37] At the right historical moment when there was a surplus of foodstuffs compared to the population, then it would make sense for certain people to seek alternative forms of employment. While it was true that 'a variety of manufactures diverts the attention of mankind from more necessary labour, and prevents the increase of the people',[38] if there were sufficient amounts of subsistence goods then this would be less of a problem.

Ultimately, however, Wallace concluded his *Dissertation* on a melancholic note. Towards the end of the text, he reiterated that modern Europe faced an urgent depopulation crisis. Wallace then reflected on how there appeared to be 'not even the smallest chance, that there shall be any sudden increase of mankind'.[39] As I have indicated, this alarmed conclusion both echoed sentiments previously expressed by thinkers such as Montesquieu and was presented as a product of an historical investigation. Yet, Wallace was also quite clear that his interest in depopulation intersected with his identity as a private citizen of Scotland. As such, Wallace's concern with poverty and population decline has to be understood in the context of the social, economic and intellectual climate that existed in Scotland between the 1690s and the start of the 1750s.

First and foremost, it is essential to highlight that Scotland's population did in fact decline in this period. This was due to three main reasons. These were famine, war and migration. The stretch of dearth and famine that took place in the last decade of the seventeenth century had lasting effects up until the period that Wallace wrote his *Dissertation*. The famine's origins lay with desperately poor weather, which had always posed a substantial risk to early modern societies predominately built around subsistence farming.[40] The famine became popularly known as King William's 'Seven Ill Years', owing to contemporary comparisons between this occasion of suffering and the seven years of Egyptian blight mentioned in the Book of Genesis. It can be more accurately dated as having started in 1695, in the wake of a deficient harvest.[41] There was also dearth in certain regions prior to this and the impact of the famine was felt long after it subsided in around 1700.[42]

In 1691, it is believed, Scotland's population had been just over 1.23 million.[43] Social and demographic historians now generally agree this figure was drastically reduced by the events of the 1690s. The famine itself caused many deaths due to both starvation and, in particular, disease. It is understood that higher levels of malnourishment left individuals more susceptible to typhus and smallpox, which spread as epidemics. In addition, one can reasonably speculate that nutritional deficiencies also had an adverse effect on fertility, pregnancies and child mortality.[44]

The effects of the famine were compounded by the realities of war. Throughout the reign of William II of Scotland and III of England, Scotland was effectively a strategic frontline state in a much larger European theatre of war.[45] This was due to the ongoing conflict with Louis XIV of France. Scotland was significant because of the threat to the stability of the British state posed by Jacobitism. War also led to an intensification in the use of punishing tariff restrictions by rival nations. The high tariffs imposed by Scotland's more powerful neighbours made it difficult for the smaller and commercially weaker country to export goods.[46]

The economic setbacks caused by international politics exacerbated the fragile conditions of a society beset with famine. It was hoped that the Darien Venture offered a chance to bring prosperity to poverty-stricken Scotland. The plan had been to set up a trading colony on the Isthmus of Panama and the first expeditionary fleet left from Leith in July 1698, with around 1,200 men.[47] No later than October 1700, however, it was confirmed that the colony had been abandoned. It had failed because of poor management, death caused by foreign illnesses and opposition from England as well as Spain. Contemporaries projected that 200,000 Scots, around one in five people, were directly or indirectly financially concerned with the project.[48] It has been estimated that between one-sixth and one-quarter of Scotland's liquid capital was lost due the failure of the Darien Venture.[49]

Together, these conditions impacted levels of migration. Economic hardship created dislocation and encouraged many to seek better prospects elsewhere.[50] As Sir Robert Sibbald observed in his account of the famine, it was not just 'wandering Beggars [...] but many House-keepers, who lived well by their Labour and their Industrie' that were 'now by Want forced to abandon their dwellings'.[51] People also moved overseas to escape the famine. Destinations included the American colonies across the Atlantic and, of course, Darien. Larger numbers even still moved to Ulster in Ireland. It has been argued that Ulster's largest seventeenth-century influx of Scots occurred in the 1690s and not during the earlier Plantation period.[52] Hostilities with the Jacobites caused many Irish tenants to desert their holdings, leaving cheap land available for Scots fleeing the famine. Thus, approximately 50,000 Scots crossed to Ulster in the years between 1690 and 1698. In total, due to migration and increased mortality, up to 15 per cent of Scotland's population was devastated as a result of this period.[53]

Overall, social historians understand that population growth stagnated in Scotland in the century prior to 1750 in a way that it did not in England. This could have been because England was comparatively wealthier, but it is also likely that Scotland's population continued to be affected by the political turmoil of the first half of the eighteenth century.[54] In short, the Jacobite Uprisings continued to have a demographic as well as a political impact on Scotland. Primarily, this would have been due to troop movements. When Stirling had been a centre of activity during the 1715 Rebellion, for example, there was an increase in mortality due to different troops overcrowding the area and spreading unfamiliar infections.[55] Furthermore, poor weather remained a constant problem for Scottish farmers. Between 1738 and 1741, poor harvests prompted danger on a national scale for the first time since the 1690s.[56] This, of course, was only a few years before Wallace first drafted his *Dissertation*.

Addressing this economic backwardness supplied the content of much intellectual discussion in the immediate decades either side of the Acts of Union being passed in 1707. In turn, this provided the impetus for the culture of improvement that took root in cities such as Edinburgh. With the loss of political institutions that the Acts of Union entailed, including the disbanding of the Scottish Parliament, participation in the country's literati and engagement in discussion about how best to improve Scotland's situation provided a new social role for an elite bereft of previous forms of public life.[57] It is within this context that learned societies such as the Rankenian Club to which Wallace belonged were formed.[58] Another notable organisation was the Society of Improvers in the Knowledge of Agriculture founded in 1723. Indeed, it has been noted that the Kirk, University of Edinburgh and these various learned societies or academies acted as an almost interlocking institutional setting for the dissemination of ideas associated with the Scottish Enlightenment.[59] As I have indicated, Wallace's personal network spanned all of these institutions. For the purposes of this chapter, particular attention has to be paid to the Edinburgh Philosophical Society as this was body where Wallace first presented the initial version of his *Dissertation*.

Established around 1737, the Edinburgh Philosophical Society sought to improve the arts and understanding of the natural world. There was a heavy emphasis on the pursuit of new truths through the experimental method and the application of knowledge.[60] Likely, many of its members saw this approach as in keeping with wider efforts to improve Scottish society. Similar organisations across Europe, including the Royal Society of London, acted as model templates. Colin MacLaurin had been the key figure in the establishment of the Edinburgh Philosophical Society. MacLaurin had been a pupil of Isaac Newton's and enjoyed an international reputation as a mathematician.[61] His appointment as Chair of Mathematics at the University of Edinburgh had been an important moment in the institution's history as a result. MacLaurin had been keen to ensure that the Edinburgh Philosophical Society was inclusive of individuals with technological, improving and historical interests as well as figures associated with natural philosophy, mathematics and medicine.[62] It is for this reason that Wallace was able to become a member of the Edinburgh Philosophical Society. In many ways, Wallace's *Dissertation* was in keeping with the society's overarching preoccupations with the search for truth through scholarly enquiry. Above all, as I shall demonstrate, all of Wallace's projects of the 1740s sought to offer practical solutions in line with Scotland's culture of improvement and in response to the country's economic distress. For Wallace, a theoretical interest in the history of human propagation coincided perfectly with a drive to eradicate poverty and increase population growth.

Despite his gloomy predictions about current rates of depopulation, Wallace's *Dissertation* offered at least some solace. In theory, Wallace maintained, the world could physically 'support a much greater number than actually live[d] upon it'.[63] Heavenly forces had, he reasoned, designed the world for it to do so. It was of paramount importance, then, that 'proper schemes were proposed for putting things on a better footing'.[64] In short, Wallace claimed that government action could viably remedy a state's level of depopulation. Moreover, he argued, this now had to take place. Although he admitted that only those 'employed in the administration of public affairs' could 'carry such schemes into execution',[65] Wallace was himself prepared to put forward plans that could be implemented to this purpose. He presented himself as a citizen able to 'employ himself in speculations, about such matters as may tend to the good of his country'.[66] This was the 'only apology' he made for finishing the *Dissertation* with 'a few observations on the state of Scotland'.[67] These observations included a proposal to tackle Scotland's levels of poverty through the creation of pension schemes. Naturally, these suggestions have to be seen in the context of Wallace's own involvement with setting up a sophisticated 'charitable design'.

As I have shown, the relationship between marriage, population growth and subsistence needs was the central preoccupation of Wallace's *Dissertation*. Indeed, it was pivotal to his political and economic thought at large. Wallace argued that, just like many other Europeans, there were many Scottish men that 'either imagine themselves not to be, or in reality are not able to maintain families'.[68] In part, this was a problem for the younger sons of nobility who could not offer potential brides the same lifestyle as could those set to inherit vast estates. More pressingly, Scottish agriculture remained too unproductive as there were 'great tracts of land [left] uncultivated'.[69] Wallace even expressed his fear that, out of the little foodstuffs that there was, too much grain was exported overseas. Furthermore, this lack of wealth and of subsistence goods meant that 'Many of our youth leave the country'.[70] Wallace speculated that these young people had felt it prudent to 'go abroad to push their fortunes, because [...] they either cannot have business at home, or cannot raise such fortunes as will satisfy their ambition'.[71] Hence, Wallace saw the route to Scottish prosperity to lie with using government to restore the confidence of those that were most likely to raise families in their native country.

Indeed, for Wallace, it was reasonable to expect governments interested in preventing depopulation to actively lift families out of conditions of poverty. In practice, it seems, this meant that it had to be a responsibility of government to assure potential providers that they would be able to fulfil their duties towards their families. Expanding the use and prevalence of pension schemes for widows would fit these criteria nicely. Wallace recognised that, even though some breadwinners may have been able to prevent their dependents from falling into poverty during their lifetimes, in many circumstances, individuals 'cannot leave a sufficient provision for their families after their death'.[72] The same intuition informed Wallace's involvement with setting up a fund for the widows and children of Scottish professors and ministers.

This project was the fruition of considerable hard work and a number of collaborators had been involved. Notably, this included Alexander Webster and Colin MacLaurin. As well as being a minister, Webster was a keen statistician who was known to his friends as Dr Bonum Magnum due to his fondness for claret.[73] Together, Wallace and Webster underwrote the actuarial basis for the fund. Extensive notes and calculations from the early 1740s still exist intact and testify to how much effort went into the realisation of this project. A letter from MacLaurin, who had provided assistance with setting up the fund, gives some indication as to how time consuming the preparations for the fund must have been. Writing to Wallace in May 1743, MacLaurin described having been 'wholly employed in pursuing the calculations'.[74] MacLaurin requested letters with additional information to be returned to him by Wallace 'or copied for me by one of your sons today'.[75]

Around the time of MacLaurin's letter, the General Assembly approved plans to set up the fund. Shortly thereafter, Wallace was able to secure the support of the Scottish MPs. Their support would ensure that the fund was granted legal status. The draft bill that Wallace read at a meeting with these MPs laid out the purpose of the scheme and the strategy to put it into execution. To set the scene, the bill's preamble explained that:

> the widows & children of the Ministers of the Church of Scotland & of the heads, Principals, & Masters, in the universities in that part of Great Britain

called Scotland are often left in indigent circumstances, without any provision for their Subsistence or Education.[76]

Evidently, the framing of the bill resonated with the key themes of Wallace's wider intellectual endeavour with its emphasis on preventing families from falling into destitution. Wallace told the Scottish MPs that 'all the Charitable designs that have heretofore been proposed, & E'ssay'd, for the supply of such widows & orphans have proved ineffectual'.[77] These proposals could be differentiated from previous attempts to assist the families of deceased ministers by the extent of their ambition and the collective commitment to their execution.

The ambition of the scheme was exemplified by its mathematical sophistication, its overall design and its enactment into legislation. In a manuscript of the bill that was taken to the House of Commons, the act stated that it would:

> oblige all the future Incumbents of Parishes in Scotland, and also all the future Principals & Heads of Colleges, Professors, & Regents or Masters of the said Universities, to contribute & pay certain annual Payments or Sums of Money therein specified, for, or towards, the erecting & compleating an annual Fund for the Relief of their Widows & Children.[78]

So, the longevity of the scheme would be secured by legally obliging members of its associated bodies to become active financial contributors. Wallace's handwritten notes sketched out how each participant would 'pay in yearly to this society what sum he thinks proper during his life & that his widow shall draw after his death a proportionable sum during her life'.[79] In this sense, the project can be understood as an early experiment in insurance. In its final form, the scheme allowed for four levels of payments that participants could choose from.[80]

Ultimately, the fund's transition into law resulted from its widespread support. MacLaurin wrote a note for Wallace in June 1743 that was seemingly meant to act as a circulated commendation of the scheme. It was enclosed with tables of sums showing how the fund would work in practice. In the note, MacLaurin explained how the 'scheme for providing an Annuity for Minster's Widows and a Stock for their children' had been presented to the General Assembly and been approved 'with the alterations and amendments made upon the scheme by the said assembly'.[81] MacLaurin found himself 'obliged to say that the Design is so good that minute objections against the perfection of the scheme seem to be improper after it has been so long under consideration'.[82] The commendation suggests that, despite a few deliberations over detail, the decision of the Assembly represented a collective endorsement of the fund's aim and scope. Crucially, as indicated by the Bill read to the Scottish MPs, the Assembly also intended for the: 'Heads, Principals, & Masters of the four Universities in that part of Great Britain called Scotland' to be 'comprehended in the aforesaid charitable design, provided that the said universities did agree thereto'.[83] The initial Bill narrated how 'the said University of Edinburgh did apply to the said General Assembly',[84] in order to be included. This was followed by 'the said Universities of St Andrews and Glasgow'[85] requesting to be involved as well. In short, this commitment to the scheme quickly extended to both the Church of Scotland and to every Scottish university of the day.

Wallace's next task was to have the scheme passed into legislation. Extracts from the records of the General Assembly indicate the gravity with which this course of action was pursued. The Assembly noted that, with the scheme approved, it 'did resolve that application be made to the King and Parliament for an Act of Parliament to render the same effectual'.[86] This was to be done 'in such manner as to the wisdom of the legislature shall see fit'.[87] To this end, the Assembly 'did nominate the Reverend Mr Robert Wallace their moderator [...] for prosecuting the said application'.[88] Wallace, as mentioned, was to be joined by another minister and fellow Rankenian from Edinburgh called George Wishart. In November 1743, the Assembly instructed Wallace and Wishart to 'repair, with all convenient Diligence, to London, and there by all lawful and Competent methods in name of this Commission',[89] convince Parliament to legally support the proposed fund. At the time, the trip to London was itself no mean feat. Much to the Assembly's delight, the Bill passed through Parliament successfully. When Grant wrote to congratulate Wallace and Wishart, he said, 'Your mission is now good as over, & I warmly congratulate you both on its success, & wish you a safe & agreeable return home.'[90]

It is fair to say that the passing of the Bill was an achievement for Wallace. The widows' fund he had envisaged and organised had been supported by the General Assembly of the Church of Scotland, every Scottish university and now the Parliament of Great Britain. It would have been reasonable to expect Wallace's ambition for the scheme to grow. Indeed, reflecting on the fund led Wallace to suggest that a more wholescale, national scheme could be implemented. This idea was explored in Wallace's *Dissertation*, which was drafted not long after the trip to London. Moreover, Wallace explicitly stated that such a scheme could copy the template of 'the model of that lately established by law, for a provision for the widows and children of the ministers of the church'.[91] A national fund could be generated by setting up:

> one large, or several small societies of married men, who should pay either all at once, or annually, during their lives, certain sums [...] as they might judge

convenient, on condition, that proportional sums be paid after their death to their widows or children.[92]

Here, Wallace's phrasing evidently evoked the wording of the legal bill that had been passed when setting up the widows' fund. It appears that Wallace's efforts to establish the fund for the widows of Scottish ministers inspired or coincided with the solutions to the broader population crisis that he had identified.

Critically, Wallace recommended the formation of more of these types of funds because: 'Such societies might be a security for the support of widows and children [...] and be a great encouragement to marriage.'[93] The primary justification for such funds, from Wallace's perspective, was that they took away the fear involved in leaving behind family members that would be unable to feed or fend themselves. In turn, consistent with Wallace's overarching logic, this would remove one of the chief obstacles to population growth. Thus, it seems fair to conclude that there was a perfect synergy between Wallace's strenuous efforts to set up the widows' fund for Scottish ministers and his drive to design a large-scale, politically structural response to depopulation.

In fact, Wallace's comments in the *Dissertation* imply that part of the success of the widows' fund for Scottish ministers rested on whether it could prove how practical and achievable national insurance schemes might be in the future. It seems that Wallace hoped the widows' fund for Scottish ministers would act as an exemplar model, which could be followed by additional government-sanctioned projects. Surely, if Parliament could legislate in favour of one insurance fund, then it could legislate in favour of others. Potentially, this could work on a national scale. In summary, insufficient attention has been paid to the links between the *Dissertation* and the context of Wallace's career as a whole. Analysing the text in relation to Wallace's relationship to the widows' fund for Scottish ministers reveals and clarifies aspects of his overall intellectual endeavour in the 1740s. Both Wallace's involvement in the fund and his *Dissertation* shared a drive to end poverty at their core. This drive was embedded in a recognition that government could and would be required to bring about a more equitable system of distribution.

The Jacobite Uprising of 1745 saw a rebellious army invading and occupying Scotland's capital. One effect of this was that it disrupted the proceedings of the Edinburgh Philosophical Society, which likely did not meet for a year as a result of these events. This means that one of the most important publications associated the Edinburgh Philosophical Society's first decade of existence was Wallace's *Dissertation*.[94] It is right, therefore, that the significance and intentions of this text are properly studied.

By situating Wallace's *Dissertation* in its proper context, this current chapter has helped to show that the aims of this text were in keeping with the Edinburgh Philosophical Society's wider endeavour. That is to say, Wallace shared in the pursuit of using fact-based enquiry to inform reforms designed to improve Scottish society. For Wallace, research into different societies across history was a terrain that could be explored in order to make conclusions about how best to facilitate population growth.

This present chapter has also demonstrated that Wallace's thought on population can be usefully understood in relation to his work on the widow's fund, which he fought to have passed into legislation in 1744. As I have shown, this was a link drawn by Wallace himself at a crucial moment in the text. This has highlighted that the amelioration of poverty was the improvement to Scottish society that Wallace was most personally preoccupied with. In this chapter, I have argued that Wallace's *Dissertation* was overarchingly concerned with how to stimulate population growth in Scotland by making it more viable for individuals to raise families. For Wallace, this had to entail a reduction in poverty through the creation of a more equitable distribution of land and resources. Wallace's work on the widow's fund was partly seen as an experiment designed to help further this goal.

At a broader historiographical level, it is now worth establishing as to whether this exploration of Wallace may have given grounds for any kind of historical re-evaluation of eighteenth-century notions about the abolition of poverty. According to Gareth Stedman Jones's influential argument, it was the convergence of late eighteenth-century political economy and ideals of democratic revolution that laid the foundations for the initial realisation that there could be an end to poverty.[95] Stedman Jones critiqued scholarship that minimised the significance of this moment, which he dated to the revolutionary years of the 1790s.[96] While this thesis may still largely hold up, it may be possible to nuance Stedman Jones's account by highlighting the importance of the attempts in the 1740s to tackle chronic want through political reform that have been discussed in this chapter.

As Christopher Berry has usefully summarised, a cultural shift in attitudes towards poverty took place over the course of the Scottish Enlightenment. This involved critiquing the early modern view that poverty was in some way redemptive in a Christian or even a republican sense.[97] Although Wallace did not accept that commerce and luxury were straightforwardly positive, his work marked a nexus point between the culture of improvement that defined early eighteenth-century Scotland and specific, detailed attempts to address the amelioration of poverty. Perhaps this emphasises the relevance of putting the earlier decades of the eighteenth century back into the picture in order to achieve a fuller historical appraisal of Enlightenment conceptualisations of poverty.

More pertinently, however, this chapter has unpacked the ways in which Wallace's discussion about poverty was shaped by his fears of depopulation. In his *Dissertation*, Wallace directly linked his work on the widow's fund to his thought on population growth. Over the course of the text, he contended that it was necessary for Scotland to reduce poverty in order to prevent further depopulation and avert catastrophe as a result. The idea that depopulation led to widespread ruination and that it was caused by poverty drove Wallace's arguments in favour of the implementation of redistributive measures. While the focus of this chapter has been on Wallace's work of the 1740s, it is worth mentioning that his later works were similarly characterised by interests in population growth and poverty.[98] Of course, the view that population growth was desirable, and that poverty could cause depopulation by affecting marriage rates, was also shared by a number of Enlightenment heavyweights including Montesquieu and Hume. It seems to me that this suggests that anxieties about depopulation may have played a much more central role in Enlightenment discussions about poverty than historians have previously acknowledged. Further research into this area would likely show that ongoing eighteenth-century debates about how best to stimulate population growth were some of the most substantial avenues through which poverty was examined.

Notes

1 General Assembly of Church of Scotland, *Extract from records of commission of General Assembly appointing Robert Wallace and George Wishart as their commissioners to apply to King and parliament for an act of parliament in favour of fund. 10th November 1743*, National Records of Scotland, Edinburgh (Hereafter NRS), CH9/17/22.
2 William Grant, *Letter from William Grant to Robert Wallace and George Wishart, Edinburgh. 3rd March 1744*, NRS CH9/17/28.
3 Nicholas Phillipson, 'Culture and Society in the 18th Century Province: The Case of Edinburgh and the Scottish Enlightenment', in Lawrence Stone (ed.), *The University in Society, Volume II: Europe, Scotland, and the United States from the 16th to the 20th Century* (Princeton, NJ: Princeton University Press, 1974), pp. 407–448.
4 John Robertson, *The Case for the Enlightenment: Scotland and Naples, 1680–1760* (Cambridge: Cambridge University Press, 2005).
5 But see Caroline Robbins, *The Eighteenth-Century Commonwealthman: Studies in the Transmission, Development and Circumstance of English Liberal Thought from the Restoration of Charles II until the War with the Thirteen Colonies* (New York, NY: Harvard University Press, 1968), pp. 199–211. The most complete review of Wallace's political thought is Robert B. Luehrs,

'Population and Utopia in the Thought of Robert Wallace', *Eighteenth-Century Studies*, 20:3 (1987), 313–335.

6 Also see: Donald Winch, *Riches and Poverty: An Intellectual History of political economy in Britain, 1750–1834* (Cambridge: Cambridge University Press, 1996), pp. 85–87; M. A. Box and Michael Silverthorne, 'The "Most Curious & Important of All Questions of Erudition": Hume's Assessment of the Populousness of Ancient Nations', in Mark G. Spencer (ed.), *David Hume: Historical Thinker, Historical Writer* (Pennsylvania, PA: The Pennsylvania State University Press, 2013), pp. 225–254; James A Harris, *Hume: An Intellectual Biography* (Cambridge: Cambridge University Press, 2015), pp. 283–286.

7 I explore this at greater length in Conor Bollins, 'Propagating the Species: Political Economy and the Population Debate, 1699–1767' (PhD Thesis, Queen Mary, University of London 2021).

8 There has been renewed interest in the Rankenian Club due to recent research on the theological debates of the Scottish Enlightenment. See, for example, Thomas Ahnert, *The Moral Culture of the Scottish Enlightenment, 1690–1805* (New Haven, CT: Yale University Press, 2015), pp. 34–65.

9 Colin Kidd, *Subverting Scotland's Past: Scottish Whig Historians and the Creation of an Anglo-British Identity 1689–1830* (Cambridge: Cambridge University Press, 1993), pp. 186–187.

10 Linda Colley, *Britons: Forging the Nation, 1707–1837* (London: Yale University Press, 1992), pp. 30–43.

11 Robert Wallace, *A Dissertation on the Numbers of Mankind in Antient and Modern Times* (Edinburgh, 1753), p. 32.

12 Ibid., p. 33.

13 For commentary on Montesquieu's thought on depopulation, see Joseph J. Spengler, *French Predecessors of Malthus: A Study in Eighteenth-Century Wage and Population Theory* (London: Routledge, Taylor & Francis Group, 1942), p. 213; Robert Shackleton, *Montesquieu: A Critical Biography* (Oxford: Oxford University Press, 1961), pp. 42–45; David B. Young, 'Libertarian Demography: Montesquieu's Essay on Depopulation in the "Lettres Persanes"', *Journal of the History of Ideas*, 36:4 (1975), 669–682; Judith N. Shklar, *Montesquieu* (Oxford: Oxford University Press, 1987), p. 46; Sylvana Tomaselli, 'Moral Philosophy and Population Questions in Eighteenth Century Europe', *Population and Development Review*, 14 (1988), 7–29; Carol Blum, *Strength in Numbers: Population, Reproduction, and Power in Eighteenth-century France* (Baltimore, MA: The John Hopkins University Press, 2002), pp. 11–20. Note that Montesquieu's ideas about the populousness of antiquity have often been neglected or even denigrated by twentieth-century scholars. For a more recent account of Montesquieu's thoughts on this subject, which seeks to offer a greater level of contextualisation, see Bollins, *Propagating the Species*, Chs 3–4.

14 Wallace, *Dissertation*, p. 2

15 Ibid. p. 114.

16 Ibid., p. 12.

17 Ibid., p. 19.

18 Ibid., p. 12.
19 Wallace also explored ideas about sex and sexuality in an unpublished pamphlet. Controversially, this text considered the benefits of more flexible divorce laws. Hypothetically, such laws could prove beneficial to population growth. See Robert Wallace, *Of Venery, or of the commerce of the sexes*, Edinburgh University Library LA.II.62012.
20 Wallace, *Dissertation*, p. 15.
21 Ibid., p. 33.
22 Ibid., p. 21.
23 Ibid., p. 18.
24 Ibid., pp. 18–19.
25 Ibid., p. 80.
26 Ibid.
27 Ibid., p. 17.
28 Ibid.
29 Ibid., p. 147.
30 Ibid.
31 Ibid., p. 115.
32 Ibid., p. 116.
33 Ibid.
34 For further discussion of Mandeville, see E. J. Hundert, *The Enlightenment's Fable: Bernard Mandeville and the Discovery of Society* (Cambridge: Cambridge University Press, 1994). For a broader overview of the luxury debate, see Istvan Hont, 'The Early Enlightenment Debate on Commerce and Luxury', in Mark Goldie and Robert Wokler (eds), *The Cambridge History of Eighteenth-Century Political Thought* (Cambridge: Cambridge University Press, 2006), pp. 379–418.
35 Wallace, *Dissertation*, p. 160.
36 Ibid., p. 160.
37 Ibid., p. 21.
38 Ibid., p. 25.
39 Ibid., p. 147.
40 Karen J. Cullen, *Famine in Scotland: the 'Ill Years' of the 1690s* (Edinburgh: Edinburgh University Press, 2010), pp. 14–19.
41 Michael Flinn (ed.), *Scottish Population History from the 17th century to the 1930s* (Cambridge: Cambridge University Press, 1977), p. 167.
42 Cullen, *Famine in Scotland*, pp. 20–22.
43 Christopher A. Whatley, *The Scots and the Union, Then and Now* (Edinburgh: Edinburgh University Press, 2014), p. 199.
44 Cullen, *Famine in Scotland*, p. 19.
45 Eric J. Graham, *A Maritime History of Scotland, 1650–1790* (East Linton: Tuckwell Press, 2002), pp. 63–65.
46 T. C. Smout, *Scottish Trade on the Eve of Union, 1660–1707* (Edinburgh: Oliver & Boyd, 1963), pp. 244–250.
47 Douglas Watt, *The Price of Scotland: Darien, Union and the Wealth of the Nations* (Edinburgh: Luath Press, 2006), pp. 132–133.

48 Ibid., pp. 82–83.
49 Smout, *Scottish Trade on the Eve of Union*, p. 252.
50 Cullen, *Famine in Scotland*, pp. 157–168.
51 Robert Sibbald, *Provision for the Poor in time of Dearth and Scarcity* (Edinburgh, 1699), p. 3.
52 Patrick Fitzgerald, '"Black '97": Reconsidering Scottish Migration to Ireland in the Seventeenth Century and the Scotch-Irish in America', in William P. Kelly and John R. Young (eds), *Ulster and Scotland, 1600–2000: History, Language and Identity* (Dublin: Four Courts Press, 2004), pp. 71–84.
53 Flinn, *Scottish Population History*, p. 164.
54 D. F. Macdonald, *Scotland's Shifting Population, 1770–1850* (Glasgow: Jackson, 1978), pp. 1–15.
55 Flinn, *Scottish Population History*, p. 212.
56 Ibid., pp. 216–223; Philipp Robinson Rössner, 'The 1738–41 Harvest Crisis in Scotland', *The Scottish Historical Review*, 90:229 (April 2011), 27–63.
57 Here, I am drawing on the influential formulation of the Scottish Enlightenment put forward by Nicholas Phillipson. See Nicholas Phillipson, 'The Scottish Enlightenment', in Roy Porter and Mikuláš Teich (eds), *The Enlightenment in National Context* (Cambridge: Cambridge University Press, 1981), pp. 19–40. For commentary on Phillipson's interpretation, see Colin Kidd, 'The Phillipsonian Enlightenment', *Modern Intellectual History*, 11:1 (2014), 175–190.
58 Phillipson also placed an emphasis on the role of the Rankenian Club. See Phillipson, 'The Case of Edinburgh', pp. 432–437.
59 Christopher J. Berry, *The Idea of Commercial Society in the Scottish Enlightenment* (Edinburgh: Edinburgh University Press, 2013), pp. 1–31.
60 Roger L. Emerson, 'The Philosophical Society of Edinburgh, 1737–1747', *The British Journal for the History of Science*, 12:41 (1979), 154–191.
61 Phillipson, 'The Case of Edinburgh', pp. 440–441.
62 Emerson, 'The Philosophical Society of Edinburgh'.
63 Wallace, *Dissertation*, p. 148.
64 Ibid.
65 Ibid.
66 Ibid.
67 Ibid.
68 Ibid., p. 150.
69 Ibid., p. 149.
70 Ibid.
71 Ibid.
72 Ibid.
73 The Scots term 'Bonum Magnum' referred to a measurement of claret. Webster was also known for his temper. For biographical details, see James Gray Kyd (ed.), *Scottish Population Statistics Including Webster's Analysis of Population 1755* (Edinburgh: Scottish Academic Press, 1952), pp. xiii–xxxiii; Thomas Thomason, *Biographical Dictionary of Eminent Scotsmen*, vol. iii, half vol. vi (Glasgow, 1875), pp. 506–508.

74 Colin MacLaurin, *Letter from Colin MacLaurin to Robert Wallace, with opinion of scheme. 24th May 1743*, NRS CH9/17/16/1.
75 Ibid.
76 Robert Wallace, *Bill read by Robert Wallace in meeting of Scots members at the House of Commons when they unanimously agreed to promote it. 1743*, NRS CH9/17/5.
77 Ibid.
78 Adam Anderson, *A bill drawn by Adam Anderson from the scheme given him by Robert Wallace and George Wishart. 1743*, NRS CH9/17/8.
79 Robert Wallace, *Proposals in Dr. Wallace's hand for raising a fund for jointures to the widows of such gentlemen as have not land estates nor great sums of money, but live by their business or yearly income which depends on their lives. 1743*, NRS CH9/17/10, p. 1.
80 For an account of Wallace and Webster with a different set of emphases, see Niall Ferguson, *The Ascent of Money: A Financial History of the World* (London: Penguin Books, 2008), pp. 190–199.
81 Colin MacLaurin, *Letter from Colin MacLaurin to Robert Wallace, with opinion of scheme. 3rd June 1743*, NRS CH9/17/16/2.
82 Ibid.
83 Wallace, *Bill read by Robert Wallace*, NRS CH9/17/5, p. 2.
84 Ibid.
85 Ibid.
86 General Assembly of Church of Scotland. NRS CH9/17/22.
87 Ibid.
88 Ibid.
89 Ibid.
90 William Grant, *Letter from William Grant to Robert Wallace and George Wishart, Edinburgh. 3rd March 1744*, NRS CH9/17/28.
91 Wallace, *Dissertation*, p. 154.
92 Ibid.
93 Ibid.
94 For an overview of the state of the Edinburgh Philosophical Society by 1747, which alluded to the significance of Wallace's contribution, see Emerson, 'The Philosophical Society of Edinburgh', pp. 180–183.
95 Gareth Stedman Jones, *An End to Poverty? A Historical Debate* (London: Profile Books, 2004).
96 For a differing account of eighteenth-century ideas of poverty, see Gertrude Himmelfarb, *The Idea of Poverty: England in the Early Industrial Age* (London: Faber and Faber, 1984).
97 Berry, *Idea of Commercial Society*, pp. 78–85.
98 For Wallace's later work, see Robert Wallace, *Characteristics of the Present Political State of Great Britain* (Dublin, 1758), and Robert Wallace, *Various Prospects of Mankind, Nature, and Providence* (London, 1761). For further analysis of these texts, see Bollins, *Propagating the Species*, Chs 9 and 11.

8

Conceptions of Polish and Russian poverty in the British Enlightenment

Ben Dew

One of the ways the Enlightenment conceptualised poverty was as a long-standing, historical problem with social, political and economic origins. This approach was of particular importance to the various narratives of human progress which characterised much British writing of the era.[1] Indeed, the major historical shifts Enlightenment authors sought to analyse – in conjectural history, man's passage through the hunting, pastoral, agricultural and commercial stages; in narrative history, the demise of the feudal system and the rise of commercial polities – involved the overcoming of particular varieties of poverty.[2] Commentators were aware, however, that movement through these developmental processes had not been the same across the globe. Such an observation paved the way for one of the defining intellectual tropes of the period: the transformation of time into space as people from other places came to be viewed as not just different, but rather 'temporally prior and backwards'.[3] The chapter that follows examines the significance of this approach for British travel writing on Poland and Russia. It has been widely noted in the existing literature that eighteenth-century accounts of these nations by 'Western' commentators emphasised their poverty and lack of development.[4] What I want to demonstrate, however, is that this poverty was conceived of in explicitly historical terms. These were states whose failures arose from their continued reliance on the feudal, non-free forms of labour which had characterised medieval 'Western Europe' and which had been much criticised in Enlightenment discourse.[5] To visit Poland and Russia was, therefore, to experience the Britain of the twelfth or thirteenth century, complete with its powerful and affluent nobles and its poor, indentured slave labour force.[6] Such ideas explicitly shaped the character of the discourse on these nations ensuring that it was dominated by reflections on the differences between slave and free labour and analysis of the political processes through which a state might move from the former system to the latter. Understanding these processes, it was assumed, necessitated a study of the mechanisms Western nations had employed to dismantle their own feudal institutions.

My discussion opens by outlining in general terms the ways that ideas about feudal and commercial societies were utilised in discussions of 'Eastern' Europe in the second half of the eighteenth century. I then move on to explore the three most detailed anglophone comparative accounts of Poland and Russia of the period. The first two texts are relatively obscure: Joseph Marshall's *Travels [...] in the Years 1768, 1769 and 1770* (1772) and John Williams' *The Rise, Progress, and Present State of the Northern Governments* (1777). The third – William Coxe's *Travels into Poland, Russia, Sweden and Denmark* (1784) – was more successful, running to five editions. This work did much to shape debates on feudalism and slavery in Eastern Europe and, by means of a series of comparisons, in the Atlantic world. Underpinning its influence, however, was a fundamental irony. Coxe conceived of the development of commercial society along British lines as normative. Later accounts, however, employed his discussions of Eastern European slavery to problematise and critique key elements of Britain's commercial empire.

For eighteenth-century British commentators, the key features of Polish and Russian society were products of the two countries' separation from the main currents of modern European history. Historical thought of the period, as J. G. A. Pocock has argued, was rooted in the idea that development in Europe could be conceptualised as an 'Enlightened narrative'. This narrative recounted the processes through which civil society had emerged out of the 'barbarism and religion' of the medieval period and it had two themes: (1) the emergence of a system of sovereign states in which 'ruling authority was competent to maintain civil government; and (2) the emergence of 'a shared civilization of manners and commerce [...] through which the independent states could be thought to constitute a confederation or republic'.[7] In accounts of these developments, the key distinction was that between feudal and commercial societies. Europe from the seventh to the eleventh centuries, it was generally agreed, had been dominated by feudal forms of property and power relations. Under this system, power had graduated towards a militarised class of nobles who were able to obtain supreme jurisdiction within their own fiefdoms. This group's independence ensured monarchs were unable to execute the laws and the continent descended into anarchy and a seemingly endless succession of conflicts. The bulk of the populace, meanwhile, was reduced to a state of servitude and, particularly in the countryside, slavery. Given this state of affairs, feudal society's core characteristics were: anarchy; gross inequality; and, as a result of the pernicious influence exerted on the spirit of industry by feudal institutions, the complete absence of commerce. A feudal society was, therefore, necessarily a poor one.

Discussions of feudalism's demise are to be found in a range of British accounts from the period, foremost among them those by David Hume,

William Robertson and Adam Smith.[8] What unites these commentaries is their insistence on the key role commerce played in undermining the power of the feudal nobility. There is, however, some difference in emphasis between them. Hume's *Essays* and Smith's *Wealth of Nations* are particularly concerned with the effects of the introduction of new luxury goods from overseas. The extensive spending of the great proprietors on these 'trinkets and baubles' served to absorb their wealth and undermine their power, and to pass both to the emerging class of merchants who furnished such goods. The narrative works of history by Hume and Robertson, meanwhile, provided an explanation of the specific political reforms which had engendered these processes. Given its direct concern with European affairs, and the fact that Coxe explicitly references it, Robertson's work is of particular significance here.[9] For Robertson, the driving force of change was a series of innovations in the government of Europe's towns and cities. The origins of this movement lay in Italy; the Italian city-states, newly enriched through the trade generated by the Crusades, had been able to shake off the 'yoke of their insolent Lords' and establish independent, municipal jurisdictions, governed by laws.[10] These innovations gave the urban population civil liberty and political power, and inspired those living in agricultural districts, often in conditions of slavery, to seek their own enfranchisement. Key to this turn of events was the growing authority of monarchs. Support from the Crown had been of central importance, Robertson argued, in enabling the cities to gain and preserve their liberties in the face of opposition from 'the domineering spirit of the nobles'.[11] Such developments helped to forge an alliance between townsfolk and their Princes. The former willingly provided the latter with 'such supplies of money as added new force to government' thereby ensuring that monarchs once again become 'the heads of the community' with wide-ranging military and legal influence.[12] These shifts in power were to prove highly beneficial: peace and order were restored; serfdom and slavery were abolished; and, perhaps most importantly, a 'spirit of industry' arose, which drove developments in commerce and manufacture.[13] Consequently, the poverty and gross inequalities of feudalism entered into abeyance as new commercial forms of society, supported by both monarchs and their non-noble subjects, emerged.

Within Robertson's model, the key mechanism for economic development was emulation. Seeing the benefits that Italy's reforms had brought about, other states soon imitated them, first France and later Germany, Spain, England and Scotland.[14] Poland and Russia played no part in Robertson's narrative; this was an exclusively 'Western' story. Commentators who were interested in these states, however, worked on the core assumption that the regulations that had brought commercial improvements elsewhere had never managed to establish themselves fully in the lands to the east of Germany. As a result, Poland and Russia continued to be governed by feudal-style institutions that resembled those of twelfth- and thirteenth-century 'Western' polities. The continued prevalence of feudalism, it was agreed, constituted the key barrier to Polish and Russian development. Feudal landowners were prevented from engaging in economic affairs by the contempt in which they held everything other than marshal occupations. Moreover, the system of serfdom – or, as British commentators generally labelled it, 'slavery' – which dominated agriculture in both Poland and Russia undermined economic efficiency.[15] In a commercial state, the prospect of self-advancement acted as a motivation to free labourers; serfs or slaves, however, could not benefit from their own endeavours and had little reason to work diligently and no capacity to invest in land or industry. Consequently, feudal polities like Poland and Russia lacked the key psychological drives which underpinned modern forms of agriculture, and the manufacture, trade and publicly beneficial forms of wealth creation they supported.

Slavery ensured that there were fundamental similarities between Russia and Poland, and notable distinctions between these countries and other European states. When accounting for the survival of feudalism and slavery, however, commentators turned to an analysis of the Polish and Russian systems of government, and here it was acknowledged there were significant differences. The core issue, given the pivotal role it had played in the demise of feudalism elsewhere, was the relationship between the nobility and the monarchy. And in their treatment of this matter, Marshall, Coxe and Williams drew on the general political typology developed by Montesquieu in *The Spirit of the Laws* (1748). States, Montesquieu had argued, could be divided into three categories: despotisms, monarchies and republics. The latter category was further subdivided into democracies and aristocracies.[16] Earlier anglophone commentators had viewed Poland as having a mixed constitution – similar in form, but massively inferior to that of Britain.[17] Enlightenment-era accounts, however, followed Montesquieu's lead in conceiving of Poland's government as an aristocracy in which, despite the presence of a ruling monarch, all meaningful political power rested with the nobility. This group did not govern collectively – as was the case with the superior form of aristocratic government practised in Venice – but held personal power over their serfs. Such a form of rule constituted, in the words of William Paley, 'the most odious' of 'all species of domination' as 'the freedom and satisfaction of private life are more constrained and harassed by it, than by the most vexatious laws, or even by the lawless will of an arbitrary monarch'.[18] The problems in Poland's political system, meanwhile, had been further worsened by two political innovations, both of which received widespread attention in British accounts. First, from the end of the sixteenth century onwards, Poland was a fully elective monarchy. As such, on the demise of a Polish monarch any prince in Christendom could submit himself for an election in which every 'noble gentleman' had a vote. Second, the reign of Jan Kazimierz (1648–1668) saw the introduction of the *liberum veto*, the infamous mechanism whereby a session of the Polish diet could be broken up by an objection from any one of its deputies. Such innovations reduced the influence of the monarchy and gave the nobility new and pernicious forms of liberty and power. The situation in Russia was very different. A Russian monarch, as the diplomat George McCartney writing in 1768 observed, could:

> without form or process of law, deprive any subject of life, liberty or estate; seize the public treasure however appropriated; raise or debase the value of the coin; make peace or war; augment or diminish her troops; frame new laws, or repeal old ones; and finally, nominate her successor to the throne [...].[19]

Russia, therefore, conformed precisely to Montesquieu's definition of a despotism; this was a state in which 'one alone, without law and without rule, draws everything along by his will and his caprices'.[20]

These analyses of the socio-economic and political frameworks did much to shape the general tenor of writing about 'Eastern' Europe and ensured that writers focused on two issues. First, they were concerned with how poor 'feudal' countries had sought in the past, and might seek in the future, to transform themselves into rich and powerful commercial polities. Such discussions provided commentary on both the existing social order – specifically the role of slavery – and Poland and Russia's contrasting political systems. The key task for writers was to establish the extent to which Polish and Russian political systems could mimic the kind of changes that had enabled 'Western' monarchs to drive development. Second, there was a need – or at least a perceived need – to provide comparative forms of analysis and explain the relevance of discussions of two distant lands to an anglophone audience. To this end authors looked at the similarities and differences between Polish and Russian, and British practices, and reflected on the ways that accounts of 'Eastern' states might constitute a useful form of knowledge. As will be demonstrated below, individual commentators came to very different conclusions on these issues.

Joseph Marshall's *Travels* provides an account of the author's trip around northern Europe in the late 1760s and early 1770s. The author's obscurity and the lack of any documentary evidence beyond the *Travels* itself that Marshall was ever physically present in the places he describes, has resulted in both eighteenth-century reviewers and modern scholars expressing doubts about the account's veracity.[21] Regardless of such issues, the work constitutes a useful example of a comparative discussion which, in spite of its awareness of the core socio-economic similarities between Russia and Poland, is primarily concerned with their contrasting historical trajectories.

Marshall travelled across Poland – or at least claimed to do so – in the late 1760s as it was in the midst of civil war.[22] The conflict, as he conceived of it, was a symptom of a wider and seemingly terminal process of national decline. At one level, the root issue was a confessional one: the antagonism which had sparked military action arose from the prevalence of a pernicious form of Catholic bigotry that sought the absolute destruction of the Protestant and Greek (Orthodox) minorities.[23] Even more significant, however, was a series of explicitly political problems. Poland's aristocratic system of government had helped to ensure that the country's slave population was tyrannised by the masters and the country lacked any strong centralised power structure; as a result, the region remained in a perpetual state of anarchy.[24] His conclusion was that: 'Poland will never see times of tolerable order, till her kings have abundantly more power.'[25] The consequences of the current state of affairs, meanwhile, were depopulation and a particularly melancholy variety of poverty: indeed, the narrative is dominated by descriptions of 'mansions in ruins'; cottages 'as mean as can be conceived'; deserted villages; and 'fields entirely waste'.[26]

Russia, for Marshall, was also a poor country. While it had three times as many inhabitants as England, it failed to produce a greater public revenue; a comparison between the two states demonstrated, therefore, that it was 'liberty, trade and manufactures' which were the key drivers of public wealth not population.[27] What distinguished Russia from Poland, however, was its government. As Tim Hochstrasser outlines in Chapter 1 in this volume, Catherine II, inspired in part by her engagement with Enlightened circles in France, had initiated a series of reforms which sought to alleviate Russian poverty. Marshall offered fulsome praise for both these measures, and those of Peter I, arguing that they had transformed the state for the better across a range of economic activities including commerce, manufacture and – most importantly given Russia's extensive, rich and largely uncultivated territories – agriculture. Indeed, it was in relation to agriculture that Catherine was proving to be a particularly effective ruler: she had given the peasant populace new liberties; introduced a scheme in which noblemen were obliged to enfranchise one of their serf families every year; and successfully encouraged Polish peasants to settle in western Russia.[28] In sharp contrast to Poland, therefore, Russia, through its despotic rulers, had something approaching the centralised form of government which had brought about reform in Western Europe. This ensured that it was a rising power.

Poland's political problems meant that there were no realistic opportunities for recovery. Rather, it seemed likely to Marshall that the superior political and economic opportunities offered by Germany and Russia would lead to increased emigration from Polish territories. The challenge for Russia, meanwhile, was to continue the process of economic development on which it had embarked. To an extent, this simply required that the country work to abolish its feudal institutions and align itself more closely with the practices of the rest of Europe.[29] For Marshall, however, such reforms constituted a very long-term goal. As things stood, Russia's agricultural labourers were so 'habituated to slavery that it would be a vain attempt to free them under all masters'.[30] Instead, what was required was the further improvement of Crown lands and a scheme which ensured that noblemen received favour at court 'in proportion to the cultivation of their estates'.[31] Marshall's contention here was that Russian landowners have the opportunity 'by means of the slavery of their peasants, to work very great effects, if they pleased to undertake them'.[32] His proposal, therefore, was to produce a distinctively Russian spur to industry; rather than relying on the self-interest of the labourers, the Tsars should appeal to the self-interest of the nobility. Russia's journey out of poverty and slavery would, as a consequence, be different to that of the rest of Europe.

In his discussions of these issues, Marshall worked on the core assumption that a description of Europe's northern nations, particularly one preoccupied with economic issues, could provide useful instruction for a British audience. However, the different historical trajectories of Poland and Russia meant that they offered contrasting lessons. Poland, for Marshall, functioned in the main as a warning, an example of how a defective political infrastructure created poverty and misery. The situation with Russia was more complicated. On occasions, Marshall explored the contrasts between Russia and Britain emphasising the differences between British liberty, civilisation and wealth, and Russian despotism, barbarism and poverty. He was also interested, however, in the resemblances between the two states as large multi-national empires, and the areas in which Russian practices were superior to British ones. This focus led him to draw on Russian inspiration for a series of proposals aimed at improving the management of Britain's own imperial territories. An account, for example, of the substantial surplus which Russia had amassed through its trade in tar, beeswax and hemp with Britain, led him to develop a scheme for sourcing these products from Britain's colonies. Similarly, a discussion of the merits of hemp growing in the Ukraine was used to justify an ambitious programme for an American hemp industry.[33] Russia's status as a feudal power did not, therefore, imply for Marshall that its practices could not be usefully imitated and emulated by Britain.

What is also worth noting here is Marshall's awareness of the wider parallels that existed with regard to labour practices in British, Russian and Polish territories. To describe the working practices of enslaved peoples in these territories, Marshall found it necessary to develop a series of comparisons with Britain. Thus, while Russian 'slaves' in the remote wastelands and forests were said to live 'tolerably' well, those in more cultivated areas are described as appearing 'very near on the same rank, as the blacks in our sugar colonies'.[34] This comparison was then extended later in the *Travels* with the observation that, 'the oppressed state of the Russian peasants is an absolute freedom' when compared to that of the lower ranks in Poland, who experience a despotism such 'as the planters in the West-Indies use over their African slaves'.[35] Importantly, therefore, the imperial perspective Marshall took with regard to British affairs served to question the notion of an absolute contrast between Eastern and Western practices.

A very different analysis of the relationship between Poland and Russia was developed by John Williams. Although Williams appears to have travelled widely across Europe, his account was in no sense a work of travel literature. Rather, he drew on a range of published histories and archival sources to provide a complete a chronological history of the states of the north: the United Provinces, Denmark, Sweden, Russia and Poland. These narratives were supplemented by shorter thematic chapters which dealt with government, manners, laws and commerce, revenues and resources, and revolutions. Williams took a broadly universalist perspective. As was explained in the preface, his account was based on the assumptions that human nature was fundamentally the same across different locales and that all governments had been established upon common principles: the 'original form of government' was an 'elective and limited monarchy' founded 'upon compact'.[36] The history of the north, as he conceived of it, was essentially the narrative of the various political revolutions through which this compact had come to be corrupted. In tracing these processes, much of Williams' approach was conventional. Russia, he argued, had quickly descended into a form of despotism, which had more in common with the practices of Turkey and Persia than those of Europe.[37] It was only during the reign of Peter I that efforts had been made to draw 'people out of that state of barbarity in which they had been involved for so many centuries'.[38] Poland, in contrast, had been a normal European state until the Catholic clergy, supported by the nobility, had transformed it into a republican aristocracy dominated by a particularly 'abject' form of 'slavery'.[39] These differing historical trajectories – one of development and one of decline – ensured that there was a sharp contrast between Russian and Polish attitudes to commerce, particularly at the level of government. Peter's reforms had sought to 'enrich and civilize' his subjects through encouraging foreign 'men of genius, merchants and traders' to settle in Russia. In Poland, however, 'not only the laws [...], but the customs and dispositions of the people are contrary to those of a commercial nation'.[40] As a result, 'Poland, which for several hundred years past has been regarded as a civilised nation, is now in a more uncultivated and more unimproved state than any part of the Russian dominions.'[41]

To an extent, such a state of affairs meant that Poland and Russia required different approaches to commercial statecraft from their governments. In Russia, commerce and the contact with the outside world were bringing wealth and with it the beginnings of refinement and civilisation. Poland's aristocratic system and its economic backwardness, however, meant the limited commerce the Commonwealth did undertake was disadvantageous. The nobility's desire for foreign luxury goods led them to 'press' their labourers to produce ever greater quantities of grain, the only product with which the Commonwealth was able to trade. Given such a situation, Williams could only endorse Montesquieu's argument that it would be better if Poland stopped trading altogether.[42] Despite this contrast, Polish and Russian social institutions remained, Williams maintained, in need of the same basic reforms. Peter's mistake had been his failure to give the Russian serfs their freedom. Had he done so, 'his dominions would at this time have been ten times as rich and flourishing as they actually are'.[43] The fact he had not, however, ensured that Russia remained, like its immediate neighbour, in a state of chronic and unnatural underdevelopment. Concluding his discussion of Polish agriculture, Williams noted:

> It is a general observation, that no kingdom can brought into a flourishing situation, in proportion to her powers, by agriculture, manufactures and commerce, while the bulk of her subjects are in a state of slavery. [...] Upon the whole therefore I must make the same observation upon Poland respecting this matter, that I have already done upon Russia, which is that this kingdom will still continue in a state of poverty and ignorance of the fine arts and manufactures till the whole system of their government is changed, and till the bulk of the people are suffered to enjoy the natural rights of mankind, and to think and act like human beings.[44]

What we see in Williams' account, therefore, is a double argument against slavery. His contention that limited government rooted in compact was the original and natural form of rule allowed him to present systems based on slavery as fundamentally 'unnatural'. Running alongside these arguments, meanwhile, was an economic case against non-free labour. Labourers, he maintained, will always be 'idle and careless' if they cannot benefit directly in material terms from their endeavours.[45] Without a free labour force agriculture, arts and manufacture would always fail regardless of the encouragement – or not – that was offered by government. As a consequence, with regard to economic development, the similarities between Poland and Russia were of more importance than the differences; until their socio-economic systems changed, they would, for Williams, inevitably be poor countries.

Williams' universalism, his belief that human nature was fundamentally the same in all locales, gave him clear grounds for arguing that an account of 'northern' European history was of direct relevance to British politics. Indeed, his preface explicitly made the point that 'speculating on foreign events', particularly those concerning the dissolution of governments, could enable people to 'provide the better and earlier against [similar dangers] which may happen at home'.[46] When he came to discuss the actual ways that knowledge of other states might be useful, Williams, theoretically at least, maintained that a more developed society might learn from a less developed one.[47] His core argument, however, was that 'sensible and civilized people' and 'barbarians' provided two distinctive types of knowledge: 'by seeing the qualities of the one [the former] they will learn to imitate them, and by seeing the faults of the other, they will learn to avoid them'.[48] In this sense a knowledge of Polish and Russian slavery, and the poverty that it produced, simply provided confirmation regarding the superiority of Britain's commercial system over the feudalism and slavery of Russia and Poland.

These ideas, however, were complicated by the repeated allusions that Williams made to the employment of slavery in Britain's imperial territories. In relation to Russia, for example, he noted that at the time of Peter's accession to the throne in 1682 'there were at least ten millions of people in the Russian dominions who were in a state of slavery equal to that of the Negroes in the West Indies'.[49] Little had improved in the intervening years. 'Seven tenths of the population' continued to be 'bought and sold in the same manner as the negro slaves are in the West-Indies'.[50] Life for Polish serfs was, if anything, even worse: 'the situation of the negroes in many of our West-India plantations is superior to theirs'.[51] Williams' argument here, it should be emphasised, is a rather slippery one. At one level, he implies that, for religious and racial reasons, Polish and Russian slavery were more unnatural than that which was taking place on British territories. The crime in Northern Europe is that people who are 'called Christians' are being treated like 'negro slaves'.[52] Despite this, he was not particularly sympathetic to slavery. His core claim – a common one in abolitionist writing – was that slavery inevitably corrupts not just the enslaved person but also the slave owner. As he noted, 'if the more civilized part of mankind were invested with such an absolute power over their fellow-creatures, from which there was no appeal, I am afraid, like many of our West-India planters and modern Nabob-Makers, they would not be much less tyrannical and oppressive'.[53] This led him to conclude that 'we must attribute the want of humanity and the social virtues in the principal part of the Polish nobility to the extreme viciousness of their government and to the infamous conduct of their clergy'.[54] The similarities between the 'tyrannical and oppressive' behaviour of the Poles and slave-owners on British territories, however, implied, by the same logic, a fundamental failure on the part of the British Government. Also of significance here were Williams' economic arguments against slavery. Indeed, when viewed alongside his comments on the connections between Britain and 'Eastern' European practices, they raise a significant question about Britain's management of its imperial workforce. If, as is stated, non-free forms of labour had served to impoverish Poland and Russia, then what were the consequences of similar methods being applied to British territories? Williams' work avoids any direct engagement with this issue but, as we shall see, later writers were to confront it head on.

The origins of a good deal of this engagement lie in the account developed by William Coxe in his *Travels into Poland Russia, Sweden and Denmark*. Coxe, an Anglican minister, travel writer and historian, based his discussion on the Grand Tour of northern Europe he completed as tutor and travelling companion to the young Earl of Pembroke in the late 1770s. Much of his commentary, like Marshall's, took the form of a day-by-day narrative describing the specific people, buildings and landscapes he encountered on his journey. This diary-style commentary, however, was 'interspersed with historical relations and political enquiries' of the sort provided by Williams.[55] The resulting work was a detailed, scholarly account, which sought to explore the complex relationship between the Polish and Russian social systems and their forms of government.

Central to Coxe's analysis was his conception of Poland and Russia as feudal polities; as such, he maintained, they were organised around a different and fundamentally inferior system of social relations to other European states. Indeed, after having witnessed Russian and Polish 'slavery', Coxe described the satisfaction he felt in Sweden to find himself 'among freemen in a kingdom where there is a more equal division of property; where there is no vassalage, where the lowest orders enjoy a security of their persons and property; and where the advantages resulting from this right are visible to the commonest observer'.[56] The survival of feudal institutions was used to explain a number of phenomena observed in the *Travels*: rural poverty, particularly in Poland, and the gross inequalities that characterised Polish and Russian towns.[57] While feudalism was the primary cause of poverty and underdevelopment in both Poland and Russia, the reason for its persistence in the two states, Coxe argued, was fundamentally different and emerged directly from their systems of government.

Poland, Coxe argued with direct reference to the account developed by William Robertson, had begun the transformation in societal relations of the sort experienced elsewhere in Europe, but these processes had been retarded by the weakness of its monarchical institutions.[58] It was these failures which led the state into decline and gave the country as a whole its 'ruined grandeur' and its sense of 'melancholy decay'.[59] Russia's problems were, in a sense, the reverse of Poland's. Russia had a highly centralised form of government, and this enabled its monarchs to pursue Enlightened programmes of reform with speed, rigour and success. As a result, Russia was, for Coxe, an advancing state in a way that Poland was not; indeed, Coxe predicted that the growing 'spirit of humanity' that had emerged in Russia would, in time, form the basis for the emergence of 'a more equal freedom' for the Tsar's subjects. However, while the power of the Tsars had initiated the process of reform, it also served to preclude the slower and deeper forms of social transformation. To become a wealthy, commercial state, Coxe assumed, Russia required a significant shift in property and power relations of the sort that had occurred in other European states during the late medieval period. Until the people enjoyed a full security in their persons and property – something that was impossible in a despotic regime – such changes could not take place. For, Coxe asked, 'what should encourage them to succeed in any art, when they do not themselves reap the benefits of their labour, but are taxed in proportion to their profits and industry?' Ultimately, therefore, political factors had, to date, functioned as a limit on socio-economic development in Russia.

The key characteristic of Coxe's account, therefore, is an awareness of the ways in which political and socio-economic causes interacted with one another in determining the wealth or poverty of a particular locale. In the main, as we have seen, such an approach served to emphasise the superiority of Russia over Poland; Coxe was appalled at Polish ideas regarding noble liberty and could not conceive of a successful polity which did not have a strong, hereditary monarch at its helm. There was one area, however, where Poland had achieved more success than its neighbour. While Coxe noted and praised measures introduced by Catherine allowing peasants on Crown lands to enrol themselves among the merchants and burghers, he was surprised to find that none of Russia's other landowners had experimented with schemes for enfranchisement. Poland, in contrast, had seen significant developments in this area. The *Travels*' key source of information here was the Polish reformer Józef Wybicki, a keen reader of the works of Montesquieu and David Hume, and a staunch opponent of non-free forms of labour. Coxe met Wybicki when in Poland and went on to quote at length from the Pole's 1777–1778 work, *Listy Patriotyczne* (*Patriotic Letters*).[60] In his account, Wybicki had provided some detailed commentary on a series of enfranchisement schemes, foremost among them that developed by Andrzej Zamoyski, a prominent Polish nobleman and Chancellor of Poland from 1764–1767. Through drawing on Wybicki's discussion, Coxe was able to provide evidence that granting peasants their liberty had substantially reduced poverty. Villages which had been enfranchised had seen landowners' revenues triple, the peasants' financial dependence on landowners reduce, and labour motivation and birth rates, a key marker of the wealth of a particular locale for eighteenth-century commentators, increase rapidly (the latter by c. 80 per cent per year).[61] In addition, Coxe emphasised that the reforms had produced genuine social benefits. Not only had drunkenness and the crime it helped to engender been reduced, but the bonds between nobility and peasants had been strengthened.[62]

Coxe himself did not attach huge importance to these reforms. The lack of any legal support for the process of enfranchisement at a national level, he argued, meant that it would be possible for them to be overturned by anyone who inherited a 'free' estate. More generally, Coxe did not see enfranchisement as a sign of a wider recovery in Poland's political and economic fortunes; he expected – correctly, as events transpired – that Poland, in time, would be swallowed up by its larger and more powerful neighbours. Underpinning Coxe's work, meanwhile, was a series of assumptions about poverty which were stated perhaps most clearly in his 1790 work *A Letter to Richard Price*. This account constituted a critical response to Price's 1789 sermon, *A Discourse on the Love of One's Country*, a defence of the French Revolution with an implicit call for constitutional reform in England.[63] Coxe's disagreement with Price was, in a sense, methodological. The ideas that underpinned Price's *Discourse* were, Coxe contended, rooted in 'speculation' and 'theory' and led by a desire to prompt the British nation to 'adopt foreign and unsettled motives, and to quit national and established principles'.[64] In place of such experiments, Coxe argued for a more evidence-based approach.[65] His own qualifications to comment on political affairs, it was emphasised, were a product of experience. He was, he reminded his readers, 'a man who has twice travelled over the greatest part of Europe; who has examined with peculiar attention, not only the different governments, but the different shades in each government; who has been careful to distinguish the practice from the theory, and has made the condition of the lower class people the particular object of his attention'.[66] Such a focus on the 'lower classes' was valuable because it demonstrated that the English constitution is 'that in which the true principles of liberty are best understood and practised'; in no other country that he had visited, Coxe concluded, did 'persons of all ranks and denominations possess such solid comforts, such real and substantial happiness'.[67] Coxe's experiences of poverty in countries like Poland and Russia, therefore, provided an empirical vindication for Britain's own constitutional arrangements.

Other writers, however, were to see things differently. By far the most frequently quoted section of the *Travels* was its description of the reforms to the serf system instigated by Zamoyski and his countrymen. Engagement with this passage was driven by debates in the 1780s and 1790s concerning the Atlantic slave trade; indeed, it was the value of Coxe's work to ongoing campaigns against slavery that led to it being deployed in a range of abolitionist pamphlets and newspaper polemics during these years.[68] Its appeal was threefold. First, it provided an economic argument against slavery. *The Times* of 27 April 1789, for example, repeated Coxe's claim that noblemen in Poland who had broken 'the fetters of slavery' had seen productivity among their labourers increase threefold and substantial growth in their incomes.[69] Given the parallels between previous Polish labour practices and 'our slavery in the west', the author concluded that such achievements provided a demonstration that abolition was in the interests not just of enslaved peoples but also of those who owned them.[70] Second, Coxe's work was used to allay fears that the abolition of slavery would lead to a rise in licentiousness and disorder. Thus *Woodfall's Register* in April 1790 repeated Coxe's account of a Polish peasant who on being told of his liberation observed: 'when we had no other property but the stick in our hands, we were destitute of all encouragements to a right conduct; but the fear of forfeiting what we shall henceforth possess, will be a constant restraint'.[71] Such comments, the author concluded, showed 'the moral effects of slavery, and of liberty rightly understood'.[72] Finally, the *Travels* were used to show the benefits of slower types of reform over more sudden kinds of change. William Dickson's work is instructive here. In his *Letters on Slavery*, after noting the that the abolition of the African trade would be an excellent preparation for the gradual annihilation of slavery itself 'in our islands', Dickson provided a lengthy footnote made up of quotations from Coxe.[73] This summarised the experiments engaged in by Zamoyski and concluded with a reference, also derived from Coxe, to a prize-winning Russian dissertation which recommended that peasants be given a '*gradual succession of privileges*, and to follow the slow, but sure method of *instruction and improvement*'.[74] Taken in sum, therefore, the value of the Zamoyski passage is clear: it provided a useful example of a transition between an inefficient slave-based economic system and an efficient 'free' one, which had increased productivity and wealth while maintaining order and a workable social hierarchy.

While these newspaper accounts draw on the same broad assumptions about slavery and free labour which underpinned accounts of the transition between feudal and commercial societies, they do not explicitly make the connection between slavery and feudalism. Other writers, however, engaged directly with this framework. The most notable example here is *The Effects of Slavery on Morals and Industry*, a 1793 work by the American lexicographer and abolitionist, Noah Webster. Webster's approach to his subject was comparative: he used a range of examples from across the world and across history to show that slavery was a fundamentally inefficient mode of labour in the sense that it impoverished enslaved individuals, landowners and governments. Examples concerning Polish and Russian poverty, all of which were derived from Coxe, played a key role in demonstrating this thesis. At one level, these countries functioned as warnings. In the twelfth century, Webster asserted, both nations had been subject to 'feudal system' and, as such, English and Polish peasants 'were nearly in the same situation'.[75] However, whereas the English 'churles', in time, become 'free tenants' with legal rights, the Poles did not.[76] This, Webster concluded referencing Robertson and Adam Smith, 'is the principal circumstance which has rendered the agriculture of England flourishing, and the farmers more intelligent, wealthy and respectable than the miserable serfs in Poland'.[77] Despite such claims, however, Webster was by no means uncritical of English practices and did not believe that states like America should seek to copy the gradual process of development which had let to the demise of feudalism. A better model was to be found in the approach taken to reform in Poland by Zamoyski and his contemporaries, which Webster summarised at length. The advantages of this approach lay in its practicality. The ultimate challenge for any abolitionist, as Webster conceived of things, was to find an approach to reform which meliorated 'the condition of the blacks', who remained 'very nearly in the situation of the villains in England under the first princes of the Norman line', without essentially injuring the enslaved person, the master and the public.[78] Zamoyski's model had achieved that aim by enriching workers and landowners and Webster concluded his discussion with a passionate plea: what America needed was its own Zamoyski who would be willing to hazard a Polish-style experiment in the Southern states. As such, Polish practices constituted a worthy object for emulation.

Conclusion

For British commentators of the latter part of the eighteenth century, Polish and Russian poverty were products of these states' feudal institutions. To an extent, such a contention enabled commentators to show the similarities between Poland and Russia and their absolute difference from, and inferiority to, the countries to the West. Two caveats, however, need to be added to such a claim. First, the key role ascribed to monarchs in the transition of 'Western' nations from the feudal societies to commercial ones meant that discussion of feudalism always contained reflections on issues relating to government. Consequently, an awareness of the sharp differences between aristocratic Poland and despotic Russia acted as a limiting factor on the development of an idea of Eastern Europe. Or, to put it another way, just as notions of feudal poverty acted as a centripetal force linking Poland and Russia together, so political analysis provided a centrifugal counter force. Writers ascribed contrasting levels of importance to these forces, and this was one of the primary differences between their analyses. Second, and even more importantly, the ideas of feudalism which underpinned discussions of poverty prevented Poland and Russia from ever being viewed as absolute 'opposites' or 'others' within British discourse. Underpinning the narrative developed by Robertson and his contemporaries was the notion that individual nations did not have their own entirely unique characters and histories. Rather there were structural affinities between the ways development had been, and continued, to be experienced by European nations; one feudal society had core similarities with another, whatever the differences in time and space that separated them. This idea was key to the way in which discussions of Russia and Poland functioned. At one level, analysis focused on the contrast, in the present, between 'Eastern' feudalism and 'Western' commerce. However, the premise of such discussions was not that Polish and Russian practices and institutions were irredeemably alien, but rather that they resembled those of medieval Britain. And even if Britain's transformation from a feudal to a commercial nation could not and should not be copied exactly, its pattern of development provided certain guidelines for other states, particularly regarding the value of slower and deeper forms of change over quicker and more superficial ones. Such a conceptualisation was, of course, based on a fundamentally normative idea of progress in which British institutions were conceived of as an ideal solution to the problems faced by less-developed, poorer nations. What is equally noteworthy, however, are the ways in which writers used discussion of feudalism and feudal poverty to identify a series of affinities between 'Western' and 'Eastern' nations. Particularly when the imperial economy was taken into consideration, British writers found parallels – and sometimes troubling ones – between feudal Russia and Poland, and the slavery utilised in British territories. Moreover, a focus on the kinds of reforms which had been undertaken on Polish and Russian territories allowed these nations to be conceived, on occasions, as worthy objects of emulation in their own right. Again, it was the idea of a shared feudalism which made such examples relevant to the anglophone world.

By paying attention to the historical ideas which underpin accounts of Poland and Russia, this chapter provides, therefore, a new perspective on Enlightenment poverty. Such a focus reveals the centrality of a sophisticated comparative framework rooted in ideas of feudalism, which could be used both to defend current practices and to express anxieties regarding them.

Notes

1 On historical writing, see Karen O'Brien, *Narratives of Enlightenment* (Cambridge: Cambridge: University Press, 1997); J. G. A. Pocock, *Barbarism and Religion*, 6 vols (Cambridge: Cambridge University Press, 1999–2015), esp. vol. ii.
2 On conjectural history, see Mark Salber Phillips, *Society and Sentiment* (Princeton, NJ: Princeton University Press, 2000); and Frank Palmeri, *State of Nature, Stages of Society* (New York, NY: Columbia University Press, 2016). On narrative history, see Phillip Hicks, *Neoclassical History and English Culture* (Basingstoke: Macmillan, 1996).
3 David L. Blaney and Naeem Inayatullah, *Savage Economics* (Abingdon: Routledge, 2010), pp. 8–10.
4 See, for example: Norman Davies, 'The Languor of So Remote an Interest': British Attitudes to Poland, 1772–1832', *Oxford Slavonic Papers*, XVI (1983), 79–90 at 81–82; Stanisław Kot, *Rzeczpospolita Polska w literaturze politycznej Zachodu* (Kraków: Nakładem Krakowskiej spółki wydawniczej, 1919), pp. 176–240. In relation to Russia, see the work of Anthony Cross, especially *Russia Under Western Eyes, 1517–1825* (London: Elek Books, 1971), pp. 39–43; and ibid., *In the Lands of the Romanovs: An Annotated Bibliography of First-hand English-language Accounts of the Russian Empire, 1613–1917* (Cambridge: Open Book Publishers, 2014). See also Larry Wolff, *Inventing Eastern Europe* (Stanford, CA: Stanford University Press, 1994).
5 For Scottish discussions, see Alison Webster, 'The Contribution of the Scottish Enlightenment to the Abandonment of the Institution of Slavery', *The European Legacy*, 8:4 (2003), 481–489. For the French debate, see Andrew S. Curran, *The Anatomy of Blackness* (Baltimore, MD: Johns Hopkins University Press, 2011).
6 The conception of 'poverty' referred to here was fundamentally different to that discussed by Istvan Hont in his hugely influential account of the 'rich country/poor country debate'. Key to the work of the authors Hont dealt with – David Hume, Adam Smith and Dugald Stewart among them – was the extent to which the abundant cheap labour and, consequently, low prices of a poor nation might enable it to 'catch-up' with more affluent polities. Poland and Russia were conceived, however, as being in a kind of second division of European polities; their feudal infrastructures, particularly their reliance on slavery, ensured they could never, without a complete social and political transformation, compete commercially with richer states. See Istvan Hont, *Jealousy of Trade* (Cambridge, MA: Harvard University Press, 2005).

7 Pocock, *Barbarism and Religion*, vol. ii, pp. 20–21.
8 Specifically David Hume, 'Of Commerce', 'Of Refinement in the Arts', *Essays, Moral, Political, Literary*, ed. Eugene F. Miller (Indianapolis, IN: Liberty Fund, 1987), pp. 253–280; David Hume, *History of England*, 6 vols (Indianapolis, IN: Liberty Fund, 1983); Adam Smith, *The Wealth of Nations*, eds R. H. Campbell, A. S. Skinner, and W. B. Todd, 2 vols (Indianapolis, IN: Liberty Fund, 1982), pp. 411–427; William Robertson, *The Progress of Society in Europe*, ed. Felix Gilbert (Chicago, IL and London: University of Chicago Press, 1972), which is the opening section of *The History of the Reign of the Emperor Charles V*, 3 vols (London, 1769).
9 Coxe, *Travels*, vol. i, p. 126, n.
10 Robertson, *Progress*, p. 29.
11 Ibid., p. 32.
12 Ibid., p. 32, p. 52.
13 Ibid., p. 32.
14 Ibid., p. 31.
15 For discussions of reform to serfdom during this period in a range of Enlightened absolutist states, see Tim Hochstrasser's Chapter 1 in this volume.
16 Montesquieu, *Spirit of the Laws*, trans. and ed. Anne M. Cohler, Basia C. Miller and Harold S. Stone (Cambridge: Cambridge University Press, 1989), p. 10.
17 See: Anna Plassart, 'Burke, Poland and the Commonwealth of Europe', *Historical Journal*, 63:4 (2020), 885–910 at 889.
18 William Paley, *The Principles of Moral and Political Philosophy*, third edition (London, 1786), p. 456. Paley was drawing upon the ideas of David Hume; for example, Hume, *Essays*, p. 17.
19 George Macartney, *An Account of Russia* (London, 1768), p. 91.
20 Montesquieu, *Spirit of the Laws*, p. 91.
21 See: *Monthly Review*, 55 (1777), 430–431; Wolff, *Inventing*, pp. 81–83; Maciej Laskowski, 'Joseph Marshall: A Traveller of "Perfect Obscurity" in Stanislavian Poland and other parts of Europe', *Polish Anglo-Saxon Studies*, 20 (2017), 5–21. Laskowski looks at claims from Danish scholars that Marshall was in fact John (or Joseph or George) Hill, a miscellaneous writer.
22 The conflict was between supporters of the monarch, Stanisław August Poniatowski and the Confederation of the Bar, an association of the nobility who were critical of Russia's influence on the King and opposed to his reformist agenda. See: Jerzy Lukowski, *Liberty's Folly* (London: Routledge, 1991), pp. 197–204.
23 Joseph Marshall, *Travels through Holland, Flanders, Germany, Denmark, Sweden, Lapland, Russia, the Ukraine, and Poland. In the years 1768, 1769, and 1770*, 3 vols (London, [1772]), vol. iii, p. 263.
24 Ibid., vol. iii, p. 188.
25 Ibid., vol. iii, p. 262 (the page is mislabelled p. 230).
26 Ibid., vol. iii, pp. 238–239.
27 Ibid., vol. iii, p. 125.
28 Ibid., vol. iii, p. 126, pp. 153–159.

29 Ibid., vol. iii, p. 146.
30 Ibid., vol. iii, p. 157.
31 Ibid., vol. iii, p. 156.
32 Ibid.
33 This was a fashionable proposition. See, for example, the similar scheme developed by Arthur Young in *Political Essays Concerning the Present State of the British Empire* (1772), p. 404. Young's work was published on 4 February (see *Daily Advertiser*, 22 January), Marshall's work was announced on 4 April of the same year (see *Gazetteer and Newly Daily Advertiser*, 4 April).
34 Marshall, *Travels*, vol. iii, p. 166.
35 Ibid., vol. iii, pp. 243–244.
36 John Williams, *The Rise, Progress, and Present State of the Northern Governments*, 2 vols (London, 1777), vol. i, pp. v–vi.
37 Ibid., vol. ii, p. 78, p. 110, p. 113.
38 Ibid., vol. ii, p. 103.
39 Ibid., vol. ii, p. 656.
40 Ibid., vol. ii, p. 645.
41 Ibid., vol. ii, pp. 645–646.
42 Ibid., vol. ii, p. 647.
43 Ibid., vol. ii, p. 206.
44 Ibid., vol. ii, pp. 650–651.
45 Ibid., vol. ii, p. 649.
46 Ibid., vol. i, p. v.
47 Ibid., vol. ii, p. 316.
48 Ibid.
49 Ibid., vol. ii, p. 205.
50 Ibid., vol. ii, pp. 316–317.
51 Ibid., vol. ii, p. 642.
52 Ibid., vol. ii, p. 205.
53 Ibid., vol. ii, p. 640.
54 Ibid.
55 William Coxe, *Travels into Poland, Russia, Sweden and Denmark*, 2 vols (London 1784), title page.
56 Ibid., vol. ii, p. 502.
57 Ibid., vol. ii, p. 137, vol. ii, p. 93.
58 Ibid., vol. i, p. 126, n.
59 Ibid., vol. i, p. 142.
60 See: Józef Wybicki, *Listy Patriotyczne*, ed. Kazmierz Opałek (Wrocław: Zakład Imienia Ossolińskich, 1955). Coxe's examples are principally taken from letter 8, pp. 174–175.
61 Coxe, *Travels*, vol. i, pp. 132–134.
62 Ibid., vol. i, p. 134.
63 William Coxe, *A Letter to the Rev. Richard Price* (1790).
64 Ibid., p. 4.

65 Coxe's claims, it should be emphasised, were polemical in nature. Price himself took an explicitly evidence-based approach in much of his work, most notably *Observations on Reversionary Payments* (1771).
66 Coxe, *Letter*, pp. 44–45.
67 Ibid., p. 45.
68 See, for example: *The Times*, 27 April 1789, 12 May 1789; *Woodfall's Register*, 23 June 1789, 18 July 1789, 16 April 1790; *Morning Post*, 17 June 1791. See also William Dickson, *Letters on Slavery* (London, 1789), pp. 89–90; Noah Webster, *Effects of Slavery on Morals and Industry* (Hartford, CT, 1793). Coxe's claims about the Zamoyski reforms were later challenged by George Burnett in his *View of the Present State of Poland* (London, 1807), pp. 106–109. The Coxe/Burnett debate was taken up in a series of later American discussions about slavery. See, for example: Thomas R. Dew, *Review of the Debate in the Virginia Legislature* (Richmond VA, 1832); *The Anti-Slavery Monthly Reporter*, 12 August 1840.
69 *The Times*, 27 April 1789.
70 Ibid.
71 *Woodfall's Register*, 16 April 1790.
72 Ibid.
73 William Dickson, *Letters on Slavery* (London, 1789), p. 89.
74 Ibid., p. 90.
75 Webster, *Effects of Slavery*, p. 22.
76 Ibid.
77 Ibid.
78 Ibid., p. 37.

9

Desolation and abundance: poverty and the Irish landscape, c. 1720–1820

James Stafford

'The want of trade in Ireland,' claimed the English diplomat and author Sir William Temple in 1673, 'proceeds from the want of people.' This, he went on,

> is not grown from any ill qualities of the climate or air, but chiefly from the frequent revolutions of so many wars and rebellions, so great slaughters and calamities of mankind, as have at several intervals of time succeeded the first conquest of this kingdom in Henry II's time, until the year 1653. Two very great plagues followed the two great wars, those of Queen Elizabeth's reign, and the last; which helped to drain the current stream of generation in the country.[1]

In depopulating the country, Ireland's seventeenth-century wars of religion had frustrated the vast natural potential suggested by its 'native fertility of the soil and seas' and 'situation so commodious for all sorts of foreign trade'.[2] Had it not been for the 'numbers of the British, which the necessity of the late wars at first drew over ... the country had by the last war and plague been left in a manner *desolate*'.[3] Nearly a century and a half later, in a letter to David Ricardo, Robert Malthus complained of the opposite problem. Population was growing too rapidly: 'greatly in excess above the demand for labour'. If Ireland's rulers were 'to give full effect to the natural resources of the country', the land had to be cleared of its excess people and consolidated into large, modern farms. It was necessary, Malthus concluded, that 'a great part of this population should be swept from the soil into large manufacturing and commercial Towns'.[4]

How was the image of Irish poverty transformed from one of desolation to one of abundance? Since it straddles the awkward gap between the economic thought of the Enlightenment and that of the 'liberal' or 'laissez-faire' nineteenth century, the question has rarely been asked. Malthus' dramatic impact on British, and subsequently European, economic thinking is usually taken as an explanation in and of itself; one in which the *Principles of Population* (1798) successfully challenged the 'populationist' consensus of the Enlightenment. Yet the variable that concerned both Temple and Malthus was not simply the raw numbers of Ireland's people, but their distribution over the island's territory – what Temple called the 'number of people in proportion to the compass of ground they inhabit'.[5] Both wrote as observers not just of Ireland's people but of its landscape, sandwiching observations on the island's potential for prosperity between remarks on its natural endowments of 'fertility' and 'a 'commodious situation' and the condition of its woods and fields.[6]

Their contrasting observations indicate something fundamental about how poverty was conceptualised in the Enlightenment: viewed, as it frequently was, from the passing carriages and brief perambulations of the travelling gentlemen who wrote about it. In an era free from statistical constructions of wealth and poverty like Gross Domestic Product, the visual aspect of a 'country' was a vital means of evaluating its poverty or prosperity, to be freely combined with those statistical measures that were available: in the case of Ireland, population figures derived from patchy hearth tax returns, the value of land (calculated as multiples of annual rental) and indications of consumption based on revenues from customs and excise. Poverty could thus be experienced as a spatial and aesthetic problem, to be set against competing visions of flourishing rural landscapes, more pleasing to the eye as well as to the patriotic and Christian conscience.

This problematic, as this chapter will show, was particularly acute in the eighteenth-century Irish Kingdom, a polity that was unique in Western Europe: both in terms of the scale and scope of demographic and agrarian change that took place in the course of the eighteenth century, and the peculiar valence of rural poverty for its Anglican, 'Anglo-Irish' ruling class, who founded their governing legitimacy in a project of disciplining and reforming both the visual aspect of the Irish countryside and the living conditions of its (largely Catholic) inhabitants. In common with other chapters in this volume, the present contribution makes the case that poverty was a central – if not *the* central – concern of Irish political-economic thought in the eighteenth century, long before the revolutionary crisis of the 1790s and the rise of Malthusianism. It was not just a grounds for articulating an Anglican paternalism, but the locus of a three-sided conflict between the Anglo-Irish governing elite, a Catholic landed gentry recovering from the conquests of the seventeenth century and British reformers of Irish Empire, who were increasingly concerned, from the last quarter of the eighteenth century, with the condition of the island's 'labouring poor'. Malthus' call for Ireland's population to be 'swept' into the towns was thus offered as sharp rejoinder to an existing Irish discourse on poverty, in which the conversion of Irish land from pasture to tillage signified the successful economic stewardship of the Irish Kingdom by its Anglican ruling class. Their vision of Irish prosperity – one of a dense and evenly distributed rural population, capable of combining wage labour on commercial grain farms with subsistence potato agriculture – was in turn a response to the depopulation and pastoralism of seventeenth and early eighteenth-century Ireland, which was blamed not only on the devastation wrought by the seventeenth century's wars of religion, but on the distorted terms of Ireland's integration into networks of European and colonial trade in the early eighteenth century.

The idea of poverty in a European colony

Ideas of poverty in Ireland tracked, therefore, the layered, many-sided structure of colonial government in a polity that had long been shaped by political and legal contestation over the ownership and uses of agricultural land. They similarly reflected the fluidity and instability of political and social authority in a society that had been completely transformed by an unusually aggressive and comprehensive program of conquest and colonisation. The political and landed elite of eighteenth-century Ireland were the beneficiaries of the dispossession of an older, Catholic aristocracy, part Gaelic, part Anglo-Norman, through successive waves of plantation, expropriation and settlement.[7] Unable to position themselves as straightforward inheritors of Ireland's medieval history and institutions, these 'New English' had frequently rested their novel claim to rule on 'improvement', rescuing the Kingdom from the 'barbaric' customs of Gaels and 'degenerate' Anglo-Normans.[8] The attractiveness of 'improvement' as a justification for conquest and colonisation persisted through the religious wars of the seventeenth century into the age of Enlightenment. When, in 1738, Samuel Madden, an Anglican priest, landowner and writer, wrote to encourage his peers to dedicate their time and money to the promotion of Irish 'manufacture and tillage', he addressed them as 'landlords ... masters of Families ... Protestants ... descended from British ancestors'.[9]

Given that the entire landed class of the country had been extirpated, resettled and replaced within living memory, it is unsurprising that eighteenth-century Irish Anglicans were able to conceive of a variety of ambitious, even utopian, 'projects' for the transformation of their society.[10] It was Ireland's shifting position in imperial and European trading networks, however, that produced a further, dramatic transformation in its human geography in the second half of the eighteenth century. As the export of beef and butter to the British Empire's Caribbean slave colonies went into decline following the War of American Independence, land use in the east and south changed rapidly. Grasslands were turned to fields of wheat, oat and barley, and grain exports, supported by a system of internal bounties and a growing network of canals and turnpike roads, overtook linen as a source of foreign earnings.[11] The population, fed overwhelmingly by the potato, expanded rapidly from mid-century, more than doubling by 1800.[12] Land hunger pushed settlement to expand into the western uplands of the island, characterised by 'rundale' cooperative farming and the proliferation of 'lazy bed' potato cultivation. The French Revolutionary Wars, which isolated Britain from Baltic grain supplies at a moment of maximum demographic and financial stress, meanwhile provided a further impetus to tillage in the south-eastern agrarian core, leading one Irish politician to assert that 'Ireland is capable of becoming the granary of Great Britain'.[13]

It was the eastern and southern agrarian core of Ireland, as opposed to the linen and smallholding economy of Ulster, or the cooperative farming of the western uplands, that witnessed the most dramatic changes in land use, and which consequently assumed an outsized importance in the economic thinking of both Irish and British elites. While this attention was partly predetermined by their relative proximity to Dublin, and their accessibility as compared to the far west, it was also because these regions were central to the new agrarian and demographic regime that emerged in eighteenth-century Ireland, and which would endure down to the catastrophic famines of 1845–1851. As demand for land pushed a growing population westwards, the eighteenth-century tillage boom created the conditions for the Malthusian vision of Irish poverty that would do so much to shape British thinking on poverty and agriculture in Ireland – and beyond. Yet it also fulfilled, in crucial respects, the ambitions of those earlier generations of Anglo-Irish settlers, who had believed tillage and proto-industry to be the indispensable means of pacifying and ordering the Irish interior, under Protestant and British tutelage. To understand the transformation of ideas of poverty in Ireland in the age of Enlightenment, therefore, we must reconstruct the dynamic interaction between rival imaginaries, both British and Anglo-Irish, of a well-ordered countryside.

The remainder of this chapter will consider first the emergence of tillage and rural population as a marker of 'improvement' meaningful to Ireland's Anglo-Irish governing class. It will then consider how the remaining Catholic gentry of the Irish Kingdom used this Protestant language of improvement to challenge post-conquest laws that restricted Catholic property holding. It will then explore how, in the era of the American and French Revolutionary Wars and the parliamentary Union of 1801, Anglo-Irish and British writers analysed the rise of the potato and the 'cottier' system as indexes of the Irish Kingdom's growing prosperity in a new imperial division of labour in which it could serve primarily as an agricultural producer for Britain's growing industrial cities. Finally, focusing on Malthus and a lesser-known agrarian writer, the Quaker land agent Edward Wakefield, it will explore how it was that the new rural dispensation created by the combination of Anglo-Irish 'improvement' and British demand came to be scorned by the new schools of demography and political economy that came to prominence in post-war Britain. The potato, for both men, guaranteed bare life, but at the cost of the varied diet, labour and social contact promised by Britain's wheat- and meat-fuelled 'commercial society'. The stage was set for the Victorian projects of social engineering that would ultimately empty the nineteenth-century Irish countryside of its 'superabundant' inhabitants in the wake of the Great Famine of 1845–1852.

Luxury and pastoralism

The distinction between a sedentary agricultural civilisation, which made private property possible and sovereign authority necessary, and an ungovernable, nomadic pastoralism, had been central to English ideologies of empire since the earliest medieval incursions into Ireland. In his *View of the State of Ireland* (1595), a dialogue on Irish colonisation that was still widely read in eighteenth-century Ireland, the Elizabethan official and poet Edmund Spenser had complained that the rebelliousness of the country could be traced by its inhabitants' attachment to the raising of cattle:

> look into all Countreys that live in such sort by keeping of Cattle, and you shall find that they are both very barbarous and uncivil, and also greatly given to War. The *Tartarians*, the *Muscovites*, the *Norwegians*, the *Goths*, the *Armenisans*, and many other do witness the same. And therefore since now we purpose to draw the *Irish* from desire of War and Tumults, to the love of Peace and Civility, it is expedient to abridge their great Custom of hardning, and augment their Trade and Tillage and Husbandry.[14]

What made the Jacobean settlement of Ireland different to its medieval predecessors, the New English attorney general Sir John Davies wrote in 1613, was the determination with which the Irish Kingdom had been 'reduced to shire-ground'.[15] For as long as English settlement had been restricted to Dublin and its environs (the 'Pale') and 'Brehon law' prevailed throughout the island, the Irish had failed to 'plant any gardens or orchards, inclose or improve their lands' or 'live together in settled villages or towns'. With the imposition of English 'sovereignty' and the extension of English law to the Irish interior, the foundations for 'peace, plenty and civility', the end goals of a 'perfect conquest', had finally been laid.[16] Over a century later, the Scottish jurist and historian John Millar attributed the 'limited appropriation of land' in pre-conquest Ireland to the persistence of 'pastoral manners', under which the old Irish 'without confining themselves to fixed residence [...] wander, with their cattle, from place to place'.[17] The colonial division of civilised settler from barbarous nomad was recast in the terms of Enlightenment stadial history.

As Ian McBride has recently argued in a pathbreaking reconstruction of the contexts for Jonathan Swift's *Modest Proposal* (1729), however, the eighteenth-century Anglo-Irish passion for tillage was rooted in something more than a generic preference for sedentarisation as a tool of colonial governance. What preoccupied Swift and his fellow Irish Anglican churchmen, in a decade marked by famine and increasing emigration to Britain's north American colonies, was the recurring problem of what Davies had called 'degeneracy': the tendency of Ireland's colonisers to recreate the 'barbarous' social structures they had supposedly extirpated among the native population and their own antecedents in the labour of settlement.[18] Absent the full introduction of agricultural techniques modelled on those of the south-east of England, the work of colonisation would never be completed. 'I have often wondered,' the Irish Whig Robert Molesworth wrote in a tract of 1723

> when I consider how long it is since this Kingdom of *Ireland* has been united and annexed to the Crown of *England*, and the *English* customs, as to Habit, Language, and Religion, have been encouraged and enjoyn'd by Laws how it comes to pass, that we should be so long a time, and so universally Ignorant of the *English* manner of managing our Tillage and Lands as we now are; or if we formerly knew them, how we came to fall off from that Knowledge and the Practice of it to such a degree, that the *English* Tenants who pay double the Rent to their Landlords for their Acres (which are much shorter than the *Irish* Acres) are able notwithstanding to supply us with Corn at a moderate price.[19]

Early eighteenth-century Ireland might no longer be a land of nomads, but Swift and his contemporaries feared that fertile land in the south and east of the country was increasingly being turned to sheep and cattle grazing, making vagrants and rebels of Irish farmers, diminishing tithe revenues, and increasing the country's susceptibility to famine. The booming trade in beef, butter and raw wool, commodities vital to the maintenance of Britain's slave colonies in the Caribbean and its domestic textile industries, was held by Swift and others to place an unacceptable strain on arable farming in the Irish west and south. The colonial equation of tillage with civilisation was here joined to a humanist critique, traceable to Thomas More, of the social devastation wrought by the expansion of grazing. Ireland's unbalanced pattern of trade, agriculture and industry fed the luxury consumption of a small elite while condemning the land and its people to poverty and desolation. 'There is no country in Europe', observed one of the founders of the Dublin Society, the merchant Thomas Prior, which produces, and exports so great a Quantity of *Beef*, Butter, Tallow, Hydes and Wool, as Ireland does; and yet our Common People are very poorly Cloath'd, go bare-legged half the Year, and very rarely taste of that Flesh meat, with which we so much abound; we pinch ourselves in every Article of Life, and export more, than we can well spare, with no other Effect or Advantage, than to enable our *Gentlemen* and *Ladies* to live more luxuriously abroad.[20]

While Prior's attack on the graziers centred on the manner in which their profits were supposedly sucked out of Ireland by the absentee expenditure of the Anglo-Irish aristocracy in their London townhouses, others decried its tendency to degrade the visual aspect of the countryside. In his *Querist* (1735–1737), a remarkable piece of monetary philosophy which argued for the total reorientation of Ireland's economy from 'foreign' to 'domestic' trade, George Berkeley suggested that it was 'a sure Sign or Effect of a Country's thriving, to see it well cultivated, and full of inhabitants'. A 'great Quantity of Sheep-walk', by contrast, was 'ruinous to a Country, rendering it waste, and thinly inhabited'.[21] Here, Berkeley's location in County Cork, the centre of the eighteenth-century Irish provisioning trade, undoubtedly influenced his analysis. Luxury in a poor country, Berkeley observed, left Ireland trapped in an entirely retrograde trade pattern, exporting beef and butter in return for foreign luxuries. Irish luxury consumption was 'madness', the result of a 'poor nation' seeking to imitate the fashions of richer ones. Pastoralism was incapable of supporting or employing the majority of its population. Berkeley set out on an impassioned line of reasoning in the *Querist*:

Q147 Whether a Woman of Fashion ought not to be declared a public Enemy?
Q148 Whether it not be certain, that from the single Town of Cork were exported, last Year, no less than 107,161 barrels of beef, 7379 barrels of Pork, 13,461 Casks, and 85,727 Firkins of Butter? And what hands were employed in this Manufacture?
Q149 Whether a Foreigner could imagine, that one half of the People were starving, in a Country which sent out such Plenty of Provisions?
Q150 Whether an Irish Lady, set out with French Silks, and Flanders lace, may not be said to consume more Beef and Butter than Fifty of our labouring Peasants?
Q151 Whether nine Tenths of our foreign Trade be not singly to support the Article of Vanity?.[22]

The purpose of Berkeley's proposed monetary revolution, which would see an Irish paper currency backed by a mixture of land and gold and silver goods donated by the wealthy of the Irish Kingdom, was to promote employment and 'industry' among the Irish poor. The sparseness of rural habitation under the rule of the graziers was part of a general aversion to industry that left land unimproved, and the diets and consumption of the poor sharply constrained, even as the rich profited.

In the introduction to the first English translation of Melon's *Essai Politique sur la Commerce* (1736), a major intervention in the early eighteenth-century European debate on commerce and luxury, the Irish merchant and economic writer David Bindon emphasised that Melon's qualified defence of luxury in a French context could hardly be applicable to Ireland's circumstances.[23] In the 'Principles' of his *Essai*, Melon had set out a clear hierarchy of human needs. Bread – and therefore corn – was of the 'first necessity'; 'wine, salt, linen and the like' were of the 'second necessity' and 'silk, sugar and tobacco' were of 'luxurious necessity'. Luxury could be defined as 'necessary' because it was required to sustain the industry of countries that had reached a position of 'superfluity' and 'superabundance' in the first two types of commodities.[24] 'Workmen, will not be employed about Works for Luxury, until there be enough of the Commodities of second Necessity; and, in like manner, they will not be employed about these, until the Products of absolute Necessity, be fully supplied.'[25] Envious prestige consumption was a necessary spur to industry above a certain level of subsistence.[26] In order to fulfil this vital function for an advanced economy, however, luxury had to be founded on domestic production. 'Luxury ought not to be confounded with the wearing of Indian goods, prohibited by the Council of Trade', warned Melon.[27]

Ireland's retrograde pastoral trading pattern, Bindon argued, meant that this ideal order of necessities had been confused in Ireland. The luxury of the elite was sustaining the kingdom's poverty, instead of inspiring its industry. 'What our Author saith of Luxury, may be perfectly right with respect to *France*', he said. But 'the Luxury of *Ireland* consisteth in the Consumption of the Products of foreign Lands ... the Degrees of Necessities are so ill distinguished, that we run in to the most extravagant Luxuries, at the same Time that there is a constant Scarcity of Corn, and of other Things of absolute Necessity'.[28] The great problem of pastoralism, Irish writers agreed, was that it granted wealth without promoting the kind of broad-based industry or social discipline that would render the island's population both prosperous and governable. Bindon condemned the 'lazy method of employing large Tracts of Land in grazing of Cattle, which prevaileth in the most fertile Provinces', demanding 'more active kinds of Husbandry' carried out on smaller arable farms.[29] 'The chief Articles of Export from *Ireland*,' he went on,

> are the Products of Land with very little additional Value from the Labour or Industry of Man. The Wealth of the Kingdom is engrossed into the Hands of

a few very opulent Landlords, overgrown Farmers, and other Persons, who neither labour nor exercise any Industry, that contributeth to encrease the Riches of the nation.[30]

Like Melon and the economic thinkers of the Scottish Enlightenment, the early eighteenth-century school of Irish improving political economists were disparaging of sweeping moralistic condemnations of material well-being as a force for the enervation of political or military virtue. The alternative to a regime of luxury and laziness, which sacrificed the education of the Catholic poor into English habits of industry to the self-interest of the landed aristocracy, was an agricultural regime of small arable farms and as much textile weaving as British restrictions on the export of Irish manufactures would permit. Prior speculated that 'our Gentlemen' might be brought to once again reside in Ireland either through a tax on absenteeism, or through the equalisation of fortunes brought about by the application of partitive inheritance ('gavelkind') to the largest Protestant estates. "Tis true Policy,' he claimed,

> and would tend much to the Benefit of remote Provinces, if Property were more equally divided among the Inhabitants; large overgrown Estates are generally consumed, either abroad or at the Capital, and may be reckon'd as so much Tribute, in Effect, drawn from the Provinces; while small Fortunes are spent in the Place where they arise, with more Virtue, and Advantage to the Country.[31]

Berkeley, for his part, asked his readers 'whether large Farms under few Hands, or small ones under many, are likely to be made most of? And whether Flax and Tillage do not naturally multiply Hands, and divide Land into small Holdings and well improved?'[32]

Property and the Catholic question

Anglo-Irish improvers were divided on the question of how to sufficiently discipline a Catholic tenantry into the best practices of English agrarianism. Molesworth complained that 'every Tenant does with his Farm as he pleases ... and that is what his Laziness, his Ignorance, or Dishonesty prompts him to, without regard to Covenants'. Not possessed of the capital to improve farms themselves, tenants sublet to 'cottagers' or 'partners' who vandalised the land: 'they plow up three Parts of four of the Land, without regard to Seasons or Manuring. They sow false Crops, Pill-fallow, break Fences, cut down Quicksetts and other Trees, for Fireing, or to mend their Carrs, spoil Copses, dig their Turf irregularly in Pitts and Hay.' 'No tenant,' Molesworth argued, should posess 'a greater Farm than he and his own Family or Servants can manage and wield after a husbandly Manner, with his own Stock and Subtance; without his Letting any part of it off to others.'[33] Keeping tenants on a tighter leash, through shorter leases, was the principal means available to Irish landlords for the promotion of agricultural improvement, which was itself a sufficient motivation to encourage patriotic landlords to forego the exploitation of good tenants by excessive rents. 'If there be any Landlord so griping as to turn an old improving good Tenant out of his Farm, at the expiration of his Lease,' Molesworth cautioned, 'let him suffer under the Obloquy of his Country.'[34]

Arthur Dobbs, an Antrim landholder and MP who was another of the founding circle of the Dublin Society, took precisely the opposite view. It was the Anglo-Irish landlords themselves, he cautioned, rather than their head tenants, who were responsible for the disordered state of Irish tillage. 'Short leases of 21 years', Dobbs argued, were a great 'discouragement to Improvements', since they gave tenants little incentive to invest labour or capital in their farms while encouraging 'extravagant' landlords to let out land at rack-rents. The agents of absentee noblemen, Dobbs warned, were the greatest offenders. 'Industry and Improvements go very heavily on, when we think we are not to have the Property in either', Dobbs observed. 'What can be expected then from Covenants to improve and plant, when the Person to do it, knows he is to have no Property in them?' The solution was not to follow Molesworth in pursuing the ever-tighter discipline of tenants through shorter leases, but to convert existing leases into a lifelong, renewable tenancies, in which the size and subdivision of the plot were strictly regulated, but the incentives to improvement maximised.[35] It was through the creation of a free 'yeomanry', not a more disciplined and precarious tenantry, that the ordered and settled rural landscape sought by the promoters of Irish tillage could be brought into being:

> What an Improvement such Tenures would procure to the Kingdom, every one at first View may observe. Here would be a fixt property in a Farm, sufficient to find employment for a large Family in improving it to the utmost. Then all lands capable of Improvement would be inclos'd, fenc'd, drain'd, manur'd, till'd or planted with every thing to the best advantage ... The whole Country would appear like a regular Plantation or Garden, by the industry and frugality of the People: And Nature would seem always to smile.[36]

Dobbs' speculations about the relationship between the security of tenure and the productivity of tillage land raised uncomfortable questions about the sectarian property settlement that was the dominant feature of Irish landed society from the seventeenth century down to independence. Following the expropriation of Ireland's Catholic aristocracy in the seventeenth century, the Anglican-dominated Parliament at Dublin had passed a series of statutes – collectively referred to as the 'Penal Laws' – that aimed to restrict the Catholic majority's access to public worship, civil or military officeholding, arms, property and credit.[37] The 1704 'Act to Prevent the Further Growth of Popery' was central to the eighteenth-century Irish debate on the of Irish tillage and the restraint of pastoralism. Under the terms of the act, Catholics were barred from inheriting from Protestants, acquiring land by purchase, or leasing land for more than thirty-one years. Land in Catholic hands was subject to the same law of 'gavelkind' – mandatory partitive inheritance – endorsed by Prior in his *List of the Absentees of Ireland*. The purpose of the provision was facilitate the breakup of Catholic estates and their sale into Anglican hands. The first male Anglican convert within a Catholic landed family was permitted to claim an estate in its entirety, rendering his siblings and parents his tenants; Protestant 'discoverers' of illegal Catholic land purchases, meanwhile, could be awarded the property themselves.[38]

Prior, Dobbs and Berkeley had tacitly acknowledged the confessional politics buried just beneath the surface of controversies over agrarian improvement in their responses to the crises of the 1720s. Prior's endorsement of 'gavelkind' for Protestants, like Dobbs' demand for lifetime tenancies, signalled an underlying dissatisfaction with the terms of the 1704 Act. Berkeley, meanwhile, had argued in more general terms that any prosperity 'exclusive of the Bulk of the Natives' would be illusory, arguing that an Irish paper money scheme would distribute economic 'power' to 'each Member' of a 'well govern'd state … according to his just Pretensions and Industry' while vindicating the political, moral and religious leadership of the Anglican church.[39] It was evidently difficult to reconcile a patriotic and inclusive rhetoric of improvement – requiring not just the acquiescence but the active support of a majority Catholic population – with the colonial and sectarian realities of Irish politics.

This tension within the Anglican discourse of improvement was seized upon by the increasingly confident Catholic movement for reform or abolition of the Penal Laws. While much of the energy of the Catholic Committee founded in 1756 by the Roscommon landlord and antiquarian Charles O'Connor of Belangere was focused on rebutting the charge that Catholics could not be loyal subjects to a Protestant king, arguments for reform also drew on the same critique of pastoralism that had animated the economic writings of Anglican improvers a generation earlier. In his *Case of the Roman Catholics of Ireland* (1755), O'Connor claimed that the Penal Laws lay at the root of Ireland's recurring currency and subsistence crises, producing a national economy that was excessively skewed towards pastoral agriculture.

Like Swift and Berkeley, O'Conor argued that prosperity that lacked a secure basis in tillage was illusory. In good years, it 'furnished us with the

Specie to purchase the Luxuries, and even the Corn of other countries', but could not do so when export markets turned against Ireland. O'Conor blamed Ireland's continuing dependence on corn imports on laws limiting the length of Catholic tenures. 'It is evident to Demonstration,' he argued, 'that such an Occupation as the Improvement of Land is no Way suited to a transient and insecure interest, but that the wasteful Method of pasturage is so.' Partitive inheritance and the conferral of estates on Protestant descendants prevented wealthier Catholics – whether merchants or land agents – from fixing their property in land. The Penal Laws, O'Conor warned, 'tempt them, above all other People, to quit a Country with which they have but little Connexion, and retire into some other with the Prospect of a more benign Climate, and a more ascertained Property'.[40]

In a 1771 pamphlet published to coincide with a later push for reform of the penal statutes, O'Connor's close associate, the historian and physician John Curry, similarly claimed that the insecurity of property and tenures by the Penal Laws created a pervasive aversion to improvement and a consequent preference for pasture among Catholic landholders. In an obvious reference to Edmund Spenser, Curry quipped that it was the ban on Catholics purchasing landed property that had 'converted our Popish landholders, into a huge tribe of graziers, like our Scythian ancestors'.[41] Curry was an acute observer of 'Whiteboy' agrarian violence in during the 1760s, arguing that it represented a set of specific economic grievances around the competition for potato plots rather than a fixed disposition to revolt among the Catholic peasantry.[42] In his writing on the Penal Laws, he repeated longstanding criticisms of the social dislocation produced by the expansion of pasture: 'these Graziers have no intereft in the culture of land, they expel the poor labourers into mountains, into towns, and into the neighbouring kingdom [...] the wives and children of the greater part infest every quarter of the island, in the shape of naked beggars'. Taming the disorder of the Irish countryside required the security of tenure necessary to convince Catholic tenants to invest in turning their 'waste' pasture to fertile tillage land.[43]

A 'great manufacture'

By the time Curry was writing in the 1770s, Ireland was on the cusp of the turn to tillage that would reshape its demography, human geography and political economy in the era of the French and American revolutionary wars. Tithe returns and estate records from Cork and South Munster – a region in which grazing, cattle fattening and tillage had long co-existed on fertile soils – show a decisive increase in grain production in the last quarter of the eighteenth century.[44] Yields per acre remained constant even as population expanded and cultivation expanded onto more marginal land, encouraged by the increasingly systematic use of lime, sand and manure as fertilisers. Crop rotations became more sophisticated and prowess in ploughing a competitive sport.[45] Some areas, such as County Wexford, were repeatedly praised by observers for their commitment to new agricultural techniques.

The principal causes for rising production, however, lay outside the control of improving landlords. Market integration within Ireland was enabled by the expansion of a system of turnpike roads capable of sustaining the bulk transport of wheat, barley and oats, as well as lime and sand for manuring. At the same time, industrial take-off in Britain, as well as repeated wartime distortions of European grain markets, boosted demand for Irish grain.[46] The commercialisation of tillage generated, in turn, new settlement patterns around the large wheat farms of the south and east of the island. Farmers and labourers increasingly lived apart, with the latter occupying cabins with accompanying potato gardens, living from a combination of the wages they could earn and the potatoes they could grow.[47] Given the demands on their labour time and the pressure, it is unsurprising that these 'cottiers' increasingly chose to plant 'lumper' varieties that required little additional work to cultivate and could be planted and harvested throughout the year.[48] The versatility and resilience of the potato was such that it enabled mass migration to the upland west of the country, where land unsuited to commercial tillage could nonetheless be used to grow potatoes through cooperative 'rundale' farming, comparatively free from the attentions of landlords and agents. On the eve of the famine, it was these marginal uplands, rather than the fertile south and east of the island, where population density was greatest. Consumption of milk, cheese and oats, mainstays of the Irish diet across much of the country down to the end of the eighteenth century, went into a precipitous decline. 'By the 1830s, one-third of the Irish population relied on potatoes for over ninety per cent of their calorie intake.'[49]

The rise of tillage fulfilled the reforming ambitions of early eighteenth-century Irish improvers. Yet the simultaneous emergence of cottierism and the potato as a primary means of organising labour and supporting population presented a striking paradox for observers of Ireland's increasingly dynamic agrarian economy. Ireland was turning to tillage, but it was not, in the process, replicating an English path to 'improvement', like that desired by older reformers like Molesworth or Dobbs. The proliferation of cottier subtenancies represented a different kind of 'proletarianisation' of agricultural labour to the enclosure and live-in service that was reshaping rural life in arable regions of England by the last decades of the eighteenth century.[50]

The association of Irish cottierism and the potato diet with poverty – so self-evident to British observers like Malthus by the 1820s – was by no means straightforward for earlier observers of Ireland's rural economy. The poor housing and clothing of Irish cottiers was frequently discussed and sensationalised in texts like Richard Twiss' *Tour of Ireland in 1775* (1776).[51] Yet it was not clear to more careful observers of Ireland that this necessarily meant the 'labouring poor' were worse off than their English counterparts. In his *Wealth of Nations* (1776), Adam Smith observed that the potato was a much more efficient crop than wheat, rice or oats for the production of 'nourishment'. 'The strongest men and the most beautiful women perhaps in the British dominions,' Smith claimed, 'are said to be ... from the lowest rank of people in Ireland, who are generally fed with this root. No food can afford a more decisive proof of its nourishing quality, or of its being peculiarly suitable to the health of the human condition.'[52] In his *Tour in Ireland* (1780), the English agrarian reformer Arthur Young had cast a similarly sceptical eye over any automatic assumption that Ireland's emergent cottier economy condemned farm labourers to a low standard of living. 'I found upon various occasions,' Young remarked,

> that some gentlemen in Ireland are infected with the rage of adopting the systems as well as the shoes of England: with one party the poor are all starving, with the other they are deemed in a very tolerable situation, and a third, who look with an evil eye on the administration of the British Government, are fond of exclaiming at poverty and rags as proofs of the cruel treatment of Ireland.[53]

The payment of agricultural labour with land and potatoes, Young argued, was an inevitability in Ireland until such time as 'a great increase of national wealth has introduced a more general circulation of money'.[54] It was by no means clear, however, that payment in cash wages, which could be frittered away on vices and luxuries, was really preferable to the steady and nourishing diet afforded by the potato. Irish 'idleness' was attributable to political oppression, not the enervating effects of a potato diet. Indeed, the relative insulation of Irish peasants from the market price of grain made them more obedient and pliable than their English counterparts: 'In England complaints rise even to riots when the rates of provisions are high, but in Ireland the poor have nothing to do with prices; they depend not on prices, but crops of a vegetable very regular in its produce.' In the absence of the purchasing power afforded by cash wages, meanwhile, the labouring poor were far less liable to fall into the kind of vice and corruption that caused English poverty. 'Do we not see numbers of half-starved and half-cloathed families owing to the superfluities of ale and brandy, tea and sugar?', Young asked of his English readers. 'An Irishman cannot do this in any degree; he can neither drink whiskey from his potatoes, nor milk it from his cow.'[55]

Young's remarks were not intended as an unqualified defence of cottier subtenancies. In keeping with the overall argument of the *Tour*, they sought to correct British ignorance about Ireland while undermining an Irish rhetoric of patriotic complaint about the poverty inflicted by imperial restrictions on the Irish Kingdom's foreign trade.[56] During the revival of Irish political economy and demography that followed the Kingdom's 'legislative independence' from Britain in 1782, however, the potato-fed subtenant became the hero of a celebratory narrative of demographic and economic growth under the custodianship of a sovereign Irish Parliament. In a paper read to the newly established Royal Irish Academy in 1789, the Anglo-Irish MP and revenue commissioner Gervaise Parker Bushe surveyed with satisfaction the rapid growth in Irish population enabled by the potato. Taking William Petty's *New Anatomy of Ireland* (1672) as his baseline, Bushe sought to calculate the Irish population of his own day by combining an estimate of total households – suggested by the records of collectors of the Irish 'hearth tax' – with qualitative observations of the mode of living among Irish 'peasants' that could provide a rough guide to the likely number of inhabitants in each household.'

'We may contemplate with pleasure the progress of Irish prosperity', Bushe observed at the outset of his investigation.[57] In the time of William Petty, Ireland had been a 'country of pasturage', with houses too shoddy for the large multigenerational families – complete with servants – who could be accommodated now that 'tillage was becoming very general'.[58] In these areas, Bushe observed with satisfaction, the 'peasants ... generally marry young; and potatoes being their general food, they are under no apprehensions of being unable to support their children; perhaps too for children there is no food so good'.[59] The greater quality, but also the greater expense, of housing meant that numerous young couples often continued to live with their parents, using any savings to acquire more land rather than expand their dwellings. This was a mark, Bushe claimed, of the 'industrious' nature of the Irish peasant 'where tillage has taken root'. Peasants' choices not to invest in building larger or sturdier houses, dictated by the insecurity of tenures and the rapacity of middlemen, could not refute the ample evidence of a healthy and rapidly growing population.

Bushe's assessment of the demographic benefits of the turn to tillage were echoed and amplified in a larger and more substantive work of Irish demography written by another Patriot politician, the Cork MP Thomas Newenham, at the height of the Napoleonic boom in Irish grain exports.[60] Newenham offered a rhapsodic account of the shift away from grazing and towards more civilised, and productive, tillage agriculture.[61] By increasing opportunities for agricultural employment, this had reduced the tide of emigration out of Ireland and facilitated rapid population growth. Irish farming was more labour intensive than its English equivalent; a factor that Newenham, following Adam Smith, identified as crucial to the promotion of population. The efficiency of the Irish staple diet of potatoes and oats ensured a relative absence of scarcity. It had been the stubborn persistence of wheat consumption among the newly settled Anglo-Irish, Newenham claimed, that had produced the famines of the early eighteenth century.[62] Ireland's modern population, by contrast, had attained a high level of density without succumbing to the vices of urbanisation. 'Instead of England being competent to maintain a greater proportionate population than Ireland,' Newenham asserted,

> we shall find that, independently of the acknowledged superiority of the latter, with regard to natural and general fertility of soil, the nature of the food on which the great majority of its inhabitants habitually subsist ... render it competent to support an infinitely more dense population than the former.[63]

Tillage, Newenham claimed, should be considered 'an immense manufacture'; it was a civilising process that had driven Ireland's ascent from a predominantly pastoral economy in the course of the eighteenth century.[64] Echoing Spenser's association of pastoralism with rebellion, he regarded seventeenth-century Ireland as having been in the 'shepherd state, which, next to the hunter state, disposes and qualifies a people most for war'.[65] Even in a modern age of commerce, a society focused on rural grain production was more likely to be stable and prosperous than one in which urban workers formed a growing, and increasingly dangerous, political constituency:

> In places where extensive manufactories are established, and those engaged in them crowded together, the morals of the people are less pure; principles hostile to the public peace are more easily propagated; and contingencies, calculated to excite popular clamour, are more to be apprehended, than is the case in those districts, where, however dense the population, the people are assiduously employed in the culture of the land. Such, for the most part, is the actual condition of the people of Ireland, and it deserves to be considered whether it would not be much more prudent to direct the attention of the Irish to agriculture, than to manufactures for export.[66]

The Anglo-Irish had long regarded manufacturing for export as a means of raising Catholic living standards and defusing social tension. The potato held the key to the cultivation of grain as a 'manufacture'. As an efficient primary staple crop that could readily be consumed by subsistence farmers on small plots of land, it ensured that grain was available to export to

Britain, in return for the manufactured goods and luxuries that were imported into Ireland. 'As there exists, and is likely to exist,' he observed, 'a great void in the British corn-market, which must be supplied from some quarter or other; it seems eminently conducive to the welfare of Britain that the tillage of Ireland be seasonably improved and extended.' The Irish peasantry's reliance on the potato ensured that while in 'other countries' grain was a 'mere necessary of life: here, it is rather an exportable manufacture, by the foreign vent whereof, those who labour in preparing it for market are enabled to purchase that article of food which they have been in the habit of using'. The combination of tillage and the potato was the key to the achievement of a novel kind of Irish prosperity, defined not by the luxury, vice and manufactures of an increasingly urban Britain, but by the steady industry and flourishing population of a teeming, intensively cultivated Irish countryside.

The potato and the poor law

For some observers in the early decades of the nineteenth century, Ireland's peculiar path to a tillage revolution represented a stable form of prosperity that contrasted favourably with the disruptions wrought by enclosure and estate consolidation in English agriculture. Robert Fraser, a Dublin Society surveyor who had earlier undertaken comparable investigations of Devon and Cornwall, noted approvingly that the flourishing small-scale agriculture of Wexford was analogous to 'that state, in which England was in the middle of the last century': before enclosures, clearances and the growth of manufacturing towns had destroyed the country's capacity to feed itself.[67] Even in Britain itself, participants in the increasingly fraught debate over reform of the English poor law cited Ireland as an example of a society that had contained and managed rural poverty more successfully than England, where rising poor rates and the near constant dependence of rural populations on the parish for labour and subsistence were beginning to cause serious resentment among the gentry.[68] Poverty, observed Young's friend and fellow English improver John Christian Curwen in the British Commons in 1817, was a thoroughly subjective experience. 'We hear perpetually of the wretched state in which the Irish peasant is doomed to exist ... accustomed, as we are, to see a more liberal distribution of the comforts of life among the lower orders', Curwen observed. Yet 'those who have the courage to examine more minutely into the condition of this hardy race, and to judge by *their own* feelings, and by ours, may draw conclusions very opposite'.[69] The virtue and comparative independence of the Irish peasant meant that 'amidst all his wants and sufferings', his condition was 'far superior to the unhappy victim of pauperism in this country'. The 'envy and jealousy' engendered among the English poor by their dependence on the parish had destroyed their capacity to participate in the 'social affections' that Curwen, following William Paley, regarded as the essence of 'happiness'.[70]

Curwen's remarks on Ireland were a preface to the case he made for a universal levy on the earnings of the poor to fund their own relief, something which he believed would both educate them into greater foresight and reduce the poor rates.[71] The threat the Irish model posed to English poor law reformers convinced of the rectitude of Robert Malthus' new theory of population, however, was that the combination of potatoes and paternalistic schemes for the accommodation of the rural poor in cottages – measures advocated by Young, among others, as a solution to the crisis of the Old Poor Law – would produce immiseration on a grand scale.[72] Malthus' attention was turned briefly to Ireland in 1808–1809 when, reviewing Newenham's works, he attributed the rapid increase in Ireland's population and the dependency on the potato as a lingering legacy of the political oppression of the Penal era, which had prevented the Irish poor from acquiring the self-respect to demand wheaten bread – an evidently superior foodstuff – as the customary basis of their diet.[73]

It was another compendious Irish travel account, authored by Edward Wakefield, an English Quaker land agent, that marked the vital intellectual turning point that led nineteenth-century British economists to anathemise the potato and cottier tenancies in their treatments of the problem of Irish poverty.[74] Wakefield's *Account* offered a radically pessimistic view of the Irish agricultural boom. While English demand was leading to increased output, farms remained small and undercapitalised. Cottier tenures were becoming more, not less, prevalent as Ireland became more thoroughly integrated into the British economic system. Worse, leading Irish improvers – Wakefield cited the examples of the Limerick physician Samuel Crumpe and the Cork land agent Horatio Townshend – seemed not to have noticed that this labour-intensive, undercapitalised form of agriculture betokened stagnation at a low level of social complexity. Their fetishisation of tillage was profoundly mistaken:

> So far from believing, that it would be beneficial to the kingdom to convert the rich grazing lands of that country into corn fields, I freely confess, that better arguments in favour of this change than I have yet heard must be adduced, before I can be convinced of its utility. When the scheme of dividing the land into small allotments, which would cramp circulation, and oblige every man to produce for himself, and to be satisfied with a bare subsistence, without any surplus, is considered in all its consequences, it will be found, that instead of making the state of agriculture more flourishing, it will have a quite contrary effect.[75]

Where Young had understood cottier tenure as a side effect of Irish poverty, Wakefield regarded it as one of its central causes. His *Account* privileged agricultural productivity over mere population, arguing that Ireland's utility to the empire would be increased if its numerous peasant smallholdings were converted into well-capitalised tenant farms on the English model. Arthur Young's *Political Arithmetic* (1774), rather than his Irish *Tour*, provided the crucial inspiration for this argument, which recalled Young's position in the English population controversies of the 1770s. In the fevered atmosphere of the American crisis, Young had dismissed Richard Price's dire warnings that enclosures and estate clearances were depopulating the countryside and destroying the military virtue of the old English yeomanry. Efficient modern agriculture enabled capital investment and economies of scale, which, combined with a growing manufacturing population, would ultimately render the nation more resilient in war and more flourishing in peacetime. 'My politicks of classing national wealth before population, needs no exception', Young declared.[76]

Wakefield urged Ireland's assimilation to this English logic of commercial diversification and agricultural investment. The potato, Wakefield claimed, was a food best suited for farm animals; it had been known to produce 'desspepsia [sic.]' and 'fluxes' among the Scottish peasantry.[77] More damaging still were the stifling psychological and civilisational confines of subsistence agriculture. In Ireland, Wakefield claimed, the 'division of labour is scarcely known'. In this 'degraded state of society', there was a 'want of encouragement to every species of ingenuity'. The nature of the 'cottier system' was to

> approximate man to the state of the savage, where the insulated being is obliged to supply himself by his own labour ... yet, I have been told, "these people are happy, they have every thing within themselves". They may enjoy the bliss of insensibility, but they are many degrees removed from that exalted happiness which gives man his proper dignity, and which always prevails in a country where the arts and moral improvement, keep an equal pace.[78]

Wakefield argued for a new spatial imaginary of Irish society, challenging Newenham's account of the even distribution of population across a densely populated countryside. 'One of the principal causes of the miserable state of society in Ireland,' he claimed, 'arises from the manner in which the country is peopled. In the interior, there are no cities or large towns to give employment to the surplus hands.'[79] In spite of the 'great wretchedness among the poor, in crowded and manufacturing towns', English urbanisation represented a superior alternative to Irish stagnation. Food for the English towns was 'obtained by the produce of labour fairly brought to market'; if the cities were drained and their population returned to the land, 'no greater quantity of food would be created; and the whole industry of this part of the community ... would be lost in a general cessation from labour'.[80] If Ireland under the control of eighteenth-century Anglo-Irish had been remodelled as a laboratory for labour-intensive agrarianism, it would, under the conditions created by the Great Famine and championed by the British economists who followed Wakefield, be returned to the pastoral, sparsely populated island encountered by Swift, Berkeley and Dobbs at the start of the eighteenth century.[81]

An end to paternalism?

Wakefield's condemnation of cottier tenancies served to sharply illustrate the gap between the 'improvement' desired by eighteenth-century Anglo-Irish agrarian writers and the 'savage' conditions of a life characterised by 'bare subsistence'. Much of nineteenth-century Irish politics would be shaped by rival projects of social engineering to end cottier tenancies and replace them either with large, well-capitalised farms – on an English model – or free peasant smallholdings, on precedents suggested by both Ulster and post-revolutionary France.[82] The potato failures of 1845–1852 were ruthlessly exploited by a succession of British politicians as an occasion to bring about the insertion of the stagnant, isolated Irish peasantry perceived by Wakefield into the civilising circuits of the wage labour and commercial society. By the later nineteenth century, the sharp reduction of Ireland's population by starvation and emigration had created conditions under which 'strong' tenant farmers – often producing beef, cattle and dairy products for export to Britain – could form the backbone of a political coalition dedicated to the redistribution of Irish property to those who farmed it.[83] The nationalist politics of land reform were frequently and self-consciously opposed to the devastating precedent set by the Famine and its attendant estate clearances. Both paradigms of agrarian change, however, represented attempts to chart a route out of the apparent economic and political cul-de-sac of the cottier system, which fatally severed subsistence from property relations in ways offensive to both British liberal and republican-nationalist conceptions of political economy. The cottier system, as we have seen, was not the natural condition of a timeless Irish peasantry, but rather the product of the lopsided development undergone by the Irish Kingdom in the second half of the eighteenth century. In producing a densely peopled and cultivated landscape, Irish population growth seemed to betoken an end to the poverty of desolation created by the seventeenth century's wars of religion, only to give rise to another: one of (over)abundance, understood by Malthus, Wakefield and their later followers as a proliferation of bare life at the edges of subsistence.

This represented a failure of the civilising mission in Ireland, because it did not create in Irish subjects the capacity to engage in the complex forms of labour and consumption that defined personal autonomy in a mature 'commercial society'. As such, these early nineteenth-century critiques should be read not as radical departures from earlier, eighteenth-century ideas about Irish poverty. Instead, they served to expose the gap that existed between earlier Anglo-Irish aspirations to the 'improvement' of the Irish landscape and population and the distinctive, unruly and even threatening agglomeration of rural population that resulted from the demographic, economic and ecological juncture of the late eighteenth century. Ideas of poverty in Ireland were formed in a crucible of political contest between different local and imperial elites, within a context of dramatic – and ultimately fatal – economic and agrarian transformations.

Notes

1 William Temple, 'An Essay upon the Advancement of Trade in Ireland. Written to the Earl of Essex, Lord Lieutenant of That Kingdom (1673)', in *The Works of Sir William Temple, Bart*, 4 vols (London, 1814), vol. iii, pp. 1–28, at p. 3.
2 Temple, 'Advancement of Trade', p. 4.
3 Ibid., p. 3.
4 Robert Malthus to David Ricardo 17 August 1817, *The Works and Correspondence of David Ricardo*, eds Maurice Dobb and Piero Sraffa, 11 vols (Cambridge: Cambridge University Press, [1817] 1973), vol. vii, p. 175.
5 Temple, 'Advancement of Trade', p. 2.
6 Ibid., pp. 4–5; Malthus to Ricardo 17 August 1817, *Works of David Ricardo*, vol. vii, p. 175.
7 Jane H. Ohlmeyer, 'Conquest, Civilization, Colonization: Ireland, 1540–1660', in Ian McBride and Richard Bourke (eds), *The Princeton History of Modern Ireland* (Princeton, NJ: Princeton University Press, 2016), pp. 21–47.
8 Nicholas Canny, 'Identity Formation in Ireland: The Emergence of the Anglo-Irish', in Nicholas Canny and Anthony Pagden (eds), *Colonial Identity in the Atlantic World, 1500–1800* (Princeton, NJ: Princeton University Press, 1989), pp. 159–213; T. C. Barnard, *Improving Ireland? Projectors, Prophets and Profiteers, 1641–1786* (Dublin: Four Courts, 2008).
9 Samuel Madden, *Reflections and Resolutions Proper for the Gentlemen of Ireland, as to Their Conduct for the Service of Their Country, as Landlords, as Masters of Families* (Dublin, 1738).
10 Deirdre Ní Chuanacháin, *Utopianism in Eighteenth-Century Ireland* (Cork: Cork University Press, 2015).
11 David Dickson, *Old World Colony: Cork and South Munster, 1660–1830* (Cork: Cork University Press, 2015); Patrick Kelly, 'The Politics of Political Economy

in Mid-Eighteenth-Century Ireland', in Sean J. Connolly (ed.), *Political Ideas in Eighteenth-Century Ireland* (Dublin: Four Courts, 2000), pp. 109–118 at p. 109.
12 Cormac Ó Gráda, *Ireland: A New Economic History, 1780–1939* (Oxford: Clarendon Press, 1994) pp. 5–13.
13 William Cobbett, *The Parliamentary History of England from the Earliest Period to the Year 1803*, 36 vols (London, 1806), vol. xv, p. 1274; Thomas, Brinley, 'Feeding England during the Industrial Revolution: A View from the Celtic Fringe', *Agricultural History*, 56:1 (1982), 328–342.
14 Emund Spenser, 'A View of the Present State of Ireland' in *The Works of Spenser*, 6 vols (London, [1595] 1750), vol. vi, p. 207.
15 John Davies, 'A Discovery of the True Causes Why Ireland Was Never Brought under Obedience of the Crown of England, until His Late Majesty's Happy Reign', in *Historical Tracts by Sir John Davies* (London, [1613] 1786), pp. 1–227 at p. 197.
16 Ibid., p. 99.
17 John Millar, *An Historical View of the English Government, From the Settlement of the Saxons in Britain to the Revolution in 1688* (Indianapolis, IN: Liberty Fund, [1803] 2006), pp. 673–674.
18 Ian McBride, 'The Politics of A Modest Proposal: Swift and the Irish Crisis of the Late 1720s', *Past & Present*, 244:1 (2019), 89–122, at 107–108.
19 Robert Molesworth, *Some Considerations for the Promoting of Agriculture and Employing the Poor* (Dublin, 1723) pp. 4–5.
20 Thomas Prior, *A List of the Absentees of Ireland, and the Yearly Value of their Estates and Incomes Spent Abroad* (Dublin, 1729), p. 32.
21 George Berkeley, *The Querist, Part 2* (London, 1736), p. 12.
22 George Berkeley, *The Querist, Part 1* (London, 1736), pp. 17–18.
23 Istvan Hont, 'The 'Rich Country-Poor Country' Debate Revisited: The Irish Origins and French Reception of the Hume Paradox', in Carl Wennerlind and Margaret Schabas (eds), *David Hume's Political Economy* (London: Routledge, 2008), pp. 243–323.
24 Jean-François Melon, *A Political Essay Upon Commerce*, trans. David Bindon (Dublin, 1738), p. 5.
25 Ibid., p. 188.
26 Ibid., p. 176.
27 Ibid., p. 195.
28 David Bindon, 'Editor's Introduction' in Melon, 'Essay upon Commerce', p. xvii.
29 Ibid., p. xi.
30 Ibid., p. xiii.
31 Prior, *Absentees of Ireland*, pp. 80–81.
32 Berkeley, *The Querist Part 2*, p. 13
33 Molesworth, *Some Considerations*, p. 12.
34 Ibid., p. 7.
35 Arthur Dobbs, *An Essay on the Trade and Improvement of Ireland* (Dublin, 1729) pp. 80–81.

36 Ibid., p. 82.
37 Sean J. Connolly, *Religion, Law and Power: The Making of Protestant Ireland, 1660–1760* (Oxford: Oxford University Press, 1992), pp. 263–264.
38 W. N. Osborough, 'Catholics, Land and the Popery Acts of Anne', in Thomas P. Power and Kevin Whelan (eds), *Endurance and Emergence: Catholics in Ireland in the Eighteenth Century* (Dublin: Irish Academic Press, 1990), pp. 21–56; Emma Lyons, 'To "Elude the Design and Intention" of the Penal Laws: Collusion and Discovery in Eighteenth-Century Ireland – A Case Study', in Kevin Costello and Niamh Howlin (eds), *Law and Religion in Ireland, 1700–1970* (Basingstoke: Palgrave MacMillan, 2021), pp. 49–75 at p. 50.
39 Berkeley, *The Querist, Part 1*, p. 2, pp. 36–38; James Livesey, 'Berkeley, Ireland and Eighteenth-Century Intellectual History', *Modern Intellectual History*, 12 (2015), 453–473.
40 Charles O'Connor, *Case of the Roman Catholics of Ireland* (Dublin, 1755), pp. 56–57.
41 John Curry, *Observations on the Popery Laws* (Dublin, 1771), p. 30.
42 John Curry, *A Candid Enquiry Into the Causes and Motives of the Late Riots in the Province of Munster: In Ireland; by the People Called White-Boys Or Levellers. With an Appendix* (London, 1767).
43 Curry, *Observations on the Popery Laws*, pp. 31–32.
44 Dickson, *Old World Colony*, pp. 284–288.
45 Ibid., pp. 290–297.
46 Kevin Whelan, 'The Modern Landscape', in F. H. A. Aalen, Matthew Stout and Kevin Whelan (eds), *Atlas of the Irish Rural Landscape*, second edition (Cork: Cork University Press, 2011), pp. 73–111, at pp. 80–81.
47 Ibid., p. 83.
48 Ibid., p. 93.
49 Ibid., p. 96.
50 Leigh Shaw-Taylor, 'Parliamentary Enclosure and the Emergence of an English Agricultural Proletariat', *The Journal of Economic History*, 61:3 (2001), 640–662.
51 Richard Twiss, *A Tour in Ireland in 1775* (London, 1776).
52 Adam Smith, *An Inquiry into the Nature and Causes of the Wealth of Nations*, eds R. H. Campbell. A. S. Skinner and W. B. Todd, 2 vols (Indianapolis IN: Liberty Fund, [1776] 1981), vol. i, p. 177.
53 Arthur Young, *A Tour in Ireland*, 2 vols (Dublin, 1770–1780), vol. ii, p. 25.
54 Ibid., vol. ii, p. 32.
55 Ibid., vol. ii, p. 31.
56 James Stafford, *The Case of Ireland: Commerce, Empire and the European Order, 1750–1848* (Cambridge: Cambridge University Press, 2022), pp. 52–56.
57 Gervase Parker Bushe, 'An Essay towards Ascertaining the Population of Ireland. In a Letter to the Right Honourable the Earl of Charlemont, President of the Royal Irish Academy', *The Transactions of the Royal Irish Academy*, 3 (1789), 145–155 at 151.
58 Ibid., 151, 153.

59 Ibid., 151–152.
60 Thomas Newenham, *A Stastistical and Historical Inquiry into the Progress and Magnitude of the Population of Ireland* (London, 1805); ibid., *A View of the Natural, Political and Commercial Circumstances of Ireland* (London, 1809).
61 Newenham, *Progress and Magnitude*, pp. 44–45.
62 Ibid., pp. 337–338.
63 Ibid.
64 Newenham, *Circumstances of Ireland*, p. 17, pp. 57–58.
65 Ibid., p 306.
66 Ibid., pp. 306–307.
67 Robert Fraser, *Statistical Survey of the County of Wexford* (Dublin, 1807), p. 61.
68 Peter Mandler, 'The Making of the New Poor Law Redivivus', *Past & Present*, 117 (1987), 131–157; Sarah Lloyd, 'Cottage Conversations: Poverty and Manly Independence in Eighteenth-Century England', *Past & Present*, 184 (2004), 69–109.
69 John Christian Curwen, *Speech ... in the House of Commons, on the 21st of February 1817, on a Motion for a Committee to Take into Consideration the Poor Laws* (London, 1817).
70 Ibid., p. 55.
71 Ibid., pp. 61–65.
72 John Riddoch Poynter, *Society and Pauperism: English Ideas on Poor Relief, 1795–1834* (London: Routledge & Kegan Paul, 1969), pp. 91–105; T. R. Malthus, *An Essay on the Principle of Population: The 1803 Edition*, ed. Shannon C. Stimson (London: Yale University Press, 2018) pp. 446–456.
73 Stafford, *Case of Ireland*, pp. 200–205.
74 Edward Wakefield. *An Account of Ireland, Statistical and Political*, 2 vols (London, 1812); David Lloyd, 'The Political Economy of the Potato', *Nineteenth Century Contexts*, 29 (2007), 311–335.
75 Wakefield, *Account of Ireland*, vol. i, p. 579.
76 Arthur Young, *Political Arithmetic* (London, 1774), p. 288.
77 Wakefield, *Account of Ireland*, vol. ii, p. 716.
78 Ibid., vol. ii, p. 721.
79 Ibid., vol. ii, pp. 719–720.
80 Ibid., vol. ii, p. 720.
81 David P. Nally, *Human Encumbrances: Political Violence and the Great Irish Famine* (Notre Dame, IN: University of Notre Dame Press, 2011).
82 Stafford, *The Case of Ireland*, pp. 210–253.
83 Peter Gray, 'Famine and Land, 1845–80', in *Oxford Handbook of Modern Irish History*, ed. Alvin Jackson (Oxford: Oxford University Press, 2013), pp. 545–558.

10

A new moral economy: the early reception of Malthus

Niall O'Flaherty

The historian wishing to characterise T. R. Malthus's influence on ideas of poverty is confronted with a paradox.[1] It is universally agreed, on the one hand, that his *Essay on the Principle of Population* (1798) had a profound impact on the way poverty was conceived in the nineteenth century and beyond. At the same time, scholars have unanimously echoed the lament of Malthus's biographer William Empson that no book of its stature has been 'so frequently misunderstood'.[2] The effect of recent scholarship has been to accentuate the gap between Malthus's intentions in the *Essay* and the 'historical' Malthus. In a ground-breaking study, Robert Mayhew has revealed the remarkable variety of ways in which the arguments of the *Essay* have been used and abused over the two centuries since its publication; while a recent collection of essays shows that France, Spain, the United States, Japan, Brazil, Russia and Italy each had their own Malthus, and often more than one.[3] With so many varieties of Malthusianism, it is tempting to conclude that the countless projects and policies advanced in Malthus's name have borne only the loosest relationship to his actual ideas. My aim in this chapter is to show that this was by no means the case in the decade after its publication. A survey of responses to the *Essay* in periodicals, pamphlets, books and parliamentary speeches in this period reveals that while some writers missed the point of the book altogether, a sizeable majority demonstrated a firm grasp of its core arguments. There was a solid basis, in other words, for a truly orthodox Malthusianism.

Naturally, it is the role of Malthus's ideas in the controversy over the poor laws in early nineteenth-century England that has received most scholarly attention. In this context, he has frequently been portrayed as 'the arch-demoraliser', plotting to supplant 'the moral economy' which had previously governed attitudes to the poor with a 'political economy' which reduced such relations to questions of cost benefit.[4] Two variations on this theme – which originated in E. P. Thompson's attempt to demonstrate the political nature of food riots in England – have proven particularly influential among historians.[5] In Gertrude Himmelfarb's iteration, the first edition of the *Essay on the Principle of Population* (1798) put paid to the humanitarian revisioning of political economy inaugurated by Adam Smith by exploding his optimistic view of the prospects of the poor in commercial society, the lesson being that the iron law of population rendered all efforts to ameliorate hardship self-defeating.[6] A more recent version of the narrative casts Malthus alongside Smith as helping mastermind a wider conspiracy to supplant 'paternalist' notions of poverty relief, which gave scope to the agency of the poor as negotiators in the application process, with a 'science of poverty' which 'submerged' their 'individual narrative[s] in statistics, input/output ratios, and institutional accounts', obscuring their pain. The invocation of scientific method was, by this logic, simply a means of rationalising cutbacks to relief, thus rendering them guilt-free.[7]

Donald Winch led the way in challenging this binary characterisation, arguing that, far from wishing to divorce economic reasoning from ethical concerns, Malthus was committed to a version of the new science that framed 'economic' questions in terms of the moral and religious precepts of so-called Anglican utilitarianism.[8] While Winch treated the *Essay* primarily as a contribution to the ideological struggles that followed in the wake of the French Revolution, I have argued elsewhere that Malthus's magnum opus is best understood as a contribution to debates about poverty relief triggered by the scarcities of 1795–1796 and 1800–1801. Though the arguments were entwined with political questions, Malthus's principal goal in the much-expanded and definitive second edition of the *Essay* (1803) was to explain the underlying causes of poverty, to provide the first rigorous anatomy of its manifestations and to advertise what he took to be its only cure.[9] The fact that many found the medicine bitter – involving, as it did, the gradual abolition of the poor laws – does not detract from the fact that it was ultimately intended to release working people from the population trap that had condemned them to periodical distress throughout all history.

But this, of itself, does not settle the matter. For, according to Himmelfarb, the more hopeful verdict on the poor's prospects set out in the second edition made no impression on public opinion, so deep and wide was the gloomy shadow cast by the first. The bleak vision held sway, blotting out both Smithian optimism and paternalist humanitarianism.[10] Of course, if this is right, it weakens one of the strongest arguments against the demoralising thesis. The goal of the first half of this chapter is to show that it is wrong on two counts. Far from falling on deaf ears, first of all, the message of the 1803 edition made a profound impression on the public imagination, supplanting that of the first *Essay*; and second, while most readers had some reservations about Malthus's practical proposals, they generally appreciated the thrust of his analysis of poverty and even some of the finer points – all of which is to say that the historical Malthus in this period was very much the moderately optimistic poverty theorist of the second *Essay*. Part of our aim in the second half of the chapter is merely to sketch Malthus's influence on political and intellectual culture in the decade after the publication of the *Essay*, since this part of the reception has been neglected. By revealing, in the first place, that many Malthusians were no more intent on rigidly separating morals and economics than the writer himself; and, in the second, how blurred the lines could often be between so-called paternalism and the 'dismal science', such an account raises further doubts about the Manichean view of social thought in the period.

Admittedly, the arguments of first *Essay* did not vanish immediately from the public consciousness on the publication of the 'Great Quarto' of 1803. Malthus's objective in 1798 had been to show that the principle of population – the tendency of population to outstrip the food supply – precluded the possibility that any country could become an egalitarian paradise on the models of William Godwin or Condorcet.[11] The principle was clearly illustrated by the wage cycles of the English labouring people, according to Malthus. In times of plenty, poor couples felt confident about their ability to raise a family, and population soon ran ahead of the food supply. With the labour market overstocked, wages fell, causing hardship, which in turn made working folk think twice about procreation. When the demand for labour once again exceeded the supply, the good times returned, and the vicious cycle resumed.[12] With subsistence guaranteed and fewer restrictions on sexual conduct, the citizens of Godwin's commonwealth would soon multiply beyond their food levels, leading to a struggle for resources which would ultimately force them to reintroduce private property and marriage.[13] Because the oscillations were perpetual, moreover, Malthus believed that there could be no decided improvement in the condition of the poor.[14] By 1803, however, he had reached a much more optimistic conclusion about the prospects of working people. The statistics for northern and central European countries revealed an increasing tendency among peasants to delay marriage for prudential reasons, that is, to ensure that they were able to support a family. The higher wages resulting from restricting the labour supply raised living standards, with the result that a larger proportion of children made it to adulthood; and, of course, they were happier and healthier than their counterparts in countries with higher crude birth rates. Although this trend already had a momentum of its own, according to Malthus, it was the duty of the political nation to try to accelerate it. His main goal, then, was to show how this could be achieved.[15] It is true that the Romantics remained preoccupied with the attack on Godwin long after it had become a side-issue for Malthus, still smarting, apparently, from the demolition of the muse of their youth, even after they had come to reject his political vision.[16] But even while they continued to frame their attacks in terms of the debate about perfectibility, they saved most of their ire for Malthus's proposals for tackling poverty, or, as Robert Southey styled it, his campaign 'to starve the poor into celibacy'.[17] It was this programme and not the critique of Godwin that invariably preoccupied the commentators who went to print with their views on Malthus between 1803 and 1815. And though the first *Essay* undoubtedly made a splash in the highest political circles, only two journals (the *Analytical Review* and the *Monthly Review*) deemed it worthy of review; whereas the second prompted a deluge of responses, from reviews to quarto volumes to parliamentary speeches, leaving aside countless sundry references.[18]

Needless to say, the early response to Malthus's second *Essay* did not unfold in a political vacuum. It was unquestionably shaped, for example, by the ideological warfare which raged between the staunchly Whig *Edinburgh Review* and the resolutely ministerial *Quarterly Review*.[19] The Edinburgh reviewers celebrated the unleashing of market forces in commercial society and the resulting reconfiguration of society. Viewing political economy as an indispensable guide to right policy in these conditions, furthermore, they were predisposed to accept apparently irrefutable economic arguments for reducing interference in the labour market.[20] Contributors to the *Quarterly* disdained what they took to be the cutthroat individualism of this credo, which they worried would undermine the bonds of mutual interdependence between rich and poor. They were highly sceptical, moreover, about the value of economic analysis as a tool of governance.[21] The *Essay*, for them, was the apogee of this 'selfish' and 'sensual' mentality.[22] It is unlikely that Whitbread's Poor Laws Bill of 1807, which did so much to bring Malthus's ideas into public view, would have seen the light of day were it not for the short-lived Grenville coalition in which the opposition Whigs shared power after nearly quarter of a century out of office.[23] There is little sense, however, in the literary responses to Malthus or the Commons debate on Whitbread's Bill that the issue was thought of as a party political matter.[24] J. R. Poynter was surely right, indeed, in observing that responses to the problem of want at this time were much less ideologically charged than they would become after 1815. The fact that relative prosperity after the dearth of 1800–1801 made the problem feel less urgent, while it removed the spur to reform the relief system, also allowed scope for explorative thinking.[25] The majority of the protagonists were capable of changing their views when presented with contrary evidence and they generally assumed the good faith of their opponents. Apart from the diatribes of William Cobbett and William Hazlitt, indeed, the most heated exchanges were over the utility of particular relief measures such as cottage-building and the provision of work for relief applicants.

For sure, the early commentaries contained some gross misrepresentations of Malthus's ideas. The worst offenders were those who saw the principle of population merely as an ideological gambit for keeping the poor in their place and generally preserving the status quo. Hazlitt, for example, charged Malthus with rehashing Robert Wallace's demographic theory which postulated a problem with overpopulation when the country had reached the absolute limits of its cultivation, missing the crucial point that the effects of the principle of population were 'imminent and immediate'.[26] The same misunderstanding was obviously behind Robert Ingram's rejection of the principle on the grounds that the worst distress occurred among sparsely populated hunter-gatherer peoples.[27] He clearly had not read the opening chapters of the book where Malthus explained that it was precisely among such societies that the checks to population were at their most dreadful. It seems clear, also, that misinterpretations abounded in household discussions of the book, as several of them figured among the objections 'urged in conversation' that Malthus responded to in the Appendix to the 1806 edition.[28] Sympathetic reviewers of the book unanimously bemoaned such misreading.[29] Ironically, however, the fact that so many writers were intent on correcting them undermines their claim that miscomprehension was ubiquitous.

There is little question that the reviews in the *Monthly Review*, the *British Critic*, the *Edinburgh Review* and the *Quarterly Review* did ample justice to Malthus's intentions in the book; while even a somewhat opaque discussion in the *Gentleman's Magazine* captured many of the key points. Certainly, none of these reviewers made the basic mistake of confounding Malthus's theory with Wallace's. As the *Gentleman's Magazine* observed, 'the chief point' on which Malthus differed from previous writers who had raised the spectre of overpopulation was in his belief that the oscillations were a constant in the lives of the poor, having existed 'almost from the first creation of the world'.[30] They had a good understanding, too, of the basic structure of the second *Essay*, recognising that the practical proposals for ameliorating want expounded in book four were derived from the historical analysis of poverty (i.e. population checks) narrated in books one and two. It was acknowledged that while many writers had understood that population growth was checked by the level of subsistence, Malthus was the first to examine the nature of these checks; to provide, in other words, a pathology of poverty.[31] There were, as the reviewers explained, three main ways in which population was kept down to the level of the food supply: disease, war and so-called vicious customs.[32] Among 'savage' peoples, 'vicious habits with respect to the female sex, the difficulty of raising children, and the nearly continual state of warfare' all played their part in repressing population.[33] Of course, the need for concision meant that some of the finer details of Malthus's analysis were lost, such as his explanation of the sequence in which checks were inclined to occur – with war, for example, stepping in to mop up the surplus numbers not extirpated by brutal customs in relation to women and children.[34] Yet they clearly got the main point that dearth assumed many faces and shared Malthus's sense that in revealing them he was putting the subject on a whole new footing.

It is evident, furthermore, that early commentators readily appreciated the take-home message of Malthus's histories of poverty. The population statistics for northern Europe gave mathematical certainly to the thesis – emerging from the histories – that high birth rates invariably gave rise to distress in its many forms; and, conversely, that the low birth rates that occurred where peasants married later produced healthier and happier children, who were more likely to make it to adulthood.[35] In explaining how Malthus reached this conclusion, the more careful reviewers were true to the logic of the argument as it appeared in the histories. The lesson of his account of the barbarian invasions of the Roman Empire, for example, was that there was a profound difference between 'a redundant population and one actually great', between peoples condemned to perpetual struggle by their very multiplicity and those who could expect to flourish because their numbers were calibrated to the food supply.[36] The writers homed in, at the same time, on the pivotal contrast illustrating this distinction between nations where the poor managed to escape poverty through prudential restraint: Norway, Switzerland and Britain; and those whose heedless reproduction trapped them in the vicious cycle between happiness and misery: Sweden, Ireland and France. It was understood that in bringing these success stories to light, Malthus was revealing what he took to be the only way of tackling poverty at its roots.[37]

The reviews also captured well the spirit of Malthus's plan for accelerating the trend of later marriage in Britain.[38] To encourage the poor to defer marriage until they were sure to be able to support a family, one had to instil what Malthus called 'decent and proper pride'. There was 'in every country a certain standard of wretchedness' below which poor folk would be unwilling to fall for the sake of marrying; the goal was 'to raise this standard'.[39] Nor was there any confusion about how Malthus believed the character of the labourer could be thus elevated. A taste for the luxury, comfort and cleanliness was the lifeblood of decent pride; while the best way to nurture it further was by raising the intellectual level of the poor. It was to these ends that Malthus's called for the introduction of a system of national education on the model recommended by Adam Smith, though with an added emphasis on basic political economy.[40] As well as nurturing the cultural attitudes that made the poor defer marriage, the educated classes were obliged to do everything in their power to encourage prudential restraint directly, by explaining the benefits of having fewer children, naturally, but also by bringing them to understand that it was *their* duty, and no one else's, to support their children. For where a right to relief from the community was assumed, the motives for delaying the big day were greatly compromised, along with the attitudes that raised 'the standard of wretchedness'.[41] It is notable, furthermore, that the most accurate portrayals of Malthus's policy proposals could be found in the *Edinburgh Review*, suggesting that disciples north of the border were every bit as faithful to the true credo as their English counterparts.

There was, confessedly, one aspect of Malthus's programme which engendered conflicting interpretations, even among writers who had read the *Essay* attentively; they differed over whether he was calling for 'moral restraint', the delaying of marriage accompanied by sexual abstinence; or merely 'prudential restraint', the same, but potentially involving premarital sexual encounters. The writers for the *Monthly Review* and *Edinburgh Review* focused almost entirely of his efforts to increase preventive checks, as if the issue of 'promiscuous intercourse' was immaterial. The former treated moral restraint merely as a synonym for prudential checks, briefly observing that Malthus strongly disapproved of any increase in sexual vice that might occur as a result of delayed marriage.[42] The latter ignored the issue of sexual morality entirely. Conversely, both the *Gentleman's Magazine* and the *Annals of Agriculture* took Malthus to be calling for *moral* restraint or nothing.[43] The fact is, however, that his explication of the issue was not without ambiguity. Ultimately, his position was that the additional happiness redounding to the poor from an increase in prudential restraint would greatly outweigh the additional misery added to their lot by the extra vice it might occasion.[44] But a reasonable case could be made for either interpretation. The clear moral of the history of population and the defence of the practical programme in the second half of book four was that the prospects of the poor depended on the prevalence of prudential marriage customs per se. Yet it was the obligation to practice *moral restraint* that Malthus expressly defended in the opening chapters of the same book, even if most of the benefits he ascribed to it were those resulting from having fewer children. Moreover, the discrepancies did not prevent the writers from communicating the substance of his proposals; for they all saw that his main focus was on promoting later marriages.

There is some evidence, too, that this acquaintance with the core arguments of the second *Essay* extended beyond the scribes, most notably to the more literate members of parliament. When the social campaigner Samuel Whitbread rose in the House of Commons to present his Poor Laws Bill in 1807, he returned to Malthus repeatedly, as the 'one philosopher' who had 'gone deeply into the causes of our present situation'. He assured the House that he had 'studied the works of this author with as much attention' as he was 'capable of bestowing upon any subject' – to good effect, apparently, since his own views on the cultural dimensions of the poverty question embodied the true spirit of Malthus's teachings.[45] His plans, for one, were expressly framed by the conviction that the future prospects of the poor depended above all else on infusing them with 'proper pride', the watchword of Malthus's prescription for poverty. He drew on the historical as well as the practical books of the *Essay*, exhorting those who objected to his scheme for exalting the character of the poor man through education to read Malthus's description of 'the character of savage, uncivilised man' to see how far ignorance was conducive to social improvement. When revealing the measures in the Bill for building more cottages for the poor, he insisted that 'the limitations and restrictions' he placed on the scheme would provide assurance for 'those who have stated that scarcity of habitations is the only preventive check to the morbid increase of population'.[46] That he ascribed such views to a plurality suggests that he believed that even the more intricate applications of Malthus's principle had currency.[47] Although, undoubtedly, he had an inflated sense of how assiduously honourable members kept abreast of the latest developments in political science, his assumption that colleagues were au fait with the arguments provides a counterweight to the impression created by Malthus and his admirers that miscomprehension of the *Essay* reigned supreme in parlour-room discussions. All in all, the core arguments of the second edition of the *Essay* were ably represented in the periodical literature, high-political debate and even, it seems, in the conversations of the educated. But it remains to be explained how far early readers actually embraced his vision.

Most of those who were not utterly hostile were clearly persuaded by Malthus's diagnosis of poverty. Whitbread thought it 'incontrovertible', as did the Edinburgh reviewers, whose aim was less to offer a critical assessment of Malthus's arguments than to expose the distortions of his critics.[48] Though he raged against the practical programme of the *Essay*, Arthur Young tacitly accepted the account of poverty at its heart. He expended much energy, for example, on disproving Malthus's claim that his own scheme for furnishing labourers with land, cottages and livestock would undermine prudential attitudes and create surplus population. While they adopted a more detached attitude to the *Essay* than their counterparts in the *Edinburgh*, the reviewers for the *Monthly Review* and *British Critic* were no less convinced of the soundness of his reasoning.[49] There was a consensus, furthermore, that the 1803 edition marked a watershed moment in the history of thinking about poverty and, indeed, government in general. 'All former systems are ... overturned by his principles', was the verdict of the *British Critic*. He had, according to the *Monthly Review*, rendered political economy 'a ground furnishing new questions of vast importance to society', correcting 'the errors sanctioned by such high names as those of Montesquieu, Hume, Smith, Price and Robertson'.[50] There is little question, then, not only that the second *Essay* made a powerful impression on the intellectual landscape of the period, eclipsing the first edition, but that the science of poverty which it sought to inaugurate was ably and accurately represented in political discourse, at least by those who were not ideologically allergic to it.

The impact of the *Essay*

Few were better placed than Whitbread to gauge attitudes to poor relief among the political elite, having been in the thick of the debate about poverty since bringing forward his ill-fated Wages Bill in 1795; and he thought it obvious that there had been 'a great revolution in the public mind' on the question. Whereas the 43rd of Elizabeth – the legislative foundation of the poor laws – had long been considered 'the *bible* on the subject', the recent scarcities had brought home the tendency of the poor laws to increase the suffering of the poor by degrading their character.[51] While it is difficult to measure how far Malthus was responsible for the sea change, Whitbread was again probably right to say that the *Essay* had 'completed that change of opinion ... which had in some measure already begun'.[52] Complaints about the ever-increasing cost of the poor laws and their alleged tendency to create dependency resounded throughout the eighteenth century, with the building of workhouses often featuring among the proposed remedies. Such concerns increased in the last two decades of the century. When a parliamentary inquiry of 1787 revealed that the welfare bill had doubled in only a decade, a growing body of writers began to reason that rising poverty was actually a function of the increasing amounts spent on relief, a diagnosis given traction by the crises of 1795–1796 which seemed to confirm that the soaring amounts spent on relief did little to check the rise in distress.[53] Among those intent on remedying these ills were Joseph Townsend, Thomas Ruggles and Frederick Eden.[54] The nub of the problem, as they saw it, was that parish handouts, especially the provision of outdoor relief to able-bodied supplicants, had eroded industrious habits among the poor; everything rested, therefore, on restoring the work ethic.

On the other side of the argument, John Howlett and David Davies saw the hike in the poor rate as indicative of the hardship arising from structural economic causes, particularly the lagging of wages behind bread prices, factors over which poor families themselves had no control.[55] By way of relieving their immediate distress, Davies proposed allowing the Justices in each district to rate wages in line with the living costs of an average size family or pegging them to the price of bread.[56] In his *Principles of Moral and Political Philosophy* (1785), William Paley launched a stout defence of the commitment underpinning these arguments, the idea that the poor had a right to relief. What Malthus saw as the core doctrine of the philosophy of 'governing too much' – styled 'paternalism' in much of the literature – was thus enshrined in a Cambridge textbook, widely revered as a sage guide to quotidian moral questions.[57] Moreover, the widespread adoption of Speemhamland-type allowances and other 'paternalist' measures in the crises of 1795 and 1800 appeared to signal that such thinking had become the prevailing ethos of the poor laws themselves.

Because they echoed Malthus so closely, Whitbread's complaints that the parish laws 'hold out hopes that cannot be realised' and 'produce surplus population', alongside his abiding concern with nurturing 'honest pride', strongly suggest that the *Essay* played an important role in persuading him of the need to remodel the parish laws along lines the opposite of those which had governed his proposals in the scarcity of 1795 for ensuring wages were commensurate with food prices.[58] There is evidence, however, that Townsend and especially Eden played a significant role in hardening opinion against existing welfare provision. In his hugely influential lectures on political economy in the University of Edinburgh in 1802–1803, Dugald Stewart drew his critique of the English poor laws largely from Eden and Townend's arguments, with Daniel Defoe and Henry Fielding also featuring.[59] He cited Eden's figures demonstrating the huge and growing expense of the parish system at length and repeated his case for the establishment of Friendly Societies. But he also shared Eden's view that opinions in favour of the poor laws were so deeply rooted that it would be unwise politically to abolish them outright, and therefore that some limitation had to be imposed upon them.[60] As many of the Edinburgh reviewers had attended Stewart's lectures, and generally fallen under his spell, it is arguable that they were primed to accept arguments lending scientific force to their laissez-faire approach to poverty. Patrick Colquhoun's typology of pauperism (discussed in the next chapter) undoubtedly fed into this emerging current of thought, as did Jeremy Bentham's profuse musings on the subject.

It is important to point out, however, that not all of Malthus's cure for poverty found favour with his earlier admirers. They accepted, in the main, his explanation of why dire poverty was in retreat in Europe and of the mindset they needed to nurture to ensure that this improvement continued. But the actual expedients he put forward for encouraging prudential restraint – especially his call for the gradual abolition of the poor laws – met with a more mixed reception. Two complaints, in particular, require our attention here. Some writers questioned the humanity of cutting off systematic aid when it was well understood – including by Malthus – that periodical downturns in wages and employment were endemic to the economic system. Fuelled, no doubt, by the unrest in many localities during the recent scarcities, there was also a widespread fear that scrapping assistance that was viewed by the poor as a customary right would spark massive social upheaval. Such doubts naturally shaped practical thinking about poverty going forward. In Whitbread's case, the combination of his newly found Malthusian fervour with deeply rooted 'paternalist' sensibilities produced a hybrid of commitments – one that would prove highly fertile in the years to come. The overarching goal was a Malthusian one: fostering a spirit of independence among the poor to the extent that it rendered the parish laws 'obsolete'. Primary education was at the heart of it, complimented by a state-sponsored system of prizes and punishments, aimed at increasing the distinction accorded to independence and the stigma attached to idleness.[61] At the same time, however, Whitbread was adamant that to deny the poor 'their right to assistance' was to 'break the chain, which ... binds the different classes of society indissolubly together', potentially turning the poor into 'dangerous enemies' of the state.[62] He would not countenance refusing relief in times of hardship even to those who had brought distress upon themselves and favoured the repeal of legislation, widely ignored in practice anyway, of prohibiting outdoor relief.[63] Abolition being out of the question, Whitbread wanted to reconfigure the parish laws so that they met the basic needs of the impotent poor without eroding the prudential habits of the industrious: there had to be a renewed focus, in other words, on discriminating between the worthy and unworthy.[64] Arthur Young, similarly, accepted the need to face up to the demographic impact of relief measures – having noticed the disastrous effects of rapid population growth in France in the 1780s – and was on board with the idea of raising the aspirations of the poor.[65] But he lambasted Malthus's plan for abolition as 'a tax on every heart', predicting mass revolt if it should be enacted, and fiercely defended the mantra that the poor had a right to relief, to the point of asserting that they were justified in blaming the rich for the hardship they suffered.[66] While the second *Essay* undoubtedly helped tip the balance of public opinion against the spirit of the relief system as it had evolved since the mid-1790s, it is clear that the bipolar depictions that have often framed historical analysis of the period conceal the complexity of the intellectual landscape. There was increasing agreement on the need to curb the excesses of the parish relief system but little appetite, as yet, for renouncing the wider philosophy of public charity given as a matter of right. What complicated matters even further was that, by 1807, Malthus had reached the view that abolition ought to be deferred until his ideas had gained wider acceptance among the poor and middle classes, thus creating the curious circumstance that his most faithful acolytes were calling for abolition when Malthus himself was beginning to contemplate less drastic measures.[67]

Malthus's acknowledgement that the time was not ripe for abolition exemplifies another aspect of the debate at this time which speaks against the view of 'the science of poverty' as merely a cloak for avarice: the conversation was remarkably evidence led. It was noted earlier that Malthus's arguments appeared to have played an important role in transforming Whitbread's views on relief.[68] His journey was not unlike that of Malthus himself, who had only come to reject the allowance system on uncovering the principle of population.[69] It was partly, no doubt, simply the logic of his position that forced Malthus to backtrack on abolition, for the poor could not be left to pay the price for improvident marriage where they did not fully appreciate its consequences. It is hard to think, however, that he was not also moved by the warnings of reviewers and friends about the disastrous social and political consequences for the country of terminating, as he later put it, 'a system which has been so long interwoven into its frame'.[70] While the controversy between Malthus and Arthur Young over the wisdom of adding to the stock of cottages for labouring people did bring the issue of the right to relief to the fore, the matter ultimately turned on the question of whether such measures would promote surplus population.[71] In other words, it largely came down to empirical evidence and to questions about how to weigh it. The fact that there were significant disagreements, moreover, between advocates of a more evidence-based approach to the problem hardly supports the notion that it was all simply a plot to reduce redistribution.

Undoubtedly, the spiralling costs of relief were an important issue for all those assessing it. Indeed, there were contributors to the discussion for whom the burden of the poor rates on the landed classes was the most urgent issue.[72] Among the writers who responded favourably to the second *Essay*, however, it was a secondary concern.[73] There is no reason to disbelieve Malthus when he declared, in his response to Whitbread, that he would be happy to double the amount if it would really benefit the poor. High contributions figured in the proselytising expositions of the *Edinburgh Review* only as evidence of the tendency of the poor laws to 'strip' the poor 'of every energetic and manly quality'.[74] Ultimate motivations are inscrutable, of course, and it may be that such arguments were merely a disguise for selfish intentions. The fact is, however, that writers in this period were not shy about bemoaning the increasing economic strains placed on the landed classes. As the main source of agricultural capital, furthermore, their economic well-being was hardly a matter of indifference to the poor. It was expressly for this reason, indeed, that Malthus would make it a priority in the years to come to ensure that their welfare was not rashly sacrificed on the altar of industrial and commercial expansion. More importantly, the project of increasing preventive checks which the early Malthusians endorsed was aimed at raising the wages of the poor, countering the illicit combinations of masters to keep them down. If the complaint of William Keir that such a 'general combination of labourers' was no less subversive of the social order than the levelling schemes of Godwin and Owen exaggerated its radicalness, there was no questioning that the plan was aimed at redressing the economic balance between master and workman.[75]

According to Himmelfarb, in seeking to advance this agenda, disciples of the new political economy sought to replace the 'more generous' attitudes to relief embodied in 'the old moral economy' with a more 'punitive form' of relief.[76] But it was precisely the generosity of the system which the early disciples of Malthus questioned. Observing, in one of a number of responses to Whitbread and Malthus collectively, that it was the level of employment rather than food that regulated population, the 'paternalist' par excellence John Weyland felt that the best way to ensure the well-being of the nation was to concentrate on sustaining its lead over its competitors in industry and commerce. The poor laws were essential to this drive precisely because they encouraged the growth of a surplus population, providing the reserve of labour needed to meet sudden increases in demand. Moreover, they facilitated the low-wage economy that was wanted to remain competitive in the global market.[77] To bribe the poor to accept low wages was, in the eyes of the early Malthusians, nothing short of tyranny, since it prevented the poor from developing the only qualities that would enable them to improve their condition in the long run. If the science of poverty was calculating and consciously unsentimental, that is because its practitioners believed that humane policy was a numbers game where present benefits were often outweighed by long-term disadvantages; in the case of the parish laws, the creation of structural poverty. Hence, when the writer for the *Edinburgh Review* accused Weyland and his like of rejecting 'Enlightened philosophy' in his seemingly wilful miscomprehension of the principle of population, this what not simply a rhetorical gambit. The choice, as he saw it, was between 'erring benevolence' and the 'Enlightened humanity' modelled by Malthus.[78]

There were certainly aspects of the revised *Essay* that helped to promote pessimistic tropes of thought about the prospects of the poor, especially as the century wore on. Malthus's concern that the proportion of the dependent poor might increase, overturning the aspirational culture of their industrious neighbours, proved particularly infectious in the following decades, not least because it chimed with evangelical anxieties about moral decline. He was far from alone in railing against the rising levels of pauperism, of course. But it is hardly a coincidence that the *Report from the Select Committee on the Poor Laws* (1817) traced the sapping of 'the independent spirit' of the labouring classes to the increasing number of 'paupers' brought into the world as a result of the parish's promise 'to maintain all who may be born, without charge to the parents'.[79] Again and again, the returns to the *Poor Laws Commissioners' Report* of 1834 offered the same diagnosis, as well as echoing Malthus's prophecy about the pauperising effects of increasing the number of peasant smallholdings and the tendency of the bastardy clauses to encourage an insouciant attitude to premarital procreation.[80] It is arguable, however, that Malthus's disquiet about the rising ratio of pauperism was a function of his positive assessment of the progress the English working people had made in terms of decent pride. His worry was that excessively free-handed aid in times of scarcity or ill-judged relief initiatives like cottage-building programmes would slow down or reverse the welcome trend. On the whole, moreover, he clearly thought that the independent spirit of the English poor was still holding up against these enervating forces; this is how he explained the fact that the poor laws did not seem to be promoting early marriage to the extent one might expect.[81] Whitbread, likewise, while accepting that the deleterious influence which the relief system had on the character of the labouring classes had exacerbated their sufferings, was assured that the effect was 'gradually wearing off' and the spirit of independence returning.[82]

Not everyone appreciated the encouraging message at the heart of the *Essay*, it is true. Those who mistakenly thought Malthus wished to promote strictly *moral* restraint – and not simply preventive checks – naturally read it as presenting a less hopeful picture, in line with his admission that he was far from sanguine about the spread of such behaviour.[83] Believing that he greatly underestimated the extent to which sexual abstinence was practised among the poor between puberty and marriage, for example, the writer for the *Gentleman's Magazine* accused him of painting an excessively 'gloomy and exaggerated view' of the impact of the oscillations on 'the progress of society'.[84] There is no question either that Hazlitt's and Cobbett's characterisation of the *Essay* as the gospel of avarice and despair resonated in radical circles. Yet the overarching optimism of Malthus's prognosis was not lost on all the early readers of the *Essay*. The writer for the *Monthly Review* was clear that his history of poverty held out 'to posterity the prospect of better days'.[85] Though he rejected Malthus solution to indigence, the reviewer for the *British Critic* grasped the progressive history underlying his arguments, noting, for example, his hugely positive assessment of developments in the marriage patterns of the English poor.[86] The take-home message of the *Essay*, according to the *Edinburgh Review*, was that there was plenty of scope for improving the lives of the labouring classes. It should be the national mission therefore to pursue this goal by encouraging a spirit of independence among the poor through education and 'equal laws'.[87]

In one sense, this programme embodied a level of optimism that was rare in Enlightenment thinking about poverty, and that is in the confidence it displayed in the poor man's potential for cultural and intellectual improvement. And those who believed in the mental capabilities of the poor were confident that the spread of learning would be hugely beneficial to society, a view which, judging from the response to Whitbread's Parochial Education Bill, had limited support among the political classes. Some objected on the grounds of cost, others to the compulsory nature of the plan. Easily the main concern about educating the poor, however, was the concern that 'it would teach them to despise their lot in life' and 'render them insolent to their superiors'.[88] It was in order to persuade the house 'on the grand principle' of whether educating the poor was beneficial to the country that Whitbread persevered with his bill, and this mainly came down to showing that it made them better citizens.[89] But there is clear evidence in this instance that such arguments were framed by Malthusian imperatives. When a supporter of the measure pointed to 'the wider range' that the mind of the poor took when educated – which better equipped them to support themselves in sickness and old age – it was a rare instance of the language of liberal education being applied to the working people. The lower classes, it was being claimed, could partake in that expansion of mind usually thought to be strictly the preserve of the gentleman.[90]

But this commitment clearly sprung from his view of what constituted 'the most important end of national education', which was none other than that 'which appeared in a Letter from Mr. Malthus to the hon mover of the bill', namely 'to elevate the general character of the poor'.[91] What is more, Whitbread reaffirmed that this was the underlying goal of his Parochial Schools Bill when he announced his plan to split the Poor Laws Bill into four separate measures. His reason for trying to establish the education of the poor first was that this was 'the grand foundation' of all his other measures of poor-law reform.[92] There is no question, then, that the argument of the *Essay* gave impetus to the drive for primary education, albeit that different objectives eventually preponderated as the Anglican Church asserted jurisdiction over the matter.[93]

It is true, on the other hand, that the Malthusian sentiments expressed in the *Poor Law Commissioners' Report* of 1834 painted a foreboding picture. Evidently, many of those quizzed about conditions in their parishes treated certain of Malthus's arguments as axiomatic. So invariably did they ascribe high poor rates to imprudent marriages and the rise of pauperism, furthermore, that it is hard not to suspect high levels of confirmation bias. Simplification and adulteration are a natural part of the translation of 'scientific' ideas into social norms, of course, and Malthus may have thought that this was a price worth paying for the popularisation of his programme. What would have perturbed him was that his hopeful message – reiterated constantly after 1803 – about the rise of respectability, ambition and intellect among the poor, and the resulting transformation of their prospects, was eclipsed by anxiety and indignation about the growth of dependent poverty. It should be clear from this account, however, that it was by no means inevitable that this should have been such a significant part of his legacy in regard to the poor laws. Worsening economic conditions after 1815, resulting in popular agitation and an increasingly partisan political climate, were largely to blame, no doubt, for bringing the pessimistic cadences of the *Essay* to the fore. How far this gloomy outlook was mitigated in the long run by the wider campaign to instil decent pride and the more positive forecasts about the cultural progress of the poor is impossible to measure. What is certain is that the binary characterisation of ideas of poverty fails to capture the complexity of these developments. And while the notion of 'the moral economy' helps to convey the political nature of social unrest in the eighteenth century, it paints a misleading picture when used to create a cast of heroes and villains for our own edification. A simple revision of our *termes d'art* that may promote a more nuanced understanding of the debate would be to speak of old and new moral economies; the old committed to compensating vast inequality with relief as a matter of right, the new to scrapping such entitlements as part of a plan for raising the poor out of the poverty cycle for good. At least this would avoid the fallacy of accepting the rhetoric of one party in the dispute as definitive.

Notes

1 The research for this chapter was carried out as part of a Leverhulme Trust mid-career fellowship. Thank you to Joanna Innes for her enormously helpful comments on an earlier draft.
2 [William Empson], 'Life, Writing and Character of Mr Malthus', *Edinburgh Review*, LXIV (January 1837), 491. I include myself in this. Niall O' Flaherty, 'Malthus and the History of Population', in ed. Shannon Stimson, *An Essay on the Principle of Population*, by T. R. Malthus (London: Yale University Press, 2018), pp. 477–96 at p. 477.
3 Robert J. Mayhew, *Malthus: The Life and Legacies of an Untimely Prophet* (Cambridge, MA: The Belknap Press of Harvard University Press, 2014); Gilbert Faccarello, Masashi Izumo and Hiromi Morishita (eds), *Malthus Across Nations: The Reception of Thomas Robert Malthus in Europe, America and Japan* (Cheltenham: Edward Elgar, 2020).
4 Donald Winch, 'Robert Malthus: Christian Moral Scientist, Arch-Demoralizer or Implicit Secular Utilitarian?' *Utilitas*, 5, 2 (1993), 239–253.
5 See E. P. Thompson, 'The Moral Economy of the English Crowd in the Eighteenth Century', *Past and Present*, 50 (1971), 76–136.
6 Gertrude Himmelfarb, *The Idea of Poverty: England in the Early Industrial Age* (New York, NY: Knopf, 1984), Ch. 4.

7 Sandra Sherman, *Imagining Poverty: Quantification and the Decline of Paternalism* (Columbus, OH: Ohio State University Press, 2001), p. 3, p. 4. Sherman sees Malthus as 'reflecting' and 'transmitting' a 'prevailing imagery' which defined the poor 'by a single need: hunger'. See p. 17.
8 Donald Winch, *Riches and Poverty: An Intellectual History of Political Economy in Britain, 1750–1834* (Cambridge: Cambridge University Press, 1996), pp. 288–348.
9 Niall O'Flaherty, 'Malthus and the End of Poverty', in Robert J. Mayhew (ed.), *New Perspectives on Malthus* (Cambridge: Cambridge University Press, 2016), pp. 74–104.
10 Himmelfarb, *The Idea of Poverty*, pp. 122–144.
11 William Godwin, *An Enquiry Concerning Political Justice, and its Influence on General Virtue and Happiness*, 2 vols (1793); Condorcet, *Esquisse d'un tableau historique des progrès de l'esprit humain* (1794–1795).
12 [T. R. Malthus], *An Essay on the Principle of Population, as It Affects the Future Improvement of Society, with Remarks on the Speculations of Mr. Godwin, M. Condorcet, and Other Writers* (London, 1798), pp. 29–31. Hereafter the First *Essay*.
13 Ibid., p. 190, p. 198.
14 Ibid., p. 143, p. 29, p. 95, p. 345.
15 T. R. Malthus, *An Essay on the Principle of Population or a View of its Past and Present Effects on Human Society*, ed. P. James, 2 vols (Cambridge: Cambridge University Press, [1803] 1989). Hereafter, the Second *Essay*.
16 Winch, *Riches and Poverty*, p. 301.
17 [Robert Southey], 'Review of *An Essay on the Principle of Population*', *The Annual Review and History of Literature for 1803*, vol. 2 (1804), 300.
18 However, the first *Essay* was praised by Samuel Parr in his *A Spital Sermon, Preached at Christ Church, Upon Easter Tuesday, April 15, 1800* (1801), pp. 141–143; and by Sydney Smith in his review of Godwin's response to Parr in *Edinburgh Review*, I (Oct. 1802), 26.
19 See John Clive, *Scotch Reviewers: The Edinburgh Review, 1802–1815* (Cambridge, MA: Harvard University Press, 1957), Chs 3–4.; Frank Whitson Fetter, 'The Economic Articles in the *Quarterly Review* and Their Authors, 1809–52', *Journal of Political Economy*, 66 (1958), 47–64.
20 Whitson Fetter, 'Economic Articles in the *Quarterly Review*', 47; Biancamaria Fontana, *Rethinking the Politics of Commercial Society: The Edinburgh Review, 1802–1832* (New York, NY: Cambridge University Press, 1985), p. 7, p. 9, p. 13.
21 J. B. Sumner's knowledgeable review of the 1817 edition of the *Essay* signalled its increasing openness to political economy, however. See *Quarterly Review* (July 1817), 369–403.
22 Whitson Fetter, 'Economic Articles in the Quarterly Review', 47–52.
23 Patricia James, *Population Malthus: His Life and Times* (London: Routledge & Kegan Paul, 1979), pp. 136–7.
24 The second *Essay* received a glowing review, for example, in the pro-ministerial (Pittite) *British Critic*. See Emily Lorraine Montluzin, 'Attributions of Authorship

in the *British Critic* during the Editorial Regime of Robert Nares, 1793–1813', *Studies in Bibliography*, 51 (1998), 241–258.
25 J. R. Poynter, *Society and Pauperism: English Ideas on Poor Relief, 1795–1834* (Toronto: University of Toronto Press, 1969), pp. 198–200.
26 William Hazlitt, *Reply to the Essay on Population* (London, 1807), p. 21. First *Essay*, p. 143. See Robert Wallace, *Various Prospects of Mankind, Nature and Providence* (London, 1761), p. 115.
27 Robert Acklom Ingram, *Disquisitions on Population in which the Principles of the Essay on Population by the Rev. T. R. Malthus are Examined and Refuted* (London, 1808), p. 6, pp. 27–28.
28 T. R. Malthus, '1806 Appendix' to *An Essay on the Principle of Population* (1803), ed. P. James, 2 vols (Cambridge: Cambridge University Press, 1989), vol. ii, p. 204.
29 [Anon], 'Review of *A Short Inquiry into the Policy, Humanity, and Past Effects of the Poor Laws. By one of His Majesty's Justices of Peace for the Three Inland Counties*', *Edinburgh Review*, XI (Oct 1807), 101–102.
30 *Gentleman's Magazine*, LLXIV, part 1 (1804), 336.
31 *The Monthly Review; or Literary Journal*, XLII (Dec. 1803), 337–338; [Anon], *British Critic* (Jan. 1804), 61; (March 1804), 242–243; [Anon], 'Review of *Disquisitions on Population* by Robert Acklom Ingram and *Reply to the Essay on Population* by [William Hazlitt]', *The Edinburgh Review*, XVI (Aug. 1810), 465, 469–470.
32 *Monthly Review*, XLII (Dec. 1803), 343; *British Critic* (Jan. 1804), 61–64.
33 *British Critic* (Jan. 1804), 62.
34 Second *Essay*, vol. i, p. 34.
35 *Monthly Review* (Dec. 1803), 339–357; *British Critic* (Jan. 1804), 62–69; *Edinburgh Review* (1810), 471–472.
36 *British Critic* (Jan. 1804), 63.
37 *Monthly Review*, XLII (Dec. 1803), 345–346; *British Critic* (Jan. 1804), 68; *Edinburgh Review* (1810), 471, 474–475.
38 *Monthly Review*, XLII (Dec. 1803), 348; *British Critic* (Jan. 1804), 68–69; *Edinburgh Review* (1807), 106, 111, 114; *Edinburgh Review* (1810), 470. Though he did not describe the programme, it is clear from Arthur Young's argument that he understood it well. See Arthur Young, 'On the Application of the Principles of Population, to the Question of Assigning Land to Cottages', *Annals of Agriculture*, XLI (1804), 217–218.
39 Second *Essay*, vol. ii. p. 197, vol. ii, p. 155. *British Critic* (March 1804), 240.
40 Second *Essay*, vol. ii, pp. 193–194; vol. ii, pp. 153–155.
41 Ibid., p. 128, p. 127.
42 *Monthly Review* XLIII (Jan. 1804), 65.
43 *Gentleman's Magazine* (1804), LLXIV, part 1, 338–339; *Annals of Agriculture*, XLI (1804), 218.
44 Second *Essay*, vol. ii, pp. 111–112.
45 Samuel Whitbread, *Substance of a Speech on the Poor Laws Delivered in the House of Commons by Mr. Whitbread, Delivered on Thursday, February 19, 1807*, second edition (1807), p. 10.
46 Ibid., p. 5, p. 24.

47 See Second *Essay*, vol. ii, pp. 6–174.
48 Whitbread, *Substance of a Speech*, p. 10.
49 *Monthly Review*, XLIII (Jan. 1804), 68–70; *British Critic* (March 1804), 242–243.
50 *British Critic* (March 1804), 243; *Monthly Review*, XLII (Dec. 1803), 338.
51 Whitbread, *Substance of a Speech*, p. 4, p. 5.
52 Ibid., p. 10.
53 Joanna Innes, 'The State and the Poor: Eighteenth-Century England in European Perspective', in John Brewer and Eckhart Hellmuth (eds), *Rethinking Leviathan: The Eighteenth-Century State in Britain and Germany* (Oxford: Oxford University Press, 1999), pp. 225–280 at p. 229.
54 Joseph Townsend, *A Dissertation on the Poor Law* (London, 1786); Thomas Ruggles, *The History of the Poor: Their Rights, Duties, and the Laws Respecting Them: in a Series of Letters* (London, 1793; New Edition 1797); Frederick Eden, *The State of the Poor; or, An History of the Labouring Classes in England from the Conquest to the Present Period* (London, 1797).
55 John Howlett, *The Insufficiency of the Causes to which the Increase of our Poor and the Poor's Rates have been Generally Ascribed* (London, 1788); David Davies, *The Case of Labourers in Husbandry Stated and Considered*, 2 vols (London, 1795).
56 Davies, *Labourers in Husbandry*, pp. 106–114.
57 William Paley, *The Principles of Moral and Political Philosophy* (1785), pp. 191–214.
58 Whitbread, *Substance of a Speech*, p. 3, p. 5. See *Cobbett's Parliamentary History* (9 Dec. 1795). vol. XXXII, cols 700–716.
59 He exposited the arguments of Davies and Howlett but came down decisively against them. *Notes of Lectures on Political Oeconomy* by Professor Dugald Stewart. Edinburgh University 1802–1803. Seligman 1802E St4, Rare Book and Manuscript Library, Columbia University in the City of New York, pp. 148–200. See pp. 158–160, p. 163, pp. 165–169, p. 171, p. 184. Thank you to Lina Weber for her transcription of these notes. See also Henry Fielding, *An Enquiry into the Causes of the Late Increase of Robbers* (London, 1751) and Daniel Defoe, *Giving Alms no Charity* (London, 1704).
60 Stewart, 'Notes of Lecturers', pp. 165–186, pp. 168–169.
61 Whitbread, *Substance of a Speech*, pp. 71–72, pp. 79–80.
62 Ibid., pp. 19–20.
63 Malthus himself insisted that aid should not be denied in times of acute distress. See, for example, Second *Essay*, (1806 edition) vol. i, p. 357.
64 Whitbread, *Substance of a Speech*, p. 2, p. 85, p. 22.
65 See Arthur Young, *Travels in France During the Years 1787, 1788, 1789*, 2 vols (London, 1784), vol. i, p. 413.
66 Young, *Annals of Agriculture*, p. 220, p. 221.
67 One writer from the *Edinburgh Review*, indeed, thought six months' notice for the move was sufficient instead of the two years suggested by Malthus. *Edinburgh Review* (1807), 115.
68 Though his views were also shaped no doubt by his experiences as an energetic magistrate.

69 Empson, 'Life of *Malthus*', p. 484.
70 *Second Essay* (1817 edition) vol. ii, p. 184.
71 See '1806 Appendix', pp. 216–226; idem, *A Letter to Samuel Whitbread: On His Proposed Bill for The Amendment Of The Poor Laws* (1807), pp. 15–34. Young, 'On the Application'; Whitbread, *Substance of a Speech*, pp. 76–78.
72 These included Townsend and Ruggles.
73 This was true of Malthus himself. See *Letter to Whitbread*, p. 12.
74 *Edinburgh Review* (1807), 106, 100–115.
75 William Keir, *A Summons of Wakening* (Harwick, 1807), p. 127.
76 Himmelfarb, *Idea of Poverty*, p. 190.
77 John Weyland, *A Short Enquiry into the Policy, Humanity, and Effect of the Poor Laws* (London, 1807), p. 51, p. 42, p. 25. His position is ambiguous, however, as he claimed that low money wages would ultimately promote high real wages. See Poynter, *Society and Pauperism*, p. 181.
78 *Edinburgh Review* (1807), 101, 113.
79 *Report from the Select Committee on the Poor Laws: With the Minutes of Evidence Taken Before the Committee: and an Appendix* (London, 1817), p. 18. See, also, p. 7, p. 10, p. 21, p. 52, p. 74, p. 194, p. 223 and *passim*.
80 *Poor Law Commissioners Report of 1834* (London, 1905), p. 16, p. 66, p. 86, p. 177, pp. 182–183, p. 192, p. 240 and *passim*.
81 Malthus, Second *Essay*, vol. ii, p. 145, vol. ii, p. 363, vol. ii, p. 263.
82 Whitbread, *Substance of a Speech*, p. 5.
83 *Gentleman's Magazine*, LLXIV, part 1 (1804), 337–339; *Annals of Agriculture*, 218. See Malthus, Second *Essay*, vol. ii, p. 104.
84 *Gentleman's Magazine*, 339, 336.
85 *Monthly Review*, XLIII (Jan. 1804), 69, 70.
86 *British Critic* (Jan. 1804), 68–69.
87 *Edinburgh Review* (1810), 472.
88 See Samuel Romilly, *The Memoirs of the Life of Samuel Romilly*, 3 vols (London, 1840), vol. ii, p. 207. HC Deb (13 June 1807), vol. ix, cols 798–799. It was this fear, of course, that lay behind the mercantilist 'utility of poverty' doctrine, memorably elaborated by Bernard Mandeville, but also widely echoed throughout the century. See Tim Hochstrasser's Chapter 1 in this volume.
89 HC Deb (13 June 1807), vol ix, col. 802.
90 This needs to be distinguished from the promotion of Charity Schools, which were geared towards making the poor more pious and obedient, and from the drive to inure children to labour by placing them in 'schools of industry'. M. G. Jones, *The Charity School Movement: A Study of Eighteenth-Century Puritanism in Action* (Cambridge: Cambridge University Press, 1938), pp. 73–84.
91 HC Deb (24 April 1807), vol. ix, col. 541.
92 HC Deb (24 April 1807), vol. ix, col. 538.
93 Joanna Innes 'L'"éducation nationale" dans les îles Britanniques, 1765–1815. Variations britanniques et irlandaises sur un thème européen', *Annales. Histoire, Sciences Sociales*, 65 (2010), 1100–1104.

11

Poverty, autonomy and control: Patrick Colquhoun's *Treatise on Indigence* (1806)

Joanna Innes

Patrick Colquhoun was a Glasgow businessman who became a London stipendiary magistrate. He has earned a place in history books largely because of his imposing publications, especially his *Treatise on the Police of the Metropolis* (1796), and because he has been represented as a progenitor of modern policing. His life, as usually told, has an oddly binary character: from thrusting capitalist he appears to have become an arch-regulator, a proponent of the disciplinary state.[1]

This chapter shifts attention to another of his treatises, the 1806 *Treatise on Indigence*, and builds around that an alternative reading of his thought.[2] It is argued here that he saw people in general as having meaningful agency, and society and economy as having their own dynamic. In this context, the initiatives he supported can be seen as targeted interventions, designed to support those struggling to cope with the pressures of life in a commercial society.

To understand what was and was not distinctive about Colquhoun's thought, we need to place him among a generation of metropolitan doers and thinkers, people who tried to reconceptualise poverty and crime, and to refresh thinking about how both state and voluntary sector could engage with these challenges.[3] They were not all of one mind. Colquhoun and Jeremy Bentham worked together on projects relating to poverty, police and prisons.[4] Yet whereas Bentham was engaged by the project of designing carceral institutions – prisons, workhouses – to structure the lives of those who failed to make their way in the world, Colquhoun worried more about the striving poor: about those who might, through mischance or failures of self-discipline, slide into pauperism or crime, but who were not ineluctably doomed to follow that course. Colquhoun borrowed from Bentham a distinction between simple 'poverty' and problematic 'indigence', identifying the latter as the subject of his 1806 *Treatise*. Yet the two used the terminology in different ways, reflecting their different perspectives. Bentham drew a sharp line between simple poverty and problematic indigence; Colquhoun, by contrast, imagined the descent from poverty to indigence as a long greyscale.

This chapter has three main parts. The first surveys Colquhoun's activities in business, local government, philanthropy and data collection across his lifetime. All coloured his thinking about the poor. The second part zooms in on his encounters with poverty before he wrote his *Treatise*, sketching contexts in which he encountered, on the one hand, struggling poor people, on the other hand, policy makers, social commentators and philanthropic activists. The third section sets out the main arguments of the *Treatise on Indigence* and shows how he deployed new data to illuminate the functioning and malfunctioning of Britain's commercial society.

Colquhoun was not a major architect of the process of rethinking of poverty and responses to it that his generation undertook – a process that helped to determine that the nineteenth-century's landscape of poverty, both as policy object and as lived experience, would differ from the eighteenth century's. Still, he was a thoughtful and creative, and a notably well-networked participant in that process, and one whose inspirations and intellectual trajectory we can to some extent lay bare.

A multi-stranded career

Throughout his career, Colquhoun engaged in and sought to forge links between three forms of activity: first, business; second, the government of urban areas, especially in relation to crime and poverty; and third the collection of information, especially quantitative information, which he used to assist his thinking about these themes, and to persuade others.

He lived his life across three countries: America, Scotland and England. He was born in Scotland in 1745, the son of the sheriff substitute for Dumbartonshire, in the neighbourhood of Glasgow. Scottish sheriffs' responsibilities were broad; in effect, Colquhoun grew up in a magistrate's household. He went to Virginia as a teenager, to learn the ways of Atlantic trade, then spent two decades in Glasgow, becoming a wealthy entrepreneur and a leader in local public life. In 1789, at the age of 44, he moved to London, probably hoping to live off his capital with relatively little exertion, and to find other interesting avocations. This did not entirely work out, but he did find fresh scope for endeavour. He died at the age of 75, in 1820.

To set the scene for Colquhoun's engagement with poverty, I'll enlarge on this outline, describing in turn how he pursued each of these three main lines of activity across his life.

Colquhoun's business career took off quickly.[5] His youthful initiation into the tobacco trade was followed by association with one of Glasgow's most powerful merchant groups. His commercial ventures were diverse, including shipping foodstuffs and goods, moving people – on at least one occasion enslaved individuals, but also troops and convicts on government contracts; he also helped complete the Forth and Clyde Navigation (which cut across Scotland, linking the North to the Irish Sea). Like other businessmen, he held offices in the city of Glasgow, including serving as Lord Provost. He turned to lobbying in the aftermath of the American War of Independence, when the government sought to repair its finances and reboot the economy. Merchants and manufacturers organised to have a say in how this was done, sometimes through the newly instituted Chambers of Commerce. Colquhoun was founding president of the Glasgow Chamber. The cotton industry was then taking off in Glasgow's hinterland, prompting him to forge links with Manchester industrialists. His move to London followed long spells lobbying there, and a brief experiment in institutionalising that role. He may have hoped in the longer term to win a seat in Parliament – but if so, that ambition was not fulfilled.[6]

In London, Colquhoun maintained economic interests, but his relationship to them was increasingly mediated. His partner's bankruptcy capsized his mercantile firm, but he found uses for his capital in a series of global investments: in the Bahamas, and in northern New York state, where along with the super-wealthy Scot William Pulteney and John Hornby, a former governor of Bombay, he developed a huge tract of land. In each case he kept a close eye on the proceedings of local agents.[7]

In the new century, building on his lobbying experience and his Caribbean links, he agreed to serve as consul for some West Indian islands, then also for the Hanseatic cities of Hamburg, Bremen and Lubeck.[8] Napoleon's attempt to build a closed continental trading bloc gave relations with these cities new significance. Colquhoun built up links across north Germany and liaised between interests in the region and the British Government.

As economic warfare escalated in the last years of the war, and peace brought challenges of adjustment, many aspects of economic policy became controversial. Colquhoun took a lively interest in such matters as whether and how to rebase British currency on a gold standard, regulating East India trade and whether to retain the income tax.[9]

One might think that this would have been enough to keep anyone busy, but Colquhoun also took on challenges of urban governance, all the more vigorously and creatively after moving to London. In Glasgow (as noted), he served as Lord Provost, reportedly overseeing a clamp down on beggars and improvements to the city's house of correction.[10] In London – possibly partly to offset losses from his partner's failure – he secured appointment as one of the first metropolitan stipendiary magistrates: posts established by an act of 1792. His patron (perhaps not coincidentally a Scot) was Henry Dundas, then Home Secretary. Precursor 'trading justices' had supported themselves in discharging what was, in a busy urban area, no light task by taking fees.

Their hand-picked successors were by contrast paid to maintain 'police offices' (they also took fees, but were meant to have less incentive to stir up business for personal gain).[11] Colquhoun was initially appointed for the east London district around Shoreditch, at a salary of £600 p.a. – a tidy amount, though not equivalent to the £800 p.a. which in his later 'social table' he identified as the typical income of a lesser merchant, let alone the £2,600 that he credited to an 'eminent merchant'.[12] But this was not his only income source.

Colquhoun's vision far outreached his formal responsibilities. In 1796, he shared his ideas about how to improve the administration of criminal justice in a *Treatise* on 'the police of the metropolis', in which he argued for law reforms, more magistrates' offices and more joined up and proactive policing.[13] He also extended his ambit in practice, helping to institute a Thames-side 'Marine Police Office', where he acted as superintending magistrate with a more hands-on partner; the office oversaw a regulatory force. The 1790s saw dramatic developments on the waterfront, including a dock-building programme. Colquhoun wrote a second *Treatise* on associated problems and opportunities.[14]

One driver for Colquhoun was always the hope of growing his income from public service. He dreamed of contracting to provide marine policing services. In the late 1790s, he projected a role for himself in running a new 'Board of Police Revenue', which he suggested might generate new income by licensing activities across the metropolis.[15] It is unsurprising, given his experience, that he believed he could manage such projects. In fact, neither scheme was sanctioned as he outlined it, though he did get himself relocated from Shoreditch to the more attractive setting of Queen Square Westminster (near Russell Square).

Meanwhile – after starting work as a stipendiary, but before launching the Marine Police – Colquhoun also engaged ambitiously with metropolitan poverty. In the mid 1790s, the condition of the poor across the nation climbed up many agendas, in the context of harvest failure and catastrophic food shortage. The French Revolution emerged from its most disorderly phase, and Anglo-French peace negotiations were for the first time attempted. The propertied classes felt free to turn from enjoining the populace to stand by king and constitution to wrestle instead with the welfare crisis.[16] A London businessman who had been a leading loyalist fundraiser refocused his efforts on building a fund to relieve the poor.[17] Colquhoun served on the committee and agreed to oversee its spending. That was one spur to the part he played in building up an innovative network of 'soup kitchens' across the metropolis (self-proclaimed nutritional experts were then advocating the benefits of soup).[18]

Just as the soup-kitchen scheme was resolved upon, Colquhoun was approached to join a group of philanthropists – including MPs and bishops, London professionals and businessmen – in what proved to be a long-running philanthropic think-tank and agency, the Society for Bettering the Condition of the Poor.[19] Its leading members also undertook charity work in their neighbourhoods. Colquhoun was a founding five-guinea subscriber, and soon also a member of the General Committee. He remained active throughout the Society's twenty-year life. His interests were probably shaped by it, and perhaps he also shaped its activities. Thus, it probably nourished his existing interest in education, a major preoccupation of its moving spirit, Sir Thomas Bernard.[20] It also provided stimulus for his growing interest in contagious disease, especially typhus and smallpox.[21]

Colquhoun resigned his stipendiary post once he passed the age of 70. He was persistently keen to share his expertise and vaunt his achievements in public service. He also treasured his reputation as a philanthropist and burnished it in correspondence with admirers.[22]

Weaving through these strands of activity, and manifesting itself especially in his publications, was a third interest of Colquhoun's: the collection of quantitative data. He must have used this in his business life, and certainly did as a lobbyist: historians continue to cite his findings about the spread of cotton mills.[23] His *Treatise on Police* contained many estimates of the scale of criminal activity, and his case for river police also included data on commerce. As we will explore further shortly, new data played a vital part in his *Treatise on Indigence*. It was in that context that he first developed the estimate of income distribution that historians have set alongside other 'social tables' (by Gregory King and Joseph Massie) to explore English social structure across the long eighteenth century.[24] Colquhoun's most ambitious data assemblage was his post war *Treatise on the Wealth, Power and Resources of the British Empire*, designed to celebrate the circumstances of the state which steadfastly opposed revolutionary and Napoleonic France, and ultimately triumphed.[25]

It's true that guesswork played a large part in his estimates. Within a generation, his numbers were being mocked – for example, by J. R. McCulloch in his review of economic literature.[26] However, he liked hard evidence when he could get it, and is probably best seen as an overenthusiastic amateur. As in other aspects of his life, his aspirations ran ahead of the possible. What is clear is that – like many historians – he found numbers seductively good to think with.

As this overview has shown, Colquhoun was a notably energetic man, who retained throughout his life, though in changing mixes, interests in business, policing, philanthropy and the collection and analysis of data. All helped to shape his thinking about poverty.

Colquhoun's engagement with poverty before the *Treatise*

Colquhoun's preoccupation with the greyscale between mere poverty and helpless indigence was surely informed by his encounters with London's poor in his various capacities; also by his interactions with colleagues, though his views had some distinctive twists.

As a metropolitan magistrate from 1792, Colquhoun processed people charged with felonies, and sent them on for jury trial, potentially to imprisonment, transportation or execution.[27] But even this process will have given him insights into what he came to see as the crimogenic milieu in which poor Londoners lived: amid cheap lodging houses and low alehouses; populated by struggling individuals and families living off what work they could get and on their wits. It was a normal incident of such lives recurrently to monetise possessions with pawnbrokers, a source of temptation that these dealers asked few questions about the origins of goods. So even this part of Colquhoun's work must have taught him much about what it meant to be poor in London.

The greater part of his time was, however, probably spent on people whose lives had not reached so critical a juncture, on petty crime, regulation and miscellaneous complaints. Constables regularly hauled before magistrates members of the 'idle and disorderly' poor: a selection of the abrasive and troublesome, pilferers and prostitutes from the capital's streets. Magistrates also provided judicial back-up and administrative oversight for the poor relief system. Parish officers brought needy poor people to establish their place of settlement and, if it proved to lie elsewhere, to seek their 'removal'. Relief seekers for their part came to complain that parish officers had unreasonably denied their requests: magistrates could order relief (even poor with no local settlement could be given emergency assistance). Finally, the poor more broadly conceived loomed large among suitors at the stipendiary's court; they used it to try to sort out cheaply problems with employers, landlords, fellow lodgers or other acquaintances, such that these courts have been called 'poor men's courts'.[28] Listening to these diverse applications, day in, day out, must have impressed Colquhoun with the difficulties and temptations of this environment: in how many ways one could fail.

What could be done for the many who had not reached the point of being sent to prison for jury trial, nor had bowed to fate and entered one of London's many workhouses? In his first years in the metropolis, Colquhoun took part in various efforts to aid the striving poor. He reorganised the management of the charity school of St Leonard's Shoreditch, and wrote to Home Secretary Dundas to propose the establishment of a 'Village of Industry' for those who had come to grief: beggars and convicts. One of his responses to dearth was to raise funds for a society for the relief of pawns – helping those who had pawned belongings in order to eat to recover clothes and work implements.[29]

The dearth crisis of 1795–1796 proved a forcing house for new thinking. In important part the effect of a bad harvest, the crisis saw bread prices shoot sky-high – when bread grain could be found at all. Everyone from the royal family down experimented with alternative foods. Wages came under pressure, and the poorer struggled to afford fuel and other necessities. Many of the working poor needed help to cope. Distinctions between them and the helpless poor became even harder to maintain.[30]

Debate in the aftermath was given focus by William Pitt's attempt to reform the poor laws.[31] This was an unusual venture for a prime minister: usually such initiatives were left to backbenchers with local experience. Pitt was, however, in many respects an innovator, open to reform. He had planned for some years to engage with the poor laws; the crisis pushed the task up his agenda. He had noted with interest efforts by magistrates and others across the country to encourage the striving poor; now, he assembled some from the frontline into a think tank to help him draft proposals. The bill that emerged aimed to complement traditional relief payments with nationwide adoption of a new set of practices, including 'schools of industry' for poor children; parish-run friendly societies, in which the poor's contributions might be topped up by donations; and help for the rural poor to buy cows.

There was as yet no public debate at any level of abstraction about the proper use of state power in such matters – though Pitt's bill helped to precipitate some. Still, many thought that his proposals were overambitious, overcomplicated, liable to exploitation by unscrupulous people and likely to entail frightening levels of expense. A group of London parishes were stridently critical. They argued that they (and similar parishes elsewhere) had their affairs in hand; they bestowed upon the poor an appropriate mix of discipline and charity, and relatively inexperienced ministers and MPs should not interfere.

It was in this context that Jeremy Bentham shifted his attention from crime and punishment – from pushing the case for his 'Panopticon' prison – to poverty and its relief. Bentham responded to what he learned about the bill at various stages by critiquing it and elaborating his contrasting ideas. When it reached Parliament, he supported the London parishes who campaigned against it. His conviction that public effort should focus on incarcerating those who had given up the struggle aligned with the parishes' case.[32]

It was during these exertions that Bentham developed, in manuscripts that he shared with Colquhoun, a new lexicon to characterise poverty (a characteristic move: he thought that precise terminologies were crucial to clear thought). Key terms in this lexicon were 'pauper' and 'indigence'. Though Bentham often coined neologisms, these were old words repurposed. Pauper was Latin for poor person; it was a habitual lawyers' term, which Bentham helped to push into wider use. Indigence, a high-flown term for poverty, though taken up by Colquhoun and some others, did not catch on in the same way. Until this point, pauper and indigence had been *synonyms* for poor and poverty. Bentham used them to draw distinctions: between the ordinary striving poor, and those who had given up (paupers). He and his parochial allies thought that public effort should focus on the latter.[33] Colquhoun, by contrast, blurred the distinction, imagining indigence as a progressive condition, warranting calibrated interventions.[34]

Few defended Pitt's bill in its entirety. Pitt abandoned it, and, though he talked about reworking and reviving it, never did. But nor was there a general swing behind the London parishes' uncompromising line. In metropolitan philanthropic circles, on the contrary, there was enthusiasm for pursuing the kind of projects Pitt favoured on a voluntary basis. The Society for Bettering the Condition of the Poor, which brought together men of this mind, was conceived and launched alongside the bill, but proceeded despite its defeat. The Society seems to have been open to legislative mandates, and indeed hoped to advise on their substance, but more immediately set itself the task of experimenting with ways of aiding the striving poor. Members were asked to submit reports on initiatives undertaken by themselves or others, explaining their objectives and operation, and in this way contribute to an empirical science of social action.[35]

Many Bettering Society members had previously supported a similarly recuperative but more moralistic campaign for the 'reformation of manners'.[36] The new society's tilt to the upbeat probably owed much to the preferences of its leader, Sir Thomas Bernard, though possibly something to the exigencies of the political moment. Nonetheless, it offered an attractive home only to those at least capable of striking this optimistic note.

Although Colquhoun's involvement with the Society probably reinforced his interest in betterment projects, particular initiatives that he undertook often had other sponsors. So it was with soup kitchens, his biggest charitable endeavour during the next few years. By Colquhoun's report, these centres served cheap soup to 10,000 Londoners in a winter.[37] His work with them can only have sharpened his sense of the scale of local need, extending well into the ranks of the working poor. He was led to reflect on weaknesses in the poor relief safety net. He noted that employers, especially large employers, often lived at a distance from their workforce. Since relief funds were mostly collected and disbursed by parish, wealth generated by workers was not available to help them in hard times. He argued the case for a common metropolitan poor fund.[38]

As well as adopting Bentham's terms 'pauper' and 'indigence', Colquhoun was also an early adopter of two other reminted terms, given currency by those who sought to refresh thinking about poverty. These were 'mendicity' and 'the casual poor'.

Mendicity was possibly in origin another Bentham-ism – it has a Benthamic ring to it, and it figures in his manuscripts. Denoting the condition of being a beggar, it appears in older English dictionaries, and was perhaps more common in French. It was first inserted into English debate on social problems by Matthew Martin, secretary to the Bettering Society, whom Colquhoun must have met at this point if not before. Martin, a retired west-country merchant, transferred from spare-time natural history to beggars a passion for cataloguing and analysis. To build up knowledge about beggars, Martin persuaded supporters to give them tickets rather than cash; these could be exchanged for money at a Mendicity Enquiry Office, staffed by Martin and others, in return for answers to questions. The answers obtained (from those who submitted to the process) persuaded Martin that beggars' circumstances were often truly dire, such that parish officers would probably have relieved them if approached. Some indeed were probably entitled to relief in the place where they begged; others might have claimed it elsewhere in the metropolis – but they did not understand the system, or were frightened of being drawn into its toils (might they be confined in a workhouse, or deported from the city?), so instead sought aid from passers-by. The Bettering Society endorsed Martin's work, and Bernard reported on his initial findings. A few years later, having been aided by a Home Office grant, Martin set out further findings for the Home Secretary. Colquhoun absorbed Martin's analysis into his developing understanding of pauperising processes, no doubt appreciating its quantitative dimension.

Finally, the term 'casual poor' had long been used by parish officers to denote various categories of poor beyond regular pensioners. These included poor people formally 'settled' in the parish who were granted occasional relief only; or poor without settlement, whom parish officers nonetheless relieved either on an ongoing basis (some parishes had their own rules, determining how long one had to have lived locally to get casual relief), or as an 'emergency' (potential legal cover for longer-term payments). Sometimes, the term was applied more narrowly to beggars and vagrants who patronised designated 'casual poor' pay tables. It thus had a range of overlapping meanings, sometimes clarified by context.[39] Bernard used it in his published report on Martin's project, to denote poor without a local settlement, all too likely (as he saw it) to fail to find work and end up on the streets. Around 1800, the term began to figure in policy debate.

Thus, a failed bill of 1800 would have prevented the removal of the 'casual poor'.[40]

Colquhoun added the term to others denoting those who operated somewhere along the greyscale between poverty and indigence. He first used it in print in 1799, as he refined and extended the proposal he had made to the 1798 session of the House of Commons 'Finance Committee': that there should be a Board of Police Revenue (ideally to be run by him), to manage a variety of licensing programmes, including for alehouses, pawnbrokers and street hawkers.[41] In two small pamphlets, printed for private circulation, he further developed his ideas.[42] He proposed in the first that the metropolitan police board might be just one node in a national network, In the second (whose arguments seem to have been inspired especially by Martin's work), he reflected on and suggested remedies for problems posed by the 'casual poor' (as well as making the poverty/indigence distinction for the first time in print). What he proposed in these few dozen pages was that yet another board might be charged with obtaining an overview of metropolitan poverty, perhaps as 'Commissioners for Inquiring into the Cases and Causes of the Distress of the Poor in the Metropolis'. Though this name highlighted the function of enquiry, Colquhoun also suggested that they be given executive powers specifically in relation to vagrants and the 'casual poor', drawing on a common metropolitan fund established for this purpose. They should have power on the one hand to set up workhouses where people lacking local settlements could be employed; on the other, to direct constables to deal with troublesome behaviour.[43] Colquhoun shovelled all these new and imperfectly integrated ideas into the next, 1800 edition of his *Treatise on Police*.[44] Even as this went to print, a new harvest crisis, 1800–1801, made such matters urgent again – though Colquhoun's attempt to urge his remedies on Pitt bore no fruit, understandably given that the prime minister had a world war, the union of Britain and Ireland and a reconfiguration of the UK religious settlement on his mind.[45]

The argument of this section has been that Colquhoun's experiences in the 1790s (partly prefigured in Glasgow) aided him in developing a complex picture of the challenges facing those living poor lives in the metropolis. As a magistrate, he dealt with the more predatory among them, but from this and his philanthropic work, he also gained a sense of the challenges they faced. Like many others, he was stimulated by wartime dearth crises to think harder about how to help the poor, both for their own and for the wider society's sake. This new thinking was associated with the development (by Bentham but not only by Bentham) of a new lexicon of terms, reflecting attempts to reimagine the landscape of poverty. As someone struggling to conceptualise what he realised was a complex reality, Colquhoun was an early adopter of the new terms.

The Treatise on Indigence: *genesis and argument*

The *Treatise on Indigence* pulled together Colquhoun's thoughts about poverty up to that point and spurred him to think more about its causes and possible remedies: about how to stop people sliding from hardship into indigence. In this context, his taste for quantitative data and his business perspective came more fully into play.

As early as 1797, when he inserted a critical footnote about the poor laws in a new edition of his *Treatise on Police*, Colquhoun indicated that he intended at some point to write at greater length about poverty, but for a while, he gave other tasks precedence. His hand was finally tipped when the Whig Samuel Whitbread (also an active magistrate and promoter of social improvement) gave notice in May 1806 that he planned to bring forward a poor law reform bill. The prospect spurred several authors (including Malthus) to publicise their ideas. Colquhoun was among those jolted into action.[46]

Colquhoun's interest may also have been engaged by the release of new data. A couple of years before, Parliament had published returns to its recent survey of parish spending on the poor (from Easter to Easter, 1803–1804). There had been previous such surveys: by the Board of Trade in 1696, and three times by Parliament.[47] This one was instigated by Pitt's former Treasury Secretary and right-hand man George Rose, who had worked with Pitt on poor law reform and thought the subject too important to drop. Rose's survey sought information under more headings than its precursors – breaking relief recipients into categories, by age, disability and whether relieved 'outdoors' or 'indoors' (in a workhouse), as well as asking about relief of the casual poor, numbers of schools of industry and friendly societies. Rose employed an amateur enthusiast, Thomas Poole, to analyse the results, with the aid of other datasets: population data from the first census (and associated historic data), acreage and tax data.[48]

Colquhoun's work with this data spurred him to further contextualising effort. He was in any case intrigued by the buoyancy of the economy at this time, despite heavy war taxation, and hoped also to shed light on that. His research proved time consuming, but by the start of the next parliamentary session, his *Treatise* was in print.[49]

In the *Treatise*, Colquhoun used data from the returns in two, complementary ways. First, to construct a cross-section. He combined the snapshot of poverty and its relief in one year which the returns provided with other data to construct a social table, an estimate of numbers of households categorised by income source and size, as first attempted by Gregory King in 1696. (The secretary to the Board of Trade, George Chalmers, had recently discovered King's workings in the British Museum.) Colquhoun also aimed to shed light on economic and social dynamics: on the amount of capital available to support employment, and on how effectively that was being used to support production and prosperity.[50] He did not take it for granted that it was used to full effect. It was, for example, possible that the poor laws operated perversely, to inhibit full employment.

Colquhoun began his *Treatise* by reflecting on the causes of 'indigence', in the sense of relief dependency, echoing some parts of Bentham's discussion, but also drawing on his own observations and data from the returns. As he saw it, some indigence was structural and unavoidable: it arose from youth, age or physical or mental impairment. Other forms were in other ways 'innocent'. They arose, at least initially, from misfortunes such as lack of work, perhaps in a context of economic downturn; or from sickness, including epidemic sickness; or from the inadequacies of the support systems for those who migrated to large cities. Such innocent poor could and should (in his view) be helped by 'timely props'.[51] However, he thought that even hard luck cases often had a culpable element. He hypothesised that three-quarters of adult relief recipients wasted some of their meagre resources in alehouses. Even friendly societies, meant to encourage providence, routinely met in pubs and held annual feasts: in tallying thousands of these societies, the returns ironically hinted at a morass of extravagant sociability. Finally, however initially caused, being indigent was itself degrading, such that the innocently indigent quickly transmuted into the culpably dependent.[52] In that context it was fortunate, Colquhoun thought, that the English were of better character than (notably) the French. Otherwise, the scale and depth of degradation would have been still greater.[53]

One simple lesson that could be drawn from the 1803 returns, when compared to earlier estimates, was that indigence was growing. Colquhoun, however, argued that when spending was contextualised, there were no grounds for panic. Things did seem to be getting worse: population growth could not explain the growth in spending. Nonetheless, Britain was a rich country, and growing richer: poor relief was not absorbing a *frightening* amount of economic surplus. Average spending was manageable given the rental value of land on which poor rates were charged. Still, it was not good to leave the land burdened, or the able-bodied idle: that was bad for them and implied an underuse of human resource. Forty percent of relief recipients were (the returns showed) *not* young, elderly or seriously incapacitated, but putatively fit to work. The scale of income generated each year across the nation suggested a huge and growing amount of capital available to undergird production; means to employ more people did exist.[54]

Why were these means not deployed? Why were so many able-bodied people relief-dependent? And why had their number increased, at a faster rate than population, as England had grown wealthier? Colquhoun argued that 'civilisation' operated in various ways to produce indigence, through a mix of material and moral causes, exacerbated by bad policies.

On the material side, he was especially intrigued by significant variations in spending on the poor by region. Both the ratio of relief to the rate-base and the ratio of the relief dependent to the local population varied. Colquhoun reported his findings about numbers of relief claimants in relation to population by county in a table.[55] I have put his data into a thematic map: Figure 11.1. They suggest that ratios of paupers to population were generally higher in the corn-growing south, and above all in Wiltshire and Sussex. That they were low in Middlesex should not surprise us; per capita expenditure on the poor was generally lower in urban districts, perhaps because there were more support options, but also because these places drew more 'unsettled' immigrants, at best scantily relieved as 'casual poor'. (Some of these immigrants will have been supported by remittances from distant parishes. Where they appear in the data is not clear. They complicate any attempt to map poverty spatially.)

A long tradition of thought, dating back to the early years of the poor law, held that the able-bodied workless should be given work. During the eighteenth century, doubts had grown about whether it was possible to create jobs at will: to sidestep market forces.[56] Colquhoun's perspective was that of an entrepreneur who embraced the substantial autonomy of the economy and aimed to strategise in that context. The main object, he thought, should be to grow the economy, to facilitate the operation of the labour market and to address market deficiencies. What evidence he had led him to conclude that the economy was growing; that was not the problem. Uneven spending on the poor suggested to him instead that (as Adam Smith had posited) the benefits of growth were unevenly shared, because the settlement laws obstructed the free (and putatively optimal) flow of labour. He hypothesised that the later seventeenth-century codification of these laws accounted for much of the increase in indigence between Gregory King's time and his own. He urged, unusually (though this was also the view of Thomas Paine) that, to make it possible to relax these rules, relief should be paid from a national fund, without regard to where a claimant lived. (Neither Paine nor Colquhoun addressed the standard objection: that this would remove from local paymasters a pressing incentive to control relief spending and might make them more lax in dealing with welfare dependency.)[57]

Although Colquhoun repeated standard phrases about allowing wages to 'find their own level', he acknowledged that the market did not sort everything out – though he was short in suggestions about how to deal with these failures. He suggested, thus, that farmers often colluded to drive labourers'

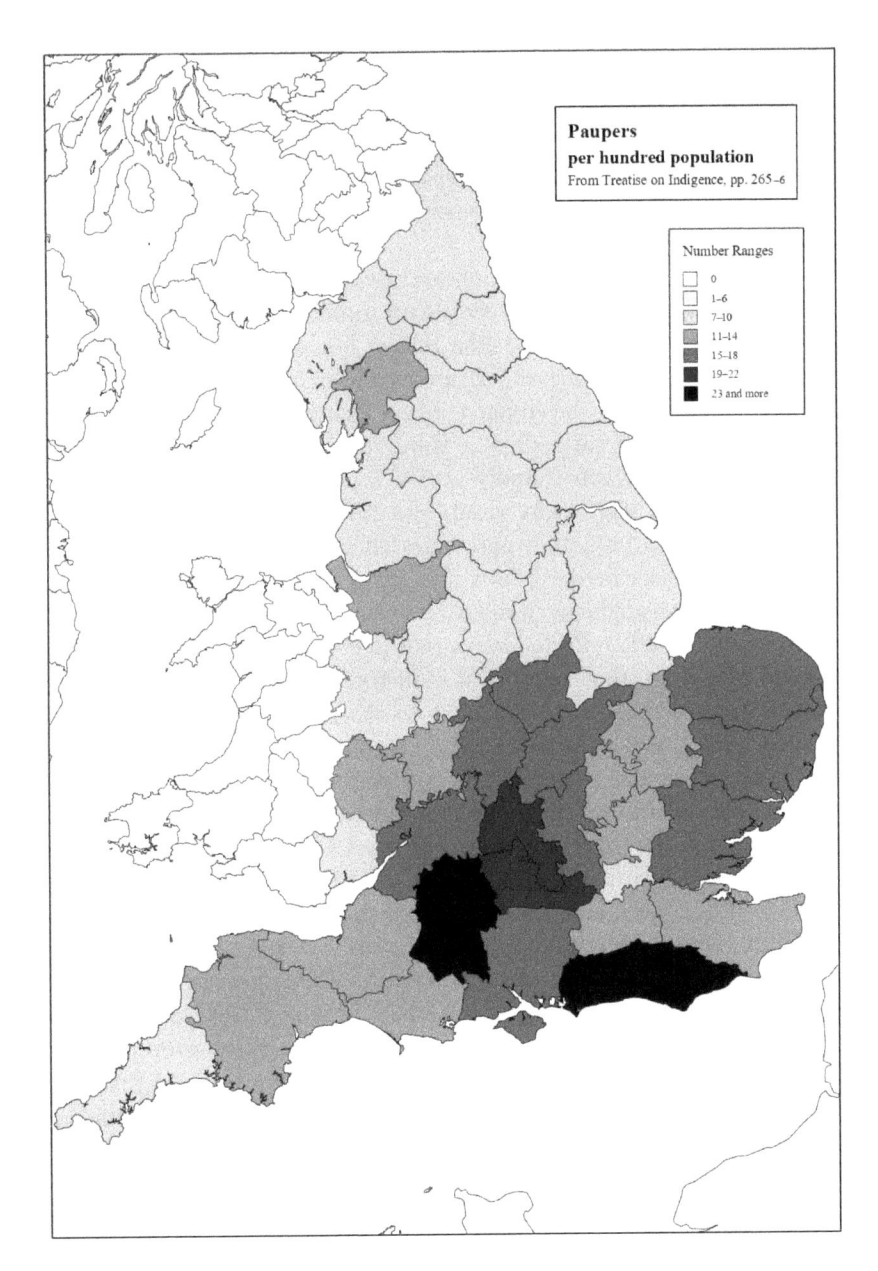

Poverty, autonomy, control: Colquhoun's Treatise 245

Figure 11.1 Map of paupers per hundred population. From Colquhoun's *Treatise on Indigence*, pp. 265–66.

wages below their natural level, deeming this 'worthy of inquiry'. Similarly, he noted that the economy was subject to occasional systemic downturns, when thousands were thrown out of work, though argued that they were usually better placed than employers to relocate.[58] He recognised in relation to apprenticeship that it was not always easy to learn about available work, but his solution – systematising information flows – related to apprenticeship alone.[59]

In relation to moral issues, Colquhoun advocated several 'timely props'.[60] One was a network of district schools on monitorial principles (allowing large numbers of children to be educated at low cost). They should equip the young both with both sound attitudes and marketable skills, which he thought the children of the indigent often lacked. A second involved the reinvigoration of apprenticeship; a third, the foundation of a 'national deposit bank' into which friendly societies might channel contributions. Societies operating in this way would not foster wasteful alehouse revels. These proposals all built on approaches championed by 'reformation of manners' enthusiasts in the 1780s and carried forward by the Bettering Society – not surprisingly given the carry-over in membership.[61] Changes of detail since the 1780s reflected ways that debate had moved on. Whereas first Sunday schools, then schools of industry, had been championed, now monitorial day schools were the rage; to the reinvigoration of service in husbandry, the reinvigoration of apprenticeship was now added; support for friendly societies as a species was now narrowed to support only those that funnelled contributions into savings banks.

Always a fan of superintending bodies, Colquhoun proposed three. One would be a National Deposit Bank for friendly societies.[62] Another, a Board of Education, roughly paralleling the recently founded Board of Agriculture, would superintend the education and training of the children of the poor.[63] Third he proposed a mash-up of his previously proposed Board of Police Revenue and Commission for the Cases and Causes of Distress, in the form of a 'Board of General and Internal Police'. This would be a 'police' body in the broad contemporary sense of providing public services. But it would be solely 'inquisitorial' – unlike much of what Colquhoun had previously discussed under the rubric of 'police'.[64] It would collect information on various poverty-related topics: in effect extending the work of the 1803 survey. It would set out some of its findings in a *Police Gazette*, in which statistical data, police bulletins, short informative and improving essays and anecdotes would appear in a form that a wide readership would find engaging and salutary.[65] This Police Board would be most actively managerial in relation to licensing: by leasing out responsibility for issuing various licences, it would generate its own income stream.

Overall, the tone of the *Treatise on Indigence* is strikingly upbeat, at least as compared with Colquhoun's previous 'treatises'. It is, to be sure, haunted by fear of the poor's susceptibility to corruption and moral decline. Yet it argues that many forms of mitigation were available. I have argued that there was consistently a recuperative and optimistic strand in Colquhoun's thought. The dominance of this within this treatise surely reflected what he saw as its genre. It was in his eyes an exercise in 'political economy' – offering reflections on the management of economy and society. As Colquhoun saw it, solutions to problems of production and consumption lay partly beyond, though partly within, the reach of the poor. His treatise acknowledged limits to the poor's power, but focused on what they could do. Political economy was, as he saw it, an action-oriented analysis, embodying a particular approach to such matters: 'The great desideratum in political economy is to lead the poor, by gentle and practicable means, *into the way of helping themselves.*'[66] Colquhoun in effect agreed with Adam Smith that human beings were naturally impelled to try to better their condition – though he did not think this so powerful an impulse as to operate under all conditions; it could be choked or corrupted. In the seventh and final edition of his *Treatise on Police*, published in the same year as the *Treatise on Indigence*, he continued to brood on how to respond to corruption, once that had set in.

Conclusions, implications

Colquhoun rarely if ever entirely let go of an idea. On the contrary, he constantly remixed the ones he had. In 1815, he laid ideas floated both in his 1799 pamphlet *The State of Indigence* and in his 1806 *Treatise on Indigence* before the parliamentary select committee convened to consider 'mendicity' in the metropolis – which may have been assembled with a view to recommending something like his pauper 'Commission', but if so, lost its nerve. In 1816, he similarly recycled before the select committee on the police of the metropolis ideas about the prevalence of depravity and the need for more and better laws, policing and punishments.[67]

Historians have mostly emphasised these latter ideas. I have tried to bring out other elements of his thought and practice, elements that cohere with other aspects of his life: his business career; his work alongside metropolitan philanthropists; and his fascination with data, especially numerical data, and hopes (or fantasies) about using that to illuminate economy and society. Those ideas had been present in germ in his early thought and practice. In his *Treatise on Indigence*, he developed them further.

Some features of Colquhoun's mind and temperament infused all his writings, those focussing on 'indigence' among others. His instincts were synthetic and pragmatic. It is symptomatic that he repeatedly compiled 'treatises': *omnium gatherums* of information and ideas, aimed at building support for programmes of action. His proposals often had reimagined institutions at their core, but were otherwise multi-pronged. Few were taken up – the Marine Police represent the chief exception (the current Metropolitan Police's Marine Policing Unit descends from them). But Colquhoun's hope was always that they *would* be taken up: that his writings would convince people across a spectrum of opinion, but above all in government, that the institutional landscape should be rearranged in line with his prescriptions.

Colquhoun was not, like Bentham or Malthus, a controversialist. Of course, he sometimes took sides. He thought friendly societies a decidedly mixed blessing; he was for his day unusual in not just questioning the merits of the parish as a relief unit, but advocating a national relief fund. Still, his proposals rarely entailed blistering attacks on existing institutions. The note that he liked to strike was rather 'Surely we could do better?' It is typical of Colquhoun that he took up a vocabulary that Bentham devised to facilitate the making of distinctions – pauper/indigence as opposed to poor/poverty – and blurred its edges.

Colquhoun's treatise on 'Police' was internationally read and cited – though more for its call for systematic thinking about institutions and laws than for its detail. The *Treatise on Indigence* made much less impact. It was a source book for the next generation of commentators, but one on which people drew to suit their own purposes: they did not treat is as a focused intervention with whose arguments they needed to engage.

The interest of this *Treatise*, as I have sought to show, lies partly in the light it sheds on Colquhoun; but also, as I've indicated and would like to stress in conclusion, in the many ways in which it reflected wider currents of thought eddying around in Colquhoun's milieu. Colquhoun directed these currents through the channels of his own preoccupations, but they flowed back from thence into these wider waters. Though drawing on his own experience, and presented in distinctive ways, many elements of his thought were not peculiar to him, but were on the contrary common among a generation of policy makers, social commentators and philanthropic activists, scattered across the country. Building on the efforts of earlier generations of charity-entrepreneurs and moral reformers, these men and women sought to understand poverty and the challenges it presented in ways that broke with the relatively restrictive vision of the poor laws.[68] This generation's reimaginings were clearly in their own way stereotyping and problematic. Yet they were consequential. They helped to shape new patterns of thought and new programmes of action, that would make the nineteenth-century's landscape of poverty – both as policy object and as lived experience – different from the eighteenth century's.

Notes

1 For Colquhoun on his achievements, London Metropolitan Archives, London ACC/1230/007; The National Archives, London (Hereafter TNA), HO 42/66, fols 105–129. He is memorialised in Westminster Abbey: www.westminsterabbey.org/abbey-commemorations/commemorations/patrick-colquhoun. Accessed 20 October 2023. General overviews include, Ruth Paley 'Colquhoun, Patrick (1745–1820), Magistrate and a Founder of the Thames Police', *Oxford Dictionary of National Biography* (revised 2008); 'Iatros' [his son in law, D. G. Yeats], *A Biographical Sketch of the Life and Writings of Patrick Colquhoun* (London, 1818); Norman Gash, ' Glaswegian criminologist: Patrick Colquhoun, 1745–1820' in ibid., *Pillars of Government and Other Essays on State and Society c1780–1880* (London: Edward Arnold, 1986), pp. 139–152; and Ralph Pieris, 'The Contributions of Patrick Colquhoun to Social Theory and Social Philosophy', *Asian Journal of Social Science*, 35:3 (2007), 288–320. The influential Leon Radzinowicz, *History of English Criminal Law and its Administration from 1750*, 5 vols (London: Stevens, 1948–86), esp. vols ii–iii, arguably overstated his contribution to policing. He features in several social-theoretical accounts: Mark Neocleous, 'Social Police and the Mechanisms of Prevention. Patrick Colquhoun and the Condition of Poverty', *British Journal of Criminology*, 40:4 (2000), 710–726 and Mitchell Dean, *The Constitution of Poverty: Toward a Genealogy of Liberal Government* (London: Routledge, 1991), pp. 53–67, pp. 193–210, are closest to my concerns, though I think too schematic on the man and the milieu.
2 Patrick Colquhoun, *A Treatise on Indigence* (London, 1806). Henceforth, *Indigence*.
3 J. R. Poynter, *Society and Pauperism; English Ideas on Poor Relief 1795–1834* (London: Routledge and Kegan Paul, 1969); on Colquhoun, pp. 200–207; David Filtness, 'Poverty, Savings Banks and the Development of Self-Help, c. 1776–1834' (PhD dissertation, University of Cambridge, 2013) and ibid., 'Poverty's Policeman: Patrick Colquhoun', *History Today*, 64:2 (2016), 32–34.
4 Michael Quinn, 'Bentham on Preventive Police: The Calendar of Delinquency in Evaluation of Policy and the Police Gazette in Manipulation of Opinion', *International Criminal Justice Review*, 20:10 (2019), 1–28 explores their relationship.
5 Michael E. Scorgie, 'Patrick Colquhoun: Accountant and Reformer', *Abacus*, 31:2 (1995), 93–112; Carolyn Marie Peters, 'The Tobacco Lords: An Examination of Wealth Creators in the Eighteenth Century' (PhD thesis, University of Glasgow, 1990); 'Patrick Colquhoun of Kelvingrove', https://glasgowmuseumsslavery.co.uk/2021/03/10/patrick-colquhoun-of-kelvingrove/. Accessed 1 February

2022; H. Hamilton, 'The Founding of the Glasgow Chamber of Commerce', *Scottish Journal of Political Economy*, 1:1 (1954), 33–48; Stanley D. Chapman, 'Arkwright's Mills: Colquhoun's Survey of 1788 and Archaeological Evidence', *Industrial Archaeology Review*, 6:1 (1981), 5–27.

6 For his lobbying roles, Yeats, *Biographical Sketch*, pp. 9–16; Robert J. Bennett, *Local Business Voice. The History of Chambers of Commerce in Britain, Ireland and Revolutionary America, 1760–2011* (Oxford: Oxford University Press, 2011), pp. 295–296. For his parliamentary ambitions, British Library Add mss 22900, fols 49–50, Charles Taylor to George Chalmers, Manchester 13 January 1789, Thanks to Julian Hoppit for this reference.

7 Scorgie, 'Patrick Colquhoun', 105–106; Emma Rothschild, 'What is Capital?', *Capitalism: A Journal of History and Economics*, 2:2 (2021), 291–371, at 311, 313–314; Orasmus Turner, *History of the Pioneer Settlement of Phelps and Gorham's Purchase* (Rochester, 1851). For Colquhoun on the last, Jeremy Bentham, *The Correspondence of Jeremy Bentham*, 12 vols (Oxford: Oxford University Press, 1968–2006), vol. vi, p. 102.

8 Yeats, *Biographical Sketch*, pp. 44–45.

9 Pieris, 'Contributions', p. 290 for bullion; Patrick Colquhoun, *A Treatise on the Wealth, Power and Resources of the British Empire*, second edition (London, 1815), pp. 57–60 for the East India Company; ibid., *Strong Reasons for the Continuance of the Property Tax* (London, 1814).

10 Irene Maver, 'The Guardianship of the Community: Civic Authority before 1833', in T. M. Devine and Gordon Jackson (eds) *Glasgow: Beginnings to 1830* (Manchester: Manchester University Press, 1995), pp. 239–277; David Barrie, 'Patrick Colquhoun, the Scottish Enlightenment and Police Reform in Glasgow in the Late Eighteenth Century', *Crime, histoire et sociétés*, 12:2 (2008), 59–79.

11 Norma Landau, 'The Trading Justice's Trade' in ibid. (ed.), *Law, Crime and English Society, 1660–1830* (Cambridge: Cambridge University Press, 2002), pp. 46–70.

12 Richard Stone, *Some British Empiricists in the Social Sciences 1650–1900* (Cambridge: Cambridge University Press, 1988), pp. 183–204; P. G. Lindert and J. H. Williamson, 'Revising England's Social Tables 1688–1812', *Explorations in Economic History*, 19:4 (1982), 385–408.

13 *Treatise on the Police of the Metropolis*, 7 editions London, 1796–1806, also published in America (1798) and in German and French translations (1800–1805, 1807). Quinn, 'Bentham on Preventive Police', 3–4 suggests that the phrase was Bentham's; Colquhoun used it only from the sixth edition of his *Treatise on Police*.

14 Patrick Colquhoun, *Treatise on the Commerce and Police of the River Thames* (London, 1800). William J. Ashworth, *Customs and Excise: Trade, Production and Consumption in England 1640–1845* (Oxford: Oxford University Press, 2003), Part III, and ibid., '"System of Terror": Samuel Bentham, Accountability and Dockyard Reform during the Napoleonic Wars', *Social History*, 23:1 (1998), 63–79.

15 *Reports from Committees of the House of Commons*, 16 vols, 1803, XIII, '28th Report of the Select Committee on Finance: Police, including Convict Establishments' (1798), esp. appendices B and D [henceforth *Reports*, XIII, Finance: Police]. Colquhoun also published his evidence as *A General View of the National Police System* (London, 1799).
16 Roger A. E. Wells, *Wretched Faces: Famine in Wartime England, 1793–1801* (Gloucester: Alan Sutton, 1988).
17 D. R. Fisher, 'Devaynes, William' in R. Thorne (ed.), *The History of Parliament: The House of Commons 1790–1820*, 5 vols (London: Secker and Warburg, 1986). For Devaynes as loyalist *inter alia* TNA: HO 42/24/187, 195; 42/28/123; 42/33/51; 43/5 f. 147. And the poor: TNA HO 42/34/18; 42/34/179; PRO 30/8/308 f.147, 155.
18 [Patrick Colquhoun], *An Account of a Meat and Soup Charity, Established in the Metropolis, in the Year 1797* (London, 1797).
19 Poynter, *Society and Pauperism*, pp. 91–98. The Society's reports were published in 6 vols 1814–15; a fortieth report in 1817.
20 Patrick Colquhoun, *A New and Appropriate System of Education for... Children Admitted into the Free School... Westminster* (London, 1806).
21 T. J. Pettigrew (ed.), *Memoirs of the Life and Writings of the Late Thomas Coakley Lettsom*, 3 vols (London, 1817), vol. ii, pp. 358–361.
22 See n. 1 above. Yeats' celebratory *Biographical Sketch* marked Colquhoun's retirement; Pettigrew, *Memoirs of Lettsom*, vol. ii, pp. 353–358. Samuel L. Knapp, *The Life of Thomas Eddy* (New York, NY, 1834), pp. 179–230, pp. 248–258, pp. 271–281.
23 Chapman, 'Arkwright's Mills'.
24 Stone, *Some British Empiricists*; Lindert and Williamson, 'Revising England's Social Tables'.
25 Patrick Colquhoun, *A Treatise on the Wealth, Power, and Resources of the British Empire* (London, 2 editions 1814–1815). Also published in German in 1815.
26 J. R. McCulloch, *The Literature of Political Economy* (London, 1845), p. 218, called his *Treatise on Wealth* a 'tissue of extravagant hypotheses and exaggerations'.
27 See n. 12 above and Kiran Mehta, 'Summary Justice in Eighteenth and Nineteenth-Century Southwark', *Crime, Histoire & Sociétés/Crime, History & Societies*, 24:1 (2020), pp. 55–90.
28 David Green, *Pauper Capital: London and the Poor Law, 1790–1870* (Farnham: Ashgate, 2010), Ch. 5.
29 Patrick Colquhoun, *An Account of the Rise and Progress and Present State of the Charity School, in the Parish of St Leonard's, Shoreditch* (London, 1793); *A Plan for Affording Extensive Relief to the Poor, by ... Redeeming Pledges ...* (London: [1795?]). For the 'village': *Reports*, XIII, Finance: Police, App. D, response to Q. 10; *PP* 1814–15 III (473), pp. 55–56.
30 Wells, *Wretched Faces*.
31 Poynter, *Society and Pauperism*, pp. 62–76. Also Michael Quinn, 'Editorial Introduction' to Jeremy Bentham, *Writings on the Poor Laws*, ed. Michael

Quinn, 2 vols (Oxford: Clarendon Press, 2002–10), vol. i, pp. xli–vii. For the think tank, Thomas Ruggles, *History of the Poor*, second edition (London, 1797), pp. 424–426.

32 Jeremy Bentham, *Writings on the Poor Laws*, vol. i, especially 'Editorial Introduction' on prompts for his writing.

33 Bentham, 'Definitions and Distinctions', in Bentham *Writings on the Poor Laws*, vol. i, pp. 3–7 and pp. 255–263. He did suggest that 'collateral uses' of industry houses (pp. 66–140) might serve the 'Independent Poor' by providing loans against chattels (pawn-broking), banking facilities, travel accommodation and out-patient provision, but his aim was surely to strengthen his primary case, or why offer these facilities only in 200 Industry Houses?

34 For their correspondence 1796–1800 and 1806–1807, Bentham, *Correspondence of Jeremy Bentham*, vols v–vii, esp. vol. v, p. 349, vol. v, pp. 353–54 and vol. vii, p. 405. For Colquhoun's grandiose, Bentham-influenced 1797 proposal – which he did not later pursue – that a hundred men of 'business and education' from across the country should manage the poor, set them to work and liaise with Parliament: University College London Bentham mss 151 fols 40–43 (accessible online through UCL Digital www.ucl.ac.uk/library/digital-collections/collections/bentham).

35 See n. 20 above.

36 For the earlier 'Proclamation' society, see Joanna Innes, *Inferior Politics: Social Problems and Social Policies in Eighteenth-Century Britain* (Oxford: Oxford University Press, 2009), pp. 192–215.

37 See n. 19 above. [Patrick Colquhoun], *Account of a Meat and Soup Charity* (London, 1797), p. 6 for numbers.

38 [Colquhoun], *Meat and Soup Charity*; Patrick Colquhoun, *Treatise on Police*, fifth edition (London, 1797), p. 33n.

39 The category of 'casual poor' is the subject of some of my work in progress.

40 Bill: *Commons Journal*, vol. 55 (1799–1800), p. 310, p. 321, p. 353, p. 360, p. 369 and p. 372. Returns: *Parliamentary Papers*, 1803–1804. XIII (175) *Abstract of the Answers and Returns ... relative to the Expense and Maintenance of the Poor in England*. Colquhoun perhaps suggested the question: see his letter to Pitt TNA: PRO 30.8.308 f. 149. Martin, *Letter*, pp. 21–22, suggested spending data might help calibrate parish contributions to a common metropolitan fund.

41 *Reports*, XIII, Finance: Police.

42 Patrick Colquhoun, *General View of the National Police System; The state of Indigence and the Situation of the Casual Poor* (London, 1799) – the first 46pp, the second 34pp.

43 I suspect that he was also influenced, via the Bettering Society, by Count Rumford's schemes: Franz Redlich, 'Count Rumford and His Followers', *International Review of Social History*, 16 (1971), 184–216. Relatedly, Bettering Society: *Reports* (1798), vol. i, pp. 125–128, and James Baker, *Life of Sir Thomas Bernard, Baronet* (London, 1819), pp. 47–49.

44 Colquhoun, *Treatise on Police*, sixth edition, Ch. 13, pp. 351–380.

45 [Colquhoun] to Pitt, Nov. 1799: PRO 30/8/308, fols 149–154.
46 Colquhoun, *Treatise on Police*, fifth edition, p. 33n; [Yeats], *Biographical Sketch*, pp. 45–46.
47 1803–04. XIII (175) *Abstract;* George Rose, *Observations on the Poor Laws... Arising from a Consideration of the Returns...* (London, 1805, 2 editions). Innes, *Inferior Politics*, p. 123, p. 140, pp. 157–158.
48 Margaret E. Sandford, *Thomas Poole and his Friends*, 2 vols (London, 1888), vol. ii, pp. 106–140.
49 Yeats, *Biographical Sketch*, p. 46; [Hansard], *House of Commons Debates*, vol. vii cols 292–293. For Whitbread, Poynter, *Society and Pauperism*, pp. 207–222. For Colquhoun's statistical speculations in 1806, see Knapp, *Life of Eddy*, pp. 216–219.
50 Colquhoun, *Indigence*, pp. 25–32.
51 Ibid., pp. 10–12, pp. 68–69, for Martin-derived insights into causes of mendicity. For 'props' and 'timely props', p. 8, p. 12, p. 62, p. 94, p. 108, p. 198, p. 228, p. 229. See n. 34 for Bentham and the terminology.
52 Ibid., pp. 230–240. For problems with friendly societies, pp. 115–117.
53 Ibid., p. 43.
54 Ibid., pp. 19–39. He returned to the subject pp. 182–183, where he also considered but decided against inflation, 'the decrease in the value of money', being a cause.
55 Ibid., pp. 265–268.
56 For example, [Daniel Defoe], *Giving Alms no Charity, and Employing the Poor a Grievance to the Nation* (London, 1704).
57 Colquhoun, *Indigence*, pp. 179–215 criticise settlement laws – before Colquhoun returns in his conclusion to attempt to demonstrate their effects: pp. 18–19, pp. 262–269; pp. 264–267 make the case for a national fund. Thomas Paine, *Rights of Man* [orig. London, 1792] proposed that funds be 'remitted' out of national taxes.
58 Ibid., pp. 14–16, p. 280.
59 Ibid. pp. 172–173, p. 176.
60 Ibid., pp. 110–229.
61 Innes, *Inferior Politics*, pp. 179–226.
62 Colquhoun, *Indigence*, pp. 122–134.
63 Ibid., pp. 140–156; p. 164.
64 Ibid., pp. 79–109. See pp. 82–83 for this concept of 'police'.
65 Quinn, 'Bentham on Preventive Police' argues that the *Police Gazette* was Bentham's idea.
66 Colquhoun, *Indigence*, p. 122. Italics in original. Cf. pp. 178–179.
67 *PP* 1814–15 III (473), pp. 34–58; 1816 V (510), pp. 45–51. Also *PP* 1819 VIII (585), pp. 65–67, he argued against capital punishment for minor crimes.
68 See n. 2 above.

Index

able-bodied poor 19, 21–22, 41, 43–44, 48, 75, 76, 96, 129, 133, 134, 137, 141, 220, 243–244
absentee aristocracy 194, 196, 197
  see also idle nobility
absolutist monarchy 3, 24
  Enlightened absolutism 8, 10
agricultural societies *see* economic societies
agriculture 23, 24, 78–79, 93, 117, 152, 157–158, 171, 173, 174, 176, 189–191, 193, 196, 246
  agricultural civilization 192
  grazing 193–194
  pasture to tillage 191, 193, 199–200, 202–204, 204–207
Aguirre, Manuel de 96–97, 100
alms *see* poor relief
Anzano, Tomás 87, 90, 91–92, 93, 96, 100
arbitristas 86–87
Armstrong, George 78

Baudeau, abbé Nicolas 36, 42–43, 44, 45, 90
Beccaria, Cesare 61–67, 69, 73–76, 77, 78, 79, 85
begging 18, 21–22, 24, 37–38, 39, 43, 47, 69, 74, 76, 89, 94, 96, 155, 199, 234, 237, 240
  see also vagrancy
Bentham, Jeremy 232, 238–239, 241, 248
Berkeley, George 136, 194–195, 196, 198

Bielfeld, Jakob F. von 85, 92
bienfaisance 9–10, 20, 21, 36–51
Bindon, David 195
Bohemia 30, 32
Britain 95, 108–109, 112, 130–131, 138–142
Buquoy, Count Johann Nepomuk 31, 77
Burke, Edmund 11, 128–133, 137, 142–143
Bushe, Gervaise Parker 202

Cabarrús, Francisco de 96, 97–98, 100
Cadalso, José 84, 99
Calvinism 108, 120, 122, 150
cameralism 5, 23–24, 29, 32, 74
Campillo, José del 87–88, 91
Campomanes, Count of, 85, 87, 91, 92–95, 98, 100
capitalism 4, 6, 7, 48
Carlos III (Spain) 92
Carlos IV (Spain) 98
'casual poor' 240–241, 242, 244
Catherine II (Russia) 8, 23, 25–28, 47, 173, 179
Catholic Church 4, 10, 29, 31, 37, 47, 84, 85–86, 97, 99, 175
Catholics (Ireland) 189, 190–191, 196–199, 203
Ceruti, Giacomo 69–73, 76–77
charity 9, 20, 45–46, 75, 76, 84, 86–87, 97–98, 108–110, 115, 129, 131, 143
  and *bienfaisance* 36–37, 49
  charity schools 93–94, 95, 110–111

criticised 9, 20, 38, 39–40, 43, 75–76, 110, 111–112, 115–116, 134–135
children 21, 24, 39, 48, 76, 153, 158–161, 202, 216–218, 238, 246
child labour 93, 94, 111–112
China 40–41
Christianity 8–9, 21
clergy 10, 19, 32, 97, 175, 178
Colbert, Jean-Baptiste 134
Colquhoun, Patrick 13, 221, 232–249
'soup kitchens' 239–240
commercial society 4, 11, 21, 37, 47, 48, 49, 110–112, 113, 130, 133, 143, 169, 170, 175–176, 183–184, 192, 204, 207–208, 213, 215, 232, 233
compassion 38–39, 48–49, 50, 51, 111
see also bienfaisance
consumerism 22
consumption 108, 112, 115, 136, 153, 189, 193–195, 208, 247
cottiers 12, 191, 200–208
Coxe, William 169, 170, 171, 178–181, 182
crime 13, 42, 43, 64–67, 69, 79, 232, 237, 238
Curry, John 199

Davies, Sir John 192
Defoe, Daniel 134, 221
demography 11, 192, 202
populousness of the ancient world 149
dépôts de mendicité 21, 22, 38, 42, 43
depopulation 11, 86, 149–159, 161, 163, 173, 190
deserving poor 21–22, 75, 84, 134, 237
indigence (Benthamite) 239, 241, 242–243
destigmatisation of the poor 38, 40
Diderot, Denis 20, 25–26
disease 74, 78, 155, 216, 236
division of labour 191, 206
Dobbs, Arthur 197
Doria, Paolo Mattia, 66

Du Pont, Pierre-Samuel 37, 43–46, 45, 46, 47–49, 51, 98
Dusquenoy, Adrien 99
Dutch Republic 4, 10, 106–122
'absence of poverty' 108–110

economic growth 21, 25, 40, 43, 61, 113, 116, 137, 138, 202, 244
'economic patriotism' (Dutch Republic) 115–117
Oeconomische Tak 117
'economic regalism' (Spain) 10, 84–86, 87–92, 99–100
economic societies 42, 47, 90, 91, 93–96
Économistes see Physiocracy
economistic conception of poverty 3, 84, 91, 115, 168, 213
see also structural poverty
Eden, Frederick 11, 220, 221
education 6, 10, 22, 26, 27, 29, 31–32, 47, 51, 66–67, 75, 78, 79, 91, 92, 94–95, 111–112, 196, 217, 219, 222, 226, 246
egalitarianism 9–10, 61, 130, 132, 133, 214
employment 9, 37–38, 40, 44, 46, 48, 77, 86, 93, 114, 118, 129, 131, 135, 203, 246
labour mobility 30
poverty as absence of work 143
enclosures 138, 204, 206
Enlightenment, the 1–6, 7–8, 13–14, 20, 28, 84, 99, 128–129, 149, 168, 188–189
and social democracy 4–5
equality 4
economic 153
human 64
legal and political 61, 66, 69, 97, 117
of opportunity 63
exploitation 5, 12, 19, 197, 238

famine 19, 60–61, 78, 108, 154–155, 193, 200
Felbiger, Abbot Johann Ignaz von 23

feudalism 12, 22, 97, 168–184
  see also slavery
'First Poverty Enlightenment' 1–3, 61
fiscal-military state 7, 18, 24–25
food prices 81, 41, 109, 131, 132, 138, 140–141, 201–202, 220, 221, 238
Foucault, Michel 5, 42, 76
foundlings 27, 29, 41, 43, 49
Franklin, Benjamin 140
Frederick II (Prussia) 8, 23, 24–25
free markets 4, 6, 9, 11, 28, 38, 41–42, 128
  labour 131–132
  liberalisation of markets 40
  market competition 66, 110
free trade 26, 43, 47, 66, 120, 137, 140
French Revolution 11, 30, 37, 128, 130, 132–133, 143, 180, 213, 235
friendly societies 221, 238, 242, 243, 246, 248
frugality 69, 110–112, 133–34, 138, 139
  see also luxury

Gee, Joshua 108, 110
geographical mobility 95
Genovesi, Antonio 66
Godwin, William 214–215, 224
government type and poverty 171, 173, 174, 178–179, 183–184
grain trade 9, 21, 24, 26, 40–41, 45, 47, 108, 131–132, 140, 141, 158, 176, 190, 191, 199–200, 201, 203–204
  see also food prices
'Great Divergence' 7
guilds 30, 86, 87, 88, 92, 94, 95, 114

Habsburg Monarchy 4, 8, 9–10, 24, 28–30, 60–79, 109
Hamburg 24
Heuvel, Herman Hendrik van den 117
Hogendorp, Gijsbert Karel van 117–118, 120–121
Hospicios 85, 88–92, 93–96
  see also workhouses

Hume, David 112, 113, 149, 163, 169–170, 179, 220

idle nobility 66, 67, 68–69, 87–88
  see also absentee aristocracy
idle poor 9, 11, 19, 21–22, 29, 75, 76, 88, 109, 134, 138, 176, 237, 243
  causes of idleness 135, 201
Il Caffè 67–69, 73–74
improvement 12, 18, 21, 24, 29, 33, 67–68, 116, 149, 156–157, 162, 174, 181, 190, 191, 192, 198–199, 207–208
  moral improvement of the poor 224–226
individual rights 10, 64, 77, 78
  right to property 29, 65, 67
  right to relief 51, 77, 79, 97, 116, 218, 221, 222–223
  right to work 77, 79
  see also social contract
Industrial Revolution 4, 7, 106
industry (production) 30, 74, 88, 90, 93, 94, 98, 112, 115, 171, 174, 191, 193, 195, 224, 234
industry (work ethic) 10, 12, 65–66, 76, 77, 84, 89, 108–109, 136, 137, 143, 153, 169–170, 174, 179, 182, 194, 194–198, 204, 206, 237, 238, 242, 246
inequality (economic) 1, 4–5, 7, 49–50, 50–51, 63, 65, 97, 109, 110, 112, 119, 169, 227
interest rates 114
international trade 109, 111, 113
  see also mercantilism
investment 39, 40, 43, 46, 47, 48, 89–90, 113–114, 206
Ireland 12, 155, 188–208
  confessional politics vs. agrarian improvement 197–198
Israel, Jonathan 1, 4–5

Joseph II (Habsburg Empire) 8, 18, 28–33, 75, 77
Institute for the Poor 31–32

Justi, Johann Heinrich Gottlob von 8, 20, 23

Kaunitz, Prince, Wenzel Anton 8, 29, 75

labour *see* employment
'labouring poor' 11, 17, 19, 128–143, 189, 201
Lambertenghi, Luigi 74, 75, 76
landownership 26, 29, 40, 46, 47, 48, 50, 51, 65, 97, 171, 174, 179–180, 182, 196–197
see also property
landscape (as indicator of prosperity) 189–190, 194
Le Trosne, Guillaume-François 37, 42–43
Leopold I (Grand Duchy of Tuscany) 47
liberalism 3, 6, 10, 11, 107, 118, 120, 128
Lombardy 9, 60–79
Lombard Enlightenment 9–10, 61–62, 67, 73–76, 79
Loen, Johann von 23
Louis XIV (France) 109, 134, 155
Louis XVI (France) 21, 37
luxury 22, 24, 46, 63, 68–69, 97, 107–108, 112, 113–114, 137, 153–154, 162, 170, 176, 193, 194, 195–196, 204, 217
see also frugality

Madden, Samuel 190
MacLurin, Colin 156–157, 158–159
Malthus, T. R. 11, 13, 188–189, 191–192, 212–227
Mandeville, Bernard 17, 107, 110–113, 134–135, 139, 142, 153–154
manufacturing 29, 30, 60, 77, 88, 93, 96, 114, 135, 141, 173, 188, 203–204, 206
Manzoni, Alessandro 60–61, 78–79
Maria Theresia, Walburga Amalia Christina (Habsburg Monarchy) 29–30, 77

marriage 30, 41, 68, 151–152, 157–158, 217–218, 226
see also procreation
Marshall, Alfred 1
Marshall, Joseph 169, 172–175
Meléndez Valdés, Juan 96–97, 100
McCartney, George 172
Melon, Jean-François 37–38, 113, 135, 195–196
mercantilism 37–38, 86, 135, 137, 140
utility of poverty 135, 138, 142–42
merchants 6, 89, 98, 108, 170, 175–176, 179, 234
migration 71, 155, 174, 200, 203
Milanese Enlightenment *see* Lombard Enlightenment
Millar, John 192–193
Mirabeau, Victor de Riqueti, Marquis de 36, 37, 39–41, 42, 45–46, 48–49
Mitterpacher, Ludwig 78
Molesworth, Robert 193, 196–197
Montesquieu, Charles Louis de Secondat, Baron de 11, 37–38, 40, 113, 129, 136–138, 139, 142–143, 151, 171, 176, 179, 219–220
moral corruption 128, 201, 247
moral economy 5, 10, 21, 23, 24–25, 46, 212–213, 224, 226

Necker, Jacques 37, 45, 112
Newenham, Thomas 202–204

O'Connor of Belangere, Charles 198–199

Paine, Thomas 2, 6, 244
Paley, William 171, 205, 220–221
Parini, Giuseppe 68–69, 74
pastoralism 190, 192–194, 195–196, 198, 203
paternalism 2, 5, 11, 40, 50–51, 189, 207–208, 212–214, 221, 224
anti-paternalism 13, 128
pensions 24, 31, 157–158, 161
see also social insurance
Peter I (Russia) 173, 175

philosophical history 12, 168–184
physiocracy 1, 9, 23, 26, 31, 36–51, 90, 97, 139–140
Pinto, Isaac de 107, 112–114
Pitt, William (the Younger) 131, 238–239, 241, 242
Poland, 12, 168–169, 170–184
policing 232, 234–235, 236, 237, 241, 246–247, 248
political corruption 6, 27, 60
political economy 1, 2, 3, 4–5, 5–6, 9–10, 11, 13, 17, 23, 84–85, 87, 99, 120, 129, 132, 134, 149, 162, 189, 192, 199–200, 207, 212–213, 215, 217, 219–220, 221, 224, 247
polizei (police) 5, 22–23, 24, 40, 73–74, 138
Poor Laws (England) 3, 5–6, 13, 86, 116, 128–130, 132–133, 139, 142–143, 204–207, 212–213, 215, 218–219, 220–227, 242, 244
   Report from the Select Committee on the Poor Laws (1817) 224–225, 247
   Poor Law Commissioners' Report (1834) 224–225, 226–227
poorhouses *see* workhouses
poor relief 10, 17–33, 44, 48, 61–62, 71, 76, 77–79, 87, 94, 106, 107, 115–116, 118, 138, 142, 220, 222, 237, 239, 242–244
population 18–19, 23, 24, 116, 149, 162, 188–189, 191, 212, 223–225
potatoes 192, 200–204, 204–207
Price, Richard 180
Prior, Thomas 193–194, 198
privilege 4–5, 9–10, 48, 50, 60, 61–62, 63, 65–66, 67, 79, 85–86, 97–98, 133, 181
procreation 214, 218, 225
   see also marriage
property 26, 29, 31, 39, 42, 43, 47, 65, 66, 67, 97, 114–117, 178–179, 181, 191, 192, 196–199, 207, 214
   see also landownership
Prussia *see* Frederick II

public health 17, 18, 19, 23, 24–25, 74–75, 78, 139, 141, 201
   health care provision 10, 24, 44, 79
public works 21, 43–44, 47–48, 50, 93–95, 98

quantifying poverty 75, 89, 93, 236, 242–244
Quesnay, François 30–31, 36, 36–37, 39–42, 43, 140

Raab, F. A. 30
Rankenian Club 156
Ravallion, Martin *see* 'First Poverty Enlightenment'
religious bigotry 173
residual poverty 41
revaluation of poverty 61, 64, 69–73, 132–133, 142–143, 162
rhetoric 11, 38–39, 45–51, 224
Richardson, Samuel 138
Robertson, John 149
Robertson, William 169–171, 179, 182, 183, 200
Rose, George 242
Rousseau, Jean-Jacques 17, 20, 97, 135
Rumford, Benjamin Thompson, Count, 85, 99
rural poverty 19, 22, 25, 30–31, 71, 74–75, 77–78, 94, 178, 189–190, 191–192, 200–201, 204–205, 208, 238
Russia 25–28, 168–169, 170–184
Russo-Turkish War (1768–1774) 28

Saint-Pierre, Charles-Irénée Castel de, abbé 36
Schama, Simon 108
schools *see* education
Scotland 11, 148–50, 154–56
   Scottish Enlightenment 130, 148–149, 156–157, 161
secularization 3, 4, 8–9, 10, 20, 24, 27, 28, 37, 62, 75–76, 84, 86, 88
self-interest 25, 32, 38–39, 48–49, 50, 97, 111, 120–121, 174, 196

serfdom 12, 25–26, 29, 30–31, 171, 176, 179–180
   opposition to reform 25, 27–28
   see also slavery
Seven Years War (1756–1763) 25, 42
slavery 12, 169, 172, 173, 174, 176–177
   serfdom and Atlantic slavery 175, 177–178, 181–182
   see also serfdom
Smith, Adam 5–6, 95, 114, 128, 129–130, 131–132, 137, 139, 141–142, 143, 170, 201, 212–213
social contract 10, 61, 62–64, 64–65, 67, 79, 97
social insurance 10, 11, 148
socialism 3, 4, 6, 10, 121
social mobility 17, 23, 25, 61–62
social parasitism *see* privileges
Society for Bettering the Condition of the Poor (Britain) 236, 239, 240
Sonnenfels, Joseph von 20, 29
Spain 10, 21, 84–100
   Spanish Enlightenment 84, 87, 96–97, 99
Spenser, Edmund 192, 199, 203
stadial history 168, 193
   see also philosophical history
state administration 19, 21–22, 23, 26–27, 30–31, 73–75, 78, 91, 96, 97–98, 137–138
   colonial administration 190
   utilising the poor 10, 115, 119, 135
state emulation 24, 170
statistics 3, 20, 23, 141, 189, 213, 214, 217, 246
Stedman Jones, Gareth 4, 162
Stewart, Dugald 221
structural poverty vs conjunctural poverty 19, 41, 61, 136–137
superstition 78
Swift, Jonathan 193

taxation 7, 30–31, 39, 42, 43, 50, 88–89, 92, 94, 98, 108–109, 112, 114–115, 135, 179, 189, 196, 202, 234, 242

technology 77–78, 112, 116–117, 157
Temple, William 109–110, 188–189
textiles 93, 196
theodicy 48–50
Thompson, E. P. 5, 23, 212
Thorbecke, Johan Rudolph 118–119, 120
Tocqueville, Alexis de 17, 19
Townsend, Joseph 135, 139, 220, 221
Trivulzio, Prince Antonio Tolomeo Gallio 76
Turgot, Anne-Robert-Jacques 8, 20–22, 31, 37–38, 41, 43–44, 45
Tydeman, Hendrik Willem 118–120, 121

unemployment *see* employment
urbanisation 109, 203, 206
urban poverty 19, 69–71, 74, 234, 241, 244

vagrancy 22, 38, 41–43, 71, 87–88, 94, 96, 109, 193, 240–241
   mendicity 240
   see also begging
valorisation of commerce 48, 138
Vanderlint, Jacob 136
Verri, Pietro 66–67, 68–69, 71, 76–77, 117
Visconti, Attilio Lampugnani 76
Voltaire, François-Marie 20, 48

wages 17, 30–31, 40–41, 65–66, 71, 75, 85, 94, 98, 108–109, 114, 128, 131–132, 135, 136–137, 139, 141–142, 190, 200–201, 207, 214, 220–221, 223–224, 238, 244–246
Wakefield, Edward 191, 205–207
Wallace, Robert 11, 148–163, 216
   Scottish widows fund 148, 157–161
war 155, 200, 216
Ward, Bernardo 84–90, 91, 95–96, 99–100
War of the Spanish Succession (1701–1714) 87, 107, 110, 114
wealth 7, 22, 65–66, 77, 113, 114, 148
   Redistribution 132

Webster, Alexander 150, 158
Webster, Noah 182
Weyland, John 224
Whitbread, Samuel 218–219, 220–223, 226, 242
Williams, John 169
women 47, 68, 69, 71, 91, 93–94, 95, 201, 216–217, 248

workhouses 19, 22, 29, 38, 71, 85, 88–92, 115–116, 129, 134, 138, 220, 232, 237, 241
Wybicki, Józef 179–180

Young, Arthur 131, 135, 140–142, 201, 206, 219, 222, 223

Milton Keynes UK
Ingram Content Group UK Ltd.
UKHW022155300524
443399UK00006B/62